Fostering Foreign Language Teaching and Learning Environments With Contemporary Technologies

Zeynep Çetin Köroğlu
Aksaray University, Turkey

Abdulvahit Çakır
Ufuk University, Turkey

A volume in the Advances in Educational Technologies and Instructional Design (AETID) Book Series

Published in the United States of America by
    IGI Global
    Information Science Reference (an imprint of IGI Global)
    701 E. Chocolate Avenue
    Hershey PA, USA 17033
    Tel: 717-533-8845
    Fax: 717-533-8661
    E-mail: cust@igi-global.com
    Web site: http://www.igi-global.com

Copyright © 2024 by IGI Global. All rights reserved. No part of this publication may be reproduced, stored or distributed in any form or by any means, electronic or mechanical, including photocopying, without written permission from the publisher.
Product or company names used in this set are for identification purposes only. Inclusion of the names of the products or companies does not indicate a claim of ownership by IGI Global of the trademark or registered trademark.

Library of Congress Cataloging-in-Publication Data

Names: Çetin Köroğlu, Zeynep, 1986- editor. | Çakır, Abdulvahit, 1953-
   editor.
Title: Fostering foreign language teaching and learning environments with
   contemporary technologies / edited by: Zeynep Çetin Köroğlu,
   Abdulvahit Çakır.
Description: Hershey, PA : Information Science Reference, 2024. | Includes
   bibliographical references and index. | Summary: "The aim of this book
   is to present how to enrich foreign language learning and teaching
   environments with emerging technologies through examples of practice and
   research in different contexts"-- Provided by publisher.
Identifiers: LCCN 2023041792 (print) | LCCN 2023041793 (ebook) | ISBN
   9798369303535 (hardcover) | ISBN 9798369303542 (paperback) | ISBN
   9798369303559 (ebook)
Subjects: LCSH: Language and languages--Study and teaching--Technological
   innovations. | Language and languages--Computer-assisted instruction. |
   LCGFT: Essays.
Classification: LCC P53.855 .F67 2024 (print) | LCC P53.855 (ebook) | DDC
   418.0078/5--dc23/eng/20231204
LC record available at https://lccn.loc.gov/2023041792
LC ebook record available at https://lccn.loc.gov/2023041793

This book is published in the IGI Global book series Advances in Educational Technologies and Instructional Design (AETID) (ISSN: 2326-8905; eISSN: 2326-8913)

British Cataloguing in Publication Data
A Cataloguing in Publication record for this book is available from the British Library.
All work contributed to this book is new, previously-unpublished material.
The views expressed in this book are those of the authors, but not necessarily of the publisher.
For electronic access to this publication, please contact: eresources@igi-global.com.

Advances in Educational Technologies and Instructional Design (AETID) Book Series

Lawrence A. Tomei
Robert Morris University, USA

ISSN:2326-8905
EISSN:2326-8913

MISSION

Education has undergone, and continues to undergo, immense changes in the way it is enacted and distributed to both child and adult learners. In modern education, the traditional classroom learning experience has evolved to include technological resources and to provide online classroom opportunities to students of all ages regardless of their geographical locations. From distance education, Massive-Open-Online-Courses (MOOCs), and electronic tablets in the classroom, technology is now an integral part of learning and is also affecting the way educators communicate information to students.

The **Advances in Educational Technologies & Instructional Design (AETID) Book Series** explores new research and theories for facilitating learning and improving educational performance utilizing technological processes and resources. The series examines technologies that can be integrated into K-12 classrooms to improve skills and learning abilities in all subjects including STEM education and language learning. Additionally, it studies the emergence of fully online classrooms for young and adult learners alike, and the communication and accountability challenges that can arise. Trending topics that are covered include adaptive learning, game-based learning, virtual school environments, and social media effects. School administrators, educators, academicians, researchers, and students will find this series to be an excellent resource for the effective design and implementation of learning technologies in their classes.

COVERAGE

- Digital Divide in Education
- Instructional Design
- Adaptive Learning
- Collaboration Tools
- Higher Education Technologies
- Educational Telecommunications
- Online Media in Classrooms
- Social Media Effects on Education
- Hybrid Learning
- Web 2.0 and Education

IGI Global is currently accepting manuscripts for publication within this series. To submit a proposal for a volume in this series, please contact our Acquisition Editors at Acquisitions@igi-global.com or visit: http://www.igi-global.com/publish/.

The Advances in Educational Technologies and Instructional Design (AETID) Book Series (ISSN 2326-8905) is published by IGI Global, 701 E. Chocolate Avenue, Hershey, PA 17033-1240, USA, www.igi-global.com. This series is composed of titles available for purchase individually; each title is edited to be contextually exclusive from any other title within the series. For pricing and ordering information please visit http://www.igi-global.com/book-series/advances-educational-technologies-instructional-design/73678. Postmaster: Send all address changes to above address. Copyright © 2024 IGI Global. All rights, including translation in other languages reserved by the publisher. No part of this series may be reproduced or used in any form or by any means – graphics, electronic, or mechanical, including photocopying, recording, taping, or information and retrieval systems – without written permission from the publisher, except for non commercial, educational use, including classroom teaching purposes. The views expressed in this series are those of the authors, but not necessarily of IGI Global.

Titles in this Series

For a list of additional titles in this series, please visit: http://www.igi-global.com/book-series/

Restructuring General Education and Core Curricula Requirements
Julie Christina Tatlock (Mount Mary University USA)
Information Science Reference • © 2024 • 300pp • H/C (ISBN: 9798369303856) • US $230.00

Generative AI in Teaching and Learning
Shalin Hai-Jew (Hutchinson Community College USA)
Information Science Reference • © 2024 • 435pp • H/C (ISBN: 9798369300749) • US $230.00

Architecture and Technological Advancements of Education 4.0
Rajiv Pandey (Amity University, India) Nidhi Srivastava (Amity University, India) and Parag Chatterjee (National Technological University Buenos Aires, Argentina)
Information Science Reference • © 2024 • 479pp • H/C (ISBN: 9781668492857) • US $225.00

Strategies and Digital Advances for Outcome-Based Adult Learning
Janice E. Jones (Carroll University, USA) and Mette L. Baran (Cardinal Stritch University, USA)
Information Science Reference • © 2024 • 335pp • H/C (ISBN: 9781799847489) • US $215.00

Cases on Effective Universal Design for Learning Implementation Across Schools
Frederic Fovet (Royal Roads University, Canada)
Information Science Reference • © 2024 • 300pp • H/C (ISBN: 9781668447505) • US $215.00

Practices That Promote Innovation for Talented Students
Julia Nyberg (Purdue University Global, USA) and Jessica A. Manzone (Northern Arizona University, USA)
Information Science Reference • © 2024 • 271pp • H/C (ISBN: 9781668458068) • US $215.00

701 East Chocolate Avenue, Hershey, PA 17033, USA
Tel: 717-533-8845 x100 • Fax: 717-533-8661
E-Mail: cust@igi-global.com • www.igi-global.com

List of Reviewers

Burak Asma, *Akdeniz University, Turkey*
Hande Çetin, *Tokat Gaziosmanpaşa University, Turkey*
Farzaneh Dehghan, *Amirkabir University of Technology, Iran*
Emrah Dolgunsöz, *Bayburt University, Turkey*
Devrim Höl, *Pamukkale University, Turkey*
Sibel Kahraman Özkurt, *Pamukkale University, Turkey*
Galip Kartal, *Necmettin Erbakan University, Turkey*
Fatma Kimsesiz, *Kırşehir Ahi Evran University, Turkey*
Betül Kınık, *İnönü University, Turkey*
Mourad Majdoub, *Université Laval, Canada*
Şenol Orakci, *Aksaray University, Turkey*
Gülşah Öz, *Aksaray University, Turkey*
Burcu Şentürk, *Bartın University, Turkey*
Hanieh Shafiee Rad, *Shahrekord University, Iran*
Tuğba Elif Toprak Yildiz, *İzmir Demokrasi University, Turkey*
Ümran Üstünbaş, *Zonguldak Bülent Ecevit Üniversitesi, Turkey*
Erkan Yüce, *Aksaray University, Turkey*
Mohamad Zreik, *Sun Yat-sen University, China*

Table of Contents

Preface xiv

Chapter 1
Artificial Intelligence and the Future of Chinese Language Pedagogy: An In-Depth Analysis 1
    Mohamad Zreik, Sun Yat-sen University, China

Chapter 2
Autonomous Learning in Distance Education Theories: Autonomy in Foreign Language Learning 21
    Şenol Orakcı, Aksaray University, Turkey
    Yücel Gelişli, Gazi University, Turkey

Chapter 3
ChatGPT as a Personalized Professional Development Tool: Voices of English Teachers 48
    Galip Kartal, Necmettin Erbakan University, Turkey

Chapter 4
Demystifying the Unknown: ChatGPT and Foreign Language Classrooms in the Voices of EFL Teachers 70
    Farzaneh Dehghan, Amirkabir University of Technology, Iran

Chapter 5
Designing Achievement Tests for Language Learners Through Contemporary Technologies 91
    Sibel Kahraman-Ozkurt, Pamukkale University, Turkey

Chapter 6
EFL Learners' Views About the Use of Artificial Intelligence in Giving
Corrective Feedback on Writing: A Case Study 115
    Ümran Üstünbaş, Zonguldak Bülent Ecevit University, Turkey

Chapter 7
How Does Gamified L2 Learning Enhance Motivation and Engagement: A
Literature Review 134
    Mourad Majdoub, Université Laval, Canada
    Géraldine Heilporn, Université Laval, Canada

Chapter 8
Integration of Digital Picture Books Into Young Learners' Language
Classrooms: A Novel Way to Develop Vocabulary Knowledge 174
    Zeynep Çetin Köroğlu, Aksaray University, Turkey

Chapter 9
Human vs. AI: The Use of ChatGPT in Writing Assessment...........................194
    Betul Kınık, Inonu University, Turkey
    Hande Çetin, Tokat Gaziosmanpasa University, Turkey

Chapter 10
Natural Language Processing Applications in Language Assessment: The
Use of Automated Speech Scoring 216
    Tuğba Elif Toprak-Yıldız, Izmir Democracy University, Turkey &
       University of Hamburg, Germany

Chapter 11
Hybrid Flexible (HyFlex) Teaching in Foreign Language Education:
Enhancing Equity, Inclusion, and Accessibility Through an Innovative
Digital Pedagogy...235
    Gülşah Öz, Aksaray University, Turkey

Chapter 12
EFL Learners' Digitalized Practices in Promoting Vocabulary Learning at the
Higher Education Level 260
    Fatma Kimsesiz, Kırşehir Ahi Evran University, Turkey

Compilation of References 281

About the Contributors 332

Index...336

Detailed Table of Contents

Preface xiv

Chapter 1
Artificial Intelligence and the Future of Chinese Language Pedagogy: An In-Depth Analysis 1
Mohamad Zreik, Sun Yat-sen University, China

This chapter explores the function of cutting-edge technologies including artificial intelligence, augmented reality, and the metaverse in teaching Chinese as a foreign language. It's an example of how AI is being put to use in tailor-made programs for mastering Chinese and all its subtleties. The chapter covers how to use augmented reality and how it can help you have more meaningful conversations with others. The potential of ChatGPT and the metaverse as interactive learning environments is also discussed in this chapter. The effects on educational policy and teacher preparation, as well as an examination of students' independence in technologically advanced classrooms, are discussed in the last section.

Chapter 2
Autonomous Learning in Distance Education Theories: Autonomy in Foreign Language Learning 21
Şenol Orakcı, Aksaray University, Turkey
Yücel Gelişli, Gazi University, Turkey

Individuals who live in the information age need to know the ways to access information to be able to use the information they have accessed and to produce new information. In order for individuals to have these qualities, they need to learn how to learn. Within this context, learner autonomy is very important in distance education system and lifelong learning. This research focuses on autonomous learning skills in foreign language learning in the context of distance education, which is widely discussed in the 21st century education system. The main purpose of this study is to investigate the autonomous learning skills that enable learners to learn on their own in terms of distance learning learners as well as aiming to examine the emergence of the concept of student autonomy in distance education within the framework of basic theories discussing language learning autonomy in this context. For these purposes, "Autonomy in Foreign Language Teaching," "Autonomous Learner Features in Foreign Language Learning," "Teacher and Student Roles in Autonomous Learning," "The role of Teacher in Autonomous Learning," "The Role of the Student in Autonomous Learning," "Autonomous Learning in Distance Education," "Areas and Approaches in Foreign Language Learning in Which Autonomous Learners Can Improve Themselves," and "Distance Education Theories" in the field of open and distance education were addressed. Finally, the chapter presented recent technologies to foster autonomous learning in distance education.

Chapter 3
ChatGPT as a Personalized Professional Development Tool: Voices of
English Teachers 48
    Galip Kartal, Necmettin Erbakan University, Turkey

This study explored the experiences of in-service English teachers using ChatGPT, an advanced AI language model, as a professional development tool. Adopting an exploratory case study approach, findings revealed a positive perception of ChatGPT's potential for personalized learning and professional growth. However, challenges related to technical issues, understanding complex queries, and accuracy concerns were identified. Recommendations include structured training for educators and refining AI models to better understand educational contexts. This research contributes to the discourse on AI's role in education and professional development.

Chapter 4
Demystifying the Unknown: ChatGPT and Foreign Language Classrooms in
the Voices of EFL Teachers 70
    Farzaneh Dehghan, Amirkabir University of Technology, Iran

Since its introduction, artificial intelligence (AI) has had inevitable effects on education including foreign language learning. ChatGPT, as the most advanced form of AI, has brought about many concerns and opportunities for both language teachers and learners. This chapter tries to probe more deeply into the concerns expressed over the use of ChatGPT in foreign language classrooms in the voices of teachers with an emphasis on finding ways to address those concerns. The results of the inductive analysis of interview data revealed a new concern in addition to the previously identified concerns, i.e. threats to teachers' and students' creativity. It is concluded that ChatGPT, with all its differences, can be regarded as a disrupter of a constant, traditional routine rather than a disrupter of education itself and that, to deal with it, like any other new technology, the only way ahead of teachers is adaptation and changing threats into opportunities.

Chapter 5
Designing Achievement Tests for Language Learners Through Contemporary
Technologies 91
  Sibel Kahraman-Ozkurt, Pamukkale University, Turkey

The chapter aims at giving insights to English as a foreign language (EFL) teachers
on creating and designing achievement tests through digital tools for checking their
student' progress and teaching/learning process. As language learners may have
concerns and barriers regarding the assessment and testing issues, the administration
of digital tools for that purpose is believed to contribute to both students' development
by lowering their anxiety levels and accordingly teachers' future practices. Based
on the feedback on students' performance gathered through digital tools, teachers
and other stakeholders can find the opportunity to re-organize teaching materials,
tasks, or the coursebooks. EFL teachers may also be provoked to use some other
digital tools not included in that chapter by following the procedures in the activity
plans for their future assessment practices.

Chapter 6
EFL Learners' Views About the Use of Artificial Intelligence in Giving
Corrective Feedback on Writing: A Case Study 115
  Ümran Üstünbaş, Zonguldak Bülent Ecevit University, Turkey

This chapter presents a qualitative study the aim of which is to explore EFL learners'
views about the use of artificial intelligence for giving corrective feedback on their
written works. Artificial intelligence use was addressed through one of recent and
popular chatbots: ChatGPT. The data were gathered through semi-structured and
stimulated-recall interviews, also videorecording of the participants' ChatGPT use for
writing feedback. In the interviews, the participants reflected on their individualized
language studies, and also having practiced the use of artificial intelligence in receiving
corrective feedback on their writing assignments via ChatGPT for five weeks, they
expressed their thoughts about this experience. The findings indicated codes and
themes about learner characteristics and preferences, and benefits and pitfalls of
artificial intelligence use for corrective feedback, which leads to several language
teaching implications specifically concerning writing to be proposed in the chapter.

Chapter 7
How Does Gamified L2 Learning Enhance Motivation and Engagement: A
Literature Review...134
  Mourad Majdoub, Université Laval, Canada
  Géraldine Heilporn, Université Laval, Canada

In recent years, the popularity of gamification has gained momentum with the
growing numbers of publications as well as the mass appeal among learners for its

potential to stimulate motivation, engagement, and positive experiences. However, this vein of research has mainly focused on the effects of game mechanics and how they can be incorporated within a gamified learning context to enhance users' positive experiences. In L2 teaching and learning, the literature states that most studies on gamification lack theoretical principles that can guide the design of gamified learning experiences that promote learners' motivation and engagement. To make the picture more coherent, this chapter synthesizes the existing literature on gamification L2 learning, focusing on empirical findings related to factors affecting L2 learning, current L2 gamified design models, gamification affordances, and their inherent motivational and engagement outcomes. For this review, thematic and content analysis of 73 publications dating from 2017 to late 2022 were examined.

Chapter 8
Integration of Digital Picture Books Into Young Learners' Language
Classrooms: A Novel Way to Develop Vocabulary Knowledge 174
    Zeynep Çetin Köroğlu, Aksaray University, Turkey

The world we live in now is more technological than in the past and continues to change and develop day by day. Our children, who are accepted as 'digital natives,' start to live a life intertwined with technology from the first years of their lives. To prepare them for the age they are in and the lives that await them in the future, digital picture books should be used effectively, especially in early childhood. This chapter discusses the use and importance of picture books in early childhood foreign language learning, the features and usage areas of digital picture books, the role and importance of digital picture books in vocabulary teaching, examples of well-designed digital picture books, websites and applications that offer these examples, and the effects of digital picture books on young learners' foreign language learning.

Chapter 9
Human vs. AI: The Use of ChatGPT in Writing Assessment 194
    Betul Kınık, Inonu University, Turkey
    Hande Çetin, Tokat Gaziosmanpasa University, Turkey

The current study seeks to investigate whether ChatGPT 3.5 can be used as an aid to help diminish the teachers' workload in assessing writing. To this aim, a mixed-methods research design was employed for the study. Randomly selected, 20 descriptive essays written by freshman student teachers of English Language Teaching were scored by an experienced human rater and ChatGPT 3.5. An adapted 'descriptive essay rubric' by the researchers was used to assess the descriptive essays of the student teachers. The quantitative aspect of the study involved frequency and percentage analysis, while the qualitative dimension centered on analyzing the written feedback provided by both ChatGPT and the human rater. The findings showed that there is a disagreement between ChatGPT 3.5 and the human rater. Furthermore, there are some problems with the written feedback it provides. It is clear that it is rapid in terms of providing feedback. Thus, it is recommended that ChatGPT 3.5 can be employed as a tool under the supervision of teachers.

Chapter 10
Natural Language Processing Applications in Language Assessment: The Use of Automated Speech Scoring 216
Tuğba Elif Toprak-Yıldız, Izmir Democracy University, Turkey &
University of Hamburg, Germany

Natural language processing is a subfield of artificial intelligence investigating how computers can be utilised to understand and process natural language text or speech to accomplish useful things in various areas, and it draws on various disciplines, such as computer science, linguistics, and robotics. Natural language processing applications, including automated speech recognition and scoring, have several exciting prospects for language testing and assessment practices. These prospects include addressing practical constraints associated with test administration and scoring, securing standardisation in test delivery, ensuring objectiveness and reliability in scoring procedures, and providing personalised feedback for learning. This chapter focuses on automated speech scoring and its applications in language testing and assessment and discusses how these systems can be employed in assessment contexts. The chapter also discusses the potential benefits and drawbacks of automated speech scoring while focusing on construct-related and practical challenges surrounding such systems.

Chapter 11
Hybrid Flexible (HyFlex) Teaching in Foreign Language Education: Enhancing Equity, Inclusion, and Accessibility Through an Innovative Digital Pedagogy...235
Gülşah Öz, Aksaray University, Turkey

Hybrid flexible (HyFlex) teaching, which is assumed as a much more flexible and learner-centered instruction mode, has received great attention from educators and researchers in recent years. In HyFlex learning and teaching environment, learners can make decisions on how they attend lessons i.e., face-to-face in a real classroom, online synchronously, or asynchronously after the allotted real lesson time. The present chapter aims to introduce HyFlex teaching as a new digital pedagogical and technological approach to the mode of instruction in relation to the foreign language learning and teaching field. In addition, this chapter discusses the benefits of EFL teaching in HyFlex classroom environments along with some challenges and possible solutions proposed by instructors in the light of the current relevant literature and empirical research. Furthermore, HyFlex teaching can promote equal, inclusive, and accessible learning conditions for all students regardless of their diverse backgrounds are addressed, in turn fostering foreign language learning and teaching processes.

Chapter 12
EFL Learners' Digitalized Practices in Promoting Vocabulary Learning at the
Higher Education Level 260
Fatma Kimsesiz, Kırşehir Ahi Evran University, Turkey

Technology has become an integral part of education; and language instruction, which is communicative in nature, has a share in the whole unit. The widespread use of portable devices has also transformed language learning through diverse accessible facilities that can alternatively be evaluated in an out-of-school context. This paved the way for self-directed learning practices that enable learners to advance their language skills and vocabulary. This study aimed to investigate these self-directed practices for learning vocabulary in English. 120 EFL learners at diverse departments at a state university in Turkiye participated in the study. For data collection, a survey was employed that interrogated the self-directed vocabulary learning practices of the participants in digital contexts. The results of the study showed that learners use mobile technology for English language practices and adopt different strategies in vocabulary learning supplied by a variety of digital applications and facilities. The results are discussed and related implications are addressed based on the findings.

Compilation of References 281

About the Contributors 332

Index 336

Preface

Our world is transforming into a more technological one day by day. Education is not an exception to this steady transformation. As a branch of education, foreign language education is also changing and adapting to technological developments. Emerging technologies have a positive impact on both foreign language learners and teachers (Mansor, 2001). Recently conducted research shows that technology not only improves teaching and learning methods but also broadens language learners' knowledge (Miner, 2004; Timucin, 2006). Accessing knowledge outside classrooms without limit and self-regulation of learning may be accepted as major benefits of using technology for language learning. We can mention several positive aspects of using technology in foreign language teaching and learning. First, its use in classrooms engages language learners as active participants and increases their motivation to complete the tasks (Lee, 2001). Second, technology enhances overall academic success and language proficiency (Dunkel, 1990). Third, it causes a rapid paradigm shift in teaching and learning. With the use of technologies, a shift in teaching methodology is in progress from teacher-centeredness to learner-centeredness. Language teachers have been adapting their new roles as facilitators and guides rather than only sources of information. Fourth, it has improved assessment. Implementation of technology in language classrooms enables language learners to assess their own language product in a more meaningful way and makes them ready to receive feedback willingly. There has been a shift to self and peer assessment (DEECD, 2010). The fifth positive aspects of utilizing technology in foreign language teaching is that it provides collaborative learning opportunities to language learners. Gillespie (2006) states that students access information and interact with resources. Students are connected to others through the internet and technology (DEECD,2010). The last but not the least advantage of using technology in foreign language classroom is that it diminishes language learners' anxiety level (Chapelle, 2001). The use of technology in English language teaching and learning has been increasing recently (Nawaila, Kanbul, & Alhamroni, 2020).

Preface

Highlighting the positive impacts of technologies on foreign language teaching and learning, the current book entitled '*Fostering Foreign Language Teaching and Learning Environments With Contemporary Technologies*' aims to present how to enrich foreign language learning and teaching environments with emerging technologies through examples of practice and research in different contexts. It also aims to provide examples of how to use modern technologies in the assessment of language skills. The book aims to provide the most modern and recently developed methods and materials so that foreign language teachers and foreign language learners as well as administrators, policymakers, teacher trainers, and researchers in the field of foreign language education keep abreast of state-of-the-art developments. It compiles conceptual, empirical, and theoretical research that contributes to the understanding of using contemporary technologies integration into language learning environments.

Today's technological developments include the metaverse, augmented reality, and artificial intelligence. '*Fostering Foreign Language Teaching and Learning Environments With Contemporary Technologies*' presents exemplary practices of contemporary technologies' use and their management in foreign language learning and teaching environments. The book also presents how emerging technologies can be used both in traditional classroom settings and in distance learning environments.

Dr. Mohamad Zreik is the author of the chapter entitled 'Artificial Intelligence and the Future of Chinese Language Pedagogy: An In-Depth Analysis': This chapter explores the functions of cutting-edge technologies including artificial intelligence, augmented reality, and the metaverse in teaching Chinese as a foreign language. It is an example of how AI is being put to use in tailor-made programs for mastering Chinese with all its subtleties. The chapter covers how to use augmented reality and how it can help you have more meaningful conversations with others. The potential of ChatGPT and the metaverse as interactive learning environments is also discussed in this chapter. Their effects on educational policies and teacher preparation, as well as their contribution to students' independence in technologically advanced classrooms, are discussed in the last section.

Dr. Şenol Orakcı & Dr. Yücel Gelişli are the authors of the chapter entitled 'Autonomous Learning in Distance Education Theories': Individuals who live in the information age need to know the ways to access information, to be able to use the information they have accessed and to produce new information. In order for individuals to have these qualities, they need to learn how to learn. Learner autonomy is very important in distance education systems and lifelong learning. This research focuses on autonomous learning skills in foreign language learning in the context of distance education, which is widely discussed in the 21st century education system. The main purpose of this study is to investigate the autonomous learning skills that enable learners to learn on their own, especially distance learning learners as well as to examine the emergence of the concept of student autonomy in distance education within the framework of basic theories pertaining to language learning autonomy. For these purposes, "Autonomy in Foreign Language Teaching", "Autonomous Learner Features in Foreign Language Learning", "Teacher and Student Roles in Autonomous Learning", "The role of Teacher in Autonomous Learning", "The Role of the Student in Autonomous Learning", "Autonomous Learning in Distance Education", "Areas and Approaches in Foreign Language Learning in which Autonomous Learners Can Improve Themselves" and "Distance Education Theories" in relation to open and distance education are addressed. Finally, the chapter presents recent technologies that foster autonomous learning in distance education.

Dr. Galip Kartal is the author of the chapter entitled 'ChatGPT as a Personalized Professional Development Tool Voices of English Teachers': The 21st century has seen advancements in technology, including Artificial Intelligence (AI), which has the potential to revolutionize teaching and learning. AI language models like ChatGPT, which use machine learning algorithms to generate text responses that mirror human-like qualities, can potentially serve as innovative tools for the professional development of English language educators. However, there are challenges such as lack of privacy and resistance from educators regarding data privacy. The chapter explores both the potential advantages and challenges of integrating chatbots into English language teachers' professional development activities. It aims to provide educators with an informed perspective on the potential advantages and challenges, as well as examples of best practices employing AI tools in professional development. The chapter explores the experiences, perceptions, and recommendations of English teachers who have integrated chatGPT into their teaching activities to foster professional growth, refine teaching methodologies, and enhance language learning experiences in classrooms. The insights derived from this exploration can refine the adoption and integration of AI-infused educational tools, enhancing EFL teaching by addressing educators' optimism and reservations. The chapter seeks to enrich the wider discourse concerning the confluence of AI and foreign language education.

Dr. Farzaneh Dehghan is the author of the chapter entitled 'Demystifying the unknown: ChatGPT and foreign language classrooms in the voices of EFL teachers': Since its introduction, Artificial Intelligence (AI) has had inevitable effects on education including foreign language learning. ChatGPT as the most advanced form of AI, has brought about many concerns and opportunities for both language teachers and learners. This chapter tries to probe more deeply into the concerns of teachers expressed over the use of ChatGPT in foreign language classrooms. The focus is on finding ways to address those concerns. The results of the inductive analysis of the interview data show that there are threats to teachers'

xvi

Preface

and students' creativity, in addition to previously expressed concerns. It is concluded that ChatGPT, with all its differences, can be regarded as a disrupter of a constant, traditional routine rather than a disrupter of education itself and that, to deal with it, like any other new technology, the only way ahead of teachers is adaptation and changing threats into opportunities.

Dr. Sibel Kahraman Özkurt is the author of the chapter entitled 'Designing Achievement Tests for Language Learners Through Contemporary Technologies': This chapter aims at giving insights to teachers of English as a Foreign Language (EFL) on creating and designing achievement tests through digital tools for checking their student' progress and teaching/learning process. As language learners may have concerns and barriers regarding the assessment and testing issues, the administration of digital tools for that purpose is believed to contribute to both students' development by lowering their anxiety levels and accordingly teachers' future practices. Based on the feedback on students' performance gathered through digital tools, teachers and other stakeholders can find the opportunity to re-organize teaching materials, tasks or the course books. EFL teachers may also be provoked to use some other digital tools not included in that chapter by following the procedures in the activity plans for their future assessment practices.

Dr. Ümran Üstünbaş is the author of the chapter entitled 'EFL Learners' Views about the Use of Artificial Intelligence in Giving Corrective Feedback on Writing: A Case Study': This chapter presents a qualitative study aiming to explore EFL learners' views about their teachers' use of artificial intelligence for giving them corrective feedback on their written works. Artificial intelligence use was addressed through one of recent and popular chatbots: ChatGPT. The data were gathered through semi-structured and stimulated-recall interviews, also video recording of the participants' ChatGPT use for writing feedback. In the interviews, the participants reflected on their individualized language studies, and also having practiced the use of artificial intelligence in receiving corrective feedback on their writing assignments via ChatGPT for five weeks, they expressed their thoughts about this experience. The findings indicated codes and themes about learner characteristics and preferences, and benefits and pitfalls of artificial intelligence use for corrective feedback, which leads to several language teaching implications specifically concerning writing to be proposed in the chapter.

Mourad Majdoub & Dr. Géraldine Heilporn are the authors of the chapter entitled 'How does gamified L2 learning enhance motivation and engagement A literature review': In recent years, the popularity of gamification has gained momentum with the growing numbers of publications as well as the mass appeal among learners for its potential to stimulate motivation, engagement and positive experiences. However, this vein of research has mainly focused on the effects of game mechanics and how they can be incorporated within a gamified learning context

xvii

Preface

to enhance users' positive experiences. In L2 teaching and learning, the literature states that most studies on gamification lack theoretical principles that can guide the design of gamified learning experiences that promote learners' motivation and engagement. To make the picture more coherent, this paper synthesizes the existing literature on gamification L2 learning, focusing on empirical findings related to factors affecting L2 learning, current L2 gamified design models, gamification affordances and their inherent motivational and engagement outcomes. For this review, thematic and content analysis of 73 publications dating from 2017 to late 2022 were examined. The main contribution of the present study consists in critically evaluating the various findings of the current literature and suggesting several future research directions for gamifying L2 learning.

Dr. Zeynep Çetin Köroğlu is the author of the chapter entitled 'Integration of Digital Picture Books into Young Learners' Language Classrooms; A Novel Way to Develop Vocabulary Knowledge': The world we live in now is more technological than in the past and continues to change and develop day by day. Our children, who are accepted as 'digital natives', start to live a life intertwined with technology from the first years of their lives. To prepare them for the age they are in and the lives that await them in the future, digital picture books should be used effectively, especially in early childhood. This chapter discusses the use and importance of picture books in early childhood foreign language learning, the features and usage areas of digital picture books, the role and importance of digital picture books in vocabulary teaching, examples of well-designed digital picture books, websites and applications that offer these examples, and the effects of digital picture books on young learners' foreign language learning.

Dr. Betül Kınık & Dr. Hande Çetin are the authors of the chapter entitled 'Human vs. AI: The Use of ChatGPT in Writing Assessment': The current study seeks to investigate whether ChatGPT 3.5 can be used as an aid to help diminish the teachers' workload in assessing writing. To this aim, a mixed-methods research design was employed for the study. Randomly selected 20 descriptive essays written by freshman student teachers of English Language Teaching were scored by an experienced human rater and ChatGPT 3.5. An adapted 'Descriptive Essay Rubric' by the researchers was used to assess the descriptive essays of the student teachers. The quantitative aspect of the study involved frequency and percentage analysis, while the qualitative dimension centered on analyzing the written feedback provided by both ChatGPT and the human rater. The findings showed that there is a disagreement between ChatGPT 3.5 and the human rater. Furthermore, there are some problems with the written feedback it provides. ChatGPT 3.5 is much faster than the human rater as expected in terms of providing feedback. Thus, it is recommended that ChatGPT 3.5 can be employed as a tool under the supervision of teachers.

Preface

Dr. Tuğba Elif Toprak Yıldız is the author of the chapter entitled 'Natural Language Processing Applications in Language Assessment: The Use of Automated Speech Scoring': Natural language processing is a subfield of artificial intelligence investigating how computers can be utilized to understand and process natural language texts or speeches to accomplish useful things in various areas, and it draws on various disciplines, such as computer science, linguistics, and robotics. Natural language processing applications, including automated speech recognition and scoring, have several exciting prospects for language testing and assessment practices. These prospects include addressing practical constraints associated with test administration and scoring, securing standardization in test delivery, ensuring objectiveness and reliability in scoring procedures, and providing personalized feedback for learning. This chapter focuses on automated speech scoring and its applications in language testing and assessment and discusses how these systems can be employed in assessment contexts. The chapter also discusses the potential benefits and drawbacks of automated speech scoring while focusing on construct-related and practical challenges surrounding such systems.

Dr. Fatma Kimsesiz is the author of the chapter entitled 'EFL Learners' Digitalized Practices in Promoting Vocabulary Learning at the Higher Education Level': Technology has become an integral part of education and language instruction which is communicative in nature. The widespread use of portable devices like smart phones or tablet computers has also transformed language learning through diverse accessible facilities that can alternatively be evaluated in an out-of-school context. This paved the way for self-directed learning practices that enable learners to advance their language skills and vocabulary. This study aimed to investigate these self-directed practices for learning vocabulary in English. 120 EFL learners at diverse departments at a state university in Turkiye participated in the study. For data collection, a survey was employed that interrogated the self-directed vocabulary learning practices of the participants in digital contexts. The results of the study showed that learners use mobile technology for English language practices and adopt different strategies in vocabulary learning supplied by a variety of digital applications and facilities. The results are discussed and related implications are addressed based on the findings.

Gülşah ÖZ is the author of the chapter entitled 'Hybrid Flexible (HyFlex) Teaching in Foreign Language Education: Enhancing Equity, Inclusion, and Accessibility through an Innovative Digital Pedagogy': Hybrid Flexible (HyFlex) teaching, which is assumed to be a much more flexible and learner-centered instruction mode, has received great attention from educators and researchers in recent years. In HyFlex learning and teaching environment, learners can make decisions on how they attend lessons i.e., face-to-face in a real classroom, online synchronously, or asynchronously after the allotted real lesson time. The present chapter aims to introduce HyFlex teaching as a new digital pedagogical and technological mode of instruction in the field of foreign language learning and teaching. In addition, this chapter discusses the benefits of EFL teaching in HyFlex classroom environments along with some challenges and possible solutions proposed by instructors in light of the current relevant literature. Furthermore, how HyFlex teaching can promote equal, inclusive, and accessible learning conditions for all students regardless of their diverse backgrounds fostering the language learning and teaching process is addressed.

IN SUMMARY

Fostering Foreign Language Teaching and Learning Environments With Contemporary Technologies shares research and reviews on how foreign language teachers, foreign language learners, and teacher educators integrate emerging technologies in their language learning and teaching processes. It raises awareness of the experiences and challenges of emerging technologies in foreign language learning environments and demonstrates how language educators draw upon contemporary technologies, their own experiences, and students' needs as resources in language teaching and learning.

Including topics such as digitalized practices of vocabulary teaching, natural language processing applications in language assessment, the use of ChatGBT for assessing writing, digital picture books to teach vocabulary to young learners, gamified L2 learning and its relation to motivation and engagement, artificial intelligence in giving corrective feedback on writing, designing achievement tests through novel technologies, ChatGBT and English language teacher candidates, autonomous learning in distance education theories, artificial intelligence and Chinese' language pedagogy, and hybrid flexible teaching in foreign language education, the current book constitutes a primary source of reference for foreign language educators of all levels, teacher trainers and all the other stakeholders.

As a whole the chapters in this edited book provide a thorough, timely and novel overview of current technologies in foreign language teaching and learning. Adapting today's foreign language classes to the technological equipment of our era means we can create learning environments tailored to our students' needs and desires. Changes in foreign language classes are inevitable, given that students' digital capabilities and skills are changing with these changing technologies and lifestyles. This book was created to prevent foreign language teachers from overlooking or standing up to these changes and to make them part of such innovations.

As the editors of this book, we extend our heartfelt thanks to all our authors who have contributed to the book. We would like to extend our appreciation to the readers, including educators, researchers, practitioners, and learners, who will actively participate in the exploration of this collection and apply its insights to their educational environments, research endeavors, and policy dialogues.

Preface

Zeynep Çetin Köroğlu
Aksaray University, Turkey

Abdulvahit Çakir
Ufuk University, Turkey

REFERENCES

Chapelle, C. A. (2001). *Computer applications in second language acquisition foundations for teaching, testing, and research.* Cambridge University. doi:10.1017/CBO9781139524681

Department of Education and Early Childhood Development. (2010). *Teaching and learning with Web 2.0 technologies. State of Victoria.* DoEECD. https://www.education.vic.gov.au/edulibrary/public/teachlearn/innovation/technology/web2report.pd

Dunkel, P. (1990). Implications of the CAI effectiveness research for limited English proficient learners. *Computers in the Schools, 7*(1/2), 31–52. doi:10.1300/J025v07n01_02

Gillespie, H. (2006). *Unlocking learning and teaching with ICT: Identifying and overcoming barriers.* David Fulton.

Lee, K. W. (2000). English teachers' barriers to the use of computer-assisted language learning. *TESL Journal, 6*(12). http://iteslj.org/Articles/Lee-CALLbarriers.html

Mansor, N. (2007). Collaborative learning via email discussion: Strategies for ESL writing classroom. *The Internet ESL Journal, 13*(3). http://iteslj.org/Techniques/Mansor-EmailDiscussion

Miner, T. (2004). *Using technology to enhance learning: Instructor-or student-moderated discussion boards: Which are more effective?* CCONE. http://www.cccone.org/scholars/0405/TomMiner_final_report.pdf

Nawaila, N. M., Kanbul, S., & Alhamroni, R. (2020). Technology and English Language Teaching and Learning: A Content Analysis. *Journal of Learning and Teaching in Digital Age, 5*(1), 16–23.

Timucin, M. (2006). Implementing CALL in the EFL context. *ELT Journal, 60*(3), 262–271. doi:10.1093/elt/ccl006

Chapter 1
Artificial Intelligence and the Future of Chinese Language Pedagogy:
An In-Depth Analysis

Mohamad Zreik
 https://orcid.org/0000-0002-6812-6529
Sun Yat-sen University, China

ABSTRACT

This chapter explores the function of cutting-edge technologies including artificial intelligence, augmented reality, and the metaverse in teaching Chinese as a foreign language. It's an example of how AI is being put to use in tailor-made programs for mastering Chinese and all its subtleties. The chapter covers how to use augmented reality and how it can help you have more meaningful conversations with others. The potential of ChatGPT and the metaverse as interactive learning environments is also discussed in this chapter. The effects on educational policy and teacher preparation, as well as an examination of students' independence in technologically advanced classrooms, are discussed in the last section.

INTRODUCTION

The educational system has been radically transformed by the digital age, which is marked by rapid technology developments and digital change. Learning has become more adaptable, personalized, and interactive thanks to the widespread adoption of digital technology during the past few decades. The importance of knowing how

DOI: 10.4018/979-8-3693-0353-5.ch001

Copyright © 2024, IGI Global. Copying or distributing in print or electronic forms without written permission of IGI Global is prohibited.

to fully utilize technological tools in the classroom is only going to grow as we progress farther into this era.

In particular, these changes have had a profound impact on language study. There has been a shift away from the more traditional language classroom, where teachers and students would sit face-to-face and use textbooks to study the language. Having instantaneous access to resources for self-paced learning means that learning a language now also involves comprehending cultural nuances, practicing conversational skills in real-time, and studying at one's own pace (Serrano et al., 2019). The essential role that new technologies will play in the future of language education is reflected in the fact that they are the primary facilitators of these broader learning opportunities.

New language-learning technology aren't just another passing fad; they're an absolute must for any serious language student. With the use of technologies like AI, AR, and the metaverse, language classes can be adapted to each student's unique learning style and speed. For instance, augmented reality (AR) may generate immersive, contextual learning experiences that traditional classrooms may not deliver, and AI can give individualized learning pathways based on a learner's performance and progress (Sharma, 2022). Because of its ability for virtual interaction and exploration, the metaverse has great promise for fostering active participation in language acquisition (Zhang, 2023).

This chapter was inspired by the realization that, thanks to the advent of the information age, technology has permeated nearly every facet of modern life, including the classroom. It aims to explore the usage and promise of technology in Chinese language education and specifically highlights the growing role of technology in language learning. This chapter is both timely and important because of the growing digitalization of education and the widespread interest in learning Chinese.

There are three goals to accomplish in this chapter. While there is a broad understanding of the value of technology in the classroom, a closer look at how it might be utilized to improve language instruction is warranted. Second, there is a need for more in-depth scholarly investigation on the role that technology plays in Chinese language teaching despite its development over time. Last but not least, the frontiers of artificial intelligence, augmented reality, and the metaverse are rich in educational possibilities. The field of language teaching urgently requires more investigation of these cutting-edge resources.

Therefore, the purpose of this chapter is to investigate how artificial intelligence, augmented reality, and the metaverse might be used to improve Chinese language education. It'll take a close look at how these tools are being used in Chinese language classes and analyze their implications for improving students' linguistic abilities and their knowledge of China's history, geography, and culture.

It'll take a close look at how students and educators view these new tools, as well as how they could be used to foster student independence. Also discussed will be the effects of technology on educational policy and teacher preparation, as well as the function of digital assessment tools in language acquisition.

APPLICATION OF ARTIFICIAL INTELLIGENCE IN CHINESE LANGUAGE EDUCATION

Case Studies of AI Utilization in Chinese Language Classrooms

In recent years, there has been a surge in the use of AI in the classroom, and Chinese language classes are no exception. The potential for AI's machine learning and cognitive computing to personalize training, increase learner engagement, and improve outcomes is substantial (Oda Abunamous et al., 2022).

The novel application of AI in Chinese language classes is demonstrated by several case examples. One study, for instance, details how intelligent tutoring systems (ITSs) were included into the instruction of Mandarin. A student's current skill level, preferred learning style, and problem areas can all be identified by these ITS. Data-driven adjustments to teaching methods allowed the systems to provide students with individualized lessons covering anything from learning new characters and words to constructing more complicated sentences. The study found that students who used ITS to learn were more proficient overall, especially in previously difficult subject areas, demonstrating the personalized learning opportunities provided by AI (Nye, 2015).

Another study focused on the effectiveness of artificial intelligence (AI) language apps that employ machine learning to enhance students' articulation and intonation. Because of its tonal nature, learning Chinese can be particularly difficult for those who are not native speakers. The app's AI features allowed students to video themselves speaking Mandarin, with subsequent real-time feedback from machine learning algorithms on pronunciation, tone, and inflection (Varatharaj, 2020).

In yet another instance, chatbots driven by artificial intelligence were employed to make language practice more engaging and effective. The purpose of these chatbots is to provide learners with a way to practice their listening and speaking abilities in Chinese outside of the classroom (Kohnke, 2023).

These examples show that the practical use of AI goes much beyond what has previously been imagined. They provide specific examples of how AI may make learning Chinese more individualized, efficient, and interesting. The use of AI in Chinese language schools has already advanced to a point where it can improve many facets of the teaching and learning processes.

Examination of AI's Role in Teaching Speaking, Reading, Writing, Listening Skills, Vocabulary, Grammar, and Pronunciation

The use of AI in language instruction is having far-reaching effects on all facets of the study of linguistics, from phonology to syntax to pronunciation. Because of the specific difficulties associated with learning Chinese, AI has proven to be especially useful in the context of language instruction in the language (Yuan, 2022).

The impact of AI on language proficiency is varied. For example, with the help of AI-powered language apps, students of Chinese can connect with intelligent bots that can understand, reply, and provide instantaneous feedback on their spoken language skills (Pokrivcakova, 2019). Learners of Chinese can use these chatbots to practice conversing like a native speaker and to improve their pronunciation, tone, and inflection, all of which are essential elements of the language.

Artificial intelligence technologies can instantly recognize Chinese characters and deliver translations, assisting students in grasping the meaning and context of words and phrases as they are being taught to read. Some AI programs also provide reading comprehension tests and exercises, during which the program evaluates the student's grasp of the material and provides constructive criticism and tips for future study (Zawacki-Richter et al., 2019).

Writing in Chinese can also be improved with the help of AI. The stroke sequence of Chinese letters is essential when writing in Chinese, and intelligent teaching programs can guide students through the process step by step. Predictive text and auto-correction capabilities enabled by AI can also aid students in strengthening their sentence structure and grammar (Qian, Owen, & Bax, 2018).

AI can also be used to improve one's listening abilities. Some AI tools include simulations of real-world situations in which students can develop their listening comprehension skills (Kessler, 2018). These systems are smart enough to modify the challenges presented to students based on their current level of knowledge and skill.

The AI's capacity for adaptive learning shines through when it comes to vocabulary and grammar. Artificial intelligence systems can personalize vocabulary and grammar exercises based on a learner's progress and difficulties, helping to reinforce learning and fill in knowledge gaps (Chen et al., 2022). Learners of Chinese can benefit from the AI's ability to provide them with continuous, repeating practice in order to grasp the language's complicated grammatical structures and large vocabulary.

Artificial intelligence can help with pronunciation, which is particularly difficult when learning Chinese because of the language's tonal nature. Apps that use artificial intelligence to analyze speech can help students improve their tone and pronunciation (Fendji et al.,2022).

Empirical Insights Into Personalized Learning Through AI Platforms

Research into the application of AI in education has shown promising results, particularly in the area of delivering individualized instruction for languages. These findings shed light on how AI can be used in the classroom to improve Chinese language instruction and student achievement.

AI's data-analysis skills are what allow it to deliver individualized education. Information on a student's preferred method of study, rate of progress, and current skill level can be collected, analyzed, and applied by an AI platform. A language learning tool powered by AI, for instance, can monitor a user's progress across reading, writing, listening, and speaking. Using this information, the program can modify its lessons to provide extra help where the student needs it most and go more quickly through material where they already know the material. AI is a powerful tool because it allows teachers to adapt their lessons to the specific needs of their students.

The results of empirical investigations suggest that this individualized strategy for language learning is highly effective. For instance, one study on the application of AI in Chinese language classes found that students who used a personalized AI tool to study the language had a deeper understanding of Chinese characters, vocabulary, and grammar rules than their peers who had used more conventional methods of instruction. Moreover, these students reported increased levels of interest and motivation, supporting the premise that individualized learning might improve not only academic performance but also students' attitudes towards learning (Chen et al., 2021).

Learning doesn't have to stop when school does, thanks to AI platforms. Students can interact with AI tools whenever they like, at their own speed, and with immediate feedback on their exercises (Hwang & Chien, 2022). This adaptability further improves the individualization of education by allowing students to study when and where it is most convenient for them.

IMPLEMENTATION OF AUGMENTED REALITY IN CHINESE LANGUAGE CLASSROOMS

Overview of AR Applications in Language Learning

Language instruction will undergo a radical transformation with the introduction of Augmented Reality (AR) technology. Because AR can superimpose digital data onto the real world, it creates a setting that is both engaging and conducive to learning.

The use of this technology in classrooms teaching Chinese has already begun to revolutionize the discipline.

The application of augmented reality to the study of Chinese is broad and varied. Teaching Chinese characters is one of the most common uses of augmented reality technology. When a pupil aims their smartphone at a character, augmented reality applications can superimpose information regarding the character's stroke sequence, pronunciation, and meaning (Wang, 2017). Using this visual and participatory approach of learning, the characters and their structure will stick in your mind.

Vocabulary study may also benefit from the use of AR applications. Some augmented reality apps, for instance, may pick out real-world items and show the student the corresponding Chinese name and pronunciation (Santos et al., 2017). Learning new words in this context, where they are associated with real-world items, can greatly improve retention and comprehension.

Chinese language classrooms also benefit from the use of interactive storybooks enhanced with augmented reality technology. These augmented reality books may bring the pages to life with audio, video, and interactive features (Challenor & Ma, 2019). This not only keeps students interested, but also enhances their reading, comprehension, and sensitivity to other cultures.

In addition, students can hone their communication and listening skills in simulated real-world settings made possible by augmented reality technology. For example, students can get real-world conversational practice with a native Chinese speaker through augmented reality-powered simulated discussion.

Augmented reality can provide pupils with a first-hand look at aspects of Chinese culture. This broader cultural context strengthens the language learning experience by allowing students to virtually visit Chinese monuments, experience Chinese holidays, and even participate in traditional Chinese activities (Anderson, 2019).

Detailed Examples of AR's Role in Teaching Chinese Language Skills and Understanding Culture, History, and Geography

When it comes to teaching Chinese language skills and boosting awareness of Chinese culture, history, and geography, augmented reality plays a game-changing role. Augmented reality aids Chinese language and culture study by allowing students to participate in realistic simulations of authentic situations (Wei et al., 2015).

Augmented reality apps can mimic real-world discussions to help students practice their speaking and listening abilities. An application may, for instance, create an augmented reality (AR) avatar of a native Chinese speaker and allow the student to converse with the avatar (Wang et al., 2018). The student's speaking and listening abilities can be honed by providing them with opportunities to listen to native speakers, interact with them in real time, and receive immediate feedback on their pronunciation and grammar.

Augmented reality can make learning to read and write Chinese characters more engaging. By scanning a character from their textbook with their mobile devices, students can receive contextualized information about the character's stroke order, pronunciation, and meaning from an augmented reality application. It can also show how the character changed through time, from traditional to simplified Chinese, which can help shed light on the character's importance and background (Huang et al., 2021).

Innovative approaches to teaching vocabulary and grammar are also available through AR. For instance, an augmented reality app may use the device's camera to name and display the pronunciation and example sentence usage of real-world things in Chinese. Putting new words into their appropriate context aids memorization and comprehension (Booton, Hodgkiss, & Murphy, 2023).

Augmented reality's ability to generate immersive experiences makes it particularly well-suited to improving students' familiarity with China's history, geography, and culture. Students can get an up-close and personal look at cultural and historical events like the Great Wall of China and the Lantern Festival without ever having to leave the classroom. Learning Chinese in this way expands beyond the classroom and into the wider, more nuanced world of Chinese culture, where a better grasp and enjoyment of the language can flourish.

POTENTIAL OF CHATGPT AND THE METAVERSE IN CHINESE LANGUAGE EDUCATION

Exploration of ChatGPT and the Metaverse as New Learning Platforms

New educational tools like ChatGPT and the metaverse have evolved as a result of technological development. Using cutting-edge technologies like AI, VR, and social engagement, these platforms usher in a new era in Chinese language instruction and study.

OpenAI's ChatGPT artificial intelligence language model is helpful for teaching Mandarin Chinese. It can have natural conversations in Chinese with students, answering their questions and providing explanations. In this way, students can increase their command of the Chinese language through frequent, low-stakes speaking and listening practice (Houston & Corrado, 2023). As an added bonus, the AI in ChatGPT allows it to tailor its responses to each individual student based on their current level of knowledge. Learners can get immediate comments on their grammar, vocabulary, and pronunciation to help them improve (Mallik & Gangopadhyay, 2023).

The metaverse, a collective virtual shared place formed by the merger of augmented reality and persistent virtual reality, could also be useful in teaching Chinese. The atmosphere it creates for learning Chinese can be wholly immersive, interactive, and social. Students can engage in virtual Chinese cultural events, practice speaking with other students, and interact with AI tutors. Learners can use the metaverse to practice authentic scenarios, such as making a reservation at a Chinese restaurant, navigating a Chinese city, or taking part in a traditional Chinese ceremony (Guodong, Huanhuan, & Yuanzhong, 2021). These simulations have the potential to greatly improve language learning results by making the learning process more interesting, applicable, and relevant.

Analysis of Learner and Teacher Perceptions Towards These Platforms

It is essential for the successful adoption of innovative learning platforms like ChatGPT and the metaverse in Chinese language education to understand how students and teachers feel about them. These biases can affect how well these tools are received, used, and ultimately successful in improving language learning results.

The majority of students have a favorable impression of educational technology tools like ChatGPT and the metaverse. Students prefer these platforms because they are participatory and immersive, making studying Chinese fun and interesting. They appreciate the customized feedback provided by ChatGPT and other AI teachers, as well as the low-stakes, frequent opportunities to practice speaking and listening. In addition, the metaverse's contextual learning experiences, such virtual tours of Chinese landmarks or simulated talks in Chinese scenarios, are highly valued by students because they deepen their familiarity with Chinese culture and improve their ability to use the language in real-world contexts (Kaplan, 2023).

However, there are problems as well. Some students, especially those with low levels of computer literacy, may feel lost in the complex features of these sites. Some students may prefer online learning, while others may long for the personal attention and contact that can only come from a classroom setting.

How professors feel about various mediums is equally important. Many educators believe that ChatGPT and other metaverse tools can help them better reach and engage today's generation of digital natives in the classroom. They value the platforms' potential to facilitate independent study outside of scheduled class times and to facilitate lifelong learning. In addition, teachers' workloads can be lightened thanks to these platforms' immediate feedback on students' exercises, freeing them up to concentrate on more strategic areas of instruction (Srinivasa, Kurni, & Saritha, 2022).

Artificial Intelligence and the Future of Chinese Language Pedagogy

Nonetheless, some educators may have reservations about using such sites in the classroom. Due to a lack of training or a fear of technology, some teachers may be hesitant to include these tools into their lessons. Some teachers may be wary of these platforms because they fear they would undermine their position in the classroom, but this is not the intention (Kulikowski, Przytuła, & Sułkowski, 2022).

Practical Examples of Engagement and Interactivity in Language Learning Through These Platforms

When it comes to teaching Chinese, ChatGPT and the metaverse provide opportunities for interaction and immersion that go well beyond the approaches often used in the classroom. Some real-world applications of these systems are provided below.

A learner learning Chinese with ChatGPT might first ask the AI instructor to break down a tricky grammatical rule or demonstrate how to properly use a particular character. The responses from the AI tutor are straightforward, with the aid of examples and even interactive tasks to further cement comprehension. The student can then use ChatGPT to practice speaking and listening in Chinese through conversation. The student's language abilities will be enhanced in a tailored and engaging fashion thanks to the AI tutor's ability to adjust the conversation's complexity based on the student's current level of competence.

ChatGPT can also serve as a storyteller's companion, delivering fables and anecdotes in Chinese to students. The AI can have conversations with the students, who can pose questions and offer suggestions for the story (Lo, 2023). This method has been shown to boost students' critical thinking abilities and cultural awareness in addition to their language proficiency.

The interaction and participation in the metaverse are on a whole other level. Students can learn to write Chinese characters, for instance, by utilizing a digital brush and ink in a simulated classroom setting. They can also practice their bargaining abilities with a virtual Chinese market seller driven by artificial intelligence (Li, Wang, & Xu, 2022).

Students may also go on a virtual field trip to a Chinese city in the metaverse, where they would be able to explore the streets, read signs, ask for directions, and engage with virtual inhabitants. Their linguistic proficiency and cultural understanding will both benefit from this fully immersing event.

The Lunar New Year and the Mid-Autumn Festival are two examples of Chinese cultural occasions that students can experience virtually and learn about the traditions, customs, and language related with. They have a deeper appreciation for the Chinese language and culture as a result of this hands-on experience (Zreik, 2021).

These real-world scenarios illustrate how virtual environments (such as ChatGPT and the metaverse) can facilitate interesting, dynamic, and contextualized language study. These platforms can considerably improve the efficiency and pleasure of studying Chinese by providing students with the opportunity to do it in an immersive, engaging, and realistic setting.

LEARNER AUTONOMY AND TECHNOLOGICAL ASSESSMENT IN A MODERN CLASSROOM

Discussion on Independent and Self-Directed Learning in Tech-Enhanced Classrooms

Technology such as ChatGPT, the metaverse, and other artificial intelligence and augmented reality tools are revolutionizing Chinese language schools, empowering students to learn on their own terms (Zreik, 2023).

Learner autonomy, when applied to the study of languages, describes students' degrees of independence in directing their own education. Students are responsible for determining their own learning objectives, choosing effective methods of study, keeping track of their progress, and modifying their methods as needed. The use of technology in the classroom greatly aids in these areas of student independence.

ChatGPT, like other AI-based applications, gives students the freedom to study on their own time and in their own ways. Students have more freedom in terms of course selection, schedule, and method of practice (Liu, Lomovtseva, & Korobeynikova, 2020). They can have a dialogue with the AI, get clarification on grammar rules, and get comments on how they sound. Learners who are given greater agency in their education report higher levels of satisfaction with their experiences as a result.

The metaverse's capacity for immersion and interaction makes it an ideal platform for fostering independent learning by presenting interesting and relevant content (Lee & Hwang, 2022). Students of Chinese can, for instance, take a virtual tour of a Chinese metropolis, a virtual cookery lesson, or a virtual discussion with a native speaker. Learners get agency and intrinsic motivation from these encounters, which they may tailor to their own interests and goals.

As technology has progressed, more complex evaluation tools have been available for students to employ in tracking their own development. These resources can offer immediate responses to learners' activities, highlight improvement areas, and propose individualized study plans. The learner receives quick, individualized feedback that helps them identify areas for improvement, formulate realistic objectives, and fine-tune their approach to learning (George & George, 2023).

Artificial Intelligence and the Future of Chinese Language Pedagogy

Overview of Contemporary Technological Assessment Tools Used in Chinese Language Education

Modern evaluation techniques have emerged as a result of the widespread use of technology in Chinese language classes, allowing for more precise and efficient monitoring and improvement of students' development.

Language-study apps that use artificial intelligence are one example. These systems utilize machine learning algorithms to continuously evaluate a student's progress, offer immediate feedback, and customize the course's difficulty based on that individual's demonstrated mastery. The writing of a student, for instance, may be analyzed by an AI platform for grammar, vocabulary, and structure, with problem areas highlighted and appropriate activities provided (Bernius, Krusche, & Bruegge, 2022). By assessing a learner's pronunciation, tone, and fluency, these platforms may evaluate a speaker's potential and offer tips for improvement.

The use of Adaptive Learning Systems is another notable technology. AI is used in these systems so that lessons and tests can be tailored to each individual's skill set and rate of progress. The following task is tailored to the student based on their success in the previous one; this keeps them pushed without being too difficult (Alam, 2022). These systems can monitor a student's development over time, revealing valuable information about his or her strengths and shortcomings and recommending individualized courses of study.

There are new ways to evaluate students using AR and VR technology as well. A learner's ability to recognize and write Chinese characters, for instance, might be evaluated using an augmented reality application by superimposing the proper stroke order and comparing it to the learner's strokes (Zreik & Abunamous, 2020). Similarly, a virtual reality program may mimic a conversation with a fluent Chinese speaker and evaluate the student's pronunciation, intonation, and vocabulary usage in real time (Athugala, 2020).

Online quizzes, games, and interactive exercises are some examples of the increasingly widespread use of digital methods of evaluation. With the help of these resources, assessing students' knowledge may be both interesting and relaxing, thereby increasing students' engagement and teachers' efficiency (Sepasgozar, 2020).

IMPLICATIONS FOR EDUCATIONAL POLICY AND TEACHER TRAINING

Examination of the Effects of Emerging Technologies on Educational Policies

The ramifications of using cutting-edge tools like artificial intelligence, augmented reality, and the metaverse in teaching Chinese as a foreign language are far-reaching. Incorporating new technologies requires a reconsideration of policies about curriculum development, assessment, and allocation of resources. Incorporating digital tools into teaching and learning processes has the potential to improve interactivity, personalization, and learner autonomy, but this may necessitate adjustments to existing curricula. Digital assessment methods that provide instantaneous, in-depth, and individually relevant feedback may need to be added to assessment policies.

In addition, digital equity concerns must be factored into educational policies. The need of ensuring that all students have access to the required technology and internet connectivity increases as more educational content and interactions shift online or to digital platforms. To ensure that students from all economic situations may benefit from new technologies, policy changes must be made.

The proliferation of these technologies, from the standpoint of educator preparation, highlights the need for professional development programs that prepare educators with digital literacy abilities. Teachers must be familiar with these tools in order to effectively incorporate them into lessons and help students learn more. Effective technology integration requires both technical expertise and pedagogical tactics, both of which should be covered in training programs.

The teacher's shifting responsibilities in a tech-enhanced classroom also need to be addressed in teacher education. Teachers need to be ready to change from being the major source of knowledge to becoming facilitators of learning as AI, augmented reality, and the metaverse take on some of the instructional roles. Teachers need training in how to help students make the most of these tools, create a classroom setting that promotes independent study, and make use of digital assessment instruments to monitor students' growth and tailor their lessons to their specific needs.

Impacts on the Development of Teacher Training Programs

There are major ramifications for the future of teacher education programs resulting from the adoption of new technology in teaching the Chinese language. As these tools grow more central to education, teacher preparation must adapt to ensure that educators are prepared to help their students succeed in the digital age.

The usage of AI platforms, AR applications, and the metaverse in the classroom is becoming increasingly important, thus training programs should reflect this (Abouhashem et al., 2021). Incorporating AR applications into courses has been shown to increase student engagement, and providing immersive and context-rich learning experiences via the metaverse is another option (Belda-Medina, 2022).

As an example, educators might receive training on how to use ChatGPT and similar AI platforms to enhance their lessons and provide students more chances to use the target language outside of class. Teachers may also receive instruction in the use of AR tools for incorporating aspects of Chinese heritage and geography into lessons to make learning a foreign language more interesting and relevant to students. Also, teachers might learn how to design metaverses that mimic real-world circumstances so that language learning can take place in a natural setting.

The pedagogical implications of these technologies are an additional concern that must be addressed in teacher preparation programs. Learning how to promote learner autonomy in a technology-enhanced classroom may require making this transition from a teacher-centered to a learner-centered approach (An & Mindrila, 2020). Teachers need preparation in the use of digital assessment tools for tracking student progress and tailoring instruction, as well as in guiding students in using these technologies for self-directed learning.

In addition, educators' digital literacy needs to be enhanced through training programs, from the most fundamental abilities like using digital devices and software to the most complex, including comprehending data protection and security in online education environments. Teachers who lack these competencies will struggle to help their pupils make safe and responsible technological choices.

RECOMMENDATIONS FOR FUTURE RESEARCH AND IMPLEMENTATION

Considering the pivotal role artificial intelligence plays in modern Chinese language pedagogy as highlighted in the study, it is recommended that future research focus on evaluating the efficacy of various AI tools. Such evaluations could take the form of randomized controlled trials, which would offer more rigorous assessments of these tools' adaptability to different learning environments and their effectiveness in improving language skills.

The study discusses the importance of augmented reality (AR) in creating immersive, contextual learning experiences. Future research could delve deeper into the role AR plays in contextualizing cultural elements, such as idiomatic expressions or cultural norms, within the language learning process. Such studies would provide valuable insights into how AR can be used to enhance not just language acquisition but also cultural understanding.

Given the study's mention of the metaverse as a fertile ground for interactive learning, subsequent research should explore the development of learner autonomy within these virtual environments. Researchers could investigate how the metaverse influences students' ability to self-regulate their learning and engage in self-directed activities, providing a clearer understanding of the metaverse's potential to foster independent learning.

The study touches upon the effects of technological advancements on educational policy and teacher preparation. It is recommended that future studies explore the specifics of how educational policy could evolve to better accommodate these technologies. Questions around curriculum integration, teacher training, and resource allocation should be focal points of this research.

As the study also discusses the role of digital assessment tools in language acquisition, it would be beneficial for future work to consider the development and validation of such tools specifically for Chinese language education. Comparative studies could be undertaken to assess the advantages and disadvantages of digital assessment methods as compared to traditional testing formats.

CONCLUSION

This chapter has illuminated the pivotal function of new technologies in Chinese language education, signaling a radical change in pedagogical strategy. The use of AI, AR, and other platforms such as ChatGPT and the metaverse in language classes has not only altered the student experience but also reworked instructional strategies, course structure, evaluation criteria, and teacher preparation programs.

Artificial intelligence has shown promise in boosting several facets of Chinese language instruction, from the acquisition of phonological awareness and lexical knowledge to the enhancement of grammatical precision and pronunciation. Artificial intelligence platforms have made it possible for educators to better meet the requirements of their students by creating individualized lessons and providing instantaneous feedback.

Similarly, AR has introduced a new dimension to Chinese language schools, allowing for a more engaging and relevant experience for students studying the language. Augmented reality applications have expanded the scope of what students may do in the classroom, increasing their interest and motivation to study.

ChatGPT and the metaverse are two innovative learning systems that have been introduced into Chinese language classes to enhance students' opportunities for active participation in language acquisition. Both students and instructors have viewed these tools favorably, which bodes well for their eventual widespread implementation.

Independent and self-directed learning has been made possible in classrooms where technology has been implemented thanks to increased student autonomy made possible by these innovations. Furthermore, they have spawned modern technology evaluation tools, which provide more customized, efficient, and interesting ways to evaluate students' development.

On the policy level, incorporating new technology has prompted major changes in educational legislation and a refocusing of teacher preparation programs. They may make the most of these advancements in Chinese language teaching if they adapt to new circumstances.

Future possibilities for learning more about and making use of these technologies are tremendous. More advanced language-learning resources will undoubtedly emerge as scientists continue to investigate the potential of AI, AR, and platforms like ChatGPT and the metaverse. Additional research on the effects of these tools on student performance, student motivation, and student agency is necessary for informing policy decisions and pedagogical development.

To guarantee that teachers have the digital literacy skills and pedagogical understanding to effectively integrate these tools into their teaching, the future of Chinese language education will also require continued investment in teacher training programs.

Taking advantage of these new tools is not merely an innovative strategy for teaching Chinese in today's increasingly digitalized environment; it's also essential. The future seems bright, and if these technologies are implemented with care, they will drastically improve Chinese language learning and instruction, making it more individualized, interesting, and successful for students all around the world. In shedding light on these promising trends, this chapter seeks to pave the way for future research and growth in the field of Chinese language teaching.

REFERENCES

Abouhashem, A., Abdou, R. M., Bhadra, J., Siby, N., Ahmad, Z., & Al-Thani, N. J. (2021). Covid-19 inspired a stem-based virtual learning model for middle schools—A case study of Qatar. *Sustainability (Basel)*, *13*(5), 2799. doi:10.3390u13052799

Alam, A. (2022). Employing adaptive learning and intelligent tutoring robots for virtual classrooms and smart campuses: Reforming education in the age of artificial intelligence. *Advanced Computing and Intelligent Technologies Proceedings of ICACIT*, *2022*, 395–406.

An, Y., & Mindrila, D. (2020). Strategies and tools used for learner-centered instruction. *International Journal of Technology in Education and Science*, *4*(2), 133–143. doi:10.46328/ijtes.v4i2.74

Anderson, A. (2019). *Virtual reality, augmented reality and artificial intelligence in special education: a practical guide to supporting students with learning differences.* Routledge. doi:10.4324/9780429399503

Athugala, R. M. V. (2020). *Developing a computer-based interactive system that creates a sense of deep engagement* [Doctoral dissertation]. Faculty of Fine Arts and Music, University of Melbourne.

Belda-Medina, J. (2022). Using augmented reality (AR) as an authoring tool in EFL through mobile computer-supported collaborative learning. *Teaching English with Technology*, *22*(2), 115–135.

Bernius, J. P., Krusche, S., & Bruegge, B. (2022). Machine learning based feedback on textual student answers in large courses. *Computers and Education: Artificial Intelligence*, *3*, 100081. doi:10.1016/j.caeai.2022.100081

Booton, S. A., Hodgkiss, A., & Murphy, V. A. (2023). The impact of mobile application features on children's language and literacy learning: A systematic review. *Computer Assisted Language Learning*, *36*(3), 400–429. doi:10.1080/095 88221.2021.1930057

Challenor, J., & Ma, M. (2019). A review of augmented reality applications for history education and heritage isualization. *Multimodal Technologies and Interaction*, *3*(2), 39. doi:10.3390/mti3020039

Chen, X., Zou, D., Xie, H., & Cheng, G. (2021). Twenty years of personalized language learning. *Journal of Educational Technology & Society*, *24*(1), 205–222.

Chen, X., Zou, D., Xie, H., Cheng, G., & Liu, C. (2022). Two decades of artificial intelligence in education. *Journal of Educational Technology & Society*, *25*(1), 28–47.

Fendji, J. L. K. E., Tala, D. C., Yenke, B. O., & Atemkeng, M. (2022). Automatic speech recognition using limited vocabulary: A survey. *Applied Artificial Intelligence*, *36*(1), 2095039. doi:10.1080/08839514.2022.2095039

George, A. S., & George, A. H. (2023). A review of ChatGPT AI's impact on several business sectors. *Partners Universal International Innovation Journal*, *1*(1), 9–23.

Guodong, Z., Huanhuan, Y., & Yuanzhong, X. (2021). *Metaverse. Beijing Book Co*. Inc.

Houston, A. B., & Corrado, E. M. (2023). Embracing ChatGPT: Implications of Emergent Language Models for Academia and Libraries. *Technical Services Quarterly*, *40*(2), 76–91. doi:10.1080/07317131.2023.2187110

Huang, X., Zou, D., Cheng, G., & Xie, H. (2021). A systematic review of AR and VR enhanced language learning. *Sustainability (Basel)*, *13*(9), 4639. doi:10.3390u13094639

Hwang, G. J., & Chien, S. Y. (2022). Definition, roles, and potential research issues of the metaverse in education: An artificial intelligence perspective. *Computers and Education: Artificial Intelligence*, *3*, 100082. doi:10.1016/j.caeai.2022.100082

Kaplan, A. (2023). *Business Schools Post-COVID-19: A Blueprint for Survival.* Taylor & Francis. doi:10.4324/9781003343509

Kessler, G. (2018). Technology and the future of language teaching. *Foreign Language Annals*, *51*(1), 205–218. doi:10.1111/flan.12318

Kohnke, L. (2023). L2 learners' perceptions of a chatbot as a potential independent language learning tool. *International Journal of Mobile Learning and Organisation*, *17*(1-2), 214–226. doi:10.1504/IJMLO.2023.128339

Kulikowski, K., Przytuła, S., & Sułkowski, Ł. (2022). E-learning? Never again! On the unintended consequences of COVID-19 forced e-learning on academic teacher motivational job characteristics. *Higher Education Quarterly*, *76*(1), 174–189. doi:10.1111/hequ.12314

Lee, H., & Hwang, Y. (2022). Technology-enhanced education through VR-making and metaverse-linking to foster teacher readiness and sustainable learning. *Sustainability (Basel)*, *14*(8), 4786. doi:10.3390u14084786

Li, M., Wang, Y., & Xu, Y. Q. (2022). Computing for Chinese cultural heritage. *Visual Informatics*, *6*(1), 1–13. doi:10.1016/j.visinf.2021.12.006 PMID:36312746

Liu, Z. Y., Lomovtseva, N., & Korobeynikova, E. (2020). Online learning platforms: Reconstructing modern higher education. *International Journal of Emerging Technologies in Learning*, *15*(13), 4–21. doi:10.3991/ijet.v15i13.14645

Lo, C. K. (2023). What is the impact of ChatGPT on education? A rapid review of the literature. *Education Sciences*, *13*(4), 410. doi:10.3390/educsci13040410

Mallik, S., & Gangopadhyay, A. (2023). Proactive and reactive engagement of artificial intelligence methods for education: A review. *Frontiers in Artificial Intelligence*, *6*, 1151391. doi:10.3389/frai.2023.1151391 PMID:37215064

Nye, B. D. (2015). Intelligent tutoring systems by and for the developing world: A review of trends and approaches for educational technology in a global context. *International Journal of Artificial Intelligence in Education*, *25*(2), 177–203. doi:10.100740593-014-0028-6

Oda Abunamous, M., Boudouaia, A., Jebril, M., Diafi, S., & Zreik, M. (2022). The decay of traditional education: A case study under covid-19. *Cogent Education*, *9*(1), 2082116. doi:10.1080/2331186X.2022.2082116

Pokrivcakova, S. (2019). Preparing teachers for the application of AI-powered technologies in foreign language education. *Journal of Language and Cultural Education*, *7*(3), 135–153. doi:10.2478/jolace-2019-0025

Qian, K., Owen, N., & Bax, S. (2018). Researching mobile-assisted Chinese-character learning strategies among adult distance learners. *Innovation in Language Learning and Teaching*, *12*(1), 56–71. doi:10.1080/17501229.2018.1418633

Santos, M. E. C., Lübke, A. I. W., Taketomi, T., Yamamoto, G., Rodrigo, M. M. T., Sandor, C., & Kato, H. (2016). Augmented reality as multimedia: The case for situated vocabulary learning. *Research and Practice in Technology Enhanced Learning*, *11*(1), 1–23. doi:10.118641039-016-0028-2 PMID:30613237

Sepasgozar, S. M. (2020). Digital twin and web-based virtual gaming technologies for online education: A case of construction management and engineering. *Applied Sciences (Basel, Switzerland)*, *10*(13), 4678. doi:10.3390/app10134678

Serrano, D. R., Dea-Ayuela, M. A., Gonzalez-Burgos, E., Serrano-Gil, A., & Lalatsa, A. (2019). Technology-enhanced learning in higher education: How to enhance student engagement through blended learning. *European Journal of Education*, *54*(2), 273–286. doi:10.1111/ejed.12330

Sharma, R. C. (2022). Reshaping teaching and learning engineering through next-gen learning technologies. *Journal of Online Learning Studies*, *1*(1), 1–8.

Srinivasa, K. G., Kurni, M., & Saritha, K. (2022). Harnessing the Power of AI to Education. In *Learning, Teaching, and Assessment Methods for Contemporary Learners: Pedagogy for the Digital Generation* (pp. 311–342). Springer Nature Singapore. doi:10.1007/978-981-19-6734-4_13

Varatharaj, A. (2020). *Developing Automated Audio Assessment Tools for a Chinese Language Course* [Doctoral dissertation]. Worcester Polytechnic Institute.

Wang, M., Callaghan, V., Bernhardt, J., White, K., & Peña-Rios, A. (2018). Augmented reality in education and training: Pedagogical approaches and illustrative case studies. *Journal of Ambient Intelligence and Humanized Computing*, *9*(5), 1391–1402. doi:10.100712652-017-0547-8

Wang, Y. H. (2017). Exploring the effectiveness of integrating augmented reality-based materials to support writing activities. *Computers & Education*, *113*, 162–176. doi:10.1016/j.compedu.2017.04.013

Wei, X., Weng, D., Liu, Y., & Wang, Y. (2015). Teaching based on augmented reality for a technical creative design course. *Computers & Education*, *81*, 221–234. doi:10.1016/j.compedu.2014.10.017

Yuan, Y. (2022). Quantitative analysis of Chinese classroom teaching activity under the background of artificial intelligence. *Education and Information Technologies*, *27*(8), 11161–11177. doi:10.100710639-022-11080-x

Zawacki-Richter, O., Marín, V. I., Bond, M., & Gouverneur, F. (2019). Systematic review of research on artificial intelligence applications in higher education–where are the educators? *International Journal of Educational Technology in Higher Education*, *16*(1), 1–27. doi:10.118641239-019-0171-0

Zhang, Q. (2023). Secure Preschool Education Using Machine Learning and Metaverse Technologies. *Applied Artificial Intelligence*, *37*(1), 2222496. doi:10.1 080/08839514.2023.2222496

Zreik, M. (2021). Academic Exchange Programs between China and the Arab Region: A Means of Cultural Harmony or Indirect Chinese Influence? *Arab Studies Quarterly*, *43*(2), 172–188. doi:10.13169/arabstudquar.43.2.0172

Zreik, M. (2023). Navigating the Dragon: China's Ascent as a Global Power Through Public Diplomacy. In Global Perspectives on the Emerging Trends in Public Diplomacy (pp. 50-74). IGI Global.

Zreik, M., & Abunamous, M. O. (2020). Human thinking at the time of Covid-19 and the role of swot analysis: A case study on the Chinese and Palestinian societies. *Psychology Research on Education and Social Sciences*, *2*(1), 31–40.

KEY TERMS AND DEFINITIONS

Adaptive Learning Systems: Educational systems that use AI to personalize learning, adjusting the content and resources in real-time based on a student's performance and needs.

Artificial Intelligence (AI): A branch of computer science that enables machines to simulate human intelligence processes, including learning, reasoning, and self-correction.

Augmented Reality (AR): A technology that overlays digital information, such as images, sounds, or text, onto the real world, enhancing user interactions with their environment.

ChatGPT: An artificial intelligence language model developed by OpenAI that can engage in natural conversations with users, answering questions and providing explanations.

Digital Equity: Fair access to digital tools, resources, and technology for all individuals, eliminating barriers related to socio-economic status, location, or other factors.

Digital Literacy: The ability to use digital technology, communications tools, or networks to locate, analyze, use, and create information.

Learner Autonomy: The capacity of students to take charge of their own learning by setting objectives, selecting methods, and assessing their own progress.

Metaverse: A collective virtual shared space that merges augmented reality and persistent virtual reality, creating an immersive digital universe.

Pedagogical Strategy: A structured system or method used by educators to facilitate learning, considering both the content to be learned and the nature of the learners.

Virtual Reality (VR): A computer-generated simulation of a three-dimensional environment that can be interacted with in a seemingly real way by a user using specialized equipment.

Chapter 2
Autonomous Learning in Distance Education Theories:
Autonomy in Foreign Language Learning

Şenol Orakcı
iD https://orcid.org/0000-0003-1534-1310
Aksaray University, Turkey

Yücel Gelişli
Gazi University, Turkey

ABSTRACT

Individuals who live in the information age need to know the ways to access information to be able to use the information they have accessed and to produce new information. In order for individuals to have these qualities, they need to learn how to learn. Within this context, learner autonomy is very important in distance education system and lifelong learning. This research focuses on autonomous learning skills in foreign language learning in the context of distance education, which is widely discussed in the 21st century education system. The main purpose of this study is to investigate the autonomous learning skills that enable learners to learn on their own in terms of distance learning learners as well as aiming to examine the emergence of the concept of student autonomy in distance education within the framework of basic theories discussing language learning autonomy in this context. For these purposes, "Autonomy in Foreign Language Teaching," "Autonomous Learner Features in Foreign Language Learning," "Teacher and Student Roles in Autonomous Learning," "The role of Teacher in Autonomous Learning," "The Role of the Student in Autonomous Learning," "Autonomous Learning in Distance Education," "Areas and Approaches in Foreign Language Learning in Which Autonomous Learners Can Improve Themselves," and "Distance Education Theories" in the field of open and distance education were addressed. Finally, the chapter presented recent technologies to foster autonomous learning in distance education.

DOI: 10.4018/979-8-3693-0353-5.ch002

Copyright © 2024, IGI Global. Copying or distributing in print or electronic forms without written permission of IGI Global is prohibited.

INTRODUCTION

Autonomous learning, as defined by Knowles (1995), entails individuals willingly accepting responsibility for their own learning, reflecting the self-directed nature of the process. However, Dickinson (1992) further distinguishes autonomous learning from self-directed learning by emphasizing that autonomous learners not only assume responsibility but also act upon it, making informed decisions and implementing them, aligning their goals and strategies. Moreover, the interdependent nature of human society, as Little (2009) suggests, challenges the misconception that autonomous learning is a solitary endeavor, recognizing that individuals can benefit from collaborative and social learning experiences. Benson's (2001) delineation of the essential components of autonomous learning, including self-management, self-evaluation, and self-observation, underlines the multifaceted nature of this process. Harmer's (2001) perspective in the context of language learning extends the concept to encompass an individual's ability to independently navigate obstacles and challenges, emphasizing self-reliance. Ultimately, Holec's (1981) widely accepted definition encapsulates the essence of autonomous learning as the learner's active and self-driven involvement in every facet of the learning journey, embodying its central tenet. In fact, when the learner takes responsibility for learning, all stages of learning are mentioned. These:

- Setting goals,
- Defining content and progress,
- Choosing the methods and techniques to be used,
- Observing the acquisition process,
- The evaluation of what has been acquired.

In order to carry out his/her own learning, the individual must go through all these stages. In these stages, the individual needs some knowledge and skills. Holec (1985) described these stages in detail. While defining a goal,

- an individual should know that the activities to be implemented will help define his/her own learning goals,
- he/she should define and analyze these activities, even if they are very general,
- he/she should create a method and its sub-steps according to him/her,
- he/she should divide its main goals into smaller units,
- he/she should know how to use assessment results in transforming them into new goals.

While defining the content;

- an individual should be able to express his/her goals,
- he/she should be able to collect all learning materials,
- he/she should classify materials according to different goals,
- he/she should be able to decide with regard to the difficulty of the materials.

While defining the materials and techniques;

- an individual should be able to determine the goals of the printed course materials,
- he/she should be able to determine the effectiveness level of learning activities taught to him/her,
- he/she should be able to prepare his/her own program by using various books and materials.

While determining the place and speed of learning;

- an individual should know that each individual is different from the other,
- he/she should should determine the learning conditions himself/herself,
- he/she should know that the speed of learning can change according to the subject learned.

In the evaluation of what has been learned;

- an individual should know that self-assessment is necessary and sufficient,
- he/she should determine their own evaluation criteria,
- he/she should know that he needs to record his/her evaluations in order to monitor his/her progress.

Autonomy in Foreign Language Teaching

Research in the last quarter century has revealed the importance of autonomy in foreign language teaching. Benson (2001) states that this phenomenon first entered the field of foreign language education as the main purpose of the European Centre for Modern Languages, which offers lifelong learning opportunities to adults. The development of the Common European Framework of Reference for Languages (CEFR) is based on the influence of foreign language teachers and methodologists since the 1970s by Humanist Psychology, which emphasized views on self-concept, the assumption of personal responsibility and influencing factors in adult education.

Tudor (1993) describes that each student has a complex structure and that language teaching not only reveals the student's activity and intellectual skills as much as possible, but also relates it to the student's ongoing life experience.

Dubin and Olshtain (1986) state that some of the goals of Humanist Psychology are directly related to key factors of student autonomy. These are high respect and value given to the student, seeing learning as a way of self-actualization, valuing the student in the decision-making process, and seeing the teacher as an activity organizer (facilitator). Since the answers to the question of what autonomy is in language teaching are subjective, it is perhaps one of the most difficult questions to answer. Pemberton (1996) argues that the subjectivity in the definition of autonomy arises from the use of different terms in similar meaning or similar terms in different meanings. These terms are self-access, self-instruction learning, and individualized teaching commonly used in education.

Self-access language learning is often used as a synonym for self-directed or autonomous learning. Access to foreign language materials with self-access provides an excellent opportunity in the context of self-directed education. Benson (2001) posits self-access as a self-directed tool that leads to autonomous learning.

The understanding of autonomy in a foreign language is associated with individualization. Dickinson (1992) assumes individual teaching as a learning process adapted by the teacher or student, taking into account the characteristic differences of each individual.

Structural Psychology is another science that forms the basis of the concept of autonomy. Benson and Voller (1997) explain this as autonomy as aiding / contributing to the process of structuring the student's own target language version and consequently the student taking responsibility for his / her own learning. They also argue that the term autonomy is used in language education in five different ways. Autonomy is used in language education;

- as situations where students work entirely alone.
- as a group of skills that can be learned and applied in self-directed education
- as an innate internal capacity suppressed by institutional training
- as taking responsibility for self-learning
- as the right to orient students regarding their self-learning.

Candy (1989 cited in Benson and Voller, 1997) acknowledges that the decisions taken in the learning process of constructivist approaches support autonomy in terms of individual responsibility. However, constructivist approaches, as well as autonomy, place emphasis on creativity and interaction in the target language.

Kohonen (2012), a strong advocate of experiential learning, states that as a part of autonomous learning, students should manage their own learning and acquire a self-concept to develop skills and organize tasks consciously. He completes this definition as that students should be productive rather than consumer of the course while trying to acquire self-perception.

As the searches for language learning diversify in our world, which has shrunk with the increase of communication channels, the difference of each person as an individual and in parallel with this, increasing the efficiency in learning is possible with understanding the importance of autonomous learning, which can be referred to as a lifelong learning strategy.

Benson (1997) classifies the views on autonomy in applied linguistics under three headings; technical autonomy, psychological autonomy, political autonomy. According to Benson, three major approaches used in learning modern and social sciences; positivism, structuralism, and critical thinking (theory) overlap with the types of autonomy in language learning.

Psychological autonomy is defined as the ability of students to take responsibility for their own learning. Psychological autonomy requires internal transformation within the individual (Benson, 1997). This definition explains the close relationship between psychological autonomy and positivism, which advocates individual freedom of thought and decision-making responsibility in constructing the meaning of learning and knowledge.

On the other hand, political autonomy is defined as the ability of students to control the learning process and content. Young (1986) defines this form of autonomy as the individual's control of his or her world regardless of the opinions of others.

Autonomous Learner Features in Foreign Language Learning

Learners who have autonomous learning skills are called autonomous learners. There are certain characteristics that a learner must have in order to be an autonomous learner. One of the most important issues of interest for education researchers in recent years is to research autonomous learning and teaching methods based on it (Johnson & Johnson, 2003; Keegan, 1983; Nunan, 1997; Nunan, 2000; Nunan, 2004). Autonomous learning is learner-centered and requires the learner to be responsible for his / her own learning process (Açıkgöz, 2007; Ghaith, 2003). As Açıkgöz (2007) stated, the learner can make decisions, make self-regulation and use appropriate strategies in the autonomous learning process. Decision making, self-regulation and using appropriate strategies are among the characteristics of the autonomous learner.

According to Dickinson (1995), the characteristics of autonomous learner in foreign language learning are as follows:

Taking Responsibility: Autonomous learners assume full responsibility for their learning, recognizing that their educational journey is their own.

Self-Direction and Evaluation: They possess the ability to direct and evaluate their learning effectively, knowing when to adjust their approach and identifying areas of improvement.

Goal Setting: Autonomous learners can articulate both short-term and long-term learning objectives, providing clear direction to their language learning journey.

Strategic Choices: They demonstrate the capacity to select and employ learning strategies suited to their specific needs and the context of their learning.

Quick Comprehension: Autonomous learners grasp new concepts and language structures swiftly, enabling them to progress more efficiently.

Resource Selection: They have the discernment to choose appropriate materials, topics, and strategies that align with their learning goals.

According to Keegan (1996), autonomous learners know exactly autonomous learning. An autonomous learner chooses an active approach according to the subject to be learned. He/She is always willing to take risks. His/Her ability to guess is strong. He/She attaches importance to appropriateness as well as accuracy in structure and content.

Teacher and Student Roles in Autonomous Learning

Gardner and Miller (1999) state that the most important prerequisite for the application of autonomous learning in language teaching is that the roles of teachers and students should change. To put it more clearly, within the framework of student-centered education, responsibility passes from teacher to student. Successful implementation of autonomous learning depends on the interaction of these two groups in line with the development of teachers 'and students' perceptions of autonomy (Esh, 1996; Esh, 1997; Gardner & Miller, 1996; Gardner & Miller, 1999; Gardner & Miller, 2011; Little, 1995). There are numerous benefits to examining the roles of students and teachers in autonomous learning separately.

The role of Teacher in Autonomous Learning

The results obtained from the application of the Common European Framework (CEFR) regarding student autonomy developed in some European countries have shown how much it encourages autonomous learning (European Union, 2002). Kohonen (2001), in a study conducted under the auspices of the EU in connection with the CEF, stated that language teacher plays an important role as a resource person for autonomous language learning and that the professional development of the teacher is directly related to language learning and teaching. As a role, the autonomous teacher always defines himself/herself as a student and behaves differently from the traditional teacher who presents himself as a know-it-all (Breen & Mann, 1997). In this new role, the teacher emerges as a consultant, organizer, material developer, and evaluator. Tudor (1993), from a similar point of view, argues that the primary role of the teacher in traditional teaching settings is the information provider as the sole decision maker on what to learn and how to learn. In other words, in programs that adopt autonomous learning, teachers should assume a consultancy role that will help students to take responsibility for setting their own goals, planning implementation opportunities or evaluating the process from the role of information provider.

Oh (2002) mentions that teachers should take into account the methods by which students can learn the language more effectively and their individual characteristics that are compatible with the strengths and weaknesses of each one. According to Little (1994), the teacher needs to make a series of preparations in order to increase student autonomy. Here, the teacher must decide in which areas he or she should develop autonomy, to what extent the student should be free to set goals, to choose materials, to evaluate the learning process.

While Cotteral (2000) discusses the content of the program for students to take more responsibility, the most important feature of the program is the teacher-student dialogue provided to increase student autonomy. With the help of this dialogue, while establishing a direct relationship between these two groups, the suggestion of the teacher for the next study is taken in determining the goal and evaluating the learning process. Individual access centers established in educational institutions are suitable places where teachers can help students learn autonomously. It should be noted here that teachers can assist in accessing and using the course material according to the needs of each student.

The Role of the Student in Autonomous Learning

Autonomous students are proactive contributors to the learning process, actively seeking out diverse learning opportunities rather than merely passively observing the teacher. Linguists concur on the characteristics that define autonomous students, several of which are worth highlighting:

Holec (1985) lists the characteristics of the autonomous student as follows;

Goal and Content Determination: Autonomous students are capable of setting their own learning goals and selecting relevant content.
Material and Technique Selection: They can judiciously choose suitable course materials and learning techniques.

Management of Learning Environment: Autonomous students skillfully manage their learning environment, including their study location, study schedule, and learning pace.

Self-Evaluation: They possess the capacity to evaluate their own learning progress critically.

Dickinson (1992) emphasizes 5 points that distinguish autonomous students from traditional students:

Comprehension of Newly-Taught Concepts: They can grasp newly-introduced concepts effectively.

Goal Shaping: Autonomous students actively shape their learning objectives.

Strategic Competence: They have the ability to select and implement appropriate learning strategies.

Self-Reflectiveness: They can self-monitor their learning strategies in practice.

Conscious Self-Assessment: Autonomous students engage in deliberate self-assessment, actively gauging their progress.

Students with autonomous learning skills make great effort to apply the language skills they learn in the classroom outside the classroom. As part of their learning, they read newspapers in the target language, watch TV and do research on the Internet. In the traditional classroom environment, students become passive and perceive the teacher as the only responsible and wait for him/her to tell him what to do at any moment. Ellis and Sinclair (1989) argue that while students thus become addicted to teachers, they need to be aware of the relationship and roles of students and teachers in the learning process in order to achieve autonomy. Little (1996) states that it is difficult for students to take responsibility for self-learning in formal education institutions, but teachers can help them by providing them with appropriate lesson materials and the opportunity to practice them. In parallel with this, Esh, Schawijk, Elsen, and Satz (2000) point out that future teachers should learn the effects of autonomous learning on teaching methods and the roles of students and teachers very well, both academically and practically. They state that as a result of long discussions and research, they have integrated the processes and principles underlying autonomous learning into the teacher training curriculum. As a result, it is possible to raise foreign language teaching to higher levels, taking into account the cognitive differences of the students, the necessity of their active participation in this process, in cooperation with their teachers, by setting goals for self-learning and being autonomous learners who apply it. In this case, students will be able to

Autonomous Learning in Distance Education Theories

include out-of-school facilities in their learning processes and continue with after-school learning activities and fulfill the requirement of being a lifelong student. It should not be overlooked that the close goals (learning outcomes) of each training program will make sense if they are directed towards distant goals.

Autonomous Learning in Distance Education

Responding to the educational demands of individuals of all ages and spreading the philosophy of lifelong learning constitute the basis of distance education. In order for lifelong learning to take place, learners need to take responsibility for their own learning. The individual who guides the learner to take responsibility for his/her own learning is called autonomous learning, and the individual who guides the learner to learn with awareness of his/her learning responsibility is called autonomous learner. Autonomous learning and autonomous learner concepts are very important in distance education system and lifelong learning. Educators specified the basic components in the distance education system as eight main processes. These are as follows respectively (Holmberg, 2000); individual learning, planning the lesson, developing course materials, providing educational communication, guiding learners, developing the course, distributing course materials, creating an organizational structure suitable for distance education and evaluating the functionality of the system.

Among all these items, the most important element is the learners. Participant characteristics (age, profession, etc.) who want to benefit from the distance education system have a wider target audience than the characteristics of individuals in formal or non-formal education institutions. Having some personal characteristics of the learners participating in distance education can increase the success of the system. The fact that the participants exhibit the characteristics of an autonomous learner, planning, implementing and evaluating their own learning processes, as well as having a learning style knowledge of how to learn, developing strategies to overcome the obstacles faced by the learning activities under their responsibility is important in achieving the goals of distance education programs. In this context, it may be important for the participants who benefit from distance education to be more self-controlled (Demirel, 1998). According to Holmberg (2000), learners in distance education should be offered free choice of programs, and their autonomy and voluntary work should be supported.

Wedemeyer (1971) explains the importance of autonomous learning in distance education with the phrase "the basis of distance education is the independence of the learner". He stated that the distance education system, which includes the adoption of learner independence and the use of technology as a way of implementing this independence, has some features that it should have.

- The learner should be independent of time and place,
- The learner should take responsibility for his/her own learning, learning should be individualized,
- The learner should be able to choose suitable learning strategies and methods,
- Individual differences should be taken into account and learning opportunities should be provided accordingly,
- Limitations such as time, place and method should be eliminated during the evaluation of learners.

Areas and Approaches for Autonomous Learning in Foreign Language Education

Autonomous learning is a versatile and adaptable approach that can be applied in various contexts within foreign language education. Drawing from the insights provided by Cohen (2007), Oxford (1990, 2001), and Little (2009), here are key areas and approaches in which autonomous learners can enhance their language proficiency:

Individualized Learning Centers

- Computer Aided Foreign Language Learning
- Distance Learning
- Learning Together
- Education Abroad
- Learning Outside the Classroom
- Self-Teaching - Learning
- Blended Learning
- Learning in Virtual Learning Environments
- Accommodative Learning
- Collaborative Learning
- Project Based Learning
- Self Assessment

Autonomous learning is a desirable feature for distance and face-to-face learners. Although autonomous learning is defined as a capacity or potential, it is possible to strengthen it with opportunities and environments to be created for the individual. Benson (2001), one of the theorists contributing to autonomous learning, examined autonomous learning under six basic approaches:

Resource-based approaches emphasize independent interaction with learning materials. Individual development and individual access centers attract the most attention in resource-based applications. Benson (2001) states that autonomy is a

Autonomous Learning in Distance Education Theories

goal, learning directed by the individual himself/herself is the tool to achieve this goal, and individual access is the environment necessary to achieve the goal.

When referring to individual access, learning materials and organized systems designed for direct use by users comes to mind. There are two reasons that make up the concept of individual access. The first reason is individualization. Because each individual has his/her own needs. In addition, each individual has weaknesses that they want to work on alone, unlike others. Individuals' learning styles and preferences are also different. Therefore, learners may need to apply to individual access centers and work. The second reason is the provision of independent learning, which can be considered under the heading of ideology why (Sheerin (1997).

Individual access creates opportunities for learners to learn how to learn (Sheerin, 1997). Technology-based approaches emphasize independent interaction with educational technology. Technology-supported education offers individuals the opportunity to research and learn on their own. In simultaneous communication, individuals also participate in conversations or discussions. In asynchronous communication, individuals communicate with each other via e-mail. Thanks to the communication established over the internet, learners who are quiet or shy in the classroom can express themselves more comfortably. In addition, education through the Internet motivates the learner in terms of increasing their education and computer skills. It also reinforces the learner motivation and success due to the ability to access up-to-date texts, to easily publish and share their own productions. (Warschauer, 2001). In addition, since the applications made over the Internet are interactive; They also reinforce autonomy, as they require decision-making and choice. Learner-based approaches emphasize directly creating behavioral and psychological changes in the learner. Learner-based approaches are different from other approaches that only create opportunities for the learner, as they directly lead to behavioral and psychological changes in order for the learner to have control over their learning (Benson, 2001). When learner-based approaches are mentioned, concepts such as learner education and strategy teaching come to mind. However, Sheerin (1997) states that these concepts consist of one teaching another how to do something.

Distance Education Theories in the Field of Open and Distance Education

The field of distance education has evolved over the years, with several key theories contributing to its development. These theories have not only shaped the landscape of distance education but have also had a significant impact on autonomous learning, especially in the context of foreign language education. Here, we delve into the prominent distance education theories and their relevance to the autonomy of language learners as in shown in Table 1.

a. Independent Learning Theory
b. Self-Determination Theory
c. Equivalency Theory
d. Cooperative Freedom Theory
e. Self-Directed Learning Theory
f. Community of Inquiry Model

Table 1. Distance education theories with a learner-centred focus

Theory	Theorist(s)	Key Concepts
Independent Learning Theory	Charles Wedemeyer	Emphasis on learner autonomy and the use of technology for autonomy implementation
Self-Determination Theory	Michael Moore	Emphasis on learner autonomy, competence and determination
Equivalency Theory	Michael Simonson	learning experience, implementation process, equity, learner and learning outcomes
Cooperative Freedom Theory	Morten Flate Paulsen	the importance of freedom and cooperation
Self-Directed Learning Theory	Malcolm Knowles and D. Randy Garrison	A learner-centred education and learner responsibility
Community of Inquiry Model	D. Randy Garrison, Terry Anderson and Walter Archer	Teaching presence, cognitive presence, and social presence

These theories are generally made by researchers working in the fields of technology, communication and economics, but when it comes to communication and learning, it is seen that researchers in the field of education are not indifferent to these developments. White (2006) emphasized the lack of foreign language published on distance language learning. The author also stated that a small number of studies connect with the basic theoretical approaches emerging in the field of distance education. Therefore, it is important to discuss the above-mentioned theories and the concepts of foreign language learning autonomy in the field of foreign languages. In this study, the effect of distance education on autonomy will be discussed in detail in terms of the independent work theory proposed by Michael G. Moore (1972) and the "Transactional Distance" (TU) theory, which the author later put forward by developing this theory (Moore, 1997).

a) **Independent Learning Theory:** The theory was introduced by Wedemeyer in 1973. This theory has been a guide for other researchers, and after this date, it has also formed the basis for the formation of new models and theories based on Independent Learning Theory (Keegan, 1996). Moore introduced the autonomy theory by being influenced by Wedemeyer's Independent Learning Theory. Moore (1972) highlighted the autonomy dimension as well as the self-learning of the individual with his independent work theory. Moore (1972) determined that learners are dependent on teachers at many points over time. Based on these situations, Moore (1986; 1987) started to work on this issue by introducing the theory of autonomy and the theory was developed over time (Horzum 2011). Within the framework of this theory, according to Moore (1993), distance education can be expressed as the geographical separation of learners and trainers in its simplest definition, but Moore (1972) speaks of a "pedagogical concept" in his theory by developing this concept.

In Independent Learning Theory, Moore (1972) hypothesizes that, in distance learning scenarios, the distance between teacher and students may cause "a potential psychological gap between teachers 'behavior and learners' behavior that can lead to misunderstanding" (Moore & Greg, 1996; Horzum 2011). In other words, Transactional Distance is the feeling of emotional distance (separation) felt by the teacher or learner in face-to-face or distance education settings (Horzum 2011).

Moore (1997) explains Transactional Distance Theory as a concept that defines the universe of teacher-student relationships when learners and trainers are separated by time and / or space. The universe of these relationships can be defined as a typology shaped around the structure of the curriculum, the interaction between learners and teachers, and the degree of student autonomy, which are the most fundamental structures of the field. According to Moore (1972), distance education is divided into two as learner management and teacher management, and it particularly emphasizes on two variables: (a) Distance between teacher and learner, (b) learner responsibility and determination. Interactional distance is the conceptual space between learner and teacher in distance education. Moore (1994) stated that interactional distance is not only the geographical distance between learner and teacher, but more importantly a pedagogical idea. This idea is the universe in learner-teacher communication that emerges with distances originating from time or distance. Interactive distance is generally based on dialogue, structure, and learner autonomy. The learner, who will interpret and make sense of the learning process, will advance on the dialogue and structure in the process. In this context, the learner will benefit from autonomous learning skills. In this context, according to Moore (1997), the quality of the communication developed between instructors and learners in distance learning depends on the relationship of three factors. These factors are "dialogue", "structure" and "learner autonomy".

Dialogue encompasses more than expressing two-way communication, meaning it takes all forms of interaction into account. These forms of interaction include clearly defined educational objectives in the field of teaching, as well as collaboration and teacher dimensions. Thus, the problems faced by learners in Transactional Distance are solved by the dialogue factor, that is, communication (Giossos, Koutsouba, & Lionarakis, 2009). According to Moore (1997), in this process, not the frequency but the quality of the dialogues and their effectiveness in solving the learning problems that the distance learner may experience are important. The second factor referred to by Moore (1997) expresses the nature of the course structure defined as the level of flexibility of the course. In addition, this factor includes the pedagogical model used and the skills students should have, as well as the pre-determination of course objectives. The relationship between the dialog factor and this factor is inverse; The better a program is structured, the less the need for dialogue (Fogolin, 2012).

The third factor, autonomy, depends on the previous two factors. It refers to the sense of both independence and interdependence perceived by students. Learner autonomy is intertwined with terms such as free decision-making, self-direction, and can be influenced by first and second factors. The term autonomy refers to the determination of goals, learning activities and assessment criteria, and active participation of students (Horzum, 2011). Falloon (2011) stated that the interaction between these 3 factors is multifaceted and they affect each other. For example, an inflexible distance education course can increase students' perception of distance interaction by leading to a decrease in the quality of dialogue and motivation for learner autonomy.

In short, it is stated that the learner should be left free to determine his/her own learning goals, the learner should take responsibility for his/her own learning, learning should be individualised and progress according to his/her own pace (Gökmen et al., 2016). Thus, distance education should be organised to provide more freedom to the learner and the communication between the learner and the teacher should be strengthened (Arslantaş, 2014).

b) **Self-Determination Theory:** This theory emphasises learner autonomy as well as self-directed learning. Autonomy means that the learner decides on his/her own goals, methods and evaluations (Moore, 1993). It is stated that the fact that learning is more dependent on the teacher in the normal teaching process is not suitable for adult education, and that the learner should be autonomous in distance education because the learner is separated from the teacher in terms of time and place. At the same time, unlike the Independent Learning Theory, in non-institutional distance education environments, the components of teacher, learner and communication are discussed. Accordingly, since distance education can be implemented at a different place and time from the teacher, distance education can be successful with its autonomous structure in which the learner takes his/her own responsibility and can plan according to his/her own wishes (Keegan, 1996).

c) **Equivalence Theory:** Based on the assumption that the closer distance education is to face-to-face education, the closer the learner success will be (Simonson et al., 2006; Simonson, 1999). This theory emphasises that the outcomes of distance education and face-to-face education should be equal to each other. The variables taken as basis are learning experience, application process, equality, learner and learning outcomes (Karataş, 2005). According to this theory, although learner experiences are different in distance education and face-to-face education, equivalent learning experiences should be provided. While distance and face-to-face learning are brought closer to each other, instructional design should be planned by considering learner needs, individual characteristics, learning environment, learning materials and processes. According to this theory, if equal learning experiences can be provided, learning outcomes will be similar and distance education will achieve its purpose (Simonson & Schlosser, 2002).

d) **Cooperative Freedom Theory:** In Cooperative Freedom Theory, it is emphasised that place, time, speed, access and curriculum are important in distance education (Paulsen, 1995). It is a theory based on the concepts of co-operation and freedom. According to this theory, since freedom and learners' right to choose are important in distance education, education should be flexible. It is stated that distance education learners are individuals who can learn on their own and they need cooperation as well as freedom. Since distance learners tend to feel lonely, they need help from others. At this point, it is thought that learners' cooperation with their peers will benefit learning. In this respect, the related theory puts the learner at the centre of distance education and states the importance of freedom and cooperation (Barut Tuğtekin, 2022).

e) **Self-Directed Learning Theory:** Self-Directed Learning Theory defines a learning process in which learners determine their own learning needs and goals without the help of others, select and apply learning resources and appropriate strategies, and evaluate their own learning (Knowles, 1975). Garrison (2003), who developed self-directed learning in distance education, states that learners should be free and aware of responsibility in order to create their own learning processes. In this respect, it is stated that distance education can be carried out with a learner-centred education approach rather than a learner-centred teaching approach.

f) **Community of Inquiry Model:** Community of Inquiry Model, which provides a general framework for learning and teaching theories, is considered useful for guiding online education practices (Swan et al., 2009). In this model, even if the environment and technology change, the masses gathered for learning are considered as learning communities. This model is based on three different components for online learning experiences: teaching presence, cognitive and social presence. In these learning environments, enquiry, meaningful learning and collaboration are considered important (Anderson et al., 2001; Garrison et al., 2010). The social presence component of the Community of Inquiry Model refers to the ability of individuals to reflect their own characters to the community they are in. Cognitive presence is the ability of individuals to create a common meaning by communicating with each other. Teaching presence is the ability to direct the design, facilitation and direct instructional processes by focusing on learner and instructor roles to ensure personally and educationally meaningful learning (Anderson et al., 2001; Garrison & Arbaugh, 2007; Garrison et al., 2000).

When learner-centred theories are examined; in general, it is stated that open and distance education should be useful and the learner should gain experience by taking responsibility for his/her own learning freely in the process with the aim of closing the gap between face-to-face education. For this, it is necessary to ensure the active participation of the learner in the distance education process, and the instructor should be in the role of a guide in this process, support communication and cooperation, and at the same time take part in the rapid feedback mechanism (Barut Tuğtekin, 2022).

Recent Technologies to Foster Autonomous Learning in Distance Education

Recent reviews and empirical studies indicate that the integration of digital technology and autonomous learning has a positive impact on language learners. By utilising technology, students can acquire new skills and enhance their level of attainment (Cripps, 2020; Pratiwi et al., 2021). It also leads to a shift in language pedagogy, prioritising student-centred approaches over teacher-centred ones (Mahmud, 2018). Moreover, it provides foreign language students with opportunities for autonomous learning beyond the classroom by providing various courses, websites, videos, online lectures, e-books, and other resources (Ahmed et al., 2020; Ubaedillah & Pratiwi, 2021).

Digital technology is considered one of the most efficient tools for promoting self-directed learning, as it enables lecturers to facilitate the class (Ling et al., 2020; Sadaghian & Marandi, 2021). Digital technologies are frequently recommended for enhancing the teaching and learning process in EFL classes (Choi & Lee, 2020). Student response systems (SRS) such as Kahoot!, Canva, Quizizz, Google Classroom,

Autonomous Learning in Distance Education Theories

Google Form and Socrative are among the most widely used digital tools in EFL classrooms (Rofiah & Waluyo, 2020).

Kahoot!: An online platform Kahoot! allows students and teachers to learn interactively. Teachers are able to ask students questions and promptly see their answers while tracking their performance. Additionally, Kahoot! can be played as a multiplayer game, which permits students to partake in learning by competing against each other. Kahoot! is becoming progressively more commonly used within the education sector. Students refine their proficiency in grammar rules, vocabulary, and pronunciation by participating in Kahoot! quizzes and games. Kahoot! can be employed to enhance students' motivation to learn. Encouraging students to compete with each other can foster motivation and promote an enjoyable learning experience. This approach can increase learning efforts, academic achievement, and appreciation for the educational process (Basuki & Hidayati, 2019).

Interactive quiz games, such as Kahoot!, offer an opportunity for students to both collaborate and compete. As an icebreaker, this platform is commonly used for conducting online quizzes. A recent study revealed that Kahoot! offers numerous benefits and promotes intrinsic and extrinsic motivation in both students and teachers. The students were prompted to pay attention to the lecture owing to their desire to perform well in Kahoot!. Subsequently, they engaged with the presenter, fellow students, and course content. Within the classroom, Kahoot! fostered a competitive environment where students strived to elevate their names to the top of the scoreboard. This resulted in a rise in attentiveness during lectures and related discussions (Tan, Ganapathy, & Kaur, 2018).

Canva: Widely employed in education, Canva allows instructors to produce interactive and striking teaching resources. Canva offers iOS, Android, and Chrome applications for student use. The platform facilitates instructors in making the materials they present more visually appealing, and its pre-designed templates simplify and expedite content creation while enhancing student comprehension. Students can enhance the visual appeal of their assignments by utilising Canva. The extensive range of templates available on Canva assists students in presenting their work with greater creativity. Students may enhance their assignments by utilising Canva's selection of pre-made graphics, or by crafting their own.

Quizizz: "Quizizz" is a cooperative learning activity allowing students to collaborate using a computer, iPad, tablet, or smartphone while enjoying the process. It is among the outstanding resources for class quiz games. It is a multiplayer gaming platform that enables students to regulate their own speed while engaging in games in the classroom.

Quizizz and Kahoot! have some similarities, but Quizizz's characteristics are more noticeable. With Quizizz, students have the freedom to respond to questions at their own pace, and they can inspect their answers once they're done. Each student's screen shows their answer speed analytics. Research indicates that the use of web quizzes in conjunction with instructional strategies and teaching methodologies is advantageous. The advantages for students include increased appreciation for quizzes, academic accomplishment, motivation to learn, learning effort, and engagement in activities (Vincent, 2015).

Google Classroom: Google Classroom is an e-learning instrument used in educational facilities to manage everyday assignments, create deadlines, enhance communication between teachers and students, and document academic performances. Teachers are empowered with tools that enable them to share files and assignments, provide constructive feedback, and grade completed work using this platform. Google Classroom offers an effective submission process. Students receive bespoke assignments from their educators, who also establish deadlines and assign tasks. The automated submission process occurs once the task is complete. This method of interaction between educators and students contributes to students' growing independence and accountability for their educational progress, potentially resulting in more conscientious professional conduct in the future.

Google Forms: The Google Forms platform serves as a survey tool for collecting and evaluating responses, providing supplementary means for conducting classes. It enables document-sharing, as well as editing of documents, tables, and various forms. This feature is particularly useful for teachers aiming to assess the effectiveness of their teaching strategies. The software calculates the proportion of correct answers, providing a means to evaluate student performance. Peer evaluation and student feedback are two significant benefits. Moreover, students reflect on their past accomplishments when completing the form, which supports them in contemplating the teaching and learning process and enhancing their autonomy and responsibility for their learning.

The use of Google Classroom and Google Forms is convenient. Students receive emails or messages containing a link to their homework. Clicking the link is all they need to do to complete the task. If the students have sufficient free time or have prepared the answers, they can commence answering the questions in a singular sitting and then resume the task at a later time if necessary. Occasionally, it may be necessary for them to monitor their learning progress for a specified duration before completing the activity. This method empowers students to take charge of their education by providing flexibility in deciding when to accomplish the assignment. Students receive organizational assistance for weekly, semester-long, and yearly studies but are not prompted by teachers to complete tasks; they must individually determine sequencing and completion times. Collaborating with Google, which aligns more closely with their interests and understanding, enhances student motivation for learning in this technological era.

Autonomous Learning in Distance Education Theories

Students actively seek opportunities for professional development and set individual learning objectives to sustain their motivation after graduation. To maximise their potential, students must employ appropriate learning techniques to identify areas of strength and weakness. In order to achieve this, students are required to critically evaluate their educational tasks and reflect on acquired knowledge.

Socrative: With Socrative, students can use their smartphones or tablets to complete tests. Students have the opportunity to receive immediate feedback. Evaluating the subject in a fun way with a game immediately after the subject is covered is a useful application in terms of both tracking student development and increasing retention of the subject (Socrative, 2023). After students log in to the system by entering their name, or even a nickname if they wish, they can access the assessment content opened by the teacher and start solving the questions. At the same time, a table with each student's name is displayed on the Smart Board. Students can immediately see which questions they got right and which they got wrong. As well as giving students instant feedback, it also creates excitement, motivation and a sweet competitive atmosphere.

CONCLUSION, DISCUSSION, AND SUGGESTIONS

In cases where distance education is not possible to carry out classroom activities due to the limitations of traditional learning-teaching methods, it is a teaching method in which communication and interaction between those who plan and implement the educational activity and learners are provided from a specific center through specially prepared teaching units and various environments has been described. Autonomous learning, on the other hand, is the individual taking responsibility for his own learning. Especially in order to be successful in foreign language learning, the individual must develop himself/herself in the classroom environment and have autonomous learning skills. Autonomous learning in foreign language learning in distance education requires learners to learn completely by themselves in the learning process. For this reason, it is thought that those who learn autonomous learning skills in foreign language learning in distance education should have more than other learners.

Nowadays, it is easier for language learners to internalize and perform autonomous learning thanks to technology and programs that develop accordingly. However, in order for language learners to benefit from these opportunities, they need trainers, even institutions, who are competent in computer technologies, to guide them. Providing the aforementioned instructors with access to courses such as web design, computer programming, and writing smart phone applications to design and develop online materials can make the technology-based environments to be created more suitable in terms of educational principles. In addition, it is important that the scope of autonomy in language learning is not limited to learning alone or learning outside the classroom. People can be individually proactive (Littlewood, 1999) or externally dependent (reactive / passive) learning style, due to their emotional nature and needs. In other words, individuals' autonomous language learning capacity (Little, 1991) or responsibility (Holec, 1981) does not show a continuous upward development curve. It may increase or decrease from time to time with the effect of intrinsic and extrinsic motivations. Teachers' expressions and behaviors that increase students' interest in the target language will also contribute positively to this process in the classroom. In this process, learners will need to know the cognitive and metacognitive strategies they can use while learning autonomous language.

RECOMMENDATIONS

In order to ensure that learners participate in more course-related activities and increase their sense of responsibility, a portfolio application should be made for suitable courses. Informative and awareness-raising brochures can be prepared and informative meetings can be organized to tell learners how important autonomous learning skills are in education and their achievements in the lifelong learning process. Web-based autonomous learning courses should be designed in order to develop autonomous learning skills and raise awareness.

REFERENCES

Açıkgöz, K. Ü. (2007). *Aktif öğrenme*. İzmir: Eğitim Dünyası.

Ahmed, S. T. S., Qasem, B. T. A., & Pawar, S. V. (2020). Computer-assisted language instruction in South Yemeni context: A study of teachers' attitudes, ICT uses and challenges. *International Journal of Language Education*, *4*(1), 59–73. doi:10.26858/ijole.v4i2.10106

Anderson, T., Rourke, L., Garrison, D. R., & Archer, W. (2001). Assessing teaching presence in a computer conferencing context. *Journal of Asynchronous Learning Networks*, *5*(2), 1–17.

Aslantaş, T. (2014). *Uzaktan eğitim, uzaktan eğitim teknolojileri ve Türkiye'de bir uygulama*. Gazi Üniversitesi Fen Bilimleri Enstitüsü. Retrieved from https://www.tankutaslantas.com/wp-content/uploads/2014/04/Uzaktan-E%C4%9Fitim-Uzaktan-E%C4%9Fitim-Teknolojileri-ve-T%C3%BCrkiyede-bir-Uygulama.pdf

Barut Tuğtekin, E. (2022). Açık ve Uzaktan Öğrenme Kuramlarının Öğrenenler, Öğrenme Ortamları ve Etkileşim Açısından İncelenmesi. *Eğitim Bilim ve Araştırma Dergisi*, *3*(1), 118–137. doi:10.54637/ebad.1059890

Basuki, Y., & Hidayati, Y. (2019, April). Kahoot! or Quizizz: the Students' Perspectives. In *Proceedings of the 3rd English Language and Literature International Conference (ELLiC)* (pp. 202-211). Academic Press.

Benson, P. (1997). The philosophy and politics of learner autonomy. In Autonomy & Independence in language learning. Longman.

Benson, P. (2001). *Teaching and Researching Autonomy in Language Learning*. Longman.

Benson, P. (2006). Autonomy in language teaching and learning. *Language Teaching*, *40*(1), 21–40. doi:10.1017/S0261444806003958

Benson, P., & Voller, P. (1997). *Autonomy and Independence in Language Learning*. Longman.

Breen, M. P., & Mann, S. J. (1997). Shooting Arrows at the Sun: Perspectives on a Pedagogy for Autonomy' in Benson and Voller. In P. Benson & P. Voller (Eds.), *Autonomy and Independence in Language Learning* (pp. 132–149). Longman.

Breen, M. P., & Mann, S. J. (1997). Shooting arrows at the sun: Perspectives on a pedagogy for autonomy (Vol. 132-149). Longman.

Candy, P. C. (1991). *Self-direction for lifelong learning*. Jossey Bass.

Choi, H., & Lee, C. H. (2020). Learner autonomy in EFL reading with digital technology at secondary school level. *The Journal of AsiaTEFL*, *17*(2), 463–478. doi:10.18823/asiatefl.2020.17.4.11.1323

Cohen, A. D. (2007). Becoming a strategic language learner in CALL. *Applied Language Learning*, *17*(1-2), 57–71.

Cotterall, S. (2000). Promoting learner autonomy through the curriculum: Principles for designing language courses. *ELT Journal*, *54*(2), 109–117. doi:10.1093/elt/54.2.109

Cripps, T. (2020). We are mobile magicians but digital refugees: Helping prospective English teachers explore technology and ubiquitous learning. *Electronic Journal of Foreign Language Teaching*, *17*(S1), 168–189. doi:10.56040/tncp171a

Demirel, Ö. (1998). *Eğitimde yeni yönelimler*. Pegem Yayıncılık.

Dickinson, L. (1992). *Learning autonomy 2: Learner training for language learning*. Authentik.

Dickinson, L. (1995). Autonomy and motivation: A literature review. *System*, *23*(2), 165–174. doi:10.1016/0346-251X(95)00005-5

Dubin, F.E.O. (1986). Course Design: Developing programs and materials for language learning. *New Directions in Language Teaching, 15*(3).

Ellis, G., & Sinclair, B. (1989). *Learning to Learn English a Course in Learner Training Teacher's Book*. Cambridge University Press.

Esch, E. (1996). *Promoting learner autonomy: Criteria for the selection of appropriate methods*. Hong Kong University.

Esch, E. (1997). Learner training for autonomous language learning. In Autonomy and independence in language learning (pp. 164- 176). Longman.

Esch, K., Schalkwijk, E., Elsen, A., & Setz, W. (2000). *Autonomous Learning in Foreign Language Teacher Training*. https://lc.ust.hk/ailasc/lapi2000.html

Falloon, G. (2011). Making the connection: Moore's theory of transactional distance and its relevance to the use of a virtual classroom in postgraduate online teacher education. *Journal of Research on Technology in Education, 43*(3), 187–209. doi: 10.1080/15391523.2011.10782569

Fogolin, A. (2012). *Bildungsberatung im Fernlernen*. Beiträge aus Wissenschaft und Praxis.

Gardner, D., & Miller, L. (1996). *Tasks for independent language learning*. TESOL.

Gardner, D., & Miller, L. (1999). *Establishing Self Access: From Theory to Practice*. Cambridge University.

Gardner, D., & Miller, L. (2011). Managing self-access language learning: Principles and practice. *System*, *39*(1), 78–89. doi:10.1016/j.system.2011.01.010

Gardner, R. C., & Macintyre, P. D. (1993). A student's contributions to second language learning: Part II: Affective variables. *Language Teaching, 26*(1), 1–11. doi:10.1017/S0261444800000045

Garrison, D. R. (2003). Self-directed learning and distance education. In Handbook of Distance Education. Lawrence Erlbaum Associates.

Autonomous Learning in Distance Education Theories

Garrison, D. R., Anderson, T., & Archer, W. (2000). Critical inquiry in a text-based environment: Computer conferencing in higher education. *The Internet and Higher Education, 2*(2), 87–105.

Garrison, D. R., & Arbaugh, J. B. (2007). Researching the community of inquiry framework: Review, issues, and future directions. *The Internet and Higher Education, 10*(3), 157–172. doi:10.1016/j.iheduc.2007.04.001

Garrison, D. R., Cleveland-Innes, M., & Fung, T. S. (2010). Exploring causal relationships among teaching, cognitive and social presence: Student perceptions of the community of inquiry framework. *The Internet and Higher Education, 13*(1), 31–36. doi:10.1016/j.iheduc.2009.10.002

Ghaith, G. (2003). Effects of the learning together model of cooperative learning on English as foreign language reading achievement, academic self-esteem, and feelings of school alienation. *Bilingual Research Journal, 27*(3), 451–474. doi:10. 1080/15235882.2003.10162603

Giossos, Y., Koutsouba, M., Lionarakis, A., & Skavantzos, K. (2009). Reconsidering Moore's transactional distance theory. *European Journal of Open Distance and ELearning, 2009*(2), 1–6. https://files.eric.ed.gov/fulltext/EJ911768.pdf

Gökmen, Ö. F., Duman, İ., & Horzum, M. B. (2016). Uzaktan eğitimde kuramlar, değişimler ve yeni yönelimler. *AUAd, 2*(3), 29-51. http://auad.anadolu.edu.tr/yonetim/ icerik/makaleler/167-published.pdf

Harmer, J. (2001). *The Practice of English Language Teaching*. Longman.

Holec, H. (1981). *Autonomy in foreign language learning*. Pergamon.

Holec, H. (1985). On Autonomy: some elementary concepts. In P. Riley (Ed.), Discourse and Learning (pp. 173–190). Academic Press.

Holmberg, B. (2000). *Theory and practice of distance education* (2nd ed.). Routledge, Tylor&Francis Group.

Horzum, M. B. (2007). *İnternet tabanlı eğitimde transaksiyonel uzaklığın öğrenci başarısı, doyumu ve özyeterlilik algısına etkisi*. Yayınlanmamış Doktora Tezi, Ankara Üniversitesi, Eğitimi Bilimleri Enstitüsü.

Horzum, M. B. (2011). Transaksiyonel Uzaklık Algısı Ölçeğinin Geliştirilmesi ve Karma Öğrenme Öğrencilerinin Transaksiyonel Uzaklık Algılarının Çeşitli Değişkenler Açısından İncelenmesi. *Kuram ve Uygulamada Eğitim Bilimleri*, 1571-1587. http://toad.edam.com.tr/sites/default/files/pdf/transaksiyonel-uzaklik-algisi-olcegi-toad.pdf

Johnson, D. W., & Johnson, R. T. (2003). Studentmotivation in co-operative groups: Social interdependence theory. RoutledgeFalmer.

Karataş, S. (2005). *Deneyim eşitliğine dayalı internet temelli ve yüz yüz öğrenme sistemlerinin öğrenen başarısı ve doyumu açısından karşılaştırılması.* Yayınlanmamış Doktora Tezi, Ankara Üniversitesi.

Keegan, D. (1996). *Foundations of distance education.* Routledge.

Keegan, D. J. (1983). *On defining distance education.* St. Martin's.

Knowles, M. (1995). *Designs for Adult Learning: Practical Resources, Exercises, and Course Outlines from the Father of Adult Learning.* American Society for Training and Development.

Knowles, M. S. (1975). *Self-directed learning: A guide for learners and teachers.* Association.

Kohonen, V. (2001). Experiential language learning: Second language learning as cooperative learner education. In Collaborative language learning and teaching (pp. 14-39). Cambridge University.

Kohonen, V. (2012). Developing autonomy through ELP-oriented pedagogy: Exploring the interplay of the shallow and deep structures in a major change within language education. In B. Kühn & M. L. Pérez Cavana (Eds.), *Perspectives from the European Language Portfolio: Learner autonomy and self-assessment içinde* (pp. 22–42). Routledge.

Ling V. Sotnikova L. Rodionova I. Vasilets I. Zavjalova O. Fedorovskaya V. Datkova E. (2020). Online educational resources for students and digital barrier. *TEM Journal, 9*(1), 373-379. doi:10.18421/TEM91-51

Little, D. (1991). *Learner autonomy 1: Definitions, issues and problems.* Authentik.

Little, D. (1994). Learner autonomy: A theoretical construct and its practical application. *Die Neuere Sprache, 93*(5), 430–442.

Little, D. (1995). Learning as dialogue: The dependence of learner autonomy on teacher autonomy. *System, 23*(2), 175–182. doi:10.1016/0346-251X(95)00006-6

Little, D. (1996). Learner autonomy: Some steps in the evolution of theory and practice. *Irish Association for Applied Linguistics, 16,* 1–13.

Little, D. (2007). Reconstructing learner and teacher autonomy in language education. In Reconstructing autonomy in language education: Inquiry and Innovation (pp. 1-13). Palgrave Macmillan.

Little, D. (2009). Language learner autonomy and the European Language Portfolio: Two L2 English examples. *Language Teaching*, *42*(2), 222–233. doi:10.1017/S0261444808005636

Littlewood, W. (1997). Self-access: Why do we want it and what can it do? In P. Benson & P. Voller (Eds.), *Autonomy and independence in language learning içinde* (pp. 79–92). Longman.

Mahmud, M. M. (2018). Technology and language–what works and what does not: A meta-analysis of blended learning research. *The Journal of AsiaTEFL, 15*(2), 365-382. https://doi.org/.365 doi:10.18823/asiatefl.2018.15.2.1

Moore, M. (1997). *Theoretical Principles of Distance Education*. Routledge. http://www.c3l.uni-oldenburg.de/cde/found/moore93.pdf

Moore, M., & Greg, K. (1996). *Distance education: A systems view*. Wadsworth Publishing Company.

Moore, M. G. (1972). Learner autonomy: The second dimension of independent learning. *Convergence (Toronto)*, *5*(2), 76–88.

Moore, M. G. (1986). Self-directed learning and distance education. *Journal of Distance Education*, *1*(1), 7–24.

Moore, M. G. (1993). Theory of transactional distance. In Theoretical Principle of Distance Education. Routledge.

Moore, M. G. (1994). Autonomy and interdependence. *American Journal of Distance Education*, *8*(2), 1–5. doi:10.1080/08923649409526851

Morera, L. S., Antonio, A. A., & Laura, G. H. (2012). Analysis of Online Quizzes as a Teaching and assessment tool. *Journal of Technology and Science Education*, *2*(1), 39–45.

Nunan, D. (1997). Designing and adapting materials to encourage learner autonomy. In Autonomy and independence in language learning içinde (pp. 192-203). Longman.

Nunan, D. (2000). *Seven hypotheses about language teaching and learning*. Plenary presentation, TESOL Convention, Vancouver, Canada.

Nunan, D. (2004). *Nine steps to learner autonomy: Plenary speech*. Shantou University. 13Mart2004.www.nunan.info/presentations/steps_learner_autonomy_files/frame.htm

Oh, M. K. (2002). *Four Korean adult learners' ESL learning beliefs and learner autonomy* [Unpublished doctoral dissertation]. Faculty of the Graduate School of State University of New York at Buffalo.

Oxford, R. L. (1990). *Language learning strategies: What every teacher should know*. Heinle & Heinle.

Oxford, R. L. (2001). Language learning strategies. In The Cambridge guide to teaching English to speakers of other languages (pp. 166-172). Cambridge University.

Pemberton, R., Toogood, S., & Barfield, A. (2009). *Maintaining control: Autonomy and language learning*. Hong Kong University. doi:10.5790/hongkong/9789622099234.001.0001

Pratiwi, D. I., & Ubaedillah, U. (2021). Digital vocabulary class in English for railway mechanical technology. *Teaching English with Technology*, *21*(3), 67–88.

Rofiah, N. L., & Waluyo, B. (2020). Using socrative for vocabulary tests: Thai EFL learner acceptance and perceived risk of cheating. *Journal of Asia TEFL*, *17*(3), 966–982. doi:10.18823/asiatefl.2020.17.3.14.966

Sadaghian, S., & Marandi, S. (2021). Fostering language learner autonomy through interdependence: The power of Wikis. *Turkish Online Journal of Distance Education*, *22*(1), 194–208. doi:10.17718/tojde.849907

Sheerin, S. (1997). An exploration of the relationship between self- access and independent learning. In P. Benson & P. Voller (Eds.), *Autonomy and independence in language learning* (pp. 54–65). Longman.

Simonson, M. (1999). Equivalency theory and distance education. *TechTrends*, *43*(5), 5–8. doi:10.1007/BF02818157

Simonson, M., & Schlosser, C. (2002). *Distance education: Definition and glossary of terms*. Nova Southeastern University Fischler School of Education and Human Services.

Simonson, M., Smaldino, S., Albright, M., & Zvacek, S. (2006). Teaching and Learning at a Distance (3rd ed.). Pearson Prentice Hall.

Socrative. (2023). Retrieved from https://www.socrative.com/

Swan, K., Garrison, D. R., & Richardson, J. (2009). A constructivist approach to online learning: The community of inquiry framework. In C. R. Payne (Ed.), *Information technology and constructivism in higher education: Progressive learning frameworks*. IGI Global. doi:10.4018/978-1-60566-654-9.ch004

Tan, D. A. L., Ganapathy, M., & Kaur, M. (2018). Kahoot! It: Gamification in Higher Education. *Pertanika Journal of Social Science & Humanities*, 26(1), 565–582.

The Council of Europe's Modern Languge Project. (2002). https://www.ecml.at/efsz/files/Trim.pdf

Tudor, I. (1993). Teacher roles in the learner-centered classroom. *ELT Journal*, 47(1), 23–24. doi:10.1093/elt/47.1.22

Ubaedillah, U., & Pratiwi, D. I. (2021). Utilization of information technology during the COVID-19 pandemic: Student's perception of online lectures. *Edukatif: Jurnal Ilmu Pendidikan*, 3(2), 447-455. doi:10.31004/edukatif.v3i2.320

Vincent, T. (2015). *Class Quiz Games with Quizizz (an Alternative to Kahoot)*. Retrieved from https://learninginhand.com/blog/quiziz

Wedemeyer, C. A. (1977). Independent study. In A. S. Knowles (Ed.), *The International Encyclopedia of Higher Education*. Northeastern University.

White, C. (2006). Distance learning of foreign languages. *Language Teaching*, 39(4), 247–264. doi:10.1017/S0261444806003727

Young, R. (1986). *Personal autonomy: beyond negative and positive liberty*. Croom Helm.

KEY TERMS AND DEFINITIONS

Autonomous Learning: A process in which individuals accept responsibility for their own learning by recognizing his/her own learning characteristics, to know, choose and use the strategies used in learning.

Distance Education: A type of learning where the main elements consist of physical separation of teachers and students during instruction and the use of various technologies to ease student-teacher and student-student communication.

Foreign Language Education: The formal education process an individual takes to learn any language.

Learner Autonomy: It is a process where the learner decides about his/her actions by taking risks with self-confidence, and undertakes the responsibility of learning with active participation.

Theories of Distance Learning: Theories that focus on learner independence and autonomy, industrialization of teaching, and interaction and communication.

Chapter 3
ChatGPT as a Personalized Professional Development Tool:
Voices of English Teachers

Galip Kartal
https://orcid.org/0000-0003-4656-2108
Necmettin Erbakan University, Turkey

ABSTRACT

This study explored the experiences of in-service English teachers using ChatGPT, an advanced AI language model, as a professional development tool. Adopting an exploratory case study approach, findings revealed a positive perception of ChatGPT's potential for personalized learning and professional growth. However, challenges related to technical issues, understanding complex queries, and accuracy concerns were identified. Recommendations include structured training for educators and refining AI models to better understand educational contexts. This research contributes to the discourse on AI's role in education and professional development.

INTRODUCTION

The inception of the 21st century has been distinctly characterized by a sweeping technological revolution, instigating a profound paradigm shift that permeates various domains, notably including the realm of education. The contemporary educational landscape is perpetually molded and reconfigured by the relentless advancements in technology, catalyzing alterations in pedagogical strategies and the overall

DOI: 10.4018/979-8-3693-0353-5.ch003

Copyright © 2024, IGI Global. Copying or distributing in print or electronic forms without written permission of IGI Global is prohibited.

learning experience (Selwyn, 2011). A technology of transformative caliber that has been increasingly pervasive across diverse educational spectrums is Artificial Intelligence (AI), which harbors the potential to radically revolutionize teaching and learning through the provision of innovative instructional tools (Kartal, 2023), the personalization of learning experiences (Panigrahi, 2020), and the fostering of enhanced efficiencies (Luckin et al, 2016). Within the extensive applications of AI in education, the emergence of sophisticated AI language models, including but not limited to OpenAI's ChatGPT, Google Bard, and Microsoft Bing, has garnered substantial attention and intrigue. ChatGPT, meticulously trained utilizing machine learning algorithms on copious volumes of text, manifests the capability to generate text responses that eerily mirror human-like qualities, showcasing an astute understanding of context, grammar, and even intricate nuances of language (Deng & Lin, 2023; Kartal, 2023). Such models unfold intriguing possibilities, especially for language educators, potentially serving as innovative tools for professional development.

The pivotal importance of professional development for educators, especially those engaged in English language teaching, cannot be understated, as it is quintessential for maintaining and enhancing the quality of teaching by ensuring educators remain abreast with the latest methodologies, resources, and technological innovations in teaching. Traditional approaches to professional development have typically embraced methods such as workshops, self-monitoring, seminars, analyzing critical incidents, peer coaching, team teaching, case analyses, teacher support groups, and the maintenance of a teaching journal, among others (Richards & Farrell, 2009). However, the advancements in AI, particularly through tools like ChatGPT, present a novel opportunity for a more personalized, autonomous, and flexible professional development experience (Atlas, 2023).

In light of this, the present chapter endeavors to delve deeply into the potential and tangible realities of employing ChatGPT as a personalized professional development tool for in-service English teachers. It aims to particularly explore the experiences, perceptions, and recommendations of English teachers who have judiciously integrated ChatGPT into their professional development activities. The overarching goal is to elucidate the ways in which the AI language model ChatGPT can be effectively utilized to foster professional growth, refine teaching methodologies, and subsequently enhance the language learning experiences in classrooms. Through this investigatory lens, this chapter seeks to enrich the wider discourse concerning the confluence of AI and foreign language education, thereby providing educators, administrators, policymakers, and researchers with an informed perspective regarding the potential advantages, challenges, and best practices for employing AI tools in professional development.

Although numerous research endeavors have investigated the potential and challenges of ChatGPT within educational contexts (Adıgüzel et al., 2023; Kasneci et al., 2023), its specific role within language education remains tantalizingly underexplored. A modest number of studies have probed into its utility in language instruction (Kohnke et al.; Koraishi, 2023). While these works acknowledge ChatGPT's capacity to augment language acquisition, its specific role in English as a Foreign Language (EFL) pedagogy and the firsthand experiences of educators interfacing with it remain shrouded in ambiguity. This research seeks to unveil ChatGPT's viability in EFL pedagogy, casting a spotlight on both the opportunities and challenges that emanate from the incorporation of chatbots into language instruction. The insights derived from this exploration bear the potential to refine the adoption and integration of AI-infused educational tools, enhancing EFL teaching by addressing educators' optimism and reservations regarding ChatGPT.

Furthermore, this chapter is grounded on the premise that the integration of advanced technologies, such as AI, into the educational ecosystem is inevitably accompanied by its own set of challenges. Obstacles such as lack of technical expertise, apprehensions regarding data privacy, and resistance to change among educators have been highlighted as significant hurdles to the successful implementation of AI in education (Bingimlas, 2019; Guenole et al., 2022). Therefore, a nuanced understanding of educators' experiences and perceptions becomes paramount in addressing these challenges and facilitating a more seamless transition towards a technologically-augmented educational environment. This chapter aims not merely to underscore the positive aspects and potential of ChatGPT but also to identify and critically discuss the challenges and reservations expressed by educators, thus providing a holistic and comprehensive analysis of ChatGPT as a tool for professional development in EFL pedagogy.

In an endeavor to bridge the extant gap in the literature, this chapter seeks to explore the experiences and perceptions of in-service English teachers who have utilized ChatGPT as part of their professional development activities. The focus will coalesce around understanding the potential benefits, challenges, and recommendations for effectively integrating ChatGPT into professional development activities for English language educators. This study is poised to provide a comprehensive understanding of the role of AI language models like ChatGPT in the professional development of language teachers, thereby contributing significantly to the broader discourse on the integration of AI in education and its implications for the future trajectory of language teaching and learning.

To meet these objectives, the study is guided by the following research questions:

1. How do in-service English teachers perceive the integration of ChatGPT as a personalized professional development tool?
2. In what manners do English teachers employ ChatGPT to facilitate their professional growth and enrich their instructional practices?

3. What challenges and obstacles do English teachers encounter when incorporating ChatGPT into their professional development activities?
4. What recommendations do English teachers provide to optimize the adoption of ChatGPT in their professional development endeavors?

LITERATURE REVIEW

In recent decades, the proliferation of technology within the educational domain has not only been remarkably evident but has also become a focal point of substantial academic scrutiny and discourse. This notable infusion of technology into educational practices and methodologies is particularly salient in the context of the rapid advancements and innovations that characterize the 21st-century digital age, wherein technology is not merely seen as a tool but progressively recognized as a pivotal element that holds significant and multifaceted implications for both teaching and learning processes (Gunawan & Shieh, 2020). The advent of AI, with its profound and multifaceted capabilities, and its subsequent integration into diverse facets of the educational landscape, has garnered considerable attention, sparking both enthusiasm and skepticism among educators, policymakers, and researchers alike. AI, characterized by its ability to mimic human intelligence and perform tasks such as problem-solving, understanding natural language, and learning from experience, has permeated various sectors, and education has been no exception.

AI in Education

The incorporation of AI into educational frameworks is not just a vision of the future, but an ongoing transformation that is redefining the boundaries of pedagogical approaches and the wider educational environment. This integration presents inventive opportunities for revising and rejuvenating conventional educational methods (Chatterjee & Bhattacharjee, 2020). One of the fundamental characteristics of AI is its ability to deliver personalized learning experiences. Unlike traditional educational instruments that implement a uniform approach for all, AI systems are capable of adjusting to the distinctive learning styles, preferences, and speeds of individual learners. These systems consistently assess student interactions and achievements to modify instructional content and techniques, guaranteeing that the learning process remains pertinent and stimulating for each student (Zhang & Aslan, 2021). This level of personalization can enhance understanding, and also encourage intrinsic motivation among learners (García-Sánchez & Luján-García, 2016).

The participation of AI in education is not merely for the sake of technology. There is a mounting body of evidence that suggests that the appropriate application of AI can result in improved learning outcomes. For example, automated feedback can offer students prompt and accurate insights into their learning trajectory, enabling them to pinpoint areas for improvement, and consequently, enhance their performance. Furthermore, AI-driven learning analytics tools can forecast academic challenges faced by students, facilitating early interventions and averting potential setbacks (Zhai et al., 2021).

Outside the classroom, AI has the potential to optimize and streamline administrative tasks, thereby augmenting the overall efficacy of educational institutions. Smart systems can manage a variety of tasks from monitoring student attendance to predictive maintenance of infrastructure, freeing educators and administrative personnel from mundane tasks and allowing them to concentrate more on instructional and strategic initiatives (Lin et al.). The versatility of AI tools also provides educators with innovative techniques to captivate and engage students. From virtual teaching assistants to interactive simulations, AI can offer a plethora of resources that render learning more interactive and immersive (Kuleta et al., 2021). Such tools can be particularly advantageous in accommodating diverse learners, ensuring inclusivity, and nurturing a more comprehensive learning environment (Kashive et al., 2020).

The educational sector is on the verge of an AI revolution, poised to transform traditional pedagogies by integrating personalization, efficiency, and innovation. As AI continues to develop and integrate more deeply into education, it is crucial for stakeholders to comprehend its capabilities, challenges, and ethical considerations to effectively harness its potential. The transformative capacity of AI in education is considerable and multifaceted. By leveraging AI, it is feasible to customize learning experiences, enhance learning outcomes, and achieve higher efficiencies in educational systems (Kuleta et al., 2021). Additionally, AI tools can equip educators with novel and effective ways to engage students, thereby refining instructional practices (Zhai et al., 2021).

As the landscape of education continues to evolve, it is critical to remain cognizant of the broader implications of AI integration. While the potential benefits are significant, it is also necessary to consider potential challenges, such as data privacy, algorithmic bias, and the digital divide, which may exacerbate existing inequalities. Moreover, as AI systems become more sophisticated, there is a need for ongoing evaluation and refinement to ensure that these tools continue to support the goals of education and foster a more inclusive and effective learning environment. Ultimately, the successful integration of AI into education will require a thoughtful and collaborative approach, involving educators, administrators, policymakers, and technologists, to maximize its benefits and mitigate potential risks.

AI in Language Learning

The confluence of AI with language learning embodies one of the most thrilling crossroads of technology and pedagogy in modern times. This entrance of AI into the domain has engendered a spectrum of instructional techniques and tools that hold the potential to revolutionize language education and transform learners' experiences (Kartal, 2023). AI is instrumental in offering innovative solutions for language teaching and practice. Tools powered by AI can create personalized learning journeys, boost learner engagement, and deliver instant feedback, thereby rendering language learning more productive and interactive (Vall & Araya, 2023). Such technologies can be employed to refine pronunciation, vocabulary, grammar, and even conversational abilities, affording students the chance for more immersive and ongoing language learning experiences (Kartal, 2023).

In contrast to conventional methods, which are largely linear and rigid, AI-driven platforms employ adaptive learning algorithms to craft content specifically tailored to the linguistic capabilities and requirements of individual learners. This guarantees that instruction remains demanding yet attainable, thereby maximizing the learner's zone of proximal development, a concept that helps us comprehend and facilitate learning (Mylnikova, 2022). A crucial advantage of AI lies in its capacity to identify patterns and conduct predictive analyses. By consistently evaluating a student's performance, strengths, and areas for enhancement, AI platforms can design customized learning pathways, ensuring that language learners stay engaged and motivated (Fu et al., 2020). This adaptability instills a sense of ownership and agency among learners, as they perceive the curriculum as being specially crafted for them.

Feedback is another critical aspect where AI contributes significantly to language learning (Smutny & Schreiberova, 2020). A major limitation of traditional language learning has been the delay in feedback, which can obstruct timely correction and mastery. AI-powered tools bridge this gap by providing immediate, accurate, and contextual feedback on various linguistic components, from pronunciation and vocabulary to intricate grammatical structures. This immediacy guarantees that learners can swiftly identify and rectify their errors, hastening the learning trajectory (Kartal, 2023). Moreover, AI tools equipped with voice recognition and natural language processing capabilities facilitate the practice and enhancement of pronunciation (Neri et al., 2008). Concurrently, interactive AI-driven exercises and quizzes ensure that vocabulary (Kartal, 2023) and grammar (Kim, 2019) are effectively reinforced (Dunn, 2016). Furthermore, conversational AI, such as chatbots, provide learners with real-time conversational practice, closely resembling authentic human interactions and preparing them for real-world linguistic challenges (García-Peñalvo et al., 2020).

As global language educators and learners enthusiastically adopt these innovations, there is a tangible sense of anticipation about the future directions of language education and the unexplored potential that AI harbors in this context. The integration of AI and language learning is a promising frontier, ripe with opportunities to not only enhance the quality and efficiency of language instruction but also to empower learners with the tools and resources necessary to succeed in a linguistically diverse world. By harnessing the power of AI, educators can create more personalized, engaging, and effective learning experiences, ultimately contributing to the development of more competent and confident language learners.

Professional Development of Language Teachers

Internationally, there has been a concerted effort to ensure that students receive instruction from highly qualified teachers, with numerous countries implementing educational policies designed to enhance and assess teacher quality (Feng & Sass, 2018). The pivotal role of teacher competence in influencing student learning is underscored by the human capital theory (Aaronson et al., 2007). Darling-Hammond (2010) posited that teachers are central to student learning, a stance echoed by education policymakers worldwide who contend that teacher quality significantly impacts student learning (OECD, 2005). Moreover, researchers investigating teacher characteristics have indicated that teachers not only influence student achievements (Ronfeldt et al., 2015) but also their effectiveness (Lee et al., 2015) in multiple dimensions. Given the crucial role of teaching and teachers, professional development (PD) of teachers is of utmost importance.

Professional development for language teachers is essential for improving the quality of language instruction and ensuring teachers remain up-to-date with modern teaching methodologies and resources (Richards & Farrell, 2009). By the 1990s, the process through which teachers acquired knowledge became as critical as the content in second language teacher education (Burns & Richards, 2009). This era witnessed an increasing emphasis on teacher cognition, focusing on the influence of a teacher's beliefs, understanding, and knowledge on their classroom practices (Borg, 2009). This transition marked a departure from the behaviorist approach, acknowledging that teachers possess pre-existing beliefs and values that affect their teaching methods (Nunan & Carter, 2001). These paradigmatic shifts laid the foundation for more effective professional development.

The very nature of PD evolved, transitioning from merely "in-service training" to a broader perspective where teachers are perceived as proactive agents of change (Richardson, 2003). Darling-Hammond et al. (2017) viewed PD as learning that engenders tangible changes in teacher practices and student outcomes. This novel conceptualization of PD was influenced by a deeper understanding of teacher cognition, shaping contemporary perspectives on teacher education and learning. Research suggests that effective PD is pivotal to the success of educational reforms (Desimone, 2009). Various scholars have outlined the characteristics of effective PD, which include its relevance to teachers' needs, fostering active teacher involvement and collaboration, support from school leadership, and an emphasis on both practical and theoretical knowledge (Borg, 2015). Darling-Hammond (2017) further noted that effective PD is content-specific, encourages active learning, fosters collaboration, and is sustained over time.

While the fundamental principles of professional development for language teachers are rooted in teacher cognition and evolving teaching methodologies, the contemporary era presents a new array of challenges and opportunities. With the increasing digitization and interconnectivity of the world, there is a marked shift towards integrating technology into every aspect of education. This transition not only enhances the tools available for teacher growth but also transforms the landscape of professional development. Traditional methodologies are now merging with new-age technologies, ushering in a new era of innovations in teacher training and development.

In conclusion, the professional development of language teachers is crucial for enhancing the quality of language instruction and for ensuring that teachers are equipped with the latest teaching methodologies and resources. The evolution of PD from mere in-service training to a broader perspective that views teachers as proactive change agents reflects a deeper understanding of teacher cognition and its impact on classroom practices. As the world becomes increasingly digitized, it is imperative that professional development for language teachers evolves to incorporate new technologies and methodologies, ultimately contributing to better language instruction and more successful language learners.

Professional Development and AI

AI tools, as noted by Kartal (2023), offer a remarkable opportunity to transform language education by providing a highly personalized learning experience for students, tailored to their individual pace and proficiency levels. The advent of AI-driven content-generation models, such as ChatGPT, has inaugurated a new era in which digital media products, writing samples, and educational materials can be created instantly. The significance of such advancements has not gone unnoticed by the educational community, with many educators and students eagerly exploring their potential.

However, this technological revolution comes with its own set of challenges. Recent developments have witnessed a surge in the popularity of AI tools, with ChatGPT, for example, garnering a staggering 100 million active users just a few months after its launch (Hu, 2023). This rapid ascent, however, has been accompanied by several pressing concerns. The misuse of such technology, particularly in the educational context, can lead to a host of problems, including plagiarism, the dissemination of harmful or biased content, inequities in access, and questions about the trustworthiness of AI-generated content. For language teachers, navigating these challenges requires discernment, critical thinking, and a comprehensive understanding of the tool's capabilities and limitations.

In this context, professional development extends beyond traditional boundaries. While sporadic workshops or seminars have their merits, the evolving nature of AI in education necessitates more agile and continuous learning avenues. AI-powered platforms, offering adaptive learning modules, can enable teachers to stay current with the latest developments in language teaching methodologies and digital innovations (Trust et al., 2023). Additionally, collaborative forums have gained prominence, fostering a global community of language educators keen to share experiences, assess the effectiveness of AI tools, and collaboratively design innovative teaching modules. The Age of AI undoubtedly holds tremendous potential for transforming the landscape of professional development for language teachers. However, a cautious and informed approach is crucial. As educators incorporate these tools into their teaching repertoires, they must be equipped with the knowledge and skills to do so responsibly.

Ultimately, the integration of AI tools into language education presents both opportunities and challenges. While AI offers the potential to revolutionize language instruction by providing personalized learning experiences, it also raises concerns about plagiarism, biased content, and equitable access. To navigate these challenges effectively, language teachers must engage in continuous professional development, which includes not only traditional workshops and seminars but also adaptive learning modules and collaborative forums. By approaching the integration of AI tools with caution and a well-informed perspective, language educators can harness the power of AI to enhance their teaching while addressing potential challenges responsibly.

METHOD

In this research, an exploratory case study approach was employed to gain a deeper understanding of the experiences and perspectives of in-service English teachers using ChatGPT as a personalized professional development tool. This method facilitated a thorough investigation of the complex dynamics and helped in identifying evolving patterns within the data (Baxter & Jack, 2008). By narrowing the focus to a specific system, data was collected through in-depth interviews and introspective diaries,

ChatGPT as a Personalized Professional Development Tool

enabling a comprehensive examination of the research questions and uncovering the genuine sentiments and observations of the study's subjects (Creswell & Poth, 2016).

Participants

The study employed a purposive sampling technique to select 15 in-service English teachers, all of whom were engaged in a non-dissertation master's program focused on language pedagogy at a renowned state-run university in Türkiye. This specific sampling method was chosen to ensure that participants had a vested interest in advancing their teaching methodologies and could provide rich, relevant insights into the integration of technology, like ChatGPT, into their professional practices. The selected participants represented a wide spectrum of professional experience, ranging from three to 15 years, and were currently teaching at various educational levels from primary to high school. This diverse cohort was carefully chosen to include teachers from different regions of Türkiye, offering a broad perspective on the instructional challenges and successes in English language education across varied demographic and socioeconomic classroom settings.

The inclusion criteria for participants were designed to encompass teachers who were not only pursuing further education in a relevant field but who also were actively teaching, thus ensuring that the study benefited from practical, on-the-ground insights. These teachers' commitment to professional development and their concurrent engagement in advanced studies provided a unique opportunity to explore the multifaceted nature of English language teaching strategies and challenges. Their contributions were considered especially valuable, as they brought forth a wealth of experience and a commitment to enhancing their pedagogical practices, thereby serving as a rich source of data for identifying educational strategies and informing policy recommendations in the realm of language teachingpedagogy.

Data Collection

The qualitative analysis required careful examination of data obtained from semi-structured interviews and reflective diaries. The primary method of data collection was individual interviews, which were designed to gain a deep understanding of the subjects' experiences and views on digital fatigue and the advantages of AI tools. The questions were formulated to be open-ended, encouraging detailed responses that would provide a richer understanding of their perspectives. With the consent of the participants, interviews were audio-recorded to ensure accuracy. Reflective diaries served as another crucial source of data, maintained over a period of ten weeks. These diaries captured the educators' daily activities and reflections related to ChatGPT, online pedagogy, digital fatigue, and other AI tools. This extended duration was crucial for tracking the evolution of experiences and the phenomena under investigation. Regular interactions between the researcher and participants ensured data integrity, and ethical standards, such as informed consent and data protection, were rigorously observed. The analysis involved a detailed examination of the interview and diary data, providing a comprehensive understanding of the educators' perspectives.

Data Analysis

The qualitative data extracted from the interviews and diaries were subjected to a structured content analysis following the four-step procedure outlined by Yıldırım and Şimşek (2006). This process involved annotating the data, identifying patterns, categorizing findings, and interpreting the results (Yıldırım & Şimşek, 2006). To ensure analytical precision, two iterations of coding were performed, and the consistency between these iterations was assessed using Miles and Huberman's (1994) method, resulting in an impressive 85% agreement rate.

The relationships between the coded data were carefully examined, and overarching themes were identified (Yıldırım & Şimşek, 2006). Participant verification of the findings, or member checking, was employed to strengthen the study's credibility.

To enhance the study's robustness, stringent analytical protocols were adhered to. Trustworthiness was reinforced using member checking, prolonged engagement with participants, and data triangulation (Lincoln & Guba, 1985). The member checking phase involved revisiting the findings with the participants to ensure their accuracy, while data triangulation involved using both dialogues and diaries to validate the findings.

In compliance with ethical standards, participants were informed about the research objectives, their rights, and the guarantee of response anonymity. Each participant provided informed consent before the data collection process. Strict measures were implemented to safeguard the data, which was only accessible to the research team, thereby ensuring participant welfare and research integrity.

FINDINGS

Through a thorough thematic analysis of the interview data, several key themes emerged that provide deep insights into the experiences and perspectives of in-service English teachers using ChatGPT as a personalized professional development tool. The analysis led to the identification of four overarching themes, each capturing a critical aspect of the teachers' experiences. These themes include: (1) Perceptions of ChatGPT, (2) Usage of ChatGPT in Professional Development, (3) Challenges

ChatGPT as a Personalized Professional Development Tool

in Adopting ChatGPT, and (4) Recommendations for Optimizing ChatGPT Usage (Table 1).

Table 1. Themes and sub-themes

Themes	Sub-Themes	Representative Quotes
Perceptions of ChatGPT	Positive perception	"ChatGPT provides instant and personalized responses which makes learning more interactive and engaging."
	Value for professional development	"It significantly contributes to my professional development by offering diverse resources and perspectives."
Usage of ChatGPT in Professional Development	Clarifying concepts	"When I'm unsure about a particular teaching concept or approach, I ask ChatGPT and it provides a concise explanation."
	Brainstorming strategies	"ChatGPT helps me in brainstorming different teaching strategies. It's like having a collaborative partner available 24/7."
	Keeping up-to-date	"It provides the latest research and trends in language teaching which keeps me up-to-date in my field."
Challenges in Adopting ChatGPT	Technical issues	"Sometimes it fails to respond or takes longer than expected, which disrupts the flow of my learning."
	Contextual limitations	"It struggles with understanding complex or context-specific queries, which can be a bit frustrating."
	Accuracy concerns	"I'm not always sure if the information it provides is accurate. That can cause some uncertainty."
Recommendations for Optimizing ChatGPT Usage	Training for teachers	"We need more training on how to effectively use ChatGPT in our professional development. It will enhance our learning experiences."
	AI model improvement	"It should better understand the nuances of educational contexts. This would make it a much more powerful tool."
	Information verification	"There should be a way to verify the information provided by ChatGPT. This would help in boosting our confidence in its responses."

Perceptions of ChatGPT

The participants predominantly held a favorable perception of ChatGPT, particularly emphasizing its capacity to deliver prompt and personalized feedback. This was articulated by one participant who said, "ChatGPT provides instant and personalized responses which makes learning more interactive and engaging." This sentiment was consistently reiterated, signifying that the speed and tailoring of ChatGPT's responses play a pivotal role in enhancing the learning experience. In addition to this, educators acknowledged the value of ChatGPT in their professional advancement. They contended that the tool not only provides a vast spectrum of resources but also offers a variety of perspectives, both of which are instrumental in their professional journey. As one educator articulated, "It significantly contributes to my professional development by offering diverse resources and perspectives." This remark suggests that ChatGPT, beyond being a mere repository of information, is perceived as a platform that can facilitate well-rounded professional development.

Usage of ChatGPT in Professional Development

Educators frequently resorted to ChatGPT for elucidating various teaching concepts or methodologies. The tool's capacity to offer succinct explanations was especially valued. As shared by one participant, "When I'm unsure about a particular teaching concept or approach, I ask ChatGPT and it provides a concise explanation." This indicates that ChatGPT functions as an easily accessible reference for educators during moments of doubt or ambiguity. Another noteworthy application was the employment of ChatGPT for brainstorming. Educators perceived that interacting with ChatGPT was akin to having a collaborative partner accessible at all hours. One educator elaborated, "ChatGPT helps me in brainstorming different teaching strategies. It's like having a collaborative partner available 24/7." This observation underscores the potential of ChatGPT as a collaborative thinking tool that can aid educators in the ideation and development of strategies. Furthermore, staying updated with the latest trends and research is of paramount importance for educators. Several participants opined that ChatGPT was instrumental in this regard. One participant highlighted, "It provides the latest research and trends in language teaching which keeps me up-to-date in my field." This comment underscores ChatGPT's potential as a dynamic knowledge repository, ensuring that educators remain at the forefront of their disciplines.

Challenges in Adopting ChatGPT

Notwithstanding its myriad advantages, some educators encountered technical challenges with ChatGPT. There were sporadic reports of service interruptions or delayed responses. An educator expressed disappointment, articulating, "Sometimes it fails to respond or takes longer than expected, which disrupts the flow of my learning." Such technical glitches can obstruct the seamless integration of ChatGPT into the learning process. A recurrent challenge highlighted by the participants was ChatGPT's intermittent struggle in interpreting complex or context-specific queries. An educator observed, "It struggles with understanding complex or context-specific queries, which can be a bit frustrating." This feedback underscores the necessity

ChatGPT as a Personalized Professional Development Tool

for the tool to better comprehend the nuances of specific educational contexts. Moreover, there were apprehensions raised regarding the accuracy of the information dispensed by ChatGPT. An educator noted, "I'm not always sure if the information it provides is accurate. That can cause some uncertainty." This sentiment accentuates the importance of ensuring that AI-driven tools like ChatGPT are both reliable and trustworthy.

Recommendations for Optimizing ChatGPT Usage

In order to optimize the utility of ChatGPT, educators expressed the need for more structured training. A participant suggested, "We need more training on how to effectively use ChatGPT in our professional development. It will enhance our learning experiences." This recommendation underscores the necessity of equipping educators with the skills needed to fully leverage the potential of ChatGPT. There was a consensus among the participants regarding the need for the AI model to better comprehend the intricacies of educational contexts. An educator posited, "It should better understand the nuances of educational contexts. This would make it a much more powerful tool." This feedback indicates the need for the continuous evolution and refinement of ChatGPT to cater specifically to the needs of educators. In light of the concerns regarding accuracy, there were calls for the implementation of mechanisms to verify the information provided by ChatGPT. A participant asserted, "There should be a way to verify the information provided by ChatGPT. This would help in boosting our confidence in its responses." The implementation of such verification mechanisms could considerably enhance the credibility and trustworthiness of ChatGPT in professional development settings. In summary, while ChatGPT is perceived as a valuable resource for professional development among educators, there are areas that require improvement to further optimize its utility. Addressing these challenges and incorporating the participants' recommendations can pave the way for a more integrated and effective utilization of ChatGPT in the educational domain.

DISCUSSION

The incorporation of Artificial Intelligence (AI), particularly the advanced language models exemplified by ChatGPT, into educational contexts has sparked significant interest and multifaceted discussions among scholars and practitioners alike. The present research undertook a meticulous exploration aimed at elucidating the feasibility and efficacy of utilizing ChatGPT as a specialized professional development apparatus for in-service educators in the English language domain. The overwhelmingly positive perception of ChatGPT, as documented among participants, is not merely an isolated observation but is instead harmoniously consistent with a broader academic dialogue that postulates the transformative and revolutionary potential of AI in educational ecosystems (Kartal, 2023; Selwyn, 2011).

In a specific nod to the invaluable attributes of ChatGPT, participants underscored the rapidity and bespoke nature of the responses generated by the model, facets that align seamlessly with existing literature which extols the virtues of AI in facilitating highly individualized and adaptive learning experiences (Zhang & Aslan, 2021). García-Sánchez & Luján-García (2016) have theorized that such meticulous personalization can indeed serve as a catalyst, fostering intrinsic motivation among learners and educators alike. The emphatic belief among educators that ChatGPT significantly augments their professional development, by furnishing an expansive array of resources and myriad perspectives, further accentuates the tool's alignment with the principal objectives of AI in educational contexts, as eloquently outlined by Chatterjee & Bhattacharjee (2020).

Furthermore, the myriad ways in which educators have harnessed ChatGPT for their professional development evinces the model's multifaceted capabilities and wide-ranging applicability. The use of ChatGPT as a mechanism for clarifying complex concepts and ideating innovative teaching strategies corroborates existing literature which underscores the pivotal role AI can play in conceiving and implementing inventive instructional methodologies (Kartal, 2023; Vall & Araya, 2023;). Additionally, ChatGPT's aptitude for keeping educators meticulously informed about the most recent research developments and emergent trends in language teaching echoes the broader potential of AI to reshape traditional pedagogical paradigms by interweaving elements of personalization, efficacy, and innovation (Kuleta et al., 2021).

However, it is imperative to acknowledge that while the potential benefits of ChatGPT are palpable, the challenges highlighted by participants provide pivotal insights into aspects that necessitate further refinement and enhancement. Technical disruptions and challenges in interpreting complex inquiries echo concerns that have been articulated in broader academic dialogues concerning the limitations inherent in AI tools (Adıgüzel et al., 2023). Participants' apprehensions regarding the veracity of information mirror wider discourses on the reliability and trustworthiness of AI-generated content, underscoring the imperative for a judicious and well-informed approach in the incorporation of AI tools into educational spaces (Trust et al., 2023).

Moreover, the appeal for more comprehensive and structured training in utilizing ChatGPT dovetails with a wider understanding that, while AI tools harbor transformative potential, their efficacious incorporation demands the inculcation of pertinent skills among educators (Richardson, 2003; Darling-Hammond et al., 2017). The proposition that the AI model should cultivate a more profound understanding

ChatGPT as a Personalized Professional Development Tool

of educational contexts aligns with existing literature, which underscores the exigency for AI tools to be meticulously customized to meet the singular needs and challenges faced by educators (Kartal, 2023). The suggestion to implement mechanisms to authenticate the information provided by ChatGPT underscores the paramountcy of ensuring that AI-driven tools are not only reliable but also engender trust, a sentiment that deeply resonates with wider discourses on the role of AI in education (Hu, 2023).

In conclusion, the findings of this research proffer invaluable insights into the potential, inherent challenges, and constructive recommendations pertaining to the utilization of ChatGPT as a professional development tool for English educators. While the tool manifests significant promise, its efficacious integration into the educational milieu necessitates a meticulous consideration of the challenges identified and a steadfast adherence to the recommendations posited by educators. As the nexus between AI and education continues to evolve and mature, research of this nature becomes quintessential in shaping the discourse and guiding best practices. The journey toward the integration of AI into education, as underscored by this study, is one that is navigated with both optimism and caution, necessitating a harmonious amalgamation of innovative spirit and prudent practice.

CONCLUSION

The onset of the 21st century marked the advent of a technological revolution that has profoundly influenced various sectors, education being no exception. This investigation, anchored in an exploratory case study methodology, meticulously examined the experiences of in-service English teachers utilizing ChatGPT as a tool for professional development. This exhaustive examination, encompassing the introduction, literature review, methodology, findings, and discussion, has furnished a comprehensive understanding of the possibilities and challenges associated with the integration of AI, specifically ChatGPT, into the domain of English language instruction.

The favorable perceptions of ChatGPT, as underscored by the participants, underline the revolutionary potential of AI in education, echoing the viewpoints of Selwyn (2011) and Kartal (2023). The capability of the tool to deliver personalized, instantaneous feedback is in harmony with the broader literature which accentuates the merits of AI-driven personalization in education (Zhang & Aslan, 2021; García-Sánchez & Luján-García, 2016). The experiences of the educators, as elucidated in the findings, further accentuate the congruence of ChatGPT with the overarching goals of AI in education, as outlined by Chatterjee & Bhattacharjee (2020).

Nonetheless, akin to any technological innovation, obstacles endure. The technical difficulties, challenges in comprehending intricate queries, and apprehensions regarding accuracy, as articulated by the participants, reflect the wider concerns in the literature about the limitations and trustworthiness of AI instruments (Adıgüzel et al., 2023; Trust et al., 2023). These obstacles highlight the necessity for a judicious and informed approach to the integration of AI in educational environments.

The recommendations proffered by the educators, particularly the demand for structured training and the necessity for AI models to develop a more nuanced understanding of educational contexts, underscore the importance of perpetual evolution and refinement in the sphere of AI in education. These insights are in line with the broader literature which emphasizes the need to equip educators with the requisite skills and customize AI tools to cater to the specific needs of educators (Darling-Hammond et al., 2017; Kartal, 2023; Richardson, 2003).

In amalgamating the insights gleaned from this research, it becomes manifest that while AI, and specifically ChatGPT, harbors immense potential for transforming the landscape of professional development for English teachers, its effective incorporation necessitates a harmonious amalgamation of innovation, prudence, and continuous learning. As the educational domain stands on the brink of an AI revolution, it is of utmost importance for stakeholders to effectively harness its potential, ensuring that the journey of integrating AI into education is characterized by both optimism and caution.

In conclusion, this research serves as a testament to the revolutionary potential of AI in education, offering invaluable insights for educators, policymakers, and researchers alike. As AI continues to evolve and permeate deeper into the educational fabric, it is imperative to continually reflect, adapt, and innovate, ensuring that the integration of such tools augments the quality of education and fosters comprehensive professional development for educators.

REFERENCES

Aaronson, D., Barrow, L., & Sander, W. (2007). Teachers and student achievement in the Chicago public high schools. *Journal of Labor Economics*, *25*(1), 95–135. doi:10.1086/508733

Adıgüzel, T., Kaya, M. H., & Cansu, F. K. (2023). Revolutionizing education with AI: Exploring the transformative potential of ChatGPT. *Contemporary Educational Technology*, *15*(3), ep429. doi:10.30935/cedtech/13152

Atlas, S. (2023). *ChatGPT for higher education and professional development: A guide to conversational AI*. Retrieved from https://digitalcommons.uri.edu/cba_facpubs/548

Baxter, P., & Jack, S. (2008). Qualitative case study methodology: Study design and implementation for novice researchers. *The Qualitative Report, 13*(4), 544–559.

Borg, S. (2009). Language teacher cognition. *The Cambridge guide to second language teacher education*, 163-171. doi:10.1017/9781139042710.022

Borg, S. (2015). *Professional development for English language teachers: Perspectives from higher education in Turkey*. British Council.

Burns, A., & Richards, J. C. (2009). *Second language teacher education*. Cambridge University., doi:10.1017/9781139042710

Chatterjee, S., & Bhattacharjee, K. K. (2020). Adoption of artificial intelligence in higher education: A quantitative analysis using structural equation modelling. *Education and Information Technologies, 25*(5), 3443–3463. doi:10.100710639-020-10159-7

Creswell, J. W., & Poth, C. N. (2016). Qualitative inquiry and research design: Choosing among five approaches. *Sage (Atlanta, Ga.)*.

Darling-Hammond, L. (2010). Teacher education and the American future, *Journal of Teacher Education, 61*(1–2), 35-47. doi:10.1177/0022487109348024

Darling-Hammond, L. (2017). Teacher education around the world: What can we learn from international practice? *European Journal of Teacher Education, 40*(3), 291–309. doi:10.1080/02619768.2017.1315399

Deng, J., & Lin, Y. (2023). The cenefits and challenges of ChatGPT: An overview. *Frontiers in Computing and Intelligent Systems*. doi:10.54097/fcis.v2i2.4465

Desimone, L. M. (2009). Improving impact studies of teachers' professional development: Toward better conceptualizations and measures. *Educational Researcher, 38*(3), 181–199. doi:10.3102/0013189X08331140

Dunn, J. (2016). Computational learning of construction grammars. *Language and Cognition, 9*(2), 254–292. doi:10.1017/langcog.2016.7

Feng, L., & Sass, T. R. (2018). The impact of incentives to recruit and retain teachers in "hard-to-staff" subjects. *Journal of Policy Analysis and Management, 37*(1), 112–135. doi:10.1002/pam.22037

Fu, S., Gu, H., & Yang, B. (2020). The affordances of AI-enabled automatic scoring applications on learners' continuous learning intention: An empirical study in China. *British Journal of Educational Technology*, *51*(5), 1674–1692. doi:10.1111/bjet.12995

García-Sánchez, S., & Luján-García, C. (2016). Ubiquitous knowledge and experiences to foster EFL learning affordances. *Computer Assisted Language Learning*, *29*(7), 1169–1180. doi:10.1080/09588221.2016.1176047

Gunawan, S., & Shieh, C. (2020). Effects of the application of STEM curriculum integration model to living technology teaching on business school students' learning effectiveness. *Contemporary Educational Technology*, *12*(2), ep279. Advance online publication. doi:10.30935/cedtech/8583

Hu, K. (2023). *ChatGPT sets record for fastest-growing user base - analyst note*. Reuters. https://www.reuters.com/technology/chatgpt-sets-record-fastest-growing-user-base-analyst-note-2023-02-01

Kartal, G. (2023). Contemporary language teaching and learning with ChatGPT. *Contemporary Research in Language and Linguistics*, *1*(1), 59–70.

Kashive, N., Powale, L., & Kashive, K. (2020). Understanding user perception toward artificial intelligence (AI) enabled e-learning. *The International Journal of Information and Learning Technology*, *38*(1), 1–19. doi:10.1108/IJILT-05-2020-0090

Kasneci, E., Seßler, K., Küchemann, S., Bannert, M., Dementieva, D., Fischer, F., Gasser, U., Groh, G., Günnemann, S., Hüllermeier, E., Krusche, S., Kutyniok, G., Michaeli, T., Nerdel, C., Pfeffer, J., Poquet, O., Sailer, M., Schmidt, A., Seidel, T., ... Kasneci, G. (2023). ChatGPT for good? On opportunities and challenges of large language models for education. *Learning and Individual Differences*, *103*, 102274. doi:10.1016/j.lindif.2023.102274

Kim, N. Y. (2019). A study on the use of artificial intelligence chatbots for improving English grammar skills. *Journal of Digital Convergence*, *17*(8), 37–46.

Kohnke, L., Moorhouse, B. L., & Zou, D. (2023). ChatGPT for Language Teaching and Learning. *RELC Journal*, *54*(2), 537–550. doi:10.1177/00336882231162868

Koraishi, O. (2023). Teaching English in the age of AI: Embracing ChatGPT to optimize EFL materials and assessment. *Language Education and Technology, 3*(1).

Kuleto, V., Ilić, M., Dumangiu, M., Ranković, M., Martins, O. M., Păun, D., & Mihoreanu, L. (2021). Exploring opportunities and challenges of artificial intelligence and machine learning in higher education institutions. *Sustainability (Basel)*, *13*(18), 10424. doi:10.3390u131810424

Lee, F. L. M., Yeung, A. S., Tracey, D., & Barker, K. (2015). Inclusion of children with special needs in early childhood education: What teacher characteristics matter. *Topics in Early Childhood Special Education*, *35*(2), 79–88. doi:10.1177/0271121414566014

Lin, P., Wooders, A., Wang, J., & Yuan, W. (2018). Artificial intelligence, the missing piece of online education? *IEEE Engineering Management Review*, *46*(3), 25–28. doi:10.1109/EMR.2018.2868068

Lincoln, Y. S., & Guba, E. G. (1985). Naturalistic inquiry. *Sage (Atlanta, Ga.)*.

Luckin, R., Holmes, W., Griffiths, M., & Forcier, L. B. (2016). *Intelligence unleashed: An argument for AI in education*. Pearson London.

Miles, M. B., & Huberman, A. M. (1994). Qualitative tata analysis: An expanded sourcebook. *Sage (Atlanta, Ga.)*.

Mylnikova, S. (2022). A unity of obucheniye and vospitaniye: An unexplored unity in Vygotskian Zone of Proximal Development. *Pakistan Social Sciences Review*, *2*(6). Advance online publication. doi:10.35484/pssr.2022(6-II)70

Neri, A., Mich, O., Gerosa, M., & Giuliani, D. (2008). The effectiveness of computer assisted pronunciation training for foreign language learning by children. *Computer Assisted Language Learning*, *21*(5), 393–408. doi:10.1080/09588220802447651

Nunan, D., & Carter, R. (2001). *The Cambridge guide to teaching English to speakers of other languages*. Ernst Klett Sprachen.

OECD. (2005). *Teachers matter: Attracting, developing and retaining effective teachers*. https://www.oecd.org/education/school/34990905.pdf

Panigrahi, C., & Joshi, V. (2020). Use of artificial intelligence in education. *The Management Accountant Journal*, *55*(5), 64–67. doi:10.33516/maj.v55i5.64-67p

Richards, J., & Farrell, T. (2009). *Professional development for language teachers*. Cambridge University.

Richardson, V. (2003). Preservice teachers' beliefs. In J. Rath & A. C. McAninch (Eds.), *Advances in Teacher Education Series* (Vol. 6, pp. 1–22). Information Age.

Ronfeldt, M., Farmer, S. O., McQueen, K., & Grissom, J. A. (2015). Teacher collaboration in instructional teams and student achievement. *American Educational Research Journal*, *52*(3), 475–514. doi:10.3102/0002831215585562

Selwyn, N. (2011). *Education and technology: Key issues and debates*. Continuum International.

Smutny, P., & Schreiberova, P. (2020). Chatbot for learning: A review of educational chatbots for the Facebook messenger. *Computers & Education, 151*, 1–11. doi:10.1016/j.compedu.2020.103862

Trust, T., Whalen, J., & Mouza, C. (2023). Editorial: ChatGPT: Challenges, Opportunities, and Implications for Teacher Education. *Contemporary Issues in Technology and Teacher Education, 23*(1), 1-23. Retrieved August 15, 2023 from https://www.learntechlib.org/primary/p/222408/

Vall, R., & Araya, F. (2023). Exploring the benefits and challenges of AI-language learning tools. *International Journal of Social Sciences and Humanities Invention*. doi:10.18535/ijsshi/v10i01.02

Yaman, S., Bal-İncebacak, B., & Sarışan-Tungaç, A. (2022). Öğretmen niteliklerinin belirlenmesinde paydaşların görüşleri. *Ahmet Keleşoğlu Eğitim Fakültesi Dergisi (AKEF), 4*(2), 376–397. doi:10.38151/akef.2022.24

Yıldırım, A., & Şimşek, H. (2006). *Sosyal bilimlerde nitel araştırma yöntemleri*. Seçkin.

Zhai, X., Chu, X., Chai, C. S., Jong, M. S. Y., Istenic, A., Spector, M., Liu, J.-B., Yuan, J., & Li, Y. (2021). A Review of Artificial Intelligence (AI) in Education from 2010 to 2020. *Complexity, 2021*, 1–18. doi:10.1155/2021/8812542

Zhang, K., & Aslan, A. B. (2021). AI technologies for education: Recent research & future directions. *Computers and Education: Artificial Intelligence*, 2, 100025. doi:10.1016/j.caeai.2021.100025

KEY TERMS AND DEFINITIONS

Case Study Approach: A research methodology that involves an in-depth exploration of a specific system, phenomenon, or group, often through qualitative data collection methods, to gain profound insights into the subject of study.

ChatGPT: An advanced AI language model developed by OpenAI, designed to generate human-like text responses by understanding context, grammar, and nuances of language.

Educational Technology: The use of digital tools, software, and platforms in education to enhance learning experiences, improve instructional practices, and foster greater efficiencies.

In-Service English Teachers: Educators who are currently practicing and teaching English, either as a first language or as a foreign language, in various educational settings.

Language Pedagogy: The method and practice of teaching language, encompassing various strategies, techniques, and principles to facilitate effective language learning.

Personalized Learning Experiences: Tailored educational pathways that cater to the unique learning styles, preferences, and paces of individual students, often facilitated by adaptive technologies.

Professional Development: A continuous process of acquiring new skills, knowledge, and insights to enhance teaching quality and stay updated with the latest methodologies, resources, and technologies.

Chapter 4
Demystifying the Unknown:
ChatGPT and Foreign Language Classrooms in the Voices of EFL Teachers

Farzaneh Dehghan
Amirkabir University of Technology, Iran

ABSTRACT

Since its introduction, artificial intelligence (AI) has had inevitable effects on education including foreign language learning. ChatGPT, as the most advanced form of AI, has brought about many concerns and opportunities for both language teachers and learners. This chapter tries to probe more deeply into the concerns expressed over the use of ChatGPT in foreign language classrooms in the voices of teachers with an emphasis on finding ways to address those concerns. The results of the inductive analysis of interview data revealed a new concern in addition to the previously identified concerns, i.e. threats to teachers' and students' creativity. It is concluded that ChatGPT, with all its differences, can be regarded as a disrupter of a constant, traditional routine rather than a disrupter of education itself and that, to deal with it, like any other new technology, the only way ahead of teachers is adaptation and changing threats into opportunities.

INTRODUCTION

Open AI's newest chatbot called ChatGPT has swept the world of education since its release in December, 2022 (and March 2023 for ChatGPT-4). ChatGPT, in full chat generative pre-trained transformer, is an artificial intelligence (AI) chatbot developed by the Microsoft-supported company OpenAI, which as a cutting-edge AI

DOI: 10.4018/979-8-3693-0353-5.ch004

Copyright © 2024, IGI Global. Copying or distributing in print or electronic forms without written permission of IGI Global is prohibited.

Demystifying the Unknown

large language model (an advanced machine learning model) is not only capable of natural language processing or understanding natural language but also generating coherent, human speech-like, and contextually relevant replies and interactions in a chat-like or conversational way based on what it has learned from training data and the prompts the interactor has given to it. Upon its introduction, ChatGPT created many concerns among educators regarding its misuse in scientific research integrity (Cotton et al., 2023; Shiri, 2023) and education (Rospigliosi, 2023) to the extent that ChatGPT-4 has been banned from some educational settings and institutes all around the world. In this regard, foreign or second language classrooms seem to be a special case as grammar accuracy, writing, correction and edition, paraphrasing and proofreading are important tasks and assignments in language classes and ChatGPT has the capability to be used (and/or misused) for these purposes. In addition to the abovementioned activities, ChatGPT can also be threatful to students' development of critical thinking, creative thinking and higher order thinking skills as the necessary requirements of many writing, speaking, reading and listening activities and tasks (Putra et al, 2023). There are also concerns about students' cheating and misconduct. There are also worries about chatbots taking the place of foreign language teachers (Brown et al., 2020).

In contrast to these concerns and worries, some other studies have emphasized the use of earlier AI-powered chatbots and ChatGPT as being beneficial to language learners in triggering language learners' interest and lowering their anxiety and shyness (Fryer et al., 2017; Fryer & Carpenter, 2006; Gallacher et al., 2018; Kohnke, 2022), helping their thinking skills (Rusandi et al., 2023), providing them with a range of conversational practices and a variety of expressions, questions and vocabulary not available from human interlocutors and adjusted personalized linguistic input and immediate feedback, (Huang et al., 2022; Kuhail et al., 2023), helping in creating an authentic, interactive language-learning environment (Chiu et al., 2023) and as a result, enhancing their engagement and language skills and capabilities (Kohnke, 2023; Smutny & Schreiberova, 2020; Kim et al., 2019; Kohnke, 2022).

These controversies over the use of chatbots and ChatGPT have created a vague situation wherein teachers may not feel assured about the effects of the new technology. Taking into account these different ideas, debates and concerns and considering the emerging literature on the effect of ChatGPT on education in general and language teaching and learning in particular, this chapter tries to probe more deeply into the topics of AI and generative language models including ChatGPT in foreign language classes by including the voices and concerns of foreign language teachers and trying to find answers to those concerns.

CHATGPT AND ITS CAPABILITIES

Before examining the uses and applications of ChatGPT in language classes, let's examine what this chatbot's actual features and capabilities are. As was mentioned, the newest released chatbot in 2022 is a generative large language model which is capable of making dialogues with users in a human-like, natural and interactive way (Susnjak, 2022). As large language models use large databases to create strong connections powered by neural networks, it can be assured that the interactions are human-like, genuine and acceptable. ChatGPT has also the capability to challenge inappropriate ideas, refuse incorrect requests and acknowledge mistakes (Haleem, Javid & Singh, 2022). Also, we should note the capability to answer follow-up questions in a conversation-like manner. Texts produced by ChatGPT include various genres such as papers and essays, poems and narratives, jokes and fables, conversations and dialogues. The more feedback and input users provide, the more improved will be the performance of ChatGPT in subsequent interactions and questions.

Therefore, in contrast to the common misunderstanding, ChatGPT has no reasoning, rationality or emotion in interactions and dialogues comparable to the features of humans, but rather, in contrast to the traditional search engines, ChatGPT retrieves information from the model itself and generates the most relevant, the most frequent and the most probable answer or simply can "learn statistical associations between words rather than understand their meanings" (van Dis et al., 2023, p. 615). In other words, ChatGPT does not understand the meaning of either the input/ information it receives or uses or the texts it generates. Instead, it is able to model associations among words in a text through self-training and generate responses that are both coherent and relevant through evaluating the context (Xue et al., 2023). This outstanding performance is due to the technology's access to training data and model building, giving the language models the ability to extract numerous and various linguistic patterns, associations and relationships, hence being able to identify the relationship between language and context (Kasneci et al., 2023; Lecler et al., 2023; Wang et al., 2023). Consequently, ChatGPT is able to provide more relevant responses compared to previous AI-powered chatbots.

As ChatGPT is dependent on the feedback of the users (in particular the end user) for the accuracy of its later responses, it may produce responses that look reasonable at surface but are incorrect, non-sensical, implausible and even fabricated (Baker, Thompson & Fox, 2023; Bowman, 2022; Conroy, 2023; Rudolph, Tan & Tan, 2023; Thorp, 2023). Nevertheless, researchers agree that future developments in the technology are inevitable and the technology will soon be able to write, edit and proofread texts (van Dis et al., 2023). Therefore, like all other technologies, educators have to accept this new outbreak and try to make the most advantage out of it.

Demystifying the Unknown

BACKGROUND

Regarding ChatGPT, it seems that most concerns expressed towards the new breakthrough are related to research articles (Conroy, 2023) and writing assignments (Graham, 2022) with the latter being a most narrated concern in foreign or second language classes. Without having any premature and hasty judgement about the effects of ChatGPT on education in general and foreign language classrooms in particular and considering all the features and capabilities of the technology, an examination of both probable positive and negative effects will be discussed.

Chatbots have been common in educational contexts since 1970s (Huang et al., 2022; Petrović & Jovanović, 2021) and have been found to be beneficial to the learning process (Clarizia et al., 2018) and language learning (Jia et al. 2022). A chatbot is a computer application that acts out human-like interactions with users through text or voice (Ashfaque et al., 2020). They are also able to provide synchronous support and tutoring (Kerly et al., 2007). Tough the early generations of chatbots were not that 'intelligent' as they were not able to answer questions they were not programmed for, they have been considered as useful learning and teaching tools (Mendoza et al., 2020). However, as time passed and with the development of AI-powered technologies and systems such as natural language processing (NLP), data mining (DM), machine learning (ML) and deep learning (DL), newer generations of chatbots were able to interact with users more intelligently. They were able to learn from previous communications and interactions, get better over time and interact with users in more and more 'intelligent' ways. With the introduction of ChatGPT to the end of 2022, the technology presented the most advanced form of human-like conversational texts.

Language teaching and acquisition is the area which is heavily dependent on two important factors, i.e. interaction and input and ChatGPT can provide both conversational practice and linguistic input. Regarding interaction, it is generally accepted that interaction is critical for language learning as it provides language learners with comprehensible input, the opportunity to receive feedback on their produced output and modify it and chatbots can provide these opportunities for language learners (MacKey, 2012). Kim et al. (2021) have suggested that AI chatbots can influence and improve students' communication abilities. As the most advanced form of chatbots, ChatGPT can learn how to respond to the user's communications and inquiries due to its underlying techniques (as NLP, DL, etc.) and its ability to extract knowledge from the model itself and generates answer. These provide a good opportunity for users to communicate with the chatbot constantly and intelligently like a language-learning assistant as it is able to simulate authentic interactions (Kohnke et al., 2023). Another advantage of ChatGPT in this regard is that these interactions can take place in an autonomous way by creating adaptive and personalized contexts.

As was mentioned, since ChatGPT learns and improves based on the interactions it has with and feedbacks it receives from users, it can be regarded as an adaptable conversational agent.

As stated earlier, because of its features, ChatGPT can provide users with more coherent and relevant responses compared to previous AI-powered chatbots. The use of chatbot technology in education has been an important way to improve personalized learning. The most important feature of chatbots is their being conversational or interactive agents that can provide users with instant replies (Smutny & Schreiberova, 2020). Before the introduction of ChatGPT, while it had been suggested that chatbots could improve language input and create opportunities for language learners to improve their communicative compctence, few chatbots had been designed for the purpose of foreign language learning that were able to create a direct interaction between chatbot programs and humans (Fryer et al., 2020; Kim et al., 2019, 2021; Yin & Satar, 2020). Accordingly, Fryer et al. (2020, p. 17) had declared that "scant progress towards chatbots as substantive language learning partners have been made." These declarations were before the introduction of ChatGPT, but at the same time too they predicted, that "the golden age of language learning that chatbots promise is still on the horizon." As ChatGPT is the most advanced form of a chatbot, it is inevitable that foreign language learners can best take advantage of the new technology to have relevant personalized communication in text or in voice. Further research can examine the degree to which ChatGPT is successful in providing language learners with authentic interaction.

The other important factor essential for language learning is input. Exposure to authentic input is so important that it is regarded as a determining factor in acquiring a target language (Ellis, 2013). Chatbots can enrich language input while performing their output speech functions (Fryer et al. 2020). This reciprocity has empowered chatbots to move beyond a mere text or audio format to a more human-like interaction, which has evolved to its most developed form in ChatGPT. In addition, the interactional nature of ChatGPT can provide learners with comprehensible input and give them the opportunities to modify their output (Klímová & Ibna Seraj, 2023; Mageira et al., 2022; Yin & Satar, 2020), with these opportunities being by themselves further input to the learners.

Two points can be discussed regarding interaction and input. The first point is related to the concept of authenticity of the content produced by chatbots including ChatGPT. Is the language produced by chatbots authentic? According to the definition of authenticity as "a stretch of real language produced by a real speaker or writer for a real audience and designed to convey a real message of some sort" (Morrow, 1977, p. 13), authentic language is the linguistic content produced for a real-world purpose in contrast to the language produced for a pedagogical purpose. Taking into account these 4 criteria (real language, real speaker or writer, real audience and real

Demystifying the Unknown

message), and regarding the fact that the words *real* and *reality* (as in augmented and virtual reality) can include technology, it can be articulated that the stretch of language produced by ChatGPT is authentic. But this raises a second question: Is this stretch of language in ChatGPT-powered input and interaction natural? To answer this question, we need to consider the features of natural language. For a stretch of language to be natural, it is purposeful or have a particular function (exchange of information, showing solidarity, identity and group membership, showing emotions), includes reduced and contracted forms, slips of tongue, repetitions, false starts and self-corrections, and happens in a social and cultural context. We may think that texts produced by ChatGPT lacks some of these natural features at least regarding spoonerism, contraction and repetition, expressed in complete, full-sentence (say bookish) and accurate (grammar, vocabulary and pronunciation) structures. In spite of these perceptions, as Fryer et al. (2020, p. 16) state, an important "positive difference that even most current chatbots bring to language learning situations, which many human partners do not, is a wide variety of language." Although in-person communication in a classroom is an important tool for developing a foreign language, it is limited due to the fact that peers in a classroom are the same level and as such, the input may not be challenging enough to satisfy the comprehensible input ($i + 1$) criterion (Krashen, 1985). Consequently, ChatGPT as the most developed form of chatbots can provide language learners with a wide range linguistic input. In addition, chatbots can provide users with more immersive experiences, conducting interactions that can improve pragmatic competence. The appearance and visualization of chatbots can be possible ways to set the scene for "culturally contextualized exchanges necessary for language students to progress in the fuzzier areas of communication (i.e., beyond basic vocabulary, syntax and pronunciation)" (Fryer et al., 2020, p.17). As Xue et al. (2023) state, ChatGPT can generate responses that are both coherent and relevant by evaluating the context.

The second important point, especially regarding interaction, is the fact that human oral interaction is dependent on body language, stance, gestures, facial expressions, etc. Although human oral interaction is identified with processing the verbal language, it is believed that the most efficient communication happens usually if both verbal and non-verbal types of input are processed at the same time and in a defined context (Çakmak, 2023). ChatGPT can evaluate the context and produce immediate responses even certain feelings (getting annoyed, rejecting requests, etc.) while lacking certain metalinguistic and body language features. (Xue et al., 2023).

OPPORTUNITIES FOR USING CHATGPT IN L2 CLASSROOMS

Besides providing the two basic premises of language acquisition, i.e. interaction and input, ChatGPT has also been suggested to be improve the different skills and components of a foreign language. Kohnke et al. (2023) provide examples on the use of ChatGPT to develop different skills and components of a language. For example, in case of vocabulary learning, they show the use of ChatGPT in vocabulary acquisition by explaining new words in a text (and translating the explanations into the learners' mother tongue), providing dictionary definitions and examples and preparing vocabulary notes the first and second languages.

For developing speaking and conversational and discussion skills, ChatGPT is able to produce dialogues and subsequently adjust the complexity of the dialogue to make it more suitable for beginners or advanced learners. In addition, according to previous research, many language learners prefer practicing with chatbots to human partners and learners are not frightened of making mistakes and look incompetent (Brandtzaeg & Følstad, 2017; Fryer & Carpenter, 2006; Fryer et al., 2019). This feature of chatbots can be regarded as a positive as the affective filter is low (Krashen, 1985), and the fear to make mistakes and appear ridiculous does not hinder learners from producing language. This way, ChatGPT can help less confident or willing-to-communicate language learners to gain more motivation for language practice and develop their conversational skills in a way that would have been much more difficult in face-to-face interaction with human peers or partners in a classroom. Accordingly, ChatGPT is helpful to personalized learning, facilitating autonomous learning.

In case of writing, ChatGPT can help learners write texts of different genres like advertisements, emails and essays. Chatbots can "participate in endless practice, giving learners the chance to try out new language and solidify newly-acquired vocabulary and grammar" (Fryer et al., 2020, p. 16). Due to the novelty of the topic, the effects of ChatGPT on language learners' acquisition of the four skills (speaking, listening, reading and writing) and the components (grammar and pronunciation accuracy, vocabulary depth and breadth), learner motivation self-efficacy and confidence and willingness to communicate are amongst the unexplored areas that can be tackled by interested researchers. Different types of question prompts given to ChatGPT are important in determining the type of personalized feedback for writing assignments done with the help of the computers (Farrokhnia et al., 2023). It can also facilitate access to plausible and relevant information faster and easier (Cascella et al., 2023; Kumar, 2023).

Demystifying the Unknown

CHALLENGES AND THREATS OF USING CHATGPT IN L2 CLASSROOMS

In spite of the advantages that ChatGPT can bring to language acquisition and development, some concerns have been stated by researchers in the field. Perhaps the most important concern is about L2 writing as for unoriginal writing assignments that cannot be detected by L2 writing teachers. Besides the ethical considerations (Liebrenz et al., 2023; Mhlanga, 2023), the use of ChatGPT can become a challenge for L2 writing practice and assessment. A concern that existed about previous chatbots too (Dehouche, 2021). However, there are several points about this concern. First, all new technologies that challenge traditional methods of teaching have worried educators and teachers. L2 writing practice in form of solely giving a topic to the learners and asking them to bring their completed assignments the following session may not be a reliable way for practicing and assessing wring competence for, even if there was not such a thing as ChatGPT, learners may have copied their texts from the Net or give it to someone else to write it for them. In other words, ChatGPT has disrupted the status que and reset the ground in this regard. Secondly, while some scholars have posited that up to the present time, detecting texts produced by chatbots is not difficult (Graham, 2022; van Dis et al., 2023), others have shown that ChatGPT can write scientific reports using fake and fabricated data which reviewers cannot detect (Gao et al., 2022). It is also claimed to be able to generate research manuscripts at a publishable level (Dowling & Lucey, 2023). Third, some plagiarism check applications and sites (e.g. Turnitin) are working to add AI-generated text detection capabilities to their platforms and there are news about the development of AI-generated text detectors like GPTZero (Kohnke et al., 2023). Related to plagiarism are concerns about cheating (Cotton et al., 2023; Gašević et al., 2023) and distribution of false (Kohnke et al., 2023) or fake (Tlili et al., 2023) information.

To deal with the concern, in-class practice (even with using ChatGPT prompts) and having portfolios including different practices are more reliable ways to make teachers sure of the originality of the assignments submitted to them. As Fararzouli et al. (2023) denote, a reconsideration of their assessment practices and home examination and assignment prompts is necessary. The fact is that technology is evolving and it is, good or bad, increasingly affecting education including foreign language learning. With the potential capabilities that is being projected for ChatGPT's successor, i.e. GPT4, like being able to emulate human thinking (Adesso, 2023), teachers need to accept the new advances in technology and find ways to adapt themselves the best possible way with their effects.

LITERATURE ON THE VOICES OF TEACHERS ABOUT CHATGPT

The acceptance and development of any new technology in education depends, to a great extent, on teachers' views and attitudes (Nguyen, 2023). As such, examining teachers' voices is an important line of research which needs more studies. Some studies have recently paid particular attention to the voices of teachers and education practitioners about the use of ChatGPT. Li et al. (2023) examined the concerns expressed about ChatGPT over social media (Twitter) using a discourse analysis approach and found that most concerns over social media are expressed by education and tech users. These concerns are expressed towards academic integrity, influence on learning achievements and skill development, limited capabilities, social and policy making concerns and challenges for the workforce. Similarly, Yang and Chen (2023) examined the views of a group of pre-service teachers about the use of chatbots and found that while they were willing to use them for organizing, understanding and finding material, they showed little desire to actually use them in their classes due to their lack of familiarity with them.

Nguyen (2023) also reports that the participants of his study who were EFL university instructors were willing and motivated to use ChatGPT in their writing classes. Yet, they emphasized the importance of professional training on the possible threats of ChatGPT for teachers and instructors including informing them about the correct and ethical uses of the chatbot. Regarding chatbots, Kiptonui, Too and Mukwa (2018) examined university instructors' positive views towards using chatbots in their classes as a user-friendly tool that makes topics more attractive. For the learners and reported that instructors regarded chatbots helpful in improving students' achievements through creating a joyful learning experience and increasing their understanding. Chuah and Kabilan (2021) found that the participating instructors in their study were willing to use chatbots in their classes as beneficial to learners in increasing their social interaction and critical thinking skills and helpful to teachers as teaching assistants.

Considering the paucity of research on teachers' voices on using chatbots specially ChatGPT in foreign language classrooms, this study tried to add to the present literature by examining the voices of young language teachers (belonging to generation Z teachers) specially their voices about the levels of concerns and probable objections that this new technology can cause in education including foreign language teachers.

Demystifying the Unknown

METHODS

For the objective of this study, a qualitative case study design was chosen. The participants, selected based on purposive sampling, are five young language teachers (From 20 to 23), so we can say that they are generation Z teachers. They are teaching English at different private language institutes for 2 to 5 years, have high levels of language proficiency and are familiar with ChatGPT and use it for different purposes related to their career. Their pseudo names are John, Marta, Aida, Micheal and Rose. The researcher's getting acquainted with them happened during a larger research project.

They were interviewed over several sessions both in-person and online via Google Meet and Skype. The semi-structured interviews lasted from 48 minutes to nearly two hours depending on the direction of the discussions. The questions related to this study were their concerns about the new technology and the possible threats of ChatGPT for both students and teachers. They were free to use either their mother tongue (Persian) or English in discussions during the interviews.

All data were transcribed and the parts related to this study was separated. Those parts conducted in participants' L1 was translated into English and back-translation and member check were used to be sure of the trustworthiness of the data gathered. Inductive data analysis procedure was used to analyze data and extract the important themes expressed by the participants. According to Ary, Jacobs & Sorensen (2010, p. 494), there are three stages of inductive data coding in a data pyramid. The first stage of data codification at the bottom of this pyramid is open coding during which similar incidents or data pieces are grouped together under certain concepts. The second stage is axial coding in which main categories and subcategories and connections between them are developed. Finally the third stage (the highest in the data coding pyramid) is selective coding which includes developing connections between separate categories and bringing them together under general themes.

FINDINGS

This study was an attempt to shed light on different aspects of ChatGPT and meanwhile to benefit from the viewpoints of the younger generation of teachers who are called generation Z as they are born after 2000 and are brought up with new technologies. The first question was about the degree of their familiarity with the new technology. All the participants were completely familiar with ChatGPT and used it for many different purposes in their career specially for content creation and designing practices and tasks. In analyzing the data, the main focus was to find concern which are not highlighted in previous studies. The analysis of the interview results about the participants' concerns towards ChatGPT and its possible threats to students and teachers identified a main concern: threats to creativity on the part of both teachers and learners. It was the concern expressed by all interviewees and the point is that it was a concern about both teachers and students. Rose, a female 22-year-old teacher, stated that she has used ChatGPT for designing many activities and tasks, however,

I am concerned about myself getting lazy, of course, it is good to get ideas from ChatGPT, but I think I may lose my creativity as a teacher.

In other words, an important concern of this young teacher is that ChatGPT may induce teachers' laziness and as a result, influence their creativity. She also expresses her concern about student's laziness,

In case of brainstorming and idea provoking activities, some students have learnt to use ChatGPT for getting ideas. This is not bad in the short run, but in the long term, it may affect their creativity, creative thinking, etc.

Similarly, Michael, a 23-year-old teacher, who had 5 years of teaching foreign language experience expressed his concern in this regard in this way,

I use many of these technologies including ChatGPT in my teaching. I ask my students too to use ChatGPT for editing and proofreading their writings. The point is here: laziness. Instead of thinking and trying to find the problems, they just use AI and ChatGPT, letting it to think instead of them.

And John, a young 21-year-old teacher with three years of language teaching experience proposes the concern in this way,

This threat is more important than cheating in assignments and writing papers. AI thinks, innovates and designs instead of you.

When asked about the effect on teachers' or student' creativity, he answered,

Students need to think creatively specially in their speaking and writing activities and ChatGPT thinks instead of them. For teachers this may not be an urgent problem as teachers use textbooks and other ready-made materials. But it finally shows itself in some cases where teacher creativity is necessary.

Demystifying the Unknown

As the solution to this problem, Rose maintains that awareness is needed as the necessary condition for its use,

We need to provide our teachers and students with information and training about this particular effect of ChatGPT. I think it could be very addictive and some conscious attention on its use is needed.

Aida has a similar idea,

For all new technologies, we need training and I think, ChatGPT is completely different from everything that we had up to now. So, it needs particular awareness raising and training.

As was mentioned earlier, many other concerns were expressed by the participants including answering reading comprehension, grammar and vocabulary assignments, writing essays, cheating on exams, etc. However, as these are concerns stated in many previous studies (as reviewed before), the finding that has not been attended to in previous research was highlighted.

DISCUSSION

The results of this study highlighted that a concern to teacher's and student's creativity is another concern expressed by teachers that ChatGPT may bring to our education. This less researched topic can be, by itself, an important threat of ChatGPT to education. Many language teaching practices are dependent on students' creativity like speaking and writing and teachers' creativity play an important role in designing learning tasks and activities. AI thinks instead of teachers and students and its long-term effect could be on their creativity and critical thinking.

Many new developments and breakthroughs in technology have encountered levels of concern, disagreement and objection in the world of education. These objections, which target a wide variety of new technologies such as search engines, mobile phones and social media, may come from many different sources including lack of familiarity with the new technology, a conservative, risk-avoiding personality that protests or is pessimistic about change or anything new and finally technostress or techno-phobia. Though it is part of the human nature to be suspicious of unknown phenomena, it has been confirmed that many of these pre-mature concerns may result in accumulated levels of technophobia and a damaged mentality about the positive effects and applications of the new technology. It is evident from the fact that many of the new technologies have faced initial negative evaluations and encounters by educators (Kahn, 2011). However, many of the abovementioned technologies turned to be accepted as beneficial learning tools as technology is perhaps the most inevitable landscape of any educational system today.

A bulk of research supports the idea that many of these once pioneering technologies have had positive effects on learning, teaching and assessment. For example, search engines such as Google which were once being accused of causing people to become slow in cognitive processes, not to think or to become stupid (Carr, 2008; Salehi et al., 2018), are proved to be beneficial for students by helping them in research for classwork and papers, online learning and keeping up-to-date with and exposure to world affairs and looking for appropriate applications and sites (school apps, learning apps, etc.) (Lavidas et al., 2020), which can consequently foster students' autonomous learning and self-efficacy (Keshavarz et al., 2016). As another example, we can remember worries expressed at the onset of smartphones about their negative effects on students' spelling and ability to write complete sentences (Strain-Moritz, 2016 as cited in Hong, 2023) or their potential use for cheating and academic misconduct. Nowadays, smartphones are confirmed to be influential learning tools from developing students' ability to think critically and creatively up to enhancing their learning. Finally, Wikipedia was once accused of being an unreliable source of information for students (Meishar-Tal, 2015, however its use in teaching especially L2 writing (Dai et al., 2023) and collaborative learning (Hsu, 2019). To these, we can add concerns about the negative effects of technology on students' achievements (Flanagan, 2008; Fried, 2008; Granata, 2019; Wentworth & Middleton, 2014). These examples indicate that negative attitudes and concerns toward technologies especially the new and less known ones are not new and specific to AI systems and ChatGPT. The concerns stated about ChatGPT by educators at its onset can be as legitimate as those stated about previous technologies. Some Researchers have expressed concerns about different aspects of ChatGPT like ethical concerns about the technology (Mhlanga, 2023), its likely negative effects on assessment as cheating (Rudolph et al., 2023) and students' higher-order thinking skills (Susnjak, 2022). Of course, this does not mean that educators' concerns are not real and valid, as they often are legitimate concerns (Alhumaid, 2019). Nonetheless, we must consider the fact that premature and immature concerns combined with risk-avoiding and conservative personalities may lead to bias against technology, technostress, technophobia and letting opportunities for one's professional development and students' learning down.

CONCLUSION

New technologies have affected and will inevitably continue to influence education and teaching, learning and assessment processes. ChatGPT has triggered certain

Demystifying the Unknown

worries about education as for home assignments and research integrity. This study added a new concern expressed in teachers' voices and that is the threats to teachers' and students' creativity. Letting AI think and innovate instead of teachers and learners is a much more serious and fundamental problem of ChatGPT than that of doing assignments or research. Innovation is regarded as an important objective of education for learners of the modern era (Cator, 2010; Newton and Newton, 2014) and as such, ChatGPT may affect the achievement of this important goal altogether. In addition, teachers' innovation as the basis of many changes and developments in the educational processes. Assigning certain aspects of language teaching which requires teacher creativity to AI and ChatGPT can threaten their job totally.

On the other hand, as was discussed in this chapter, these concerns and worries are not new and have been expressed by educators and teachers upon the introduction of many recent technological breakthroughs. Even though ChatGPT provides a completely different experience and has created great concerns, it can be regarded as a disrupter of a constant, traditional routine rather than a disrupter of education itself. New ways need to be sought and followed by teachers to cope with new emerging technologies. Many areas of ChatGPT's effects on language learning has not been examined yet such as its effects on the development of different language skills (reading, writing, speaking, listening), components (grammar accuracy and use, vocabulary depth and breadth, pronunciation accuracy), the development of pragmatic and discourse competences, the development of conversational, academic and discussion skills to name just a few, which can be examined by interested researchers. To this list can be added the long-term effects ChatGPT on learner and teacher creativity.

REFERENCES

Adesso, G. (2023). Towards the ultimate brain: Exploring scientific discovery with ChatGPT AI. *AI Magazine, 44*(3), 328–342. Advance online publication. doi:10.1002/aaai.12113

Ary, D., Jacobs, L. C., & Sorensen, C. (2010). *Introduction to research in education* (8th ed.). Wadsworth.

Brandtzaeg, P. B., & Følstad, A. (2017). *Why people use chatbots.* Paper presented at the International Conference on Internet Science, Thessaloniki, Greece. 10.1007/978-3-319-70284-1_30

Brown, T. B., Mann, B., Ryder, N., Subbiah, M., Kaplan, J., Dhariwal, P., Neelakantan, A., Shyam, P., Sastry, G., Askell, A., Agarwal, S., Herbert-Voss, A., Krueger, G., Henighan, T., Child, R., Ramesh, A., Ziegler, D. M., Wu, J., Winter, C., & Amodei, D. (2020). Language models are few-shot learners. *Advances in Neural Information Processing Systems, 33*, 1877–1901. https://proceedings.neurips.cc/paper/2020

Çakmak, F. (2022). Chatbot-human interaction and its effects on EFL students' L2 speaking performance and anxiety. *Novitas-ROYAL, 16*(2), 113–131.

Carr, N. (2008). Is Google making us stupid? *Teachers College Record, 110*(14), 89–94. doi:10.1177/016146810811001427

Cascella, M., Montomoli, J., Bellini, V., & Bignami, E. (2023). Evaluating the feasibility of ChatGPT in healthcare: An analysis of multiple clinical and research scenarios. *Journal of Medical Systems, 47*(1), 1–5. doi:10.100710916-023-01925-4 PMID:36869927

Chiu, T. K. F., Moorhouse, B. L., Chai, C. S., & Ismailov, M. (2023). Teacher support and student motivation to learn with Artificial Intelligence (AI) based chatbot. *Interactive Learning Environments*, 1–17. Advance online publication. do i:10.1080/10494820.2023.2172044

Chuah, K. M., & Kabilan, M. K. (2021). Teachers' Views on the Use of Chatbots to Support. *International Journal of Emerging Technologies in Learning, 16*(20), 223–237. doi:10.3991/ijet.v16i20.24917

Clarizia, F., Colace, F., Lombardi, M., Pascale, F., & Santaniello, D. (2018). *Chatbot: An education support system for student. International symposium on cyberspace safety and security.* Springer.

Cotton, D. R., Cotton, P. A., & Shipway, J. R. (2023). Chatting and cheating: Ensuring academic integrity in the era of ChatGPT. *Innovations in Education and Teaching International*, 1–12. doi:10.1080/14703297.2023.2190148

Dai, J., Wang, L., & He, Y. (2023). Exploring the effect of wiki-based writing instruction on writing skills and writing self-efficacy of Chinese English-as-a-foreign language learners. *Frontiers in Psychology, 13*, 1069832. Advance online publication. doi:10.3389/fpsyg.2022.1069832 PMID:36704680

Dehouche, N. (2021). Plagiarism in the age of massive generative pre-trained transformers (GPT-3). *Ethics in Science and Environmental Politics, 2*, 17–23. doi:10.3354/esep00195

Dowling, M., & Lucey, B. (2023). ChatGPT for (Finance) research: The bananarama conjecture. *Finance Research Letters*, *53*, 103662. doi:10.1016/j.frl.2023.103662

Education. *Artificial Intelligence*. Advance online publication. doi:10.1016/j.caeai.2022.100119

Ellis, R. (2014). Principles of instructed second language learning. In M. Celce-Murcia, D. Brinton, & M. Snow (Eds.), *Teaching English as a second or foreign language* (4th ed., pp. 31–45). Cengage Learning.

Farazouli, A., Cerratto-Pargman, T., Bolander-Laksov, K., & McGrath, C. (2023). Hello GPT! Goodbye home examination? An exploratory study of AI chatbots impact on university teachers' assessment practices. *Assessment & Evaluation in Higher Education*, 1–13. Advance online publication. doi:10.1080/02602938.2023.2241676

Farrokhnia, M., Banihashem, S. K., Noroozi, O., & Wals, A. (2023). A SWOT analysis of ChatGPT: Implications for educational practice and research. *Innovations in Education and Teaching International*, 1–15. Advance online publication. doi:1 0.1080/14703297.2023.2195846

Flanagan, J. L. (2008). *Technology: The positive and negative effects on student achievement*. University of New York.

Fried, C. B. (2008). In-class laptop use and its effects on student learning. *Computers & Education*, *50*(3), 906–914. doi:10.1016/j.compedu.2006.09.006

Fryer, L. K., Ainley, M., Thompson, A., Gibson, A., & Sherlock, Z. (2017). Stimulating and sustaining interest in a language course: An experimental comparison of Chatbot and Human task partners. *Computers in Human Behavior*, *75*, 461–468. doi:10.1016/j.chb.2017.05.045

Fryer, L. K., & Carpenter, R. (2006). Bots as language learning tools. *Language Learning & Technology*, *10*, 8–14. http://llt.msu.edu/vol10num3/emerging/default.html

Fryer, L. K., Coniam, D., Carpenter, R., & Lăpuşneanu, D. (2020). Bots for language learning now: Current and future directions. *Language Learning & Technology*, *24*(2), 8–22.

Fryer, L. K., Nakao, K., & Thompson, A. (2019). Chatbot learning partners: Connecting learning experiences, interest and competence. *Computers in Human Behavior*, *93*, 279–289. doi:10.1016/j.chb.2018.12.023

Gašević, D., Siemens, G., & Sadiq, S. (2023). Empowering learners for the age of artificial intelligence. *Computers and Education: Artificial Intelligence, 100130,* 100130. Advance online publication. doi:10.1016/j.caeai.2023.100130

Graham, F. (2022). Daily briefing: Will ChatGPT kill the essay assignment? *Nature.* Advance online publication. doi:10.1038/d41586-022-04437-2 PMID:36517680

Granata, K. (2019). Tech may be to blame for decline in students' reading for pleasure. *Education World.* Retrieved from https://www.educationworld.com/a_news/technology-proves-negatively-effect-reading-skills

Hong, W. C. H. (2023). The impact of ChatGPT on foreign language teaching and learning. *Journal of Educational Technology and Innovation, 1*(1).

Hsu, H. C. (2019). Wiki-mediated collaboration and its association with L2 writing development: An exploratory study. *Computer Assisted Language Learning, 32*(8), 945–967. doi:10.1080/09588221.2018.1542407

Huang, W., Hew, K. F., & Fryer, L. K. (2022). Chatbots for language learning – are they really useful? A systematic review of chatbot-supported language learning. *Journal of Computer Assisted Learning, 38*(1), 237–257. doi:10.1111/jcal.12610

Jia, F., Sun, D., Ma, Q., & Looi, C.-K. (2022). Developing an AI-Based learning system for L2 learners' authentic and ubiquitous learning in English language. *Sustainability (Basel), 14*(23), 15527. doi:10.3390u142315527

Kahn, P. H. Jr. (2011). *Technological nature: Adaptation and the future of human life.* MIT. doi:10.7551/mitpress/7983.001.0001

Kasneci, E., Seller, K., & Küchemann, S. (2023). ChatGPT for good? On opportunities and challenges of large language models in education. *Learning and Individual Differences, 103*(102274). Advance online publication. doi:10.1016/j.lindif.2023.102274

Kerly, A., Hall, P., & Bull, S. (2007). Bringing chatbots into education: Towards natural language negotiation of open learner models. *Knowledge-Based Systems, 20*(2), 177–185. doi:10.1016/j.knosys.2006.11.014

Keshavarz, H., Esmaeili Givi, M., & Vafaeian, A. (2016). Students' sense of self-efficacy in searching information from the web: A PLS approach. *Webology, 13*(2), 16–31.

Kim, H.-S., Cha, Y., & Kim, N. Y. (2021). Effects of AI chatbots on EFL students' communication skills. *Korean Journal of English Language and Linguistics, 21,* 712–734. doi:10.15738/kjell.21.202108.712

Kim, N. Y., Cha, Y., & Kim, H.-S. (2019). Future English learning: Chatbots and artificial intelligence. *Multimedia Assisted Language Learning*, *22*(3), 32–53. doi:10.15702/mall.2019.22.3.32

Kiptonui, B. P., Too, J. K., & Mukwa, C. W. (2018). teacher attitude towards use of chatbots in routine teaching. *Universal Journal of Educational Research*, *6*(7), 1586–1597. doi:10.13189/ujer.2018.060719

Klímová, B., & Ibna Seraj, P. M. (2023). The use of chatbots in university EFL settings: Research trends and pedagogical implications. *Frontiers in Psychology*, *14*, 1131506. Advance online publication. doi:10.3389/fpsyg.2023.1131506 PMID:37034959

Kohnke, L. (2022). A qualitative exploration of student perspectives of chatbot use during emergency remote teaching. *International Journal of Mobile Learning and Organization*, *16*(4), 475–488. doi:10.1504/IJMLO.2022.125966

Kohnke, L., Moorhouse, B. L., & Zou, D. (2023). ChatGPT for language teaching and learning. *RELC Journal*, *54*(2), 1–14. doi:10.1177/00336882231162868

Krashen, S. (1985). *The Input Hypothesis Issues and Implications*. Longman.

Kuhail, M. A., Alturki, N., Alramlawi, S., & Alhejori, K. (2023). Interacting with educational chatbots: A systematic review. *Education and Information Technologies*, *28*(1), 973–1018. doi:10.100710639-022-11177-3

Kumar, A. H. (2023). Analysis of ChatGPT tool to assess the potential of its utility for academic writing in biomedical domain. *Biology, Engineering, Medicine and Science Reports*, *9*(1), 24–30. doi:10.5530/bems.9.1.5

Lavidas, K., Achriani, A., Athanassopoulos, S., Messinis, I., & Kotsiantis, S. (2020). University students' intention to use search engines for research purposes: A structural equation modeling approach. *Education and Information Technologies*, *25*(4), 2463–2479. doi:10.100710639-019-10071-9

Li, L., Ma, Z., Fan, L., Lee, S., Yu, L., & Hemphill, L. (2023). *ChatGPT in education: A discourse analysis of worries and concerns on social media.* arXiv, https://doi.org//arXiv.2305.02201 doi:10.48550

Liebrenz, M., Schleifer, R., Buadze, A., Bhugra, D., & Smith, A. (2023). Generating scholarly content with ChatGPT: Ethical challenges for medical publishing. *The Lancet. Digital Health*, *5*(3), 105–106. doi:10.1016/S2589-7500(23)00019-5 PMID:36754725

Mackey, A. (2012). *Input, interaction, and corrective feedback in L2 learning.* Oxford University Press.

Mageira, K., Pittou, D., Papasalouros, A., Kotis, K., Zangogianni, P., & Daradoumis, A. (2022). Educational AI chatbots for content and language integrated learning. *Applied Sciences (Basel, Switzerland), 12*(7), 3239. Advance online publication. doi:10.3390/app12073239

Meishar-Tal, H. (2015). Teachers' use of Wikipedia with their Students. *The Australian Journal of Teacher Education, 40*(12), 126–140. doi:10.14221/ajte.2015v40n12.9

Mhlanga, D. (2023). Open AI in education, the responsible and ethical use of ChatGPT towards lifelong learning. SSRN *Electronic Journal.* https://doi.org/doi:10.2139/SSRN.4354422

Morrow, K. (1977). Authentic texts in ESP. *English for Specific Purposes*, 13–17.

Nguyen, T. T. H. (2023). EFL teachers' perspectives toward the use of ChatGPT in writing classes: A case study at Van Lang University. *International Journal of Language Instruction, 2*(3), 1–47. doi:10.54855/ijli.23231

Petrović, J., & Jovanović, M. (2021). The role of chatbots in foreign language learning: the present situation and the future outlook. In E. Pap (Ed.), *Artificial Intelligence: Theory and Applications. Studies in Computational Intelligence, 973.* Springer. doi:10.1007/978-3-030-72711-6_17

Putra, F. W., Rangka, I. B., Aminah, S., & Aditama, M. H. R. (2023). ChatGPT in the higher education environment: Perspectives from the theory of high order thinking skills. *Journal of Public Health (Oxford, England), 45*(4), fdad120. Advance online publication. doi:10.1093/pubmed/fdad120 PMID:37455540

Rospigliosi, P. (2023). Artificial intelligence in teaching and learning: What questions should we ask of ChatGPT? *Interactive Learning Environments, 31*(1), 1–3. doi:10.1080/10494820.2023.2180191

Rudolph, J., Tan, S., & Tan, S. (2023). ChatGPT: Bullshit spewer or the end of traditional assessments in higher education? *Journal of Applied Learning and Teaching, 6*(1). Advance online publication. doi:10.37074/jalt.2023.6.1.9

Rusandi, M. A., Ipah Saripah, A., Yunika, D., & Mutmainnah, K. (2023). No worries with ChatGPT: Building bridges between artificial intelligence and education with critical thinking soft skills. *Journal of Public Health (Oxford, England), 45*(3), e602–e603. doi:10.1093/pubmed/fdad049 PMID:37099761

Salehi, S., Du, J. T., & Ashman, H. (2018). Use of Web search engines and personalization in information searching for educational purposes. *Information Research, 23*(2), 1–13.

Shiri, A. (2023). ChatGPT and academic integrity. SSRN *Electronic Journal*. / doi:10.2139/ssrn.4360052

Smutny, P., & Schreiberova, P. (2020). Chatbots for learning: A review of educational chatbots for the Facebook messenger. *Computers & Education*, *151*, 103862. doi:10.1016/j.compedu.2020.103862

Susnjak, T. (2022). *ChatGPT: The end of online exam integrity?* arXiv, 2212. https://doi.org//arXiv.2212.09292 doi:10.48550

Tlili, A., Shehata, B., Adarkwah, M. A., Bozkurt, A., Hickey, D. T., Huang, R., & Agyemang, B. (2023). What if the devil is my guardian angel: ChatGPT as a case study of using chatbots in education. *Smart Learning Environments*, *10*(1), 15. doi:10.118640561-023-00237-x

van Dis, E. A. M., Bollen, J., Zuidema, W., van Rooij, R., & Bockting, C. L. (2023). ChatGPT: Five priorities for research. *Nature*, *614*(7947), 224–226. doi:10.1038/d41586-023-00288-7 PMID:36737653

Wentworth, D. K., & Middleton, J. H. (2014). Technology Use and Academic Performance. *Computers & Education*, *78*, 306–311. doi:10.1016/j.compedu.2014.06.012

Xue, V. W., Lei, P., & Cho, W. C. (2023, March). medicine. *Clinical and Translational Medicine*, *13*(3), e1216. Advance online publication. doi:10.1002/ctm2.1216

Yin, Q., & Satar, M. (2020). English as a foreign language learner interaction with chatbots: Negotiation for meaning. *International Online Journal of Education & Teaching*, *7*(2), 390–410.

ADDITIONAL READING

Fütterer, T., Fischer, C., Alekseeva, A., Chen, X., Tate, T., Warschauer, M., & Gerjets, P. (2023). ChatGPT in education: Global reactions to AI innovations. *Scientific Reports*, *13*(1), 15310. Advance online publication. doi:10.103841598-023-42227-6 PMID:37714915

Gill, S. S., Xu, M., Patros, P., Wu, H., Kaur, R., Kaur, K., Fuller, S., Singh, M., Arora, P., Parlikad, A. K., Stankovski, V., Abraham, A., Ghosh, S. K., Lutfiyya, H., Kanhere, S. S., Bahsoon, R., Rana, O., Dustdar, S., Sakellariou, R., ... Buyya, R. (2023). Transformative effects of ChatGPT on modern education: Emerging era of AI chatbots. *Internet of Things and Cyber-Physical Systems*, *4*, 19–23. doi:10.1016/j.iotcps.2023.06.002

Grassini, S. (2023). Shaping the Future of Education: Exploring the Potential and Consequences of AI and ChatGPT in Educational Settings. *Education Sciences*, *13*(7), 692. Advance online publication. doi:10.3390/educsci13070692

Lin, S. M., Chung, H. H., Chung, F. L., & Lan, Y. J. (2023). Concerns about using ChatGPT in education. In Y. M. Huang & T. Rocha (Eds.), *Innovative technologies and learning* (pp. 37–49). Springer Nature. doi:10.1007/978-3-031-40113-8_4

Lo, C. K. (2023). What is the impact of ChatGPT on education? A rapid review of the literature. *Education Sciences*, *13*(4), 410. Advance online publication. doi:10.3390/educsci13040410

KEY TERMS AND DEFINITIONS

ChatGPT: In full chat generative pre-trained transformer, is an artificial intelligence (AI) chatbot developed by the Microsoft-supported company OpenAI, which as a cutting-edge AI large language model is not only capable of natural language processing or understanding natural language but also generating coherent, human speech-like, and contextually relevant replies and interactions in a chat-like or conversational way based on what it has learned from training data and the prompts the interactor has given to it (Xue et al., 2023).

Large Language Models: Refers to advanced machine learning models including the use of different statistical and probabilistic procedures to specify the probability of sequences of words occurring in a sentence based on large bodies of text data and natural language processing (NLP) and predict and generate texts as output (Kasneci et al, 2023).

Chapter 5

Designing Achievement Tests for Language Learners Through Contemporary Technologies

Sibel Kahraman-Ozkurt
Pamukkale University, Turkey

ABSTRACT

The chapter aims at giving insights to English as a foreign language (EFL) teachers on creating and designing achievement tests through digital tools for checking their student' progress and teaching/learning process. As language learners may have concerns and barriers regarding the assessment and testing issues, the administration of digital tools for that purpose is believed to contribute to both students' development by lowering their anxiety levels and accordingly teachers' future practices. Based on the feedback on students' performance gathered through digital tools, teachers and other stakeholders can find the opportunity to re-organize teaching materials, tasks, or the coursebooks. EFL teachers may also be provoked to use some other digital tools not included in that chapter by following the procedures in the activity plans for their future assessment practices.

INTRODUCTION

Tests have become commonly and popularly used language testing and assessment methods in the educational world. A test, at its simplest, can be defined as a method of measuring a person's ability or knowledge in a given domain (Brown, 2001).

DOI: 10.4018/979-8-3693-0353-5.ch005

Copyright © 2024, IGI Global. Copying or distributing in print or electronic forms without written permission of IGI Global is prohibited.

There are many kinds of tests, each with a specific purpose and a criterion to be measured. Among all the kinds of the tests, achievement tests are the most common and popular ones that are related to classes, course units or the total curriculum. They can be applied to check whether the course objectives or unit outcomes of a lesson are satisfied following a period of instruction. Most of the language teachers tend to use achievement tests to simply give some test scores to their students or, more importantly, to detect the strengths or weaknesses of their learners regarding the achievement of the course objectives. Through the achievement tests, language teachers can rearrange the techniques, materials or activities they employ in their classes in line with the underlying principles of dynamic assessment.

Despite this popularity and usefulness of achievement tests, preparing quality test items requires some great efforts and elaboration on the side of the language teachers. Creating quality and dependable tests which are administrable within the given constraints and accurately measure what they aim to measure has been a popular topic of discussion among the test developers for years. Despite the ongoing discussions on how to create and structure valid, reliable and practical tests to measure language skills and components, language learners too often feel anxious and tense when taking achievement tests, and they may get disappointed when they cannot make the expected grade. Under the influence of such feelings, many language learners may refrain from giving answers to test questions or totally avoid taking tests. Therefore, language teachers need to find some alternative ways to deal with these negative affective factors while administering tests to their students. At that point, using some contemporary technological tools can be the simplest, or the most complicated for some language teachers, solution for overcoming the barriers of anxiety and inhibition.

The use of technology for language teaching and learning has been widely accepted as an inevitable practice in today's digital age. This necessity and importance of technology use have led many professionals or organizations to elaborate on some guidelines or frameworks for the effective use of technology in and out of the classroom. As one of these organizations, TESOL Technology Standards Project Team published TESOL Technology Standards Framework (Healey et al., 2008) to provide guidance to language teachers and learners for implementing technology rather than setting barriers or unrealistic expectations about it. As one of the goals in the technology standards for teachers, it is stated in the framework that language teachers apply technology in record-keeping, feedback, and assessment. They can evaluate and implement relevant technology to aid in effective learner assessment. Therefore, they need to demonstrate familiarity with a variety of forms of assessment that employ technology. According to the performance indicators of the framework, language teachers can use technological tools for diagnostic, summative and formative testing.

Designing Achievement Tests for Language Learners

Considering the necessity and popularity of achievement tests, the concerns and barriers of the language learners regarding these tests and the use of technology for language assessment as a standard, the current chapter of the book will try to give some insights to language teachers to design and create achievement tests for their learners by using some technological tools. This chapter will suggest some Web 2.0 tools (namely, Nearpod, Wordwall and Kahoot) especially for K-12 learners at primary, lower secondary and upper secondary school levels. Sample activity plans will be given for the language teachers so that they can design and create their own diagnostic tests using these tools. Suggested Web 2.0 tools presents examples of formative assessment and dynamic media features and templates to guide teachers' performances and improve student outcomes. They employ artificial intelligence (AI) strategies in a diverse range of tasks from deciding how to lay out items on the screen to figuring out how to best switch one template into another. The current chapter will try to support English language teachers in their classroom practices and objectives by simply indicating and elaborating on the use of these digital tools with some sample activities for language assessment.

BACKGROUND

Why Language Assessment?

Assessment is broadly defined as the process of collecting information about something that one is interested in (Bachman & Palmer, 2022). In language assessment, language teachers aim to interpret some aspects of test taker's language ability to make some decisions about the test takers' performance and teaching learning process. As one of the intended uses of language assessment, these decisions are expected to lead to some beneficial consequences for quality teaching and learning processes. The importance of test interpretations, decisions and consequences related to language assessment tasks places a bigger responsibility on language teachers (Fulcher, 2012). Language teachers need to better understand the relationship between language assessment and their ways of teaching. As the decisions based on assessment are expected to have beneficial consequences, teachers can become more effective in facilitating the learning process. However, choosing, creating, or preparing quality language assessment tasks can be a challenging and demanding process for language teachers (Cheng et al., 2004; Clapham, 2000). They question how, when, and how often they need to assess their students and look for guidance on practical and digital classroom applications of language assessment. Therefore, it is crucial to equip language teachers with the knowledge and skills regarding the modes of language assessment and how these assessment modes can be realized through digital technologies.

Modes of Language Assessment

As there are expectations about language assessment from language teachers such as making decisions regarding teaching and learning process and drawing consequences, they should be well informed about the modes of assessment. When choosing appropriate language assessment tasks, teachers need to contemplate on the functions and roles of the assessment employed. Also, with the expectations from teachers regarding the use of technology for language assessment, they are required to come up with the ideas and ways to assess their students through digital ways.

Starting with incidental, unplanned comments and reactions, mentoring, and other impromptu feedback to the student, informal assessment can take a variety of forms (Brown & Abeywickrama, 2010). Informal assessment does not aim at recording the results, giving points, or making fixed judgments about students' performances. A teacher giving positive reinforcement by making comments such as 'good job!', 'well done!' or putting stickers or smileys on the assignments is making informal assessment. That type of assessment gives opportunity to teachers to identify the strengths, weaknesses and needs of individual students without regard to their ages, scores or school levels (Navarrate, 1990). Informal assessment aims at helping students continue their growth process through teacher and peer feedback when they are forming their competencies and skills on any topic. Bulletin boards or online discussion platforms of some Web 2.0 technologies give the opportunity to teachers to give informal feedback to their students.

Formal assessments, on the other hand, are systematic, deliberate strategies designed to provide teachers and students with an evaluation of student performance and achievement. Formal assessment is mostly done in a specified, relatively short time limit. Although they are not limited to end of unit quizzes or tests (Van der Mars et al., 2018), they can be given as examples of formal assessment as they are carried out to make a formal evaluation of the student performance and hence to give a score or grade for the performance. In formal assessment, students are aware that they are being tested and evaluated.

Brown and Abeywickrama (2010) define formative assessment in terms of three important components: teacher's feedback delivery on student performance, student's internalization of the feedback and formation of learning. Feedback is viewed as the essential element in formative assessment as it is the key for ongoing student progress (Black, 2009). By giving appropriate feedback on the learners' performance, teachers help students form their competencies and improve their skills in an effective way. At that point, all types of informal assessment can be regarded as formative.

Designing Achievement Tests for Language Learners

That is because when a teacher makes a comment on student performance or gives corrective feedback, the objective of such feedback is to develop students' language ability. Web 2.0 tools designed for formative assessment purposes can be regarded as influential feedback providers for the learners. They can give immediate feedback or delayed feedback to the students on their performance, and their way of giving the feedback can affect students' internalization of it and hence formation of learning. On the contrary to formative assessment, summative assessment is generally carried out at the end of a course or instructional unit as it tries to measure or summarize what a student has learned. Achievement tests and proficiency exams can be given as examples of summative assessment. All the Web 2.0 tools designed to create and apply tests can be used as summative assessment tools.

In norm-referenced testing, test taker's performance is directly related to that of other test takers. Each test taker's score is interpreted through a mean score, median or a percentile rank. For instance, if a test taker gets a score placing him or her in the top 10 per cent of test takers or she or he did better than 60 per cent of those who took the test, it means she or he is assesses through norm-referenced testing. Based on this evaluation, the result of testing does not directly tell what the students can do in the language (Hughes, 2003). In criterion-referenced testing, the results do not tell anything about how the test taker's performance compares with that of other test takers. As a result of such kind of testing, a test taker can learn what he or she can do with the language and whether he or she is able to perform a set of tasks satisfactorily. Test takers either pass or fail based on their own performances without being compared to their fellows. Therefore, such kind of testing is found more advantageous for the students as these tests set meaningful standards which do not change according to the performances of other test takers, and hence motivate and encourage students to reach the meaningful criteria determined prior to the testing. Teachers can apply criterion-referenced testing through Web 2.0 technologies when creating their tests by setting some standards or criteria for passing or failing the tests. Prior to taking the test, students are given information about the scoring criteria, and they can immediately learn their scores at the end of the test. Having such immediate feedback about the performance can be motivating for the students.

Designing Tests for Language Assessment

Covering some reasons and modes for language assessment previously in this chapter, the current part deals with the description of 'test' and test types. Language teachers can use tests as a method or instrument that requires performance on the part of the test takers. A test measures an individual's knowledge, performance, proficiency or competence. Although tests and assessment are the concepts used interchangeably in current educational practice, Brown and Abeywickrama (2010) point out that they are two different terms describing tests as a subset of assessment. Tests are one of the useful devices that teachers can use to assess students.

While teachers are designing tests for their students, they need to consider some important points. First, they need to ask themselves why they are creating the test, that is, what the major purpose of test is. After specifying the purpose, a teacher needs to decide on the objectives of the test. The objective of a test may include the reasons for testing the language abilities of the students or simply testing about the forms and structures following a course unit. As the first task of a teacher when designing a test for his or her students is to determine the purpose and objectives of the test, this specification can help teachers choose the right kind of test. Therefore, it is important and useful for the teachers to be well-informed about the test types. Hughes (2003) categorizes the tests into four according to the types of information they provide: proficiency tests, diagnostic tests, placement tests and achievement tests.

Proficiency tests aim at measuring global competence in a language to be considered as 'proficient'. For a person to be regarded as proficient in the target language, she or he needs to have sufficient command of the language for a particular purpose. Proficiency tests are mostly summative and norm-referenced. They give a score at the end for the proficiency level of the test taker, and she or he is either accepted or denied for the subsequent stage. They also do not give diagnostic feedback for students' progress as they tend to measure performance and give scores according to a norm, an average score or a percentile. Since it takes great time and money to design and create proficiency tests, it would be good for language teachers to refrain from developing a general proficiency test on their own (Zheng & Henning, 1985).

Placement tests are used to 'place' a student into a particular level of stage of language curriculum or school. Therefore, they are constructed for particular reasons for the aims of the curriculum or the school. Placement tests providing information beyond only determining class level may also be used for diagnostic reasons (Brown & Abeywickrama, 2010).

A diagnostic test, on the other hand, is designed to specify individual learner's strengths and weakness about the language skills (Leighton & Gierl, 2007). A teacher administering a diagnostic test to his or her students is trying to see what students need to work in their future studies. It aids in identifying the abilities that a person has mastered and those that still need to be learned (Gorin, 2007).

Achievement Tests

Among all the test types, achievement tests are the most often used types in education as they seem to be representative of the tasks that children perform in school (Jenkins & Pany, 1978). Achievement tests are directly related to language teachers and classes since their purpose is to establish how successful students or classes have been in

Designing Achievement Tests for Language Learners

achieving the course objectives. Such tests aim at assessing whether students have gained the necessary information and abilities and have accomplished the course objectives by the end of a certain instructional time.

Along with their popularity and frequent use among language teachers, they offer a number of advantages. First, course designers, stakeholders or teachers need to be explicit about the course objectives. Second, as test results give information how far students have achieved these objectives, it puts pressure on the stakeholders to develop the course materials, tasks or the whole teaching process (Hughes, 2003). Achievement tests can take both summative and formative roles. They can be summative as they are generally administered at the end of an instructional unit or term. However, they can be formative as well since they give feedback on the students' performances and teachers can organize their instructional processes accordingly. Achievement tests may include an infinite variety of item types or formats ranging from five-minute quizzes to three-hour examinations.

Despite their popularity and usefulness, it is not easy to create effective achievement tests. An effective achievement test must be practical. This means it needs to be cost efficient, easy to apply, time-saving and has easy and time-efficient scoring. In addition to practicality, it needs to be reliable as well. That is, it must be dependable and consistent. Giving the same test to the same student or matched students on two different occasions should give similar results. Reliability depends on a number of factors such as the student, rater, test administration or the test itself. Another principle an effective achievement test needs to have is validity. Validity can be defined as "the extent to which inferences made from assessment results are appropriate, meaningful, and useful in terms of the purpose of the assessment" (Gronlund, 1998, p. 226). In other words, if a test aims at measuring the reading ability, it needs to include items testing the reading ability, not any other items or questions regarding the other language skills or previous knowledge. An effective achievement test must be authentic. An authentic test has a natural language, contextualized rather than isolated items, meaningful topics and real-world tasks. If one claims to have authenticity in a task in their tests, that task is supposed to be enacted in the real world (Brown & Abeywickrama, 2010). The last principle an effective achievement test needs to have is washback which can be defined as the effect of testing on teaching and learning (Hughes, 2003). The washback effect gives the opportunity to both the students and teachers to diagnose the strengths and weaknesses of the test takers. Students' incorrect responses can be seen as the indicators of further study on the test items. Correct answers, on the other hand, must be praised and reinforced as they represent the success in a student's interlanguage.

Considering all these principles, that is, practicality, reliability, validity, authenticity and washback as the necessary elements of an effective achievement test, it is a challenging and demanding task for language teachers to create such a

97

test (Tsang et al., 2008). The use of digital tools such as Web 2.0 technologies would create opportunities for the teachers by making this task easier and attainable. Once teachers get into the idea and practice of using Web 2.0 tools for language assessment, they can benefit from these tools in their language teaching and assessment practices.

Technology and Language Assessment

Computer-based tests and computer-adaptive testing have long been used by designers for assessing language skills of test takers. In a computer-based test, each test-taker receives a set of questions that adhere to the test's requirements and are generally suitable for his or her level of performance. They generally include items with fixed, closed-ended responses, and students receive prompts in the form of spoken or written stimuli (Brown & Abeywickrama, 2010). A computer-based test does not have to be in the format of a computer-adaptive test. A computer-adaptive test is structured and 'adapted' based on the correct and wrong answers given by the test taker. It starts with items of moderate difficulty. Depending on the answer given to the previous item by the test-taker, the system determines the next question presented to the test-taker. Those responding incorrectly are presented with an easier item while those responding correctly are presented with a more difficult item. The popularity of computer-based tests is quite understandable as it gives more precise information about test takers' level of ability, less time is needed, scoring is faster and test-takers can take the test in more convenient times (Chalhoub-Deville & Deville, 1999; Jamieson, 2005; Madsen, 1986). Computer-based tests can serve as summative assessment tools as they give information about the test takers' abilities at a given time, which is pass or failure. They can also be used for formative assessment as teachers can make judgments about students' performances due to the immediate feedback received through the computer (Deutsch et al., 2012; Wilson et al., 2011).

On the other hand, the lack of interaction because of the human element and multiple-choice format of the computer-adaptive testing, EFL teachers cannot make use of these tests in their classes in an efficient and effective way. With the advancements in web-based technologies and multimedia, EFL teachers are offered with the potential for designing and developing web-based tests that are more authentic and interactional than their paper and pencil counterparts (Bachman, 2000). Web-based technologies work over the Internet and utilize the browsers as its interface. These systems allow teachers to quickly examine answer sheets and record scores online in addition to offering online real-time examinations and online item construction (Bonham et al., 2000). Students can take web-based tests whenever and wherever they like through the Internet with standard browsers. Bonham et al. (2000) highlights the practicality of web-based testing by stating that automatic grading, score collection, and recording are crucial for teachers because they make it easier for them to track and monitor students' learning progress than with traditional paper-and-pencil exams.

Along with the premises of web-based testing, EFL teachers need to critically evaluate the many purposes of testing on the web, what is being assessed, for whom and under what conditions. Moreover, the current focus in web-based or technology-based assessment is in exploring the possibilities of the increasingly popular rich digital media, such as web 2.0 tools and video games. At that point, it is an unignorable fact that mobile and tablet devices are also offering opportunities both for teachers and students in terms of language assessment. It should be noted that EFL teachers are not expected to develop new assessment tools, but to improve teaching and learning processes by benefiting from new assessment technologies. However, it is a questionable fact that whether EFL teachers feel ready or motivated to use contemporary technologies for language assessment in their classroom practices or they have necessary competencies, skills or knowledge required for designing and creating tests through digital tools.

EFL Teachers' Readiness of Technology Integration Into Language Assessment

The developments and changes in technology-based language assessment is not meaningful alone when teachers are not a part of that process. The way technology is used and applied for language teaching and assessment largely depends on teachers (Marshall & Cox, 2008). Although teachers are aware of the fact that they are an important factor in successful integration of technology into language teaching and assessment and that technology enhances students' motivation and enhancement (Ottenbreit-Leftwich et al., 2010; Voogt et al., 2013a), many of them have some challenges to achieve successful integration. Farjon et al. (2019) claims that even the new generation of teachers struggles with the use of technology, which is more problematic and worrisome for the educational practices. In line with this assertion, several studies (Admiraal et al., 2013; Drent & Meelissen, 2008; Tondeur et al., 2016) have found out novice teachers do not feel fully equipped and competent enough to use technological tools in their instructional practices.

Teacher education programs have a big and challenging role in providing EFL student teachers with the competencies and skills for the effective and successful technology integration. Mere digital skills such as word processing programs or the use of presentation programs are not alone sufficient to integrate technology into language teaching processes (Mouza et al., 2014). These prospective teachers need to know what digital tools to use, how to utilize them properly and how to make them pedagogically appropriate to the discipline (Kwangsawad, 2016). Mishra and Koehler (2006), grounded in the work of Schulman (1987), developed

Technological Pedagogical Content Knowledge (TPACK) as a theoretical framework for understanding the knowledge and skills teachers need for effective and efficient integration of technology. TPACK framework includes seven domains: Technology Knowledge (TK), Pedagogy Knowledge (PK), Content Knowledge (CK), Technological Content Knowledge (TCK), Technological Pedagogical Knowledge (TPK), Pedagogical Content Knowledge (PCK), and Technological Pedagogical Content Knowledge (TPACK). The framework has three main components that relate and align with one another: content (subject matter), pedagogy (teaching methodology) and technology. A successful practitioner teacher is required to understand and interpret the relations and interplay among these three components (Koehler & Mishra, 2009). Technology knowledge (TK) means that teachers must have a thorough understanding of information technology to effectively implement it in their classrooms. They must also know how to modify the goals of technologies to make better use of them. Teachers' knowledge of the procedures and methods used in teaching and learning is known as pedagogy knowledge (PK). It offers information on instructional methodologies, learner characteristics, and methods for assessing students' comprehension (Harris et al., 2009). Content knowledge (CK) is teachers' knowledge about the subject matter they teach including concepts, theories or conceptual frameworks.

Although there are some studies indicating a problematic distinction among the components of the framework (Graham, 2011; Niess, 2011; Voogt et al., 2013b), TPACK is regarded as a useful framework for describing the information that pre-service teachers must acquire to properly integrate technology into their teaching, regardless of the subject matter. A teacher grasping the underlying principles and internalizing TPACK framework can easily understand the technological concepts, pedagogical methods that effectively teach curriculum by using technology, how technology can be utilized to reinforce or expand existing epistemologies.

Another model developed by Knezek and Christensen (2008) is the will, skill and tool model which describes different influences on the integration of technology by teachers. Technology integration is explained in terms of these three constructs: will (teachers' attitudes and beliefs towards technology), skill (their competencies regarding the technology use), and tool (access to digital tools). Farjon (2019) also adds experience as the fourth contributor to the components in this model as quality and quantity of teaching experience in the teacher education programs are seen essential constructs for successful technology integration. Will, highly likely the most important component of the model, is recognized as a necessary condition for successful technology integration (Christensen & Knezek, 2008, 2009). Research indicates that positive attitudes and beliefs affect whether and how teachers integrate technology in their future classes (Agyei & Voogt, 2011; Ertmer et al., 2012; Prestridge, 2012). Teachers' willingness to use digital tools in their

Designing Achievement Tests for Language Learners

classes often determines the effective and successful integration of technology into the classroom. Therefore, teacher education programs and teacher educators need to come up with the ideas and practices to encourage positive attitudes and beliefs of student teachers for technology integration. Moreover, pre-service teachers need to get exposed to examples of successful technology integration in line with the experience contributor of the model. Teacher educators can become role models during teacher education for the student teachers, and field experience such as internship can be beneficial for them to experience the use of technology for language teaching and assessment purposes. Another component of the model, skill, requires student teachers to develop basic skills in and knowledge of various technologies and how to use them to achieve both personal and educational goals (Schmidt et al., 2009). The technology knowledge component of the TPACK framework has common grounds with the *skill* construct in this model. Lastly, the tool component can be defined as the teachers' accessibility and familiarity of technology use. The lack of access to different technologies logically plays a key role in successful technology integration and this lack is less likely to occur in Western countries (Farjon et al, 2019). For successful and efficient technology integration into language assessment, teacher education programs need to support their student teachers in terms of these four components.

Using Digital Tools for Language Assessment

In this part of the chapter, the audience of the book is presented with information about three digital tools and sample activity plans to apply these tools for language assessment purposes. Following the information about the general objectives, interface and content of the tools, activity plans are given in details including the students' levels and ages, materials and procedure.

Nearpod

Nearpod (www.nearpod.com) is a free website and application giving access to both teachers and learners to interactive slides and videos, gamification and activities. With slides and videos, teachers can find the opportunity to visualize and support student understanding. They can make use of the information from formative assessments and interactive media elements to improve the way they teach and the results of their students. With the use of formative assessment tools, teachers can rearrange the ways of their instruction or detect the misconceptions of the students as they can get immediate feedback or post-session reports from real-time data. It offers nine types of formative assessments to capture student understanding in any lesson: drag and drop, draw it, open-ended questions, polls, quizzes, time to climb, collaborate board, fill in the blanks, matching pairs.

Nearpod has a quite easy to understand interface. The overview and tutorial videos are available once the app is downloaded on the device or in the web version of the tool. To store future presentations, the teacher must first register an account with a username and password. A student code shows up at the top of the presentation after the teacher creates it. When students launch the app or go to the website, they use the code for the access to the presentations, activities or games. They can communicate via any device, live or at their convenience.

For integrating technology in a meaningful way, Nearpod can be incorporated into language teaching with little effort and increased student engagement (Burton, 2019; Delacruz, 2014; Hakami, 2020). McClean and Crowe (2017) found out in their study that instructors can use Nearpod to assist students' active learning by offering a variety of learning exercises and information even in big classes. This finding is in line with that of other researchers, who found that Nearpod made teaching their class considerably simpler than alternative app presentations. (Gallegos & Nakashima, 2018).

An Activity Plan to Apply Nearpod for Language Teaching

Prior to the activity: At the beginning of the class, the teacher gives the key vocabulary for the unit by using visuals so that the students learn the names of the kitchen tools and cooking verbs. Then, the students watch a video of an easy recipe. They will practice the vocabulary of the unit now and learn how to describe the process of cooking.

Students' level: A2
Students' age: 12-13
Aims of the activity:
- ◦ Students will be able to practice new vocabulary.
- ◦ Students will be able to improve their understanding of a simple process.
- ◦ Students will be able to use authentic materials for the context.

Duration: 30 minutes
Materials: A YouTube video and a Nearpod Mount Climbing Game

Procedure: The teacher tells students that they are going to watch a recipe and they can take notes. S/he opens the video of the recipe (https://youtu.be/H4d_lsVnjc4) and students watch it with subtitles. After watching the video, s/he asks them some questions to check their comprehension level (e.g.: What are the ingredients of the recipe?) and after getting answers s/he opens the video again. This time, teacher

Designing Achievement Tests for Language Learners

explains the key words and their meanings following the video in case some of the students do not remember them. Later, s/he asks new questions to make sure they all understand the text now. The teacher tells the students that they will play a mount climbing game. S/he says there are questions about the video in the game. Then, the teacher tells them that when they enter the code s/he has already created in given space, the teacher will start the game and they will see a question for 30 seconds and click on the correct answer. S/he also adds that the one who clicks faster and on the correct answer will be the first climbing to the top of the mountain. Then, the teacher asks the students to enter the code and when everyone comes into the waiting room, the teacher starts the game. The activity continues until all the questions are done.

Follow-up: After the quiz, teacher encourages students to speak in the target language by asking them their favorite food (e.g., Can you cook? Do you have a secret recipe? What do you like to cook?). When students talk about their experiences, s/he listens to them and gives feedback afterwards.

Assignment: S/he asks students to interview with their parents and students write their secret recipe for the next lesson. S/he tells students that they can record a video of them cooking or an audio of them talking about their recipe as well. Next lesson, students share their projects in the classroom. They discuss the recipes together. In that way, students can choose between alternatives, and they will prepare what they prefer to do. They have a chance to review the lesson by visuals, audios and reading texts that they create themselves.

Kahoot

Kahoot is a game-based student response system where the teacher acts as the owner of the game shows and students are the gamesters. When developing the platform for teachers and learners, the founders agreed that it should be simple for teachers to use to produce their own content, play quizzes, and evaluate their students. It also needs to be simple for students to join without registering, play anonymously, have fun, compete, and learn (Wang, 2015). Kahoot has a creator tool that lets the users design their own kahoots that can be a Quiz question, a True or false question, an Open-ended question, a Puzzle, a Poll, a Word cloud or a Slide. Users, highly possibly teachers, can add questions from the question bank of the tool or can import questions from a spreadsheet. When creating a question in Kahoot, teachers can set a time limit for each question, add a visual or video link to questions and specify the points awarded for each question. There are also non-game related question types including polls to gather student opinions, word clouds to collect free-form answers and slides.

In the classroom, teachers can either launch Kahoot in a web browser through the smartboard or give the game pin to the students so that they can go to the Kahoot

103

Designing Achievement Tests for Language Learners

through their mobile phones. Students can choose a nickname for themselves which allows anonymity that may enhance students' encouragement and confidence to join the activities in class (Wang & Tahir, 2020). After entering their nicknames, the students wait in the lobby playing a lobby tune to put them in the mood for the game. Students with inappropriate nicknames can be kicked out by the teacher. After all the questions are answered by the students, the game gives a scoreboard presenting the top 5 players. The game will end in a podium, and the students can also rate the quiz with one to five stars indicating whether they learnt anything, would suggest it, and whether they felt happy, neutral, or sad at the end of the game.

In terms of formative assessment, teachers can use analytics from game reports to assess class learning progress in real time. Teachers can have the snapshot of their class performances immediately following the Kahoot quiz. They can easily detect the difficult questions that require follow-up or re-teach process in line with the basic underlying of dynamic assessment (Dellos, 2015; Johns, 2015). Through polls, open-ended questions or word clouds, they can also get feedback from the students about the course content, quality or difficulty levels of the questions. Also, it would be possible for the teachers to pre-assess student knowledge, their expectations from the classes or their feelings in general so that they can arrange their classroom practices.

An Activity Plan to Apply Kahoot for Language Teaching

Prior to the activity: The teacher first introduces weather words to the students via a PowerPoint presentation to prepare them for the topic. S/he shows these words accompanied by pictures. After the weather words, this time the teacher introduces the words that describe emotions to the students. S/he also exemplifies them with pictures. Then, the teacher asks some questions to the students (e.g., What is the weather like in this picture? How do you feel when the weather is like this? Describe your feelings.). Then, students do some listening and writing activities to better understand the topic. They also complete the activities related to the unit in the workbook. In final step, the teacher gives a passage to the students. This reading text provides information about the weather in England. Students read this passage in turn. Then, the students play a Kahoot game. The teacher evaluates whether the students understand the text they are reading and the weather unit they have learned.

Students' level: A2
Students' age: 10-11
Aims of the activity:
- Students will be able to pick up specific information from short texts about weather conditions.

Designing Achievement Tests for Language Learners

- Students will be able to ask people about the weather.
- Students will be able to talk about the weather in a simple way.
- Students will be able to understand short and simple texts about the weather, weather conditions.

Materials: smart boards / computer / smart phones, pictures, text handout

Procedure: The teacher tells the students how to use Kahoot if they do not know. If the students know about and have used Kahoot before, s/he tells them that they should answer 10 questions within the given time based on the text they read. If this game is played in a classroom with computers, each student enters the game and answers the questions individually. Or, if it is played in an online course, students participate in the game from their own computers or mobile phones in the same way. In the classroom environment, games can be played through the smart board. In this case, the students can give the answer by raising their hands. The students answer the questions. Meanwhile, the teacher explains the parts, sentences and words the students do not understand or do not know. At the end of the game, the teacher evaluates the students' knowledge about the unit and topic.

Follow – up: The teacher shows the students some posters with a 5-day forecast for some cities. Then, s/he asks the students to choose a city and prepare a poster describing the next 5 days weather forecast for that city. S/he tells them to use pictures in this poster and also asks them to write sentences under that poster for the weather for each day. Then, the students bring the poster they have prepared to the classroom. Each student comes to the board in turn and shows the poster to their friends. They imagine themselves as if a weather forecaster and describe the next 5-day weather report of that city.

Wordwall

A secondary school teacher in London, United Kingdom, first had the concept for a web-based application, Wordwall.net, in 2006. She thought that teachers had a difficult time creating instructional materials with paper and posters on the classroom walls for centuries. Therefore, to assist teachers with class preparation, particularly with regard to learning materials, student engagement and interactive activities, she and her team developed an application in 2006. Wordwall.net is an educational game-based website that allows teachers to create interactive games and printed materials for their students. Teachers simply pick a template out of 33 templates on the website for their content, enter the content and the tools design the activity according to the template by using AI technologies. Techers can either print out their activities or play them on a screen in or out of class. Most of the templates of the tool are suitable for both interactive and printable activities. Interactive games or activities can be played on any web-enabled device such as a computer, tablet, or mobile phone. Students can individually do the activities on their computers or mobile phones. However, when the students do not have that opportunity, teachers can play the games on the class smartboard and students can take turns to do the activities by coming to the board. Teachers can easily change the template once they have created an activity or game using any of the templates. This saves time for the teachers and reinforce the use of Wordwall for their classroom practices (Bueno et al, 2022; Çil, 2021; Jannah & Syafryadin, 2022).

There are 60,425,524 resources on the website, and 43 languages are supported. If a teacher finds a pre-made activity for his/her students but it is not quite alright, s/he has the chance to customize the material to make it appropriate for the class, content or the teaching style. Crossword, gameshow quizz, random card, matching up, random wheel, group sort, anagram and word search are some of the activity/ game types or templates on Wordwall.net. Teachers need to sign up for creating games while students do not need to create an account for the access to the activities.

When a teacher creates an assignment, s/he gets a link for it. Through the link, students are directed to that assignment without the distraction of the main page of the website. The results or the scores of the students are recorded and made available for the teacher. There is a section called 'My Results' where teachers can check individual students' results.

An Activity Plan to Apply Wordwall for Language Teaching

Prior to the activity: They have learned Present Continuous Tense during "Animal Shelter" Unit. The teacher wants the students practice Present Continuous Tense and the vocabulary in the unit in an enjoyable and interactive way. S/he creates an unjumble activity on Wordwall for the students.

Students' level: A1
Students' age: 10-11
Aims of the activity:
- ◦ Students will be able to understand descriptions of what people/animals are doing at
the moment.
- ◦ Students will be able to make sentences using Present Continuous Tense.
- ◦ Students will be able to talk about what people/animals are doing at the moment of speaking.

Materials: The video of Animal Shelter on YouTube: https://youtu.be/ Gw9lI1yGKJI?si=GCNpD8nL2eAuTUB6

Designing Achievement Tests for Language Learners

An unjumbling activity for ordering sentences: https://wordwall.net/tr/resource/14154306

Procedure: Since students have learned present continuous tense in the previous lesson, this lesson prepared for practicing this input through listening, speaking and reading. The teacher comes to the class and greets the students. S/he tells the students they are going to watch a video and s/he will ask some questions about the video after watching. They watch the video twice. Then, the teacher asks questions such as "Which animals do you see in the video?, What is the cat doing?, What is Kartopu eating?" etc. After the discussion on questions, the teacher says it is time for the Wordwall activity. S/he goes to the link of the activity on smartboard and tells the students that they are going to drag and drop words to rearrange each sentence into its correct order. Then, s/he opens the first sentence and asks if there are any students who want to come to the board and do the first unjumbling activity. One of the students is chosen, s/he drags and drops the words to make correct sentences. The teacher gives positive reinforcement to the student by saying 'thank you, well done'.

Follow-up: At the end of lesson, the teacher asks the students go home and look at the animals in their neighborhood every day. S/he tells them they are going to write at least five sentences about these animals and their actions. S/he says s/he is going to check their sentences in the next class.

CONCLUSION

Assessing language skills can be a challenging and demanding task for EFL teachers as there are different assessment types, test types and some other factors such as test validity and reliability to consider when designing and creating tests for the student assessment. Teachers need to test and assess their students' language ability to make some decisions about their performance and teaching learning process. In line with the formative assessment processes, they can re-organize their teaching methods, materials or coursebooks for the enhancement of teaching and assessment practices. Considering the side of language learners, being tested by their teachers in the foreign language they are practising can be a stressful and worrisome experience. They may even refrain from performing in and out of classroom tasks and activities. Language teachers seeking some alternative ways to deal with these negative affective factors can use contemporary technological tools for language assessment.

The current chapter of the book tried to give information to EFL language teachers about the necessity and modes of language assessment, test types and integrating technology into language teaching and assessment. By elaborating on the TPACK framework and will, skill, tool and experience model, it focused on the importance and necessity of teachers' readiness, attitudes and beliefs on successful integration of technology into language teaching and assessment. To contribute to teachers' readiness and the enhancement of positive attitudes towards technology integration for language assessment, three digital tools and activity plans were presented. EFL teachers can benefit from these tools and sample activity plans when designing and creating language tests for their students. They can even get encouraged and enthusiastic about using some other tools not included in that chapter in their teaching and assessment practices.

REFERENCES

Admiraal, W., Louws, M., Lockhorst, D., Paas, T., Buynsters, M., Cviko, A., Janssen, C., de Jonge, M., Nouwens, S., Post, L., van der Ven, F., & Kester, L. (2017). Teachers in school-based technology innovations: A typology of their beliefs on teaching and technology. *Computers & Education*, *114*, 57–68. doi:10.1016/j.compedu.2017.06.013

Agyei, D., & Voogt, J. (2011). Exploring the potential of the Will, Skill, Tool model in Ghana: Predicting prospective and practicing teachers' use of technology. *Computers & Education*, *56*(1), 91–100. doi:10.1016/j.compedu.2010.08.017

Bachman, L., & Palmer, A. (2022). *Language assessment in practice: Developing language assessments and justifying their use in the real world*. Oxford University.

Bachman, L. F. (2000). Modern language testing at the turn of the century: Assuring that what we count counts. *Language Testing*, *17*(1), 1–42. doi:10.1177/026553220001700101

Black, P. (2009). Formative assessment issues across the curriculum: The theory and the practice. *TESOL Quarterly*, *43*(3), 519–524. doi:10.1002/j.1545-7249.2009.tb00248.x

Bonham, S. W., Beichner, R. J., Titus, A., & Martin, L. (2000). Education research using Web-based assessment systems. *Journal of Research on Computing in Education*, *33*(1), 28–45. doi:10.1080/08886504.2000.10782298

Brown, D. (2001). *Teaching by principles: An interactive approach to language pedagogy*. Pearson Education.

Brown, H. D., & Abeywickrama, P. (2010). *Language assessment: Principles and classroom practices*. Pearson Education.

Bueno, M., Perez, F., Valerio, R., & Areola, E. M. Q. (2022). A usability study on Google site and Wordwall.net: Online instructional tools for learning basic integration amid pandemic. *Journal of Global Business and Social Entrepreneurship*, *7*(23), 61–71.

Burton, R. (2019). A review of Nearpod – an interactive tool for student engagement. *Journal of Applied Learning & Teaching*, *2*(2), 95–97. doi:10.37074/jalt.2019.2.2.13

Chalhoub-Deville, M., & Deville, C. (1999). Computer adaptive testing in second language contexts. *Annual Review of Applied Linguistics*, *19*, 273–299. doi:10.1017/S0267190599190147

Cheng, L., Rogers, T., & Hu, H. (2004). ESL/EFL instructors' classroom assessment practices: Purposes, methods and procedures. *Language Testing*, *21*(3), 360–389. doi:10.1191/0265532204lt288oa

Christensen, R., & Knezek, G. (2008). Self-report measures and findings for information technology attitudes and competencies. In J. Voogt & G. Knezek (Eds.), *International handbook of information technology in primary and secondary education* (pp. 349–365). Springer. doi:10.1007/978-0-387-73315-9_21

Christensen, R., & Knezek, G. (2009). Construct validity for the teachers' attitudes toward computers questionnaire. *Journal of Computing in Teacher Education*, *25*(4), 143–155.

Çil, E. (2021). The effect of using Wordwall.net in increasing vocabulary knowledge of 5th grade EFL students. *Language Education & Technology*, *1*(1), 21–28.

Clapham, C. (2000). Assessment and testing. *Annual Review of Applied Linguistics*, *20*, 147–161. doi:10.1017/S0267190500200093

Delacruz, S. (2014). Using Nearpod in elementary guided reading groups. *TechTrends*, *58*(5), 63–70. doi:10.100711528-014-0787-9

Dellos, R. (2015). Kahoot! A digital game resource for learning. *International Journal of Instructional Technology and Distance Learning*, *12*(4), 49–52.

Deutsch, T., Herrmann, K., Frese, T., & Sandholzer, H. (2012). Implementing computer-based assessment – A web-based mock examination changes attitudes. *Computers & Education*, *58*(4), 1068–1075. doi:10.1016/j.compedu.2011.11.013

Drent, M., & Meelissen, M. (2008). Which factors obstruct or stimulate teacher educators to use ICT innovatively? *Computers & Education*, *51*(1), 187–199. doi:10.1016/j.compedu.2007.05.001

Ertmer, P., Ottenbreit-Leftwich, A., Sadik, O., Sendurur, E., & Sendurur, P. (2012). Teacher beliefs and technology integration practices: A critical relationship. *Computers & Education, 59*(2), 423–435. doi:10.1016/j.compedu.2012.02.001

Farjon, D., Smits, A., & Voogt, J. (2019). Technology integration of pre-service teachers explained by attitudes and beliefs, competency, access, and experience. *Computers & Education, 130*, 81–93. doi:10.1016/j.compedu.2018.11.010

Fulcher, G. (2012). Assessment literacy for the language classroom. *Language Assessment Quarterly, 9*(2), 113–132. doi:10.1080/15434303.2011.642041

Gallegos, C., & Nakashima, H. (2018). Mobile devices: A distraction, or a useful tool to engage nursing students? *The Journal of Nursing Education, 57*(3), 170–173. doi:10.3928/01484834-20180221-09 PMID:29505077

Gorin, J. S. (2007). Cognitive diagnostic assessment for education. In J. P. Leighton & M. J. Gierl (Eds.), *Test construction and diagnostic testing* (pp. 173–204). Cambridge University.

Graham, C. R. (2011). Theoretical considerations for understanding technological pedagogical content knowledge (TPACK). *Computers & Education, 57*(3), 1953–1960. doi:10.1016/j.compedu.2011.04.010

Gronlund, N. E. (1998). *Assessment of student achievement.* Allyn and Bacon.

Hakami, M. (2020). Using Nearpod as a tool to promote active learning in higher education in a BYOD learning environment. *Journal of Education and Learning, 9*(1), 119–126. doi:10.5539/jel.v9n1p119

Harris, J., Mishra, P., & Koehler, M. (2009). Teachers' technological pedagogical content knowledge and learning activity types. *Journal of Research on Technology in Education, 41*(4), 393–416. doi:10.1080/15391523.2009.10782536

Healey, D., Hegelheimer, V., Hubbard, P., Ioannou-Georgiou, S., Kessler, G., & Ware, P. (2008). *TESOL technology standards framework.* TESOL. Retrieved from https://www.tesol.org

Hughes, A. (2003). *Testing for language teachers.* Cambridge University.

Jamieson, J. (2005). Trends in computer-based second language assessment. *Annual Review of Applied Linguistics, 25*, 228–242. doi:10.1017/S0267190505000127

Jannah, M., & Syafryadin, S. (2022). EFL students' perspectives on the use of Wordwall.net as vocabulary learning media. *Journal of English Language Teaching, 11*(2), 115–124. doi:10.15294/elt.v11i2.57120

Jenkins, J. R., & Pany, D. (1978). Standardized achievement tests: How useful for special education? *Exceptional Children, 44*(6), 448–453. doi:10.1177/001440297804400606

Johns, K. (2015). Engaging and assessing students with technology: A review of Kahoot! *Delta Kappa Gamma Bulletin, 81*(4), 89–91.

Knezek, G., & Christensen, R. (2008). The importance of information technology attitudes and competencies in primary and secondary education. In J. Voogt & G. Knezek (Eds.), *International handbook of information technology in primary and secondary education* (pp. 321–331). Springer. doi:10.1007/978-0-387-73315-9_19

Koehler, M., & Mishra, P. (2009). What is technological pedagogical content knowledge (TPACK)? *Contemporary Issues in Technology & Teacher Education, 9*(1), 60–70. doi:10.1177/002205741319300303

Kwangsawad, T. (2016). Examining EFL pre-service teachers' TPACK trough self-report, lesson plans and actual practice. *Journal of Education and Learning, 10*(2), 103–108. doi:10.11591/edulearn.v10i2.3575

Leighton, J. P., & Gierl, M. J. (2007). Cognitive diagnostic assessment for education. In J. P. Leighton & M. J. Gierl (Eds.), *Why cognitive diagnostic assessment?* (pp. 3–18). Cambridge University. doi:10.1017/CBO9780511611186.001

Madsen, H. (1986). Evaluating a computer-adaptive ESL placement test. *CALICO Journal, 4*(2), 41–50. doi:10.1558/cj.v4i2.41-50

Marshall, G., & Cox, M. (2008). Research methods: Their design, applicability and reliability. In J. Voogt & G. Knezek (Eds.), *International handbook of information technology in primary and secondary education* (pp. 983–987). Springer. doi:10.1007/978-0-387-73315-9_62

McClean, S., & Crowe, W. (2017). Making room for interactivity: Using the cloud-based audience response system Nearpod to enhance engagement in lectures. *FEMS Microbiology Letters, 364*(6), 1–7. doi:10.1093/femsle/fnx052 PMID:28333274

Mishra, P., & Koehler, M. J. (2006). Technological pedagogical content knowledge: A new framework for teacher knowledge. *Teachers College Record, 108*(6), 1017–1054. doi:10.1111/j.1467-9620.2006.00684.x

Mouza, C., Karchmer-Klein, R., Nandakumar, R., Yilmaz Ozden, S., & Hu, L. (2014). Investigating the impact of an integrated approach to the development of preservice teachers' technological pedagogical content knowledge (TPACK). *Computers & Education, 71*, 206–221. doi:10.1016/j.compedu.2013.09.020

Navarrate, C. (1990). *Informal assessment in educational evaluation: Implications for bilingual education programs*. Educational Resources Information Center.

Niess, M. L. (2005). Preparing teachers to teach science and mathematics with technology: Developing a technology pedagogical content knowledge. *Teaching and Teacher Education, 21*(5), 509–523. doi:10.1016/j.tate.2005.03.006

Ottenbreit-Leftwich, A., Glazewski, K., Newby, T., & Ermer, P. (2010). Teacher value beliefs associated with using technology: Addressing professional and student needs. *Computers & Education, 55*(3), 1321–1335. doi:10.1016/j.compedu.2010.06.002

Prestridge, S. (2012). The beliefs behind the teacher that influences their ICT practices. *Computers & Education, 58*(1), 449–458. doi:10.1016/j.compedu.2011.08.028

Schmidt, D., Baran, E., Thompson, A., Mishra, P., Koehler, M., & Shin, T. (2009). Technological Pedagogical Content Knowledge (TPACK): The development and validation of an assessment instrument for preservice teachers. *Journal of Research on Technology in Education, 42*(2), 123–149. doi:10.1080/15391523.2009.10782544

Schulman, L. S. (1987). Knowledge and teaching: Foundations of the new form. *Harvard Educational Review, 57*(1), 1–23. doi:10.17763/haer.57.1.j463w79r56455411

Tondeur, J., van Braak, J., Siddiq, F., & Scherer, R. (2016). Time for a new approach to prepare future teachers for educational technology use: Its meaning and measurement. *Computers & Education, 94*, 134–150. doi:10.1016/j.compedu.2015.11.009

Tsang, S. L., Katz, A., & Stack, J. (2008). Achievement testing for English language learners, ready or not? *Education Policy Analysis Archives, 16*(1), 1–29. doi:10.14507/epaa.v16n1.2008

Van der Mars, H., Timken, G., & McNamee, J. B. (2018). Systematic observation of formal assessment of students by teachers (SOFAST). *Physical Educator, 75*(3), 341–373. doi:10.18666/TPE-2018-V75-I3-8113

Voogt, J., Fisser, P., Pareja Roblin, N., Tondeur, J., & Van Braak, J. (2013b). Technological Pedagogical Content Knowledge (TPACK) - a review of the literature. *Journal of Computer Assisted Learning, 29*(2), 109–121. doi:10.1111/j.1365-2729.2012.00487.x

Voogt, J., Knezek, G., Cox, M., Knezek, D., & Ten Brummelhuis, A. (2013a). Under which conditions does ICT have a positive effect on teaching and learning? A Call to Action. *Journal of Computer Assisted Learning, 29*(1), 4–14. doi:10.1111/j.1365-2729.2011.00453.x

Wang, A. I. (2015). The wear out effect of a game-based student response system. *Computers & Education, 82*, 217–227. doi:10.1016/j.compedu.2014.11.004

Wang, A. I., & Tahir, R. (2020). The effect of using Kahoot! for learning – a literature review. *Computers & Education, 149*, 1–22. doi:10.1016/j.compedu.2020.103818

Wilson, K., Boyd, C., Chen, L., & Jamal, S. (2011). Improving student performance in a first year geography course: Examining the importance of computer-assisted formative assessment. *Computers & Education, 57*(2), 1493–1500. doi:10.1016/j. compedu.2011.02.011

Zheng, C., & Henning, G. (1985). Linguistic and cultural bias in language proficiency tests. *Language Testing, 2*(2), 155–163. doi:10.1177/026553228500200204

ADDITIONAL READING

Abbitt, J. (2011). Measuring technological pedagogical content knowledge in preservice teacher education: A review of current methods and instruments. *Journal of Research on Technology in Education, 43*(4), 281–300. doi:10.1080/15391523 .2011.10782573

Bachman, L. F. (1991). What does language testing have to offer? *TESOL Quarterly, 25*(4), 671–704. doi:10.2307/3587082

Fulcher, G., & Davidson, F. (2007). *Language testing and assessment.* Routledge.

Heitink, M., Voogt, J., Verplanken, L., van Braak, J., & Fisser, P. (2016). Teachers' professional reasoning about their use of technology. *Computers & Education, 101*, 70–83. doi:10.1016/j.compedu.2016.05.009

Koehler, M. J., Mishra, P., & Yahya, K. (2007). Tracing the development of teacher knowledge in a design seminar: Integrating content, pedagogy, technology. *Computers & Education, 49*(3), 740–762. doi:10.1016/j.compedu.2005.11.012

Wang, Y. (2002). When technology meets beliefs: Preservice teachers' perception of the teacher's role in the classroom with computers. *Journal of Research on Technology in Education, 35*(1), 150–161. doi:10.1080/15391523.2002.10782376

KEY TERMS AND DEFINITIONS

Achievement Tests: They are the tests that aims to establish how successful students or classes have been in achieving the course objectives.

Assessment: It is the process of collecting information about something that we are interested in.

Formal Assessment: They are the systematic, deliberate strategies designed to provide teachers and students with an evaluation of student performance and achievement.

Formative Assessment: It is a process including teacher's feedback delivery on student performance, student's internalization of the feedback and formation of learning accordingly.

Informal Assessment: They are the incidental, unplanned comments and reactions, mentoring, and other impromptu feedback to the students.

Language Assessment: It is the process of collecting information about test takers' performance to interpret some aspects of their language ability to make some decisions about their performance and teaching learning process.

Summative Assessment: It is carried out at the end of a course or instructional unit as it tries to measure or summarize what a student has learned.

Chapter 6

EFL Learners' Views About the Use of Artificial Intelligence in Giving Corrective Feedback on Writing:
A Case Study

Ümran Üstünbaş
iD https://orcid.org/0000-0002-7382-6220
Zonguldak Bülent Ecevit University, Turkey

ABSTRACT

This chapter presents a qualitative study the aim of which is to explore EFL learners' views about the use of artificial intelligence for giving corrective feedback on their written works. Artificial intelligence use was addressed through one of recent and popular chatbots: ChatGPT. The data were gathered through semi-structured and stimulated-recall interviews, also videorecording of the participants' ChatGPT use for writing feedback. In the interviews, the participants reflected on their individualized language studies, and also having practiced the use of artificial intelligence in receiving corrective feedback on their writing assignments via ChatGPT for five weeks, they expressed their thoughts about this experience. The findings indicated codes and themes about learner characteristics and preferences, and benefits and pitfalls of artificial intelligence use for corrective feedback, which leads to several language teaching implications specifically concerning writing to be proposed in the chapter.

DOI: 10.4018/979-8-3693-0353-5.ch006

Copyright © 2024, IGI Global. Copying or distributing in print or electronic forms without written permission of IGI Global is prohibited.

INTRODUCTION

Transforming lifestyles, technological advances have led to changes in core systems of society. Thus, specific to changes reflecting in the educational system, computers and mobile tools have been integrated to support learning and/or teaching of any school subject. Thus, benefitting from becoming partially or totally online, new teaching approaches and methods such as blended learning and flipped classroom have brought about. Furthermore, bulk of digital tools and mobile applications have become part of educational programs particularly to help students conduct independent out-of-class studies. Consequently, in accordance with recent developments highlighting the beginning of a new digital era, artificial intelligence (AI) has been promoted in teaching, and ChatGPT, "a chatbot with a conversational artificial intelligence interface that was developed by OpenAI" (Tlili et al., 2023, p. 1) has currently been one of the trendiest AI tools. Since it has been a very popular AI chatbot, also considered as revolutionary, empirical research has started to provide evidence of how it is used or could be used for varied educational purposes (Lancaster, 2023). Concerning language learning and teaching, it is possible for autonomous learners to conduct self-regulated language studies by using ChatGPT to improve their vocabulary knowledge, study grammar or to practice conversational patterns (Fryer et al., 2020; Kohnke et al., 2023). As for writing practice, this chatbot could be used to generate written texts, which undoubtedly raise ethical concerns. As an acceptable use, it could be used to get feedback for written products, and it is the focus of the study presented in this chapter.

In language learning, writing is considered as the most complex language skill due to cognitive processes and social interaction involved (Ghonsooly & Shalchy, 2013). With this regard, writers activate working memory by generating and organizing ideas, monitoring while writing and evaluating the written work. Additionally, within the scope of second language (L2) learning, written corrective feedback (WCF) defined as "error correction on L2 student writing" (Bitchener, 2008, p. 102) is provided by the teacher in traditional writing classes in which L2 learners could ask the teacher for corrective feedback or give peer feedback, which contributes to constitute social dimensions of writing. Furthermore, engaging in corrective feedback includes cognitive aspects as L2 writers try to grasp what is wrong and why in their papers, and they figure out how to fix it. WCF is provided in various forms while their effects and the extent of which they are preferred by learners differ. For instance, direct/indirect corrective feedback (indicating existence of an error by underlying), metalinguistic corrective feedback (use of error code to indicate an error) are two forms that could be used to give corrective feedback on writing (Ellis, 2009), and as for students' preferences for corrective feedback on writing, there is a tendency towards benefitting from different types of feedback basically

EFL Learners' Views About the Use of Artificial Intelligence

direct corrective feedback and indicating codes (Chen et al., 2016; Saragih et al., 2021). Keeping pace with developments, WCF has included technology-integrated types such as electronic feedback in which teachers correct errors and provide links guiding students for examples of correct use of those errors (Ellis, 2009). Similarly, video feedback and screen-casting in which teachers correct students' papers on the screen and make explanations about the errors through videorecording (Demirel & Aksu, 2019) are new and digital-oriented types of WCF. In line with the most recent development in the digital world, it is inevitable that AI-driven types of WCF are emerging. To this end, ChatGPT is proposed to be used for giving corrective feedback on writing by teachers (Özçelik & Gündüz, 2023). On the other hand, the problem related to the integration of any AI tools into language learning has been reported to be the lack of social and humanistic aspects (Kushmar et al., 2022), which are considered essential aspects of writing classes (Mitchell et al. 2019). Thus, the chapter aims to provide more insight into an emerging research area. For this purpose, it proposes to address background issues with a brief introduction to artificial intelligence in language learning and teaching, benefits and drawbacks regarding the use of ChatGPT for the writing skill, and how EFL learners consider ChatGPT use for WCF.

AI Use in Language Learning and Introduction of ChatGPT

Artificial intelligence (AI), defined as an automatized information processing system that carries on tasks like humans by organizing, storing and using information when necessary, has affected all walks of life in recent years. Accordingly, it is in the operation system of machines and tools that are used on a daily basis, and it also takes a major part in the digital world and computers. Finally, it has been a part of educational technologies through smart devices and digital tools used for educational purposes that have been proposed to facilitate learning (Huang, 2021; Rool & Wylie, 2016), and it has been integrated into fields of education without exception of language learning and teaching.

While integration of AI technology into language learning and teaching is inevitable, there are issues to consider such as benefits and drawbacks. To start with, in language learning, there are several AI tools such as editing tools and text generators that could help learners conduct independent studies to improve their knowledge and skills. Thus, a scaffolded environment where the users (language learners) are supported continuously is constructed, and this may lead to an increase in self-efficacy beliefs and learner autonomy. Therefore, AI tools can be positively associated with self-regulated learning defined as a process to organize resources and environments by managing cognitive and psychological skills. On the other hand, there could be problems caused by lack of digital literacy referring to knowing how to use digital and smart tools effectively to find and analyze information. To this end, learners may not know which tools to use for their studies, they may not know how to use them effectively, or they may use them excessively, but unethically. Besides, excessive use of the tools may limit the development of higher order skills such as critical thinking, and lack of human interaction is proposed to affect motivation negatively (Özçelik & Gündüz, 2023).

In a general sense, AI tools are promoted to benefit language learners for their studies despite some concerns (Kim et al., 2022). In a narrow sense, among the tools, there is one which is particularly popular and suggested to be used for various language learning purposes: ChatGPT. It is "…a chatbot with a conversational artificial intelligence interface that was developed by OpenAI" (Tlili et al., 2023, p. 1), and it has been suggested to have positive and negative aspects like other AI tools. In this sense, it is a more efficient and accurate, cost saving AI tool (Deng & Lin, 2022). Furthermore, it has been proposed to improve vocabulary (Kartal, 2023; Kohnke et al., 2023) and writing skill by generating texts on numerous topics in various genres (Warschauer et al., 2023; Yan, 2023). Yet, as a negative aspect, it has been stated that they might be errors in the responses of the chatbot (Kartal, 2023). In addition, ethicality could be a problem when the learners totally use the AI-generated texts through ChatGPT in their writing assignments (Kılıçkaya & Kic-Drgas, 2023; McKnight & Hicks, 2023). Therefore, considering benefits and drawbacks of AI tools, this study aims to focus one specific tool and its use in writing for a different purpose: receiving corrective feedback rather than generating texts.

Written Corrective Feedback (WCF)

In language learning process, the writing skill is considered as challenging as it involves not only cognitive aspects to generate and organize ideas and structure of the product, but also social aspects in interaction with teacher or peers to seek help and ask for feedback on the product (Mitchell et al., 2019). The feedback including corrections on students' writing papers refers to written corrective feedback, and it could be in various forms some of which are direct and indirect corrective feedback or metalinguistic corrective feedback (Ellis, 2009), and the process is completed with revision of the papers based on the type of WCF (Shintani et al., 2014). As stated by Ellis (2009), while direct corrective feedback includes the teacher's providing the correct form, indirect corrective feedback includes the teacher's indication about the errors to be corrected. Another type of WCF is metalinguistic corrective feedback that involves the teacher's indication about the existence of an error by using specific symbols (See Ellis, 2009 for other types of WCF). Concurring with technological and digital developments, WCF has been in digital types such as video feedback involving the teacher's error correction through screen-casting (Demirel & Aksu,

2019). Apart from teacher feedback, in the digital world, language learners could also conduct self-regulated writing practices through machine error correction as there are AI-driven text generators to correct errors while writing. Finally, ChatGPT has been promoted as the latest AI tool to correct errors in L2 learners' papers (Özçelik & Gündüz, 2023).

Inasmuch as type of WCF is a fundamental aspect of error correction, the type of error is as important as it is. In this regard, the type of an error may determine what type of WCF language learners prefer or understand better. For example, there are lexical errors, orthographic errors, and pragmatic errors proposed (Zhang et al., 2021). In Zhang et al (2021), it is stated that while L2 learners may realize the reason for correction of lexical errors, they may not understand what is wrong with a correction on a pragmatic error as it seems grammatically correct. Seemingly, WCF is a multi-faceted process involving not only error correction but also types of errors and corrections and interpretation of L2 writers.

Regardless of WCF and error types, it has been investigated whether WCF is effective in improving L2 learners' writing, and the existing research provides evidence for its positive effect as it leads to improved accuracy in writing tasks (Bitchener, 2008; Zhang et al., 2021). For example, Bitchener (2008) explored the effect of written corrective feedback on efficacy in writing. The study in experimental design conducted with 75 low intermediate ESL learners in New Zealand revealed that the students in the experimental group who received direct written corrective feedback performed better than the students in the control group who had no feedback on their writing. Although direct corrective feedback works well for language acquisition, indirect corrective feedback was considered as more useful in the long term (Ferris et al., 2013). In a similar vein, L2 learners have been reported to have positive attitudes towards receiving WCF (Chen et al., 2016). As for type of WCF L2 leaners prefer, research findings have put forward that language proficiency is a significant background factor influencing their preferences. To this end, L2 learners with a low level of proficiency tend to prefer direct correction whereas the ones with higher levels of proficiency prefer indirect ways of indicating an error rather than the teacher's direct correction of the errors (Chen et al., 2016; Zhang et al., 2021). Additionally, AI-driven error correction has been suggested to support L2 learners' individual writing studies (Barrot, 2023; Özçelik & Gündüz, 2023; Yan, 2023). However, among AI-driven tools to use in correcting errors, ChatGPT could also explain the reasons for them. Thus, considering the related research findings and that the integration of artificial intelligence into language learning is a relatively new research field, particularly the use of ChatGPT for the purpose, it is necessary to reveal how it is really used by foreign language learners for their writing studies or if there are any background factors affecting the use of it. The following research questions are addressed within the scope of this study:

1. How do EFL learners consider the use of AI for receiving WCF?
   a) Do they have independent language study habits?
   b) What are their views about use of digital technologies for language studies?
   c) How do they use ChatGPT to receive WCF for written products?
   d) How do they reflect on the experience of using ChatGPT for getting WCF?

METHODOLOGY

Research Design

This study adopted a qualitative research design to get a deep understanding of the process (AI use). Adhering to "triangulation" principle of data collection procedures (Creswell, 2014), two types of interviews and screen-recordings were employed to collect data. To this end, interviews were held with the participants and recorded before ChatGPT writing feedback experience. In these individual interviews, the participants were asked several semi-structured questions about their language study habits that are presented in the section of findings. In a following session, ChatGPT was introduced and some guidelines on how to use the chatbot for getting feedback on writing texts were shared with the participants. Thus, two ways of error correction were suggested: direct error correction and error correction with explanations. The next step involved the learners' experiences in using ChatGPT to correct their writing papers and get explanations about their errors. In order to keep track for the researcher, this process, which lasted for five weeks with at least five sessions, was recorded by the participants. The last session was designed as a stimulated-recall interview in which the participants commented on their experience. With an assumption that it would allow the participants to express their thoughts better, the interviews were held in Turkish. Then they were translated into English by the researcher(s).

Participants

This study involved five Turkish EFL learners (3 female, 2 male) aged 18-25 studying English at School of Languages of a state university in Türkiye, in the academic year of 2022-2023. They were chosen randomly among the learners agreeing to participate in the study after being informed about research procedures in the target group. In this sense, the researcher(s) were not acquainted with any of participants. They had similar backgrounds in terms of language learning experiences considering that they had pre-intermediate language level at the program when the study was conducted, and they were false-beginner language learners when they started to the program in which they were taught English through integrated-skills. As for writing skill, they practiced various genres appropriate for their language proficiency as part of the main course. Moreover, based on the process-oriented assessment implemented in the program, they kept writing portfolios for their products. The portfolio worked in two phases. First, the students completed the writing task as a draft which their teacher checked for errors and gave feedback. Then, the students engaged in the teachers' comments and correct their papers before keeping them in their portfolios. Due to this practice, they had a chance to receive written corrective feedback on a regular basis, which made the group eligible and convenient for the research purpose of this study. To this end, it was expected that they knew how receiving WCF practice worked, and they would comment on a new AI experience on that. Thus, they were determined as the sample of the current research.

Data Analysis

The data collected through semi-structured and stimulated-recall interviews, and recordings of ChatGPT use were analyzed qualitatively through content analyses of hand coding. The raw data were categorized under common themes and related codes. Moreover, each theme was supported by the participants' responses as evidence for the emerging codes.

The Researcher's Role

According to Creswell (2014), expressing biases that could be caused by demographic and/or socio-economic reasons in researcher's interpreting the results is an important aspect of a good and effective qualitative study. To this end, the researcher(s) are expected to honestly state their background concerning research purpose and the findings that could influence the results. As for the biases involved in this qualitative research, it could be indicated that the researcher(s) have been interested in writing research and have had experience in giving corrective feedback on writing in various types for years. Since the integration of AI technologies and specifically ChatGPT into language learning is a recent development in the field, it has also been a new experience and insight for the researcher(s) to examine how it is used and considered by EFL learners. Concerning this purpose, the researcher(s) have aimed to avoid the biases by not favoring traditional WCF types that they are used to or the use of ChatGPT in any phases of data collection and analysis. Being objective has been the primary goal of the researcher(s) in this sense.

Ethical Issues

The researcher(s) considered several principles proposed by Creswell (2014) to avoid the problems that influence data collection and analysis processes and are caused by the nature of qualitative research and, thus, to ensure that the study was conducted in ethical and reliable terms. For the concern about ethicality, first, necessary approval to conduct the study was obtained from Ethics Committee of the university that the study was conducted on 28.03.2023. Second, it is necessary to note that the researcher(s) never tended to act as if they had favored and prompted the use of ChatGPT. Instead, it was merely a tool being selected to address AI use for the research purpose. Therefore, no direct or guiding question was asked in the interviews, and it was sustained by another researcher in the field who checked the interview questions after they had been worded. Besides, the researcher(s) only observed the process during the interviews without any intervention. Finally, for the concern about reliability of data analysis, the researcher(s) had the codes and themes checked through *member checking* (Creswell, 2014).

FINDINGS

The current research centered around one research question with its sub-questions addressing various probably associated aspects. Thus, the participants' views about AI use for receiving corrective feedback were targeted with questions about their independent language studies and learner autonomy, their views about the use of digital tools for language learning and their use of ChatGPT as AI tool in the study. The findings emerging through content analyses of the responses in interviews are as follows:

The first sub-question targeted the participants' language study habits, in turn, their self-regulated learning habits and autonomy. For this purpose, it was asked to the participants whether they conducted any out-of-class studies, if yes, what they studied and how much time they allocated for it. The analysis of the data revealed that except for one, they were practicing English through independent studies without any fixed time by using digital tools and resources such as games and podcasts to improve skills for which they had less self-efficacy. The responses which are to be presented in pseudonyms are as follows:

Bulut: *"I have never been a person who studies regularly, but I try to use English in my daily life. For example, the language of my mobile is English, I play computer games, and while playing, I broadcast live on digital platforms both in Turkish and English, so I chat with other players in English. Also, I have friends who have high* *level of English language proficiency, and I practice conversations with them. I watch series and films with captions in English. I have realized that even though I do not understand the language totally, I can understand it to the 80%, which has made me so happy. Sometimes, I just study for an upcoming exam. Instead, I listen to songs in English, and also I sing, and it has improved my pronunciation..."*

Çiçek: *"I practice vocabulary. It became a habit for me thanks to my teachers at the course I attended when I was high school. I have a vocabulary notebook. When I learn new words, I note them down in it. I practice vocabulary twice or three times every day. Moreover, I have a few resource books and I practice reading by using them. I try not to forget things that I have previously learned. Besides, I watch series in its original language without captions, and I try to catch words in them, I watch especially sitcoms as the language in them is easier to catch. I play games in English...."*

Doğa: *"I watch films in English. I talk to friends from other countries in English. I have bought English story books, so I am going to read them. I learn new vocabulary; I note them down and stick on the walls...."*

Güneş: *"Yes, I do study. I look up the words that I see anywhere, I speak in English by myself. Furthermore, I practice listening very often and attentively....songs, music and videos by native speakers....They are apt to my learning style..."*

Toprak: *"To be honest, I only study for the exams and I only study grammar for them"*

As seen in the responses, the participants tend to be autonomous learners who are aware of their learning needs and styles, and they regulate their studies accordingly. Moreover, as the current research is related to the writing skill, it was asked if the participants conducted any studies on writing. For that, only one participant reported that she practiced writing through extra tasks. The other participants expressed that they did not practice writing as they had negative thoughts about it. Some of the responses are as follows:

Çiçek: *"I practice writing. For portfolio, we write papers, but in addition, I do extra writing on a topic that I come up with. I show my extra studies to my teacher for feedback, and s/he corrects my paper. I write the second draft in the same way as in the portfolio process..."*

Bulut: *"Apart from portfolio assignments, I do not do any writing study, as it makes me afraid, yes, I am scared of writing, more specifically, making mistakes. I only use*

ChatGPT if I need to write anything, but if I cannot generate ideas in it, or when I have limited ideas to develop in that task. I use the ideas provided by ChatGPT. Once, I have tried it three times for the same assignment, and it has presented three different texts for the same topics. I have copied the ideas there and used them in my writing."

Doğa: *"I do not practice writing because I find it boring. It is difficult for me to reflect my ideas in writing both in Turkish and English, but I like it when I am with my teacher and classmates in the classroom. I feel as if we were in a competition in which the winner is the one who writes the best and in line with how the teacher has guided. It is fun, I think...."*

Güneş: *"I know I need to improve writing, but I do not practice enough or effectively. In fact, I like this skill, but it is getting worse as I am not practicing any more..."*

As the responses suggest, the participants are inclined to have negative thoughts about the writing skill due to its nature, which hinders their motivation to conduct studies and improve it. In reference to the response about the use of ChatGPT, it could be stated that it exemplifies a bad use of AI and digital technologies and justifies concerns about ethicality of them. As the participant referred to the use of ChatGPT in association with his views about writing, this finding is presented here. Yet, it is also an issue to be discussed about the related to other research questions.

The second sub-question targeted the participants' views about use of digital technologies for language studies. As also seen in the responses above, they use various digital tools for their language studies, which indicates their positive views about those digital tools. Except for one participant, the others expressed that they found them useful.

Toprak: *"I do not use any digital tools because I do not know which to use and how they could be helpful to me. I am not good with technology."*

Bulut: *"I use digital applications to practice English, and I sometimes use ChatGPT, but I am not competent in using it.....Most of the digital tools and applications are basic and very easy to use, but I think ChatGPT is a bit complex."*

Çiçek: *"I think digital tools are useful if you use them properly and consciously."*

Doğa: *"I think they are helpful to learn vocabulary. They are easy to use and access."*

As seen in the responses, ease of use and accessibility are important qualities of digital tools to be preferred by potential users. Furthermore, the responses put an emphasis on digital literacy to use tools effectively.

The third sub-question addressed the use of ChatGPT for receiving WCF for written products. For this purpose, individual sessions were held with the participants, and in addition to introducing ChatGPT, guidelines on how to use it to correct written products were presented. Before the sessions, the participants reported that they had not heard about or used ChatGPT. Only one participant knew it (as also shown in the responses above), but he stated that he did not know how to use it effectively. Thus, it was the first time they were introduced with a guided use of ChatGPT. After the session, the participants attempted to use the chatbot for the presented purpose and recorded their screen and studies. Finally, they commented on their use through stimulated-recall interviews. The examination of their recordings revealed several aspects in common which are demonstrated in Table 1 below:

Table 1. Aspects of ChatGPT use for WCF

The Users		ChatGPT	
Purpose in the requests	Error correction and explanations	Purpose in the responses	Error correction and/or explanations
Language of the requests	Turkish	Language of the responses	Turkish and English
Content of the requests	Short sentences only including instruction	Content of the responses	Long and complex sentences
Adequacy of the explanations in the requests	A need for clarification (of the chatbot)	Adequacy of the responses about corrections	A need for clarification (of the user)

As illustrated in Table 1, the participants' use of ChatGPT for receiving WCF centered around the same aspects. With regard to purpose of the responses, it emerged that the participants tended to write the instruction for error correction with explanations. For this purpose, they wrote the instruction in their own language in short sentences, but the chatbot did not understand it exactly, which required clarification. Thus, the participants typed alternative responses by either rewriting the same instruction or only the part that is misunderstood. Similarly, when the user did not get the responses of the chatbot, they asked for clarification. An example from the final study of a participant could be found below. As stated before, the original chat was in Turkish, so it was translated into English by the researcher(s).

Çiçek: Hello, assistant

ChatGPT: Hello, how can I help you?

Çiçek: Now, I am sending you a text in English. Can you explain my errors in it?

ChatGPT: Of course, I would love to. Send me your text and I will correct the mistakes and explain them.

Çiçek: (writes a formal letter for application for a job in English)

ChatGPT: (as the letter is in English, it makes all the corrections and explanations in English). Here are the corrections I made:

"I have worked at the university" is a more appropriate tense instead of "I have worked." Because the content suggests ongoing employment.......(continues) Overall, the content of your letter is clear, but I made some adjustments to improve grammar and phrasing.

Çiçek: Can you explain my mistakes in Turkish?

ChatGPT: Of course….. (even translates the letter in Turkish)

As seen in the dialog above, there are breakdowns in the conversation caused by the chatbot's misunderstanding. However, in this conversation and in the other recordings examined, it emerged that there were participants who found ways to solve these breakdowns by rephrasing or repeating the instructions. Furthermore, it emerged that this AI tool only made corrections without explaining why they were wrong. To conclude, when it is directed thoroughly, ChatGPT could make corrections on written products.

The last sub-question focused on the participants' reflection on the experience of using ChatGPT for getting WCF. To start with, one participant who had previously reported that he did not have experience in using digital tools stated that he could not use it at all as it was difficult for him to have a chat with the ChatGPT. The other participants highlighted positive and negative aspects dependent on their experience. The emerging themes and codes are as follows:

EFL Learners' Views About the Use of Artificial Intelligence

Table 2. Reflections about ChatGPT experience

Positive Aspects	Negative Aspects
Easily accessible	Problems in comprehension
More opportunities for feedback	Having difficulty in leading the conversation
An effective use through guiding	Lack of social aspects (a mechanic interaction)

As seen in Table 2, there were both positive and negative aspects suggested by the participants. Their responses were in line with the points that were observed related to their use in the recordings. As positive aspects, they stated that they could have more opportunities for feedback thanks to the chatbot, which was normally limited to class hours. Moreover, the participant having experience in using the tool reported that guidelines for how to use it for error correction was beneficial for him. Conversely, in addition to problems concerning ChatGPT's misunderstanding, they emphasized a need for human interaction. They mentioned that they could ask questions to their teachers, and contrary to misunderstanding of the tool, they had never had such problems with their teachers. Two of the related responses are as follows:

Bulut: *"I did not know it could be used elaborately for various purposes, especially for writing. Before, I would only use it to generate texts that I copy and paste for my assignments."*

Doğa: *"It was useful, but when it did not understand, I had to ask the question again. I realized that there were mistakes in its responses compared to the requests in my messages. We do not have this problem with our teachers."*

Overall, this qualitative research presents findings about the aspects of participants' ChatGPT use and their perceptions about it in line with background issues such as their study habits and views about digital tools. In this sense, having positive views about and experience in the use of digital tools in language learning could lead to an interest in trying a new tool. Additionally, despite pitfalls, ChatGPT provides opportunities for individualized language practices when used properly.

DISCUSSION

The findings of this qualitative research could be discussed in comparison with the existing research. First of all, that the participants had study habits based on their needs and learning styles, which could be associated with background factors of self-concepts; self-efficacy and self-regulated learning, learner autonomy and motivation. In this sense, that the participants were pre-intermediate level L2 learners could be an indicator for the fact that these concepts are not only related to higher level of language proficiency. Contrary to this, the concepts are interrelated; when a learner is motivated to learn a language, they set goals to study and organize their environments and resources, which are included in self-regulated learning and learner autonomy, and they could be conscious about their capabilities in this ongoing process (self-efficacy) no matter what proficiency level they have.

Secondly, the findings highlight significance of digital literacy, which could be augmented in the autonomy related concepts. Accordingly, it emerged that the participants were inclined to be autonomous L2 learners, and they used digital tools meeting their needs. Their search for what could work the best for them and using them effectively are associated with digital literacy. Similarly, one of the participants reported that he neither conducted any independent studies nor knew which tools to use and how to use them (this participant also had problems in using ChatGPT for the study), which supports the suggestion related to interconnection of the concepts.

Thirdly, the findings set forth that the participants used ChatGPT for error correction with explanations. They could also have used it for only error correction as they were presented the two types in the guiding session before the treatment, but they had preferred to use it for the latter purpose. This provides support for the discussion of L2 learners' preferences for WCF types (Chen et al., 2016; Saragih et al., 2021; Zhang et al., 2021). With this regard, in the literature, it has been found out that at lower levels of proficiency, the tendency is towards getting direct WCF, which was also possible using ChatGPT in the study. Furthermore, direct error correction and error correction with explanations could be included in typology of WCF (Ellis, 2009) as the two new types of AI-driven WCF. Nevertheless, it is necessary to note that ChatGPT corrects the errors and make explanations in the same way no matter what type of error it is (e.g., pragmatic errors). In addition to the type of WCF, the findings indicated positive and negative aspects related to how the chatbot operates. Thus, the examination of the recordings put forward that ChatGPT corrected the errors and explained why they were wrong to a certain extent, which relatively support the previous studies (Barrot, 2023; Özçelik & Gündüz, 2023; Yan, 2023). Yet, there were problems observed with ChatGPT's comprehension and content of the messages (long and complex explanations), which is in line with problem of ChatGPT's incorrect responses mentioned by Kartal (2023).

EFL Learners' Views About the Use of Artificial Intelligence

Lastly, the findings presented how the participants reflected on their experience in ChatGPT use for WCF. In addition to positive aspects reported by the participants and suggested in the related research abovementioned, there were other significant points to consider. The participants reported that they did not know an effective use of the tool before the guiding session. Accordingly, an instruction on how to use AI tools for the purpose or guiding sessions could be useful as not all learners would be autonomous and competent enough to learn how to use them effectively. Thus, it could contribute to deal with ethicality concerns reported with regard to generating texts by using ChatGPT for writing assignments (Kılıçkaya & Kic-Drgas, 2023; McKnight & Hicks, 2023). Besides, the participants reported a lack of human interaction as a negative aspect in relation to the use of the AI tool compared to their in-class experience for the same purpose, which was stated to impact L2 learning motivation negatively (Özçelik & Gündüz, 2023).

In sum, the research findings which were dependent on in-depth and long-term analyses of the participants' use of one of the AI-generated tools provide evidence for the discussion of positive and negative aspects concerning their use for language learning purposes and particularly for the writing skill.

CONCLUSION

This chapter has presented a qualitative study on EFL learners' use of AI tools for receiving corrective feedback on their written products. Even though ChatGPT was addressed in the study, the purpose of the chapter has been to demonstrate how AI tools are used or could be used in language learning. Focusing on the writing skill, the chapter, first, has presented an introduction into the concepts and research purpose. Then, the chapter has informed about artificial intelligence use in language learning, which is followed by the introduction of ChatGPT. Specific to the writing skill, an important aspect of it; written corrective feedback has been handled before the study is presented with its components. In reference to the significance of this research, it could be stated that despite being a small-scale study, it has provided detailed and notable findings which have emphasized issues and provided evidence for a recent research field. Based on the findings, the conclusion is that in the digital world, digital and AI tools take certain part in language education. Thus, teaching implication is to find and propose effective use of them. To this end, digital literacy is a major skill to be fostered among students. That could be possible through guiding students about ethical and proper use of digital technologies and (specific to the focus of this chapter) AI tools.

REFERENCES

Barrot, J. S. (2023). Using ChatGPT for second language writing: Pitfalls and potentials. *Assessing Writing, 57,* 100745. doi:10.1016/j.asw.2023.100745

Bitchener, J. (2008). Evidence in support of written corrective feedback. *Journal of Second Language Writing, 17*(2), 102–118. doi:10.1016/j.jslw.2007.11.004

Chen, S., Nassaji, H., & Liu, Q. (2016). EFL learners' perceptions and preferences of written corrective feedback: A case study of university students from Mainland China. *Asian-Pacific Journal of Second and Foreign Language Education, 1*(1), 5. doi:10.118640862-016-0010-y

Creswell, J. W. (2014). *Research design: Qualitative, quantitative and mixed methods approaches* (4th ed.). Sage.

Demirel, E. T., & Aksu, M. G. (2019). The application of technology to feedback in academic writing classes: The use of screencasting feedback and student attitudes. *Ufuk University Journal of Social Sciences Institute, 8*(16), 183–203. doi:10.4018/978-1-4666-9577-1.ch019

Deng, J., & Lin, Y. (2022). The benefits and challenges of ChatGPT: An overview. *Frontiers in Computing and Intelligent Systems, 2*(2), 81–83. doi:10.54097/fcis.v2i2.4465

Ellis, R. (2009). A typology of written corrective feedback types. *ELT Journal, 63*(2), 97–107. doi:10.1093/elt/ccn023

Ferris, D. R., Liu, H., Sinha, A., & Senna, M. (2013). Written corrective feedback for individual L2 writers. *Journal of Second Language Writing, 22*(3), 307–329. doi:10.1016/j.jslw.2012.09.009

Fryer, L. K., Coniam, D., Carpenter, R., & Lăpuşneanu, D. (2020). Bots for language learning now: Current and future directions. *Language Learning & Technology, 24*(2), 8–22. http://hdl.handle.net/10125/44719

Ghonsooly, B., & Shalchy, S. (2013). Cultural intelligence and writing ability: Delving into fluency, accuracy and complexity. [Research on Youth and Language]. *Novitas-ROYAL, 7*(2), 147–159.

Huang, X. (2021). Aims for cultivating students' key competencies based on artificial intelligence education in China. *Education and Information Technologies, 26*(5), 5127–5147. doi:10.100710639-021-10530-2

Kartal, G. (2023). Contemporary language teaching and learning with ChatGPT. *Contemporary Research in Language and Linguistics*, *1*(1), 59–70.

Kılıçkaya, F., & Kic-Drgas, J. (2023). Misuse of AI (Artificial Intelligence) in assignments: Can AI-written content be detected? In R. E. Ferdig, R. Hartshorne, E. Baumgartner, R. Kaplan-Rakowski, & C. Mouza (Ed.), What PreK-12 teachers should know about educational technology in 2023: A research-to-practice anthology, (pp. 145-152). AACE2023.

Kim, M. K., Kim, N. J., & Heidari, A. (2022). Learner experience in artificial intelligence-scaffolded argumentation. *Assessment & Evaluation in Higher Education*, *47*(8), 1301–1316. doi:10.1080/02602938.2022.2042792

Kohnke, L., Moorhouse, B. L., & Zou, D. (2023). ChatGPT for language teaching and learning. *RELC Journal*, 1–14. doi:10.1177/00336882231162

Kushmar, L. V., Vornachev, A. O., Korobova, I. O., & Kaida, N. O. (2022). Artificial intelligence in language learning: What are we afraid of. *Arab World English Journal (AWEJ)*, (8), 262–273. doi:10.24093/awej/call8.18

Lancaster, T. (2023). Artificial intelligence, text generation tools and ChatGPT – does digital watermarking offer a solution? *International Journal for Educational Integrity*, *19*(10), 10. Advance online publication. doi:10.100740979-023-00131-6

McKnight, L., & Hicks, T. (2023). Generative AI writing tools: How they work, what they do, and why they matter. In R. E. Ferdig, R. Hartshorne, E. Baumgartner, R. Kaplan-Rakowski, & C. Mouza (Eds.), What PreK-12 teachers should know about educational technology in 2023: A research-to-practice anthology, (pp. 117-121). AACE2023.

Mitchell, K. M., McMillan, D. E., & Rabbani, R. (2019). An exploration of writing self-efficacy and writing self-regulatory behaviours in undergraduate writing. *The Canadian Journal for the Scholarship of Teaching and Learning*, *10*(2), 1–25. doi:10.5206/cjsotl-rcacea.2019.2.8175

Özçelik, A. E., & Gündüz, Z. E. (2023). Embracing ChatGPT in foreign language writing classes: Potentials and challenges. In R. E. Ferdig, R. Hartshorne, E. Baumgartner, R. Kaplan-Rakowski, & C. Mouza (Eds.), What PreK-12 teachers should know about educational technology in 2023: A research-to-practice anthology (pp. 133-143). AACE2023.

Roll, I., & Wylie, R. (2016). Evolution and revolution in artificial intelligence in education. *International Journal of Artificial Intelligence in Education*, *26*(2), 582–599. doi:10.100740593-016-0110-3

Saragih, N. A., Madya, S., Siregar, R. A., & Saragih, W. (2021). Written corrective feedback: Students' perception and preferences. *International Online Journal of Education & Teaching*, *8*(2), 676–690.

Shintani, N., Ellis, R., & Suzuki, W. (2014). Effects of written feedback and revision on learners' accuracy in using two english grammatical structures. *Language Learning*, *64*(1), 103–131. doi:10.1111/lang.12029

Tlili, A., Shehata, B., Adarkwah, M. A., Bozkurt, A., Hickey, D. T., Huang, R., & Agyemang, B. (2023). What if the devil is my guardian angel: ChatGPT as a case study of using chatbots in education. *Smart Learning. Environments*, *10*(1), 15. doi:10.118640561-023-00237-x

WarschauerM.TsengW.YimS.WebsterT.JacobS.DuQ.TateT. (2023). *The affordances and contradictions of AI-generated text for second language writers*. doi:10.2139/ssrn.4404380

YanD. (2023). *How ChatGPT' s automatic text generation impact on learners in a L2 writing practicum: an exploratory investigation*. https://doi.org/ doi:10.35542/osf.io/s4nfz

Zhang, T., Chen, X., Hu, J., & Ketwan, P. (2021). EFL students' preferences for written corrective feedback: Do error types, language proficiency, and foreign language enjoyment matter? *Frontiers in Psychology*, *12*, 660564. doi:10.3389/fpsyg.2021.660564 PMID:33897570

ADDITIONAL READING

Dörnyei, Z. (2005). *The psychology of the language learner*. Lawrence Erlbaum Associates.

Ellis, R. (2009). A typology of written corrective feedback types. *ELT Journal*, *63*(2), 97–107. doi:10.1093/elt/ccn023

Mitchell, K. M., McMillan, D. E., & Rabbani, R. (2019). An exploration of writing self-efficacy and writing self-regulatory behaviours in undergraduate writing. *The Canadian Journal for the Scholarship of Teaching and Learning*, *10*(2), 1–25. doi:10.5206/cjsotl-rcacea.2019.2.8175

Schunk, D. H., & Zimmerman, B. J. (Eds.). (2012). *Motivation and self-regulated learning: Theory, research, and applications*. Routledge. doi:10.4324/9780203831076

Sharadgah, T. A., & Sa'di, R. A. (2022). A systematic review of research on the use of artificial intelligence in English language teaching and learning (2015-2021): What are the current effects? *Journal of Information Technology Education, 21,* 337–377. doi:10.28945/4999

KEY TERMS AND DEFINITIONS

Artificial Intelligence (AI): It is a type of computerized intelligence which enables to complete human related tasks.

ChatGPT: It is a chatbot developed by OpenAl that conducts human-like chats using AI.

Corrective Feedback: It is a signal indicating errors in spoken or written language products.

Digital Literacy: It is an ability to use digital and smart tools effectively to find and analyze knowledge.

Learner Autonomy: It is an ability for a learner to conduct self-studies in accordance with an awareness of learning needs and styles.

Self-Efficacy: It is an individual's belief in their capabilities to complete a specific task.

Self-Regulated Learning: It is a process in which a learner organizes resources and environments by managing cognitive and psychological skills.

Written Corrective Feedback: It is a type of error correction on the language learners' written products in the form of written comments.

Chapter 7
How Does Gamified L2 Learning Enhance Motivation and Engagement:
A Literature Review

Mourad Majdoub
ⓘ https://orcid.org/0000-0003-0338-9296
Université Laval, Canada

Géraldine Heilporn
ⓘ https://orcid.org/0000-0002-7951-4420
Université Laval, Canada

ABSTRACT

In recent years, the popularity of gamification has gained momentum with the growing numbers of publications as well as the mass appeal among learners for its potential to stimulate motivation, engagement, and positive experiences. However, this vein of research has mainly focused on the effects of game mechanics and how they can be incorporated within a gamified learning context to enhance users' positive experiences. In L2 teaching and learning, the literature states that most studies on gamification lack theoretical principles that can guide the design of gamified learning experiences that promote learners' motivation and engagement. To make the picture more coherent, this chapter synthesizes the existing literature on gamification L2 learning, focusing on empirical findings related to factors affecting L2 learning, current L2 gamified design models, gamification affordances, and their inherent motivational and engagement outcomes. For this review, thematic and content analysis of 73 publications dating from 2017 to late 2022 were examined.

DOI: 10.4018/979-8-3693-0353-5.ch007

Copyright © 2024, IGI Global. Copying or distributing in print or electronic forms without written permission of IGI Global is prohibited.

INTRODUCTION

A large body of extensive research into technology-based learning environments revealed that digital textbooks, multimedia, the internet, and several other forms of learning materials enhance learners' knowledge and language proficiency (Alobaid, 2021; Putri & Sari, 2020; Sari, 2020). However, the teaching of English in non-English-speaking environments (e.g. Quebec) does not escape several difficulties such as the lack of authentic contexts to practise it and the lack of motivation and engagement on the part of learners (Moghari & Marandi, 2017). This can hamper the learning process and lead to lower performance (Kruk, 2021). In this regard, the use of game-based language learning has increased significantly in recent years and has received considerable attention from educators and researchers for their potential to enhance the language learning experience. Over the past decades, several research studies have indicated that game play has positively influenced a range of factors involved in the language learning process, mainly motivation, willingness to communicate and language socialization (Reinders, 2017).

There are more and more teachers who, in search of resources to enhance the engagement of their students, introduce several elements of games into their teaching using technological supports (Goethe, 2019; Siemon & Eckardt, 2017). In this perspective, gamification is seen as an enjoyable and effective teaching methodology, the main objective of which is to provide a language learning experience that generates student engagement and interest (Nahmod, 2017; Tulloch, 2014). While several studies have revealed that gameful L2 environments can provide a sheltered, low anxiety space and opportunities for higher willingness to communicate (Reinders, 2017), there has been too little experimental work on how to design gamified teaching methods that address key issues in second/foreign language learning and how gamification can support a positive L2 learning experience. Besides, the recent scientific literature suggests that the gamified environments for learning English as a second language could enhance learners' motivation and engagement (Azzouz Boudadi & Gutiérrez-Colón, 2020; Dehghanzadeh et al., 2021; Pujolà & Appel, 2020). Nevertheless, gamifying learning through game elements can enhance or undermine motivation and engagement, depending on how they are used. In fact, more research on how gamification can address learners' motivational processes will inform future implementation and enrich design approaches to education and training. Further, more than 50 gamification design frameworks have been proposed, but it is still early to argue that the current design taxonomies and models provide clear guidelines on how to select and group gamification elements for an effective use (Azouz & Lefdaoui, 2018; Dichev & Dicheva 2017; Toda et al., 2019).

Using gamification in second/foreign language learning has been the focus of several recent literature reviews (Azzouz Boudadi & Gutiérrez-Colón, 2020;

Dehghanzadeh et al., 2021; Govender & Arnedo-Moreno, 2021; Ishaq et al., 2021; Pinto et al., 2021; Shortt et al., 2021; Yürük, 2019). However, while the growth of these publications has enriched the corpus of literature on the use of gamification, there is still a lack of a synthesized and comprehensive overview of the design principles through which gamification can enhance learners' motivation and engagement as well as the theoretical foundations that can inform the development of an engaging L2 learning content. Hence, the present review aims to synthesise state-of-the-art literature on gamification L2 learning, touching on how factors affecting L2 learning are addressed, current L2 gamified design models, gamification affordances and their inherent motivational and engagement outcomes.

LITERATURE REVIEW

Challenges in LESL

Language Anxiety

Several factors have been suggested as responsible for the difficulties usually encountered by L2 learners. Recent research has been more interested in the influence of personality traits, particularly anxiety. The meta-analysis of 67 studies by Botes et al. (2020) examined the link between foreign language classroom anxiety (FLCA) and general academic achievement as well as four competencies: reading, writing, listening and speaking. The results confirmed the negative relationship between FLCA and academic achievement in L2 classes. Among other studies exploring the relationship between L2 learning and language anxiety, the research by Šafranj and Zivlak (2019) can be mentioned. The study was carried out among 296 Serbian engineering students learning English for Specific Purposes (ESP) as a one-semester subject. Three questionnaires were administered to them: *International Personality Item Pool, Foreign Language Classroom Anxiety Scale and Fear of Negative Evaluation Scale*. The study results revealed that learners who worry more about their language performance (low in emotional stability) are likely to experience more negative emotional reactions and therefore expect negative outcomes. Similarly, the link between L2 anxiety and second language acquisition was the focus of the study of Teimouri et al. (2019). Their meta-analysis examined the relationship between anxiety and L2 achievement. The 97 analyzed studies revealed that anxiety, overall, is negatively associated with L2 achievement. The authors argue that anxiety affects, although in varying degrees, individual differences that have been explored in research literature, mainly aptitude, motivation and working memory.

Self-Confidence and Learner Scaffolding

Several other aspects of L2 learners have been highlighted in recent research as having close links with L2 achievement, including self-confidence and learner scaffolding. For instance, Bai and Wang (2020) noted that L2 learners who effectively monitor and invest efforts to regulate their learning are more likely to achieve high results. They added that self-efficacy is positively associated with second language learning strategies, namely monitoring, effort regulation, and goal setting and planning. Sun and Wang (2020), in a study on Chinese college students, tried to examine how self-efficacy and self-regulated writing strategies are related to L2 writing proficiency. Their study confirmed results from previous studies that writing self-efficacy was positively associated with writing proficiency. Participants who used note reviewing and revising as well as seeking more opportunities to practise tended to have higher writing achievements. Moreover, scaffolding students' learning has been found to be necessary and useful for effective L2 learning (Wilson, 2017). The aim of the study of Shalizar and Rezaei (2022) was to examine the benefits of applying the Zone of Proximal Development (ZPD) and explicit feedback on the L2 writing of four ESL adult learners living in Canada. The qualitative analysis showed that scaffolding learners with feedback increases their cognitive engagement through reflecting on their errors, testing their hypothesis and noticing errors and gaps in their learning by assuming responsibility and control over their learning process. In the same vein, Li and Zhang (2021) added that teacher scaffolding in L2 writing "enhances learners' understanding of L2 knowledge, raises their awareness in the writing processes and impacts their future writing practices" (p. 344). The importance of employing strategies to stimulate a learner's emotional response to L2 learning, referred to as 'emotional scaffolding', has also been the object of several studies. Alavi and Esmaeilifard (2021) aimed at examining the effect of emotional scaffolding on language achievement and willingness to communicate of EFL university students from Iran. The study findings argued that providing learners with corrective feedback indirectly using a positive and inclusive approach not only decreases their negative emotions, such anxiety, but also boosts their communicative willingness and their performance in speaking.

Motivation

Motivation has long been considered as the key variable to succeed in L2 learning. Learners without some basic level of motivation are not likely to engage in the learning process (VanPatten et al., 2020). Several theories have been formed to examine the main differences between motivated and unmotivated learners. For instance, over 300 relevant studies on Self-Determination Theory (SDT) and language learning motivation have been published since 1990, half of them within the last eight years (Noels et al., 2019). According to SDT, optimal functioning and learning depend on the satisfaction of three psychological needs: competence (belief that one's efforts will make a difference to his/her learning), autonomy (sense of being able to influence one's own learning experience) and relatedness (feeling connected to and valued by others) (Ryan & Deci, 2017). Several scholars aimed to examine the links between factors related to language learning and language learners' basic psychological needs. The results of these studies indicated that learners' autonomy, competence and sense of relatedness are related to factors such as choice (Parrish & Lanyers, 2018), advising (Shelton-Strong, 2022), well designed digital support strategies that provide various resources for learning and allow choices in digital format and sharing tools (Chiu, 2021), autonomous engagement with digital tools (Dincer, 2020), positive feelings (Liu, 2022; Shelton-Strong, 2022), technology-mediated learning environment (Alamer & Al Khateeb, 2021; Han, 2022) and relevance to a future job (Hsu, 2018).Dörnyei's (2005) L2 Motivational Self System Theory (L2MSS), on the other hand, suggests that students' learning motivation is affected by three main constructs: the ideal L2 self (to what extent they imagine themselves as highly proficient users of the target language), the ought-to L2 self (what they are aware of as external pressures throughout the learning process) and the L2 learning experience (attitudes towards the learning process) (Dörnyei, 2005). Following the elaboration of the theory, several studies have been conducted to examine its core concepts, namely the influence factors of L2MSS, which have been categorized as internal: self regulation (Zheng et al., 2018), self-efficacy (Roshandel et al., 2018), positive or negative emotions (Khany & Amiri, 2018), etc. or external: English learning experiences (Li & Liu, 2021), supportive use of technology (Lee & Lee, 2021), supportive classroom environment (Kong et al., 2018) and so on.

Despite the fact that SDT, L2MSS and other L2 motivational theories have received exceptional interest among researchers in the field, an important shift from L2 learning to L2 use has been perceived in the field, focusing more on the potential of using technology to contribute to the development of learners' intrinsic motivation (Peterson et al., 2022). In this context, game-based learning, serious games and gamification have been the subject of an impressive body of research because of their potential to enhance learners' language experience. With their open worlds, attractive designs and multiplayer features, they provide opportunities for learners to satisfy their basic psychological needs (Alamer, 2022) and their L2 motivational self-system (Aydın & Çakır, 2022).

Advantages of Gamification in L2 Learning

Definition of Gamification

The term 'Gamification' has been described in many ways. The definitions that have been largely used in the literature are: "the use of game design elements in non-game contexts" (Deterding et al., 2011, p. 10), "mechanics, dynamics, and frameworks to promote desired behaviors" (Lee & Hammer, 2011, p. 1) and "a process of enhancing a service with affordances for gameful experiences to support user's overall value creation" (Huotari & Hamari, 2012, p. 19). In this sense, using gamification in learning increases students' motivation, engagement, and performance thanks to various mechanisms, e.g., avatars, quests and challenges, badges, points, leaderboards (Popescu et al., 2022). As recent studies on foreign languages show, gamified environments could be the most enjoyable and engaging teaching method (Dehghanzadeh et al., 2021) because it generates educative dedication, commitment, responsibility, and self-learning (La Cruz et al., 2021) and reduces language anxiety (Pitoyo & Asib, 2019; Salemink et al., 2022).

Gamification and Gamified L2 Learning

Gamified learning has been reported to enhance content language learning. A study by Aditya et al. (2020) aimed to investigate the effect of gamification on the listening comprehension of 95 5th grade students. The descriptive analysis revealed that the use of audiovisual media embedded in the gamified local story encouraged the participants to listen and understand, which helped them to achieve better results. Similarly, the effect of *Snapticon*, a gamified activity, on students' speaking and listening skills was the aim of the study of Ngah et al. (2022). From the qualitative questionnaire that was administered to 25 undergraduate students from 6 different engineering faculties, the findings showed that the participants considered the application as fun, engaging and interesting because it was designed to improve their oral and listening skills. It helped them think outside the box and that it made them more confident and less anxious in their learning. Aside from a focus on listening comprehension, the impact of gamification on speaking and reading skills was also scrutinized. For instance, Hernández Prados et al. (2021) implemented and evaluated a gamified activity called *The Tik Tok School* that aimed at enhancing students' skills in economic management, entrepreneurship, communication processes, negotiation and decision-making. The use of a descriptive analysis revealed that gamification positively affects motivation and L2 learning. The authors claim that the skill the participants improved the most was speaking as they were constantly using more English than Spanish. Additional support for this claim comes from Reitz et al.

(2019) who examined the impact of a VR-based gamified platform on students' communication using EFL. With a design that uses information gaps to solve creative tasks, the gamified app enhanced students' authentic language usage. The authors observed that their framework helped the participants to step out of their comfort zone as they could express themselves and share their information using the target language. There is also evidence that the use of gamified strategies can be motivational in relation to fostering reading comprehension. With 85 students from four primary school classrooms in Spain, Prados et al. (2021) carried out a quantitative study to analyze the impact of gamification on students' reading comprehension. The study findings confirmed the potential of gamification in promoting reading skills thanks to the game mechanics integrated into the platform, mainly points, badges and leaderboards. In the same vein, Kaban (2021) investigated the perceptions and attitudes of Turkish high school EFL learners towards gamified electronic book reading. The mixed-method study findings highlighted the fact that all the participants improved their reading skills. It was argued that gamified reading helped them to accomplish their tasks easily. Writing skills and gamification have also been the focus of several research studies. Zhihao and Zhonggen (2022) evaluated the effect of gamification on L2 writing. The study participants used the *Chaoxing Xuexitong* platform to write their essays. The results revealed that gamification could improve learners' English writing skills thanks to its elements, such as points, badges and leaderboards. The same findings were confirmed by Mazhar (2019) who argued that gamified writing activities ensure learners' participation and allow them to have fun, which contributes to the development of their writing skills.

Gamification and Gamified L2 Motivation and Engagement

Current research interest in gamified L2 learning has been broadened to include the strategies gamification can offer to enhance students' motivation and engagement. Huang et al. (2019) suggest that gamified strategies positively affect students' behavioral engagement, including stimulating learners to complete more activities on time and being perseverant in their participation. Additionally, Zainuddin et al. (2020) found that the gamified experimentation kept the participants engaged and involved in their learning (e.g. paid more attention, listened intently, asked questions and interacted with their teachers and peers). In a similar study, Ding et al. (2018) concluded that gamification helps students monitor and control the progress of their academic achievements, which allows them to develop critical learning and multi-tasking skills. At the same time, Ding et al. (2018) reported that gamification improves cognitive engagement. Their study found that participants seemed to spend more time and effort writing their texts because of the desire to get badges, stay at the top of the class average, maintain their rank and receive positive feedback from their peers. The study also found that learners showed self-regulated learning in online discussions through two game mechanics, the progress bar and the ranking. Data on socio-emotional engagement have been reported by several studies, particularly by Schwartz and Plass (2020) who stated that many playful design features that include rewards, game characters, storytelling, sound, and musical score foster attitudes and beliefs that evoke emotional engagement. Zainuddin et al. (2020) also reported that participants in their study perceived the gamified formative questionnaires as fun, motivating and emotionally engaging, as they experienced feelings of pleasure, joy, interest, enthusiasm and curiosity.

A series of reviews focusing mainly on gamified L2 learning was conducted lately. The systematic review by Dehghanzadeh et al. (2021) revealed that the learners' experiences were positive when dealing with gamification, but they admitted that their study was missing common affordances and hindrances that are inherent to gamified LESL. Similarly, Boudadi and Gutiérrez-Colón (2020) conducted a literature review focusing on second language acquisition in higher education and computer-assisted language learning. They mentioned in their analysis that the use of gamification in L2 learning is a predominantly positive experience. However, they call for caution as most of the reviewed papers involve several limitations. As for Dehganzadeh and Dehganzadeh (2020), their review confirmed that using gamification helps learners enhance their personalized learning, motivation and engagement, peer and teacher interaction, positive attitude and overall L2 learning performance. They admitted the lack of clear trend regarding the types of game elements that might be appropriate for each language skill. Pinto et al. (2021) examined in their systematic review the effect of gamification on second/foreign language learning using virtual reality (VR). They argued that even though most of the reviewed studies revealed positive outcomes when using gamified VR, it is hard to affirm that this learning method is better than traditional learning approaches.

The majority of these reviews are descriptive in nature. In particular, the link between gamification affordances or features and second/foreign language theories and principles are not well established. It is not clear, for instance, how gamification can enhance the factors that are involved in teaching and learning second/foreign language skills (speaking, writing, listening, etc.). In the field of second/foreign language acquisition in particular, motivation is considered as one of the most powerful affective variables responsible for the success or failure in learning, but the recent broad claims on the effects of gamification on L2 motivation can gloss over a detailed knowledge of exactly how gamified learning could sustain learners' interest. Our literature review will address these gaps.

Current Gamified Approaches in L2 Learning

Game Elements

Several game elements are used to gamify education: points, levels/stages, badges, leaderboards, rewards, narratives, and feedback (Nah et al., 2014). According to Dicheva et al. (2015), points, badges and leaderboards are the most popular game mechanics that emerged in their systematic analysis of the use of gamification in education. Similarly, Lister (2015) reported that the most commonly implemented elements of gamification are points, badges, achievements, leaderboards, and levels. However, instead of focusing on single game elements and their impact on users' motivation and engagement, there has been a need for a systematic approach that holistically accounts for the characteristics of the gamification components and how they can be mobilized within a process for a specific purpose. Hunicke et al. (2004) and Zichermann and Cunningham (2011) suggested the MDA framework, composed of mechanics, dynamic and aesthetic elements. Werbach and Hunter (2012) proposed the DMC model (dynamics, mechanics and components). Both frameworks have been limited to identifying and characterizing game design elements without reference to the context. Other models, such as the 6Ds framework (Werbach & Hunter, 2012), have been proposed without empirical evidence on how to combine these elements properly (Toda et al., 2019).

Gamified Design Models

Several other gamified design models have emerged, and recent literature reviews have documented more than 50 frameworks used in various contexts (Toda et al., 2019). A few of them have focused on education and learning. Huang and Soman (2013) suggested a five-step process gamified model to achieve various learning objectives: understanding the audience and the surrounding context, specifying learning objectives, structuring the experience, identifying resources, and implementing gamification elements. The Reference Model for Applying Gamification in Education proposed by Simões et al. (2013) implies a process with phases for characterizing the context, identifying the instructional objectives, selecting game design elements, analyzing data and inserting content into the target activities. Similarly, Andrade et al. (2016) developed The Framework for Intelligent Gamification to guide the use of structural gamification based on 4 steps: information gathering, operation, assessment and adaptation. Nicholson (2015) developed a theoretical framework for meaningful gamification to help users find personal connections that engage them in a specific context using a set of guidelines: a) focus on game-based elements, b) create transformative opportunities through participatory activities, and c) create a playful learning space where users can explore, engage and set their own rules and goals. Nevertheless, these frameworks have been developed with a one-size-fits-all approach assuming that their application can be generalizable to other learning contexts without empirical evidence.

Developing language learning environments that engage learners requires a holistic design approach that emphasizes how content and language are selected and organized according to learners' needs and interests (Aldemir et al., 2019). Since it is an emerging practice, there are very few examples of game-based L2 learning approaches to be found in the literature, let alone gamified models. Therefore, there is still a need for gamification strategies based on theoretical foundations that can guide the process of learning by following a systematic approach that recognizes the complex and dynamic nature of L2 learning. The present review aims to synthesise state-of-the-art literature on gamified L2 learning, particularly how factors affecting L2 learning are addressed, current L2 gamified design models, gamification affordances and their inherent motivational and engagement outcomes. These will be addressed in this study by answering the following four questions:

1. How does gamification address key issues in second/foreign language learning (willingness to communicate, language anxiety, motivation and engagement)?
2. How are elements of gamification mobilized in the design of second/foreign language learning experiences and in enhancing these experiences?
3. What affordances does gamification offer to support a positive learning experience in L2 learning?
4. How intrinsic and extrinsic motivations as well as learners' engagement are approached in gamified design?

Method

Research Design

This paper used a narrative review method to examine the gamified approach in learning second/foreign languages. This method is a particularly useful means of surveying the state of knowledge in a specific topic, thus helping researchers to identify new research avenues (Paré & Kitsiou, 2017). It critically examines theories and interprets data to offer a comprehensive understanding of a particular topic (Efron & Ravid, 2019). Therefore, the choice of this approach was based on its potential to examine studies and investigate methods used in current research to provide a broad overview of the current research and applications of gamification concept carried out in the specific area of foreign language learning (Onwuegbuzie, 2016).

Searched Databases

The review included electronic databases relevant to the field of educational technology and learning and accessible by our university: EBSCOhost, ScienceDirect, SpringerLink, ERIC, Web of Science, Wiley Online Library, Google Scholar and Tyler & Francis Online.

Search Terms

Our search for literature used two sets of search terms in both English and French. The first set included terms for gamification, such as "gamification", "gamify", "gamified", "gameful", "gamifying", *"ludification"*, *"ludifier"*, *"ludifié"*, *"ludifiée"*. The other set consisted of terms related to second/foreign language learning: "second language learning", "SLA", "English as a second language", "ESL", "English as a foreign language", "EFL", "second language acquisition", "SLA", "foreign language acquisition", "FLA", "L2", *"apprentissage des langues seconde"*, *"anglais comme langue seconde"*, *"anglais comme langue étrangère"*. The Boolean operators (AND, OR) were applied to acquire the broadest scope of qualified papers.

The Inclusion and Exclusion Criteria

To ensure a rigorous process of data selection, the studies included in the review had to meet the following criteria:

1. Empirical research papers (qualitative, quantitative and mixed methods) that address the main topic of the project: learning English as a second/foreign language using gamification. Book chapters, conference proceedings, books or reviews were excluded;
2. Explicitly explore the gamification concept and gamified learning. Studies that discussed games, game-based learning, educational games, etc. were excluded.
3. Publication date not older than 5 years (from 2017 to 2022);
4. Be written in English or French;
5. Specify a level of education (primary, middle, high school or higher education).

After applying these five criteria, removing duplicate papers and scanning each article's title and abstract, 180 papers were identified as relevant to the current review: 8 articles were found in the SpringerLink database, 61 from Google Scholar, 50 from EBSCOhost, 8 from Wiley Online Library, 15 from ERIC and 38 from Web of Science. These papers were downloaded for further analysis. The detailed selection process is provided in Figure 1.

Figure 1. Paper selection process used in the present review

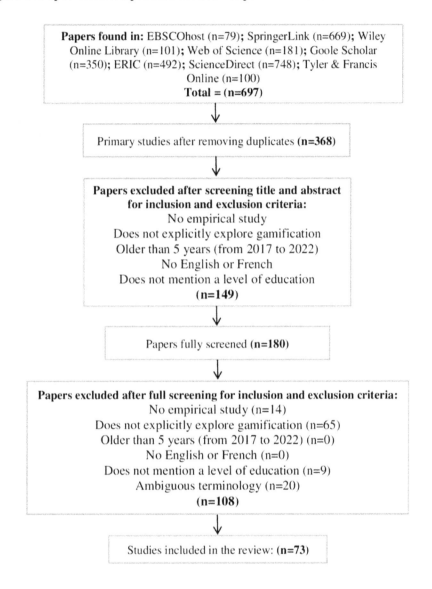

Data Analysis

The research team screened the full texts of the identified studies. Content, focus and insights of each paper were examined before deciding on its eligibility. The 73 papers judged relevant were analysed descriptively using charts and tables. The information extracted and analyzed from each paper included the purpose of the study, a synopsis of the content, context, participants, research methodology, key results, interpretation of the results, limitations and the impact of the conclusions in the field.

Data were synthesized using content and thematic analysis according to our research questions. A meticulous examination of the extracted information allowed us to identify themes and subthemes. Then, an iterative process was conducted where individual sources were analysed and clustered together to discern relationships among the patterns, variables and themes. The next step consisted of engaging in a process of comparing and contrasting groups of data. This practice enabled us to identify similarities and differences among the selected papers, such as theoretical foundations, design principles, findings and conclusions. As the analysis progressed, evidence related to each research question was carefully selected and evaluated. Regular meetings with the research team where interpretations were shared helped us refine the review findings.

Findings and Discussion

Before addressing the research questions, Table 1 presents a summary of the publications included in the analysis of this study. It includes information on authors, year of publication, purpose of the study, educational level, and data collection method.

RQ1: *How does gamification address key issues in second/foreign language learning?*

Recent research points to a potential link between gamification and lower levels of learners' anxiety. According to Lyu (2019), gamified AR (Augmented Reality) helps students overcome their language anxiety and enhance their self-confidence. It seems clear from the study's conclusions that the use of gamification creates a 'casual' environment in which learners are no longer obsessed with the fear of making mistakes. Thékes and Szilvássy (2021) who explored the impact of a gamified language learning application on students' self-regulated motivation and learning reported similar findings. Based on the participants' qualitative data, the authors point out that the application reduces stress and language anxiety. Of particular interest is their insight into the important role technology can play in helping students to have control over their emotions to enhance language learning. However, the results of both studies should be treated with considerable caution. While Thékes and Szilvássy (2021) mention that *Xeropan* is a gamified app, the study fails to explain the gamification principles adopted in its design. A number of specific game elements have been stated in their paper, such as levels, an avatar (*the Professor Max*) and narratives, but the selection and the evaluation of these elements lack empirical insight. Similarly, Lyu (2019) clearly uses gamification and games interchangeably when he states that the prototype used in his study "is a game, in which three players are locked in different rooms, not in the same room' and that 'according to the participants, the difficulty level of the puzzles in the game was acceptable" (p. 8). The reasoning here is problematic because the research conclusions are significant in the context of games, assuming that they would be generalizable to gamification. The findings presented in the two studies provide evidence on how game-based learning creates a low-anxiety learning environment, but call for further investigation to address the lack of consistency in what gamification and games clearly mean is necessary.

A number of other studies have explored how gamification explicitly addresses the relationship between language anxiety and personality dimensions. As stated by Zhang and Chen (2021), foreign language anxiety, particularly nervousness and fear of making mistakes while speaking, may be linked to learners' introverted personality or their lack of preparation. Based on their conclusions, teachers could help students to prepare for in-class learning through implementing gamification out of class in the form of flipped or blended classes. For introverted participants, gamified learning was not effective enough to lower their anxiety and motivate them to participate in the class activities. However, other scholars adhere to the view that certain gamified platforms, such as *Kahoot*, allow users to join them without registration, which sustains the anonymity of introverted learners who might be reluctant to dynamically participate in classroom tasks (Almusharraf, 2021). Govender and Arnedo-Moreno (2021) who have reviewed the current literature to better understand the game elements used in digital game-based language learning make a similar point. Although their review was not limited to gamification but covered games and serious games as well, their conclusions suggest that gamified elements, such as avatars, allow users a certain degree of anonymity. With their identities masked, language learners could chat in the target language with much confidence. This effect is thought to be due to manipulating the parameters of implementation; for instance, playing off-line or anonymously, and the game design that often appeals to different personality types and play styles, which provides a form of shelter that protects and encourages L2 learners to take risks (Reinhardt, 2018). Contrary to current literature, these findings suggest that the causal relationship between personality traits and language anxiety is still inconclusive. Although Dewaele (2017) and Ellis (2015) have mentioned that anxiety can be seen as a personality variable, they have admitted that language anxiety is a complex construct with different facets, and generalizing such findings requires further explanation. Burns and Richards (2018) also noted that situation-specific anxieties, such as second/foreign language learning, do not generally stem from a personality trait. According to the same authors, anxious language learners reported several reasons for their anxiety, mainly speaking in front of their peers and negative perceptions of their intellectual ability, of their language competence as well as of their colleagues' "superior" language ability.

How Does Gamified L2 Learning Enhance Motivation

Table 1. A summary of the publications included in the analysis of this study

Author and Year of Publication	Purpose of the Study	Educational Level	Data Collection Method
Lyu (2019)	Help Japanese second language students to overcome the barrier of speaking English by designing a game-based language learning tool that incorporates elements of Augmented Reality (AR) technology	University	Questionnaire and focus group
Thékes and Szilvássy (2021)	The impact of a pedagogical intervention is presented grounded on Xeropan, a gamified language learning application	University	Questionnaire and interview
Zhang and Chen (2021)	Investigated students' perceptions of gamification and their FLA in the preliminary stage of a gamified College English Listening and Speaking (ELS) class	College	Interviews
Almusharraf (2021)	Explored students' perception of Kahoot	University	Observation and a survey
Govender and Arnedo-Moreno (2021)	Examines and categorizes observations about game elements used in published papers		Rieview of the literature
Park et al. (2020)	Create a more efficient online, or E-learning, environment that will promote participation and enhance the learning speed of foreign languages	N/A	Test
Rueckert et al. (2020)	Measured the extent to which a gamified English as a foreign language classroom adhered to 21 principles of good education proposed by Mind, Brain, and Education	University	Questionnaire, learners' reflections and teachers' journals
Vallejo (2018)	Examines the effects of a one-semester gamified didactic experience aimed at facilitating vocabulary acquisition.	Adult education	Questionnaires and interviews
Kohnke (2020)	Investigated students' perceptions of a vocabulary learning app developed by the researcher as a tool to help them to improve their L2 receptive vocabulary	University	Interview
Yürük (2019)	Demonstrate Kahoot can be used as a Review Activity in foreign language classrooms and to gather information on students' perceptions about this application included in educational process	University	Questionnaire
Dehganzadeh and Dehganzadeh (2020)	Investigate and synthesize the trends and key findings of the studies related to gamification as a new method in the field of learning a Foreign language		Systematic review

Table 1. Continued

Author and Year of Publication	Purpose of the Study	Educational Level	Data Collection Method
Mitchell and Shachter (2021)	The effects of web-based, gamified vocabulary instruction on assessment scores and student motivation are examined	University	Tests and questionnaires
Zou (2020)	Conducted a 1-year project on gamified flipped English as a foreign language classroom	Elementary	Observations, interviews and self-reflections
Weissheimer et al. (2019)	Investigated a gamified vocabulary teaching and learning intervention	University	Observation and focus group
Bagunaid et al. (2019)	Integrates OSSM approach and gamification concepts in order to provide self-assessment for English language learners	University	Test and a survey
Homer at al. (2018)	Reports the findings of a field experiment that gamified the classroom experience of elementary school ESL students by implementing digital badges-and-points	Elementary	Tests, observations and Teacher reflection
Kohnke and Ting (2021)	Presents a gamified, discipline-specific vocabulary learning app Books vs Brains@PolyU	University	Focus group
Arce and Valdivia (2020)	A digital resource for foreign language learning was developed taking into account competitiveness and gamification	University	Tests and questionnaire
Dehghanzadeh et al. (2019)	Presents an overview of the state of the art on the use of gamification for LESL in digital environments		Systematic review
Dindar et al. (2021)	Compared how gamified cooperation and competition impact task effort, learning achievement, motivation and social relatedness in English vocabulary learning with a mobile application	University	Test and a questionnaire
Hong et al. (2020)	The effects of students posing and gamifying questions in relation to second language grammar learning are explored	Middle school	Test and questionnaires
Korosidou and Bratitsis (2019)	Assess how DS and AR can contribute to the enhancement of children's vocabulary in the FL through a number of gamified activities	Elemantary	Tests, interviews and a teacher's journal
Aljraiwi (2019)	Identify the effectiveness of gamification of web-based learning on academic achievement and creative thinking among primary school students	Elementary	Tests

Table 1. Continued

Author and Year of Publication	Purpose of the Study	Educational Level	Data Collection Method
Rajendran et al. (2019)	Stimulate pupils from a rural area in Melaka to learn English as their second language more effectively, actively and interestingly	High school	Questionnaire and interview
Veryaeva and Solovyeva (2021)	Overcome the research gap, exploring the relationships between user engagement, platform affordances, and gamification in online learning	N/A	Questionnaire
Rahmani (2020)	Displaying the results of reviewing research-based articles about gamification in the context of learning English		Review of the literature
Huang et al. (2020)			
Azzouz Boudadi and Gutiérrez- Colón (2020)	A comprehensive review of literature published in the most prominent journals		Review of the literature
Idris et al. (2020)	Examine the effectiveness of Kahoot	Elementary	Tests
Pratama (2020)	Used one online-gamification tool called 'Kahoot!' in a senior high school to promote their engagement and motivation	High school	Questionnaire
Md Yunus and Azmanuddin bin Azman (2019)	Prove that the use of Kahoot! helps the Year 3 pupils in retaining the English Irregular verbs	Elementary	Tests
Sun and Hsieh (2018)	Examined gamification effects on the intrinsic and extrinsic motivation, engagement, and attention of junior high school students when learning English	High school	Tests and questionnaires
Khalilian et al. (2021)	Employ the Kahoot to assess students' strengths and weaknesses in learning grammar	High school	Tests and questionnaires
Tan et al. (2019)	Examine the suitability of Kahoot for use among remedial tertiary-level English language learners	University	Questionnaires
Purgina et al. (2020)	Discusses gamification of learning natural language grammar with a mobile app WordBricks	University	Tests

Many scholars have suggested other factors that gamification can affect to enhance second/foreign language learning. Park et al. (2020), in their attempt to create an efficient L2 environment that enhances participation and learning speed, have argued that gamification shows promise for improving learners' memory recall. In fact, with 95% confidence, the experiment results have concluded that the gamified platform users were able to recall the tested materials later on. Rueckert et al. (2020) drew attention to the role of gamification in helping students gain a sense of control over their L2 learning. A unique feature of gamified instruction, according to them, is allowing users to work at their own pace and the ability to repeat tasks until the objectives are met, which provides ample possibilities for learners to self-correct and thus create a sense of learner autonomy. Vallejo (2018) added that gamification offers constant and immediate feedback (points, badges, leaderboards, etc.) that boosts learners' self-confidence. This, in turn, enhances their sense of control and satisfies their need for autonomy.

Figure 2. Summary of the findings for Question 1

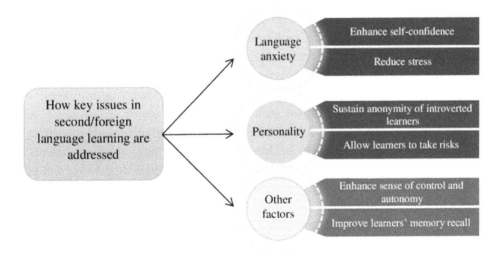

In our view, the merits of such studies are undeniable since they have focused on several individual variables that are important in language learning and have correlated the results with gamification (Figure 2). However, such an approach treats learner variables in isolation which poses a particular problem in cases where one variable depends holistically on other ones (such as motivation) forming, thus, a complex, dynamic and situated system (Griffiths & Soruç, 2020). Therefore, gaining in-depth understanding of the effects of gamified learning on language acquisition requires more rigor in identifying and conceptualizing factors that predict success in L2 learning and suggesting a comprehensive framework which can guide further research in this field. Finally, while longitudinal research is time consuming and involves several challenges, we believe that going beyond short-term intervention periods (such as the studies reported above) is needed to yield solid evidence on how gamification can be mobilised to address individual variables.

RQ2: *How are elements of gamification mobilized in the design of second/foreign language learning experiences and in enhancing these experiences?*

Gamification requires tailoring game elements to the user. Several studies have used certain mobile or web-based apps that are based on gamified design. *Kahoot, Duolingo* and *Quizlet*, for instance, have been widely used to offer users a language learning experience that generates their engagement and interest. Other apps such as *Classcraft, Quizziz, Edmodo, Classdojo, Padlet* and *Edpuzzle* have also been tried for their innovative gamified environment (Figure 3). While attempting to justify the selection of these gamified applications, several researchers have highlighted the potential of using certain game elements to provide an enjoyable learning experience. These platforms contain features such as a chat space for interactions both inside and outside the classroom, comments can be posted, messages sent, and learner progress tracked. It has been found that providing L2 students with instant feedback, for example, promotes teacher-student and student-student interactions, improves the teaching-learning process and allows students to develop a deeper understanding of the subject matter (Kohnke, 2020; Yürük, 2019). Positive, corrective and explanatory feedback has also been sought to facilitate language learning, enhance students' performance, help them progress and provide them with challenges to keep them engaged and avoid boredom (Dehganzadeh & Dehganzadeh, 2020; Mitchell & Shachter, 2021; Tsourounis & Demmans Epp, 2016; Zou, 2020). Other than the popular gamified feedback forms (points, badges and leaderboard), several other game elements emerged from the reviewed publications, such as levels, challenges, collaboration, competition, reinforcement, surprise, mission, fantasy and clear goals (Weissheimer et al., 2019), narratives, random rewards and avatars (Zhang & Chen, 2021), stars and tokens (Yamasaki, 2016), hints, curiosity and freedom to fail (Zhou et al., 2017). On closer examination, the majority of the reviewed studies used a gamified design that draws on the synergy emerging from the interaction of several game elements that, when combined, would produce a greater motivating effect, either for learners to get a proper feedback of their learning progress, to facilitate comprehension, to enhance collaboration or competition among students and to reward their efforts (Bagunaid et al., 2019; Homer et al., 2018). This effect is made possible thanks to certain innovative practices that blend materials, tools and tasks to reflect learners' needs and interests. Interestingly, Kohnke and Ting (2021) used certain adaptability measures to help learners progress. If players are stuck on a particular task, he/she has the option either to skip to the next one or to receive quick hints. Similarly, Zhou et al. (2017) propose *Adventure*, a gamified application that examines the users' pronunciation and provides instant corrective feedback to aid them explore content and gain language skills. Posting messages, exploring the virtual environment, solving puzzles and escaping rooms have also been found helpful to incorporate gamified elements in a meaningful way (Arce & Valdivia, 2020; Lyu, 2019). However, the existing literature reveals a lack of consistency by using terms such as "dynamics", "aesthetics", "mechanics", "components" and "elements" to identify gamification taxonomies. It is not clear what gamification design these categories represent. For example, in the MDA framework (Mechanics, Dynamics and Aesthetics) by Hunicke, LeBlanc and Zubek (2004), feedback is treated as a mechanic that can generate player engagement (Arce & Valdivia, 2020; Dehghanzadeh et al., 2019), while in Marczewski's Mechanics and Elements, it is treated as a gamification element that comprises many mechanics (Govender & Arnedo-Moreno, 2021). This lack of consensus in the current literature makes the selection and the evaluation of different game elements opaque for practitioners. In their systematic review, Dehghanzadeh et al. (2019) mentioned that the most used elements for gamifying L2 were feedback, challenges, points, rewards, leaderboards, and levels, while curiosity, warning signals, medals, chunking, avatars, and virtual credits are the least frequently used. However, evidence-based taxonomies would be more effective in translating research into recommendations and practical guidelines and, when implemented, can enhance learning outcomes.

One of the main requirements for the development of meaningful gamified materials is that they should be based on sound principles that articulate the aim of the learning process. Dindar et al. (2021) drew on Social Interdependence Theory to examine the impact of gamified cooperation and competition on task effort, learning achievement, motivation and social relatedness of L2 learners. According to this theory, task goals in a group setting influence one's interactions with others, creating either positive interdependence, negative interdependence or no interdependence (Johnson & Johnson, 2009). To reward participants for their cooperation or competition, the whole group of the participants received points for task completion and were presented with a leaderboard that showed their ranking. In a study of Hong et al. (2020), the authors applied Trait Activation Theory and adapted Cognitive-Affective Theory to explore the effects of gamification on second language grammar learning. Through a gamified platform, called *TipOn*, students could input their questions to create game modes and set passing scores or answer each other's questions using words, pictures or sounds. These attitudes were evaluated to analyze participants' epistemic curiosity. Korosidou and Bratitsis' (2019) experiment was based on Willis' task-based language teaching and Coyle's pluriliteracies approach to Content and Language Integrated Learning (CLIL) to evaluate how digital storytelling and augmented reality can enhance children's foreign language vocabulary. The participants were encouraged to collaborate to maximize meaningful interaction and enhance their problem-solving skills. Digital storytelling, feedback, rewards and rules have been used as a gamified design to promote creative and innovative practices. A number of other studies have applied game-based frameworks, as in the case of Aljraiwi (2019) who adopted a set of steps and procedures, whereby points, achievements, badges, and time constraints can help to achieve self-actualization, competitiveness, interactivity, and cooperation. Instructional design has also been used as in the study of Rajendran et al. (2019) to provide certain guidelines for their gamified design.

In fact, the methodologies presented in these studies offer authentic ways to address the research issue and to elicit useful data; however, little is known about how a given theory might guide the selection of gamification design elements for specific tasks and how they can be tailored to motivate and engage different types of users. Interestingly, the idea of using instructional design to create gamified experiences and address the users' needs is innovative. The challenge for future research will be to suggest strategies for adapting instructional design frameworks to map different influential variables in L2 learning, including research-based taxonomies of gamified elements, suitable theoretical foundations that can address user motivation and engagement and learners' different attributes.

Figure 3. Summary of the findings for Question 2

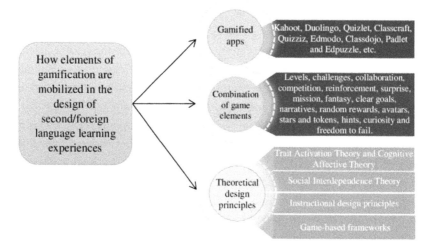

RQ3: *What affordances does gamification offer to support a positive learning experience in L2 learning?*

The review results suggest that gamification has features that can make tasks meaningful and adaptively respond to learners' specific needs to enhance their L2 learning experience (Figure 4). Exploring the relationship between user engagement, platform affordances and gamification in online learning was the objective of the research by Veryaeva and Solovyeva (2021). They argued that one of the affordances of their gamified design is the capacity of adapting the learning process to learners' own interests. It allowed the users to customize all activities according to their goals and motivations, which granted them a certain control over the course content. Aljraiwi (2019) also developed a gamified learning environment that aims at testing its effect on academic achievement and creative thinking among primary school students. The author emphasized that the possibility to access the learning materials at any time in addition to the website's gamified features, such as feedback, systematic follow-up, instant evaluation of students' responses and sharing comments increased the flexibility of learning. Similarly, Rueckert et al. (2020) claimed that gamified foreign language instruction could be a major asset to grant students a sense of control over their studies. Through the possibility to work at one's own pace and the opportunities to repeat and self-correct, learners felt greater autonomy in their learning. At the same time, some noted that gamification facilitates meaningful language use, considering their motivational qualities. For example, Aljraiwi (2019) specified that the gameful features embedded in their web-based materials made L2 activities more relevant and valuable for learners. The possibility of participating in the construction of content, building positive communication as well as cooperative relationships promoted the learners' problem-solving skills, independence and performance. Furthermore, Rahmani (2020) highlighted that several reviewed studies improved the 21st century skills, mainly critical thinking, problem-solving, creativity, innovation, media literacy, ICT literacy, flexibility, initiative and self-direction. These skills enable learners to apply new knowledge, thus empowering them to control practical and theoretical aspects of their learning. These conclusions show the potential benefits gamification can bring to educational contexts. On the other hand, little is known about how gamified elements can be operationalized to enhance meaningful learning experiences. Most of the reviewed studies don't expose the L2 pedagogical approaches that have been used, which makes it difficult to evaluate their potential in leveraging the gamified principles beyond the motivational effects of certain gamification elements. The absence of quality learning materials and pedagogical approaches combined with gamification will not necessarily enhance students' learning experience (Huang et al., 2020).

Our review has revealed that gamification contributes significantly to students' learning achievement (Figure 4). The same conclusion was revealed by the literature review led by Azzouz Boudadi and Gutiérrez-Colón (2020), who have mentioned that even though a limited number of papers matched their selection criteria, the results proved that gamified learning is able to improve students' ESL grammar and vocabulary. In their systematic review, Dehghanzadeh et al. (2019) pointed out that the majority of the reviewed publications reported positive outcomes of gamified ESL environments on learning vocabulary. Potential benefits were also reported on other language skills (writing, speaking, listening and reading) and components (pronunciation and grammar). In fact, while reviewing the current literature, one is immediately struck by the number of studies which looked into the potential and benefits of using the gamified platform *Kahoot*. Idris et al. (2020) have argued that it had a positive effect on grammar, particularly simple present tense verb learning. Yürük (2019) has outlined that *Kahoot* provides active learning and rapid thinking, gives the opportunity to access richer content and makes learning easier. This helps all types of learners to enhance their language skills. According to Tan et al. (2019), their study's participants agreed that *Kahoot* has made the learning of English grammar easier and more effective. Pratama (2020), who confirmed that the engagement and interactivity of *Kahoot* helped learners enhance their skills in grammar, vocabularies and translation, has put the same assumptions forward. Md Yunus and Azmanuddin bin Azman's study (2019) has also revealed that *Kahoot* was effective in retaining the participants' memory of the irregular verbs thanks to its relevance and to the features embedded in the application.

Figure 4. Summary of the findings for Question 3

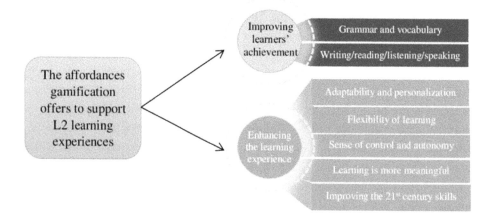

Our review conclusions suggest that no single study has reported negative findings for the use of gamification in terms of L2 content learning. This implies that all the gamified approaches being used have proven effective in second language learning. Nonetheless, taking into account that the concept of gamification is relatively new and that several studies have focused on answering questions such as does gamification have a positive impact on the learning process? Does it motivate or engage students?, further research is necessary to establish a clearer relationship between gamified approaches and learning outcomes.

RQ4: *How intrinsic and extrinsic motivations as well as learners' engagement are approached in gamified design?*

The majority of studies claim that gamification promotes motivation and engagement. Usually this argument comes from the fact that game elements have been shown to be able to evoke the interest of learners. This assumption finds an echo in several motivational frameworks that sought to incorporate mainstream psychological theories into L2 research, namely Crookes and Schmidt's (1991) theory that argues that the classroom motivational factors include activities, interest, relevance, need for affiliation, feedback, the issue of extrinsic rewards, past experiences and the effect of students' self-perception. What is common in the reviewed studies is that they contain references to several of these elements (Figure 5). Sun and Hsieh (2018), for instance, mentioned that their proposed gamified interactive response system could effectively stimulate the participants' interest and intrinsic motivation thanks to an instant feedback system, which had a positive effect on their level of emotional engagement and attention during English class. In a similar vein, Park et al. (2020) as well as Veryaeva and Solovyeva (2021) highlighted the fact that several extrinsic rewards particularly related to gamification, such as points, levels and incentives, can enhance learners' motivation and engagement. Sun and Hsieh (2018) added that using an instant feedback mechanism could not only provide learners with satisfying learning experiences but also reinforce their emotional engagement.

In recent years, a new approach has called attention to the changing nature of L2 motivation. One of these approaches has been Dörnyei's (2005) framework which sees L2 motivation as a process that is broken down into temporal segments: "initial wishes and desires are first transformed into goals and then into operationalized intentions, leading to the accomplishment of the goal and concluded by the final evaluation of the process" (Dornyei, 2005, p. 84). Our analysis of the reviewed papers revealed that gamified learning applies to some components of this model (Figure 5). It allows for the consideration of certain L2 motivational factors that are seen as effective in the L2 learning process. Such factors include expectancy of success and perceived coping potential, quality of the learning experience and sense of autonomy as well as classroom reward and goal structure. According to Khalilian et al. (2021), *Kahoot* helps the participants to enhance their grammar knowledge because it stimulates better perceptions and increases their learning expectations towards the target activities. Similarly, Almusharraf's study (2021) revealed that students felt that *Kahoot* triggered their attention and concentration as they developed a deeper understanding of English literature. The research participants reported being aware of "why they were right or wrong" through reviewing and assessing the learning content. Moreover, almost all the reviewed studies reported positive gamified learning experiences. For instance, Tan et al. (2019) point out that their study participants perceived their experience with gamification as "fun, entertaining, exciting, and useful for teaching and learning purposes". Similar arguments were brought forward by Purgina et al. (2020) who revealed that the mobile app *WordBricks* encouraged students to learn language because they "enjoyed working with the platform, found it easy to use and would like to use it as a part of their homework". Additionally, several research studies have claimed that gamified instruction enhances autonomous learning. As stated by, Rueckert et al. (2020), gamification is a major asset in helping learners gain a sense of control over their learning as it allows them opportunities to work at their own pace and to self-correct and repeat until the objectives of the assignments are met. Similar findings were reported by Dehganzadeh and Dehganzadeh (2020) who claim that gamified foreign language learning enables learners to develop autonomy by "taking responsibility for learning the course content in their own space".

L2 motivation research has provided empirical evidence of the influence of several other factors related to classroom-related processes on learner motivation (Csizér, 2017). Our review has revealed that gamification motivational affordances are related to these factors, mainly task motivation (the interaction process between the learner and the environment) and group dynamics (Figure 5). Accordingly, Dindar et al. (2021) study emphasized that the positive influence of gamification on learners' motivation is due to the cooperative aspects that facilitate positive social interactions such as mutual support, information exchange and constructive communication. Similarly, Korosidou and Bratitsis (2019) assessed the potential of gamified digital storytelling and Augmented Reality in developing children's foreign language vocabulary. Meaningful interaction was among the strategies used to help the participants retain vocabulary. They were encouraged to help each other and collaborate to find solutions to the given problems. Another potentially pivotal element that affects learners' motivation, which is closely related to collaborative learning environments, is task motivation. In fact, the majority of the reviewed studies have concluded that gamified learning positively influences learners' performance. Several explanations are deduced from their behavior while carrying out a specific task. Veryaeva and Solovyeva (2021) investigated the relationship

How Does Gamified L2 Learning Enhance Motivation

between user engagement and gamification affordances in online learning. Among the predictors of user engagement the study came up with, was the control the platform allowed to participants over primarily timing to complete the tasks as well as over the course content and process to cater for their own needs. The importance of control was also emphasized in the work of Rueckert et al. (2020) who evaluated the extent to which a gamified L2 classroom complies with the 21 principles of good education proposed by mind, brain, and education research. They found that gamified instruction could be a major asset to aid learners gain a sense of control over their L2 learning through the possibility of working at one's own pace and to repeat and self-correct. Arce and Valdivia (2020), who explored the effects of applying gamification and competitiveness in a virtual foreign language environment, present another example of task-based motivation. Based on their study results, it can also be concluded that there is a close link between gamification and students' commitment towards the course and its completion, with more motivated learners being more willing to continue learning throughout the course while being able to compete against each other.

While our analysis has revealed that several motivational affordances of gamification highlighted in the reviewed papers are grounded in well-established theories on L2 motivation, they don't provide empirically validated evidence that adheres to the principles informed by L2 research. To our knowledge, the choice and the implementation of the gamified strategies in the present review are not informed by a rich understanding of the principles and processes of L2 motivational research. Accordingly, gamified L2 learning needs to capitalize on the variety of theories and models that have been suggested in the literature to make active use of its attributes and affordances and to properly account for the nonlinearity and dynamicity of L2 motivation which differs from one learner to another.

Practical Implications

Based on the findings of this study, we suggest a set of guidelines for implementing gamification in a language classroom:

- Use gamified, flipped, or blended classes to help learners prepare for in-class activities, thereby reducing their anxiety;
- Allow learners a certain degree of anonymity to boost their self-confidence;
- Allow learners to work at their own pace and correct their own mistakes helps foster a sense of learner autonomy;
- Use a range of feedback methods to encourage meaningful interactions and improve students' performance and sense of control;

Figure 5. Summary of the findings for Question 4

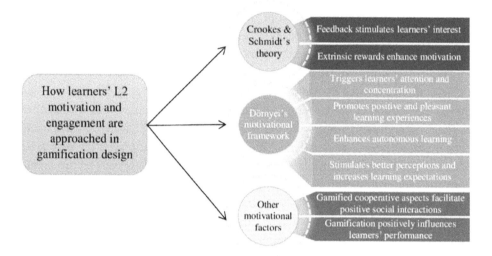

- Provide users with the ability to customize activities based on their preferences and objectives;
- Allow learners to participate in the creation of learning materials and to collaborate with their peers to promote their problem-solving skills;
- Use a variety of gamification elements that engage learners, including storytelling, puzzles, challenges, missions, etc. to produce a greater motivating effect.

Limitations and Future Directions

Our review has some limitations that require additional research. First, although our search used several academic databases, many papers were excluded because we considered only empirical work and peer-reviewed articles written in English. It would be interesting for future researchers to go beyond journal articles and explore other types of publications such as conference proceedings and book chapters. This can provide an in-depth analysis of the phenomenon under study. Second, we focused on articles published between 2017 and late 2022. Including additional recent studies would bring an added value to this field of research by suggesting further avenues on how L2 gamified environments could provide learners with enjoyable experiences and enhance their motivation and engagement. Furthermore, key issues in L2 learning addressed in this review included but not limited to personality traits, anxiety, memory, feedback and the sense of control. Future research should thus tackle additional issues such as language aptitude and willingness to communicate to provide robust findings that could be generalized to other learning contexts.

CONCLUSION

Gamification is an emerging research trend. While most of the reviews on gamified L2 learning have been quantitative in nature and focused only on how game elements can motivate L2 learners, there has been a lack of understanding of how theoretical foundations of L2 learning can be mobilized in the design of gamified learning experiences that can engage and motivate learners. We believe the results of our review contribute to the ongoing research on L2 gamification in several ways. First, we analysed how the current literature address certain key variables in L2 learning that can lead to a better understanding of the benefits of using gamification. We also synthesized the various methodologies used in the reviewed papers to design and incorporate game elements in their L2 educational settings. Our analysis can stimulate the debate on further theoretical foundations that can support solid design principles that speak directly to user motivation and engagement. Ultimately, we provided an overview of the potential advantages gamified design can bring to L2 educational contexts. It is clear from the current review results that gamification is an approach that can offer much to facilitate learning and to improve learners' participation and performance. We concluded our review by examining how motivation and engagement are addressed in current literature on gamification. We were able to document a number of studies that apply, whether directly or indirectly, theory and research to promote and enhance learners' motivation and engagement.

REFERENCES

Aditya, D. (2020). The effect of gamification based on Balinese local story. *ACITYA Journal of Teaching & Education, 2*(2), 115–128. doi:10.30650/ajte.v2i2.1368

Alamer, A. (2021). Basic psychological needs, motivational orientations, effort, and vocabulary knowledge. *Studies in Second Language Acquisition, 44*(1), 164–184. doi:10.1017/S027226312100005X

Alamer, A., & Al Khateeb, A. (2021). Effects of using the WhatsApp application on Language learners motivation: A controlled investigation using structural equation modelling. *Computer Assisted Language Learning, 36*(1-2), 149–175. doi:10.108 0/09588221.2021.1903042

Alavi, S. M., & Esmaeilifard, F. (2021). The effect of emotional scaffolding on language achievement and willingness to communicate by providing recast. *Cogent Psychology*, *8*(1), 1911093. Advance online publication. doi:10.1080/23311908.2 021.1911093

Aldemir, T., Ataş, A. H., & Celik, B. (2022). A systematic design model for gamified learning environments. *Research Anthology on Developments in Gamification and Game-Based Learning*, 214–234. doi:10.4018/978-1-6684-3710-0.ch011

Aljraiwi, S. (2019). Effectiveness of gamification of web-based learning in improving academic achievement and creative thinking among primary school students. *International Journal of Education and Practice*, *7*(3), 242–257. doi:10.18488/journal.61.2019.73.242.257

Almusharraf, N. (2021). Incorporation of a game-based approach into the EFL online classrooms: Students' perceptions. *Interactive Learning Environments*, 1–14. doi:1 0.1080/10494820.2021.1969953

Alobaid, A. (2021). ICT multimedia learning affordances: Role and impact on ESL learners' writing accuracy development. *Heliyon*, *7*(7), e07517. Advance online publication. doi:10.1016/j.heliyon.2021.e07517 PMID:34307944

Andrade, F. R., Mizoguchi, R., & Isotani, S. (2016). The bright and dark sides of Gamification. *Intelligent Tutoring Systems*, 176–186. doi:10.1007/978-3-319-39583-8_17

Arce, N. H., & Valdivia, A. C. (2020). Adapting competitiveness and gamification to a digital platform for foreign language learning. *International Journal of Emerging Technologies in Learning*, *15*(20), 194–209. doi:10.3991/ijet.v15i20.16135

Aydın, S. M., & Çakır, N. A. (2022). The effects of a game-enhanced learning intervention on Foreign Language Learning. *Educational Technology Research and Development*, *70*(5), 1809–1841. doi:10.100711423-022-10141-9

Azouz, O., & Lefdaoui, Y. (2018). Gamification design frameworks: A systematic mapping study. *2018 6th International Conference on Multimedia Computing and Systems (ICMCS)*. 10.1109/ICMCS.2018.8525900

Azzouz Boudadi, N., & Gutiérrez-Colón, M. (2020). Effect of gamification on students' motivation and learning achievement in Second language acquisition within higher education: A literature review 2011-2019. *The EuroCALL Review*, *28*(1), 40. doi:10.4995/eurocall.2020.12974

Bagunaid, W. A., Meccawy, M., Allinjawi, A., & Meccawy, Z. (2019). The Impact of Gamification on Self-Assessment for English Language Learners in Saudi Arabia. *International Journal of Educational and Pedagogical Sciences*, *13*(2), 129–134. doi:10.5281/zenodo.2571829

Bai, L., & Wang, Y. X. (2020). Pre-departure English language preparation of students on joint 2+2 programs. *System*, *90*, 102219. doi:10.1016/j.system.2020.102219

Botes, E., Dewaele, J.-M., & Greiff, S. (2020). The foreign language classroom anxiety scale and academic achievement: An overview of the prevailing literature and a meta-analysis. *Journal for the Psychology of Language Learning*, *2*(1), 26–56. doi:10.52598/jpll/2/1/3

Burns, A., & Richards, J. C. (2018). *The Cambridge Guide to learning English as a second language*. Cambridge University Press. doi:10.1017/9781009024761

Chiu, T. K. (2021). Applying the self-determination theory (SDT) to explain student engagement in online learning during the COVID-19 pandemic. *Journal of Research on Technology in Education, 54*(sup1). doi:10.1080/15391523.2021.1891998

Csizér, K. (2017). Motivation in the L2 classroom. The Routledge Handbook of Instructed Second Language Acquisition, 418–432. doi:10.4324/9781315676968-23

De La Cruz, K. M., Gebera, O. W., & Copaja, S. J. (2021). Application of gamification in higher education in the teaching of English as a foreign language. *Perspectives and Trends in Education and Technology*, 323–341. doi:10.1007/978-981-16-5063-5_27

Dehganzadeh, H., & Dehganzadeh, H. (2020). Investigating effects of digital gamification-based language learning: A systematic review. *Two Quarterly Journal of English Language Teaching and Learning University of Tabriz, 12*(25), 53–93. doi:10.22034/ELT.2020.10676

Dehghanzadeh, H., Fardanesh, H., Hatami, J., Talaee, E., & Noroozi, O. (2019). Using gamification to support learning English as a Second language: A systematic review. *Computer Assisted Language Learning*, *34*(7), 934–957. doi:10.1080/095 88221.2019.1648298

Dehghanzadeh, H., Fardanesh, H., Hatami, J., Talaee, E., & Noroozi, O. (2021). Using gamification to support learning English as a Second language: A systematic review. *Computer Assisted Language Learning*, *34*(7), 934–957. doi:10.1080/095 88221.2019.1648298

Deterding, S., Sicart, M., Nacke, L., O'Hara, K., & Dixon, D. (2011). Gamification. using game-design elements in non-gaming contexts. *CHI '11 Extended Abstracts on Human Factors in Computing Systems*. doi:10.1145/1979742.1979575

Dewaele, J.-M. (2017). Psychological dimensions and foreign language anxiety. The Routledge Handbook of Instructed Second Language Acquisition, 433–450. doi:10.4324/9781315676968-24

Dichev, C., & Dicheva, D. (2017). Gamifying education: What is known, what is believed and what remains uncertain: A critical review. *International Journal of Educational Technology in Higher Education, 14*(1), 9. Advance online publication. doi:10.118641239-017-0042-5

Dicheva, D., Dichev, C., Agre, G., & Angelova, G. (2015). Gamification in education: A systematic mapping study. *Journal of Educational Technology & Society, 18*(3), 75–88.

Dincer, A. (2020). Understanding the characteristics of English language learners' out-of-class language learning through digital practices. *IAFOR Journal of Education, 8*(2), 47–65. doi:10.22492/ije.8.2.03

Dindar, M., Ren, L., & Järvenoja, H. (2020). An experimental study on the effects of gamified cooperation and competition on English vocabulary learning. *British Journal of Educational Technology, 52*(1), 142–159. doi:10.1111/bjet.12977

Ding, L., Er, E., & Orey, M. (2018). An exploratory study of student engagement in gamified online discussions. *Computers & Education, 120*, 213–226. doi:10.1016/j.compedu.2018.02.007

Dörnyei Zoltán. (2005). *The psychology of the language learner: Individual differences in Second language acquisition*. Routledge.

Efron, S. E., & Ravid, R. (2020). *Action research in education: A practical guide*. The Guilford Press.

Ellis, R. (2019). *Understanding second language acquisition*. Oxford University Press.

Goethe, O. (2019). *Gamification mindset*. Springer. doi:10.1007/978-3-030-11078-9

Govender, T., & Arnedo-Moreno, J. (2021). An analysis of game design elements used in digital game-based language learning. *Sustainability (Basel), 13*(12), 6679. doi:10.3390u13126679

Griffiths, C., & Soruç Adem. (2020). *Individual differences in language learning: A complex systems theory perspective*. Palgrave Macmillan.

Han, S. (2023). The contribution of blog-based writing instruction to enhancing writing performance and writing motivation of Chinese EFL learners. *Frontiers in Psychology*, *13*, 1069585. Advance online publication. doi:10.3389/fpsyg.2022.1069585 PMID:36743589

Hedjazi Moghari, M., & Marandi, S. S. (2017). Triumph through texting: Restoring Learners' interest in grammar. *ReCALL*, *29*(3), 357–372. doi:10.1017/S0958344017000167

Hernández-Prados, M. Á., Belmonte, M. L., & Manzanares-Ruiz, J. C. (2021). How to run your own online business: A gamification experience in ESL. *Education Sciences*, *11*(11), 697. doi:10.3390/educsci11110697

Hong, J.-C., Hwang, M.-Y., Liu, Y.-H., & Tai, K.-H. (2020). Effects of gamifying questions on English grammar learning mediated by epistemic curiosity and language anxiety. *Computer Assisted Language Learning*, *35*(7), 1458–1482. doi:10.1080/09588221.2020.1803361

Hsu, H. T. (2018). *L2 learning motivation from the perspective of self-determination theory: A qualitative case study of hospitality and tourism students in Taiwan. In ELT in Asia in the Digital Era: Global Citizenship and Identity*. Routledge.

Huang, B., Hew, K. F., & Lo, C. K. (2019). Investigating the effects of gamification-enhanced flipped learning on undergraduate students' behavioral and cognitive engagement. *Interactive Learning Environments*, *27*(8), 1106–1126. doi:10.1080/10494820.2018.1495653

Huang, R., Ritzhaupt, A. D., Sommer, M., Zhu, J., Stephen, A., Valle, N., Hampton, J., & Li, J. (2020). The impact of gamification in educational settings on student learning outcomes: A meta-analysis. *Educational Technology Research and Development*, *68*(4), 1875–1901. doi:10.100711423-020-09807-z

Huang, W. H. Y., & Soman, D. (2013). Gamification of education. *Report Series: Behavioural Economics in Action*, *29*(4), 37.

Hunicke, R., LeBlanc, M., & Zubek, R. (2004, July). MDA: A formal approach to game design and game research. In *Proceedings of the AAAI Workshop on Challenges in Game AI* (*Vol. 4*, No. 1, p. 1722). AAAI.

Huotari, K., & Hamari, J. (2012). Defining gamification. *Proceeding of the 16th International Academic MindTrek Conference*. 10.1145/2393132.2393137

Idris, M. I., Said, N. E., & Tan, K. H. (2020). Game-based learning platform and its effects on present tense mastery: Evidence from an ESL classroom. *International Journal of Learning. Teaching and Educational Research*, *19*(5), 13–26. doi:10.26803/ijlter.19.5.2

Ishaq, K., Mat Zin, N. A., Rosdi, F., Jehanghir, M., Ishaq, S., & Abid, A. (2021). Mobile-assisted and gamification-based Language Learning: A Systematic Literature Review. *PeerJ. Computer Science*, *7*, e496. Advance online publication. doi:10.7717/peerj-cs.496 PMID:34084920

Johnson, D. W., & Johnson, R. T. (2009). An educational psychology success story: Social interdependence theory and cooperative learning. *Educational Researcher*, *38*(5), 365–379. doi:10.3102/0013189X09339057

Kaban, A. L. (2021). Gamified e-reading experiences and their impact on reading comprehension and attitude in EFL classes. *International Journal of Mobile and Blended Learning*, *13*(3), 71–90. doi:10.4018/IJMBL.2021070105

Khalilian, B., Hosseini, H., & Ghabanchi, Z. (2021). On the Effect of Employing the Online Kahoot Game-Based App on Iranian EFL Learners' Structural Ability and their Motivation. *Journal of Language Teaching and Learning*, *11*(2), 42–60. https://www.jltl.com.tr/index.php/jltl/article/view/330

Khany, R., & Amiri, M. (2016). Action control, L2 motivational self system, and motivated learning behavior in a foreign language learning context. *European Journal of Psychology of Education*, *33*(2), 337–353. doi:10.100710212-016-0325-6

Kohnke, L. (2020). Exploring learner perception, experience and motivation of using a mobile app in L2 vocabulary acquisition. *International Journal of Computer-Assisted Language Learning and Teaching*, *10*(1), 15–26. doi:10.4018/IJCALLT.2020010102

Kohnke, L., & Ting, A. (2021). ESL Students' Perceptions of Mobile Applications for Discipline-Specific Vocabulary Acquisition for Academic Purposes. *Knowledge Management & E-Learning*, *13*(1), 102–117. doi:10.34105/j.kmel.2021.13.006

Korosidou, E., & Bratitsis, T. (2019). Infusing multimodal tools and digital storytelling in developing vocabulary and intercultural communicative awareness of young EFL learners. *Lecture Notes in Computer Science*, *11899*, 191–200. doi:10.1007/978-3-030-34350-7_19

Kruk, M. A. R. I. U. S. Z. (2022). *Investigating dynamic relationships among individual difference variables in learning... English as a foreign language in a virtual world.* SPRINGER.

Lee, J. J., & Hammer, J. (2011). Gamification in education: What, how, why bother? *Academic Exchange Quarterly, 15*(2), 146. https://www.researchgate.net/publication/258697764_Gamification_in_Education_What_How_Why_Bother

Lee, J. S., & Lee, K. (2020). The role of informal digital learning of English and L2 motivational self system in foreign language enjoyment. *British Journal of Educational Technology, 52*(1), 358–373. doi:10.1111/bjet.12955

Li, H. H., & Zhang, L. J. (2021). Effects of structured small-group student talk as collaborative prewriting discussions on Chinese University EFL students' individual writing: A quasi-experimental study. *PLoS One, 16*(5), e0251569. Advance online publication. doi:10.1371/journal.pone.0251569 PMID:34048435

Li, T., & Liu, Z. (2021). Exploring effects of the Second Language Motivational Self System on chinese EFL learners' willingness to communicate in English and implications for L2 education. *Journal of Higher Education Research, 2*(4). Advance online publication. doi:10.32629/jher.v2i4.404

Lister, M. (2015). Gamification: The effect on student motivation and performance at the post-secondary level. *Issues and Trends in Educational Technology, 3*(2). Advance online publication. doi:10.2458/azu_itet_v3i2_lister

Liu, M. (2022). Exploring the motivation-engagement link: The moderating role of positive emotion. *Journal for the Psychology of Language Learning, 4*(1), 1–18. doi:10.52598/jpll/4/1/3

Lyu, Y. (2019). *Using Gamification and Augmented Reality to Encourage Japanese Second Language Students to Speak English.* Retrieved from https://www.diva-portal.org/smash/record.jsf?pid=diva2%3A1416017&dswid=2225

Mazhar, B. A. L. (2019). Use of digital games in writing education: An action research on gamification. *Contemporary Educational Technology, 10*(3), 246–271. doi:10.30935/cet.590005

Mitchell, T., & Shachter, J. (2021). The Effects of Gamified Instruction on Japanese English Language Learner Vocabulary Recall. *Language Education and Research Center Journal, 16*, 54–75.

Nah, F. F. H., Zeng, Q., Telaprolu, V. R., Ayyappa, A. P., & Eschenbrenner, B. (2014). Gamification of education: a review of literature. In *HCI in Business: First International Conference, HCIB 2014, Held as Part of HCI International 2014, Heraklion, Crete, Greece, June 22-27, 2014. Proceedings 1* (pp. 401-409). Springer International Publishing. 10.1007/978-3-319-07293-7_39

Nahmod, D. M. (2017). *Vocabulary gamification vs traditional learning instruction in an inclusive high school classroom*. Rowan University.

Ngah, E., Fauzi, W. J., Radzuan, N. R. M., Abdullah, H., Ali, A. Z. M., Abidin, N. A. Z., & Fadzillah, F. I. M. (2022). Snapticon: Developing Effective Listening Skills for Group Oral Discussion. *Asian Journal of University Education*, *18*(2), 361–374. doi:10.24191/ajue.v18i2.17991

Nicholson, S. (2015). A recipe for meaningful gamification. *Gamification in Education and Business*, 1–20. doi:10.1007/978-3-319-10208-5_1

Noels, K. A., Pelletier, L. G., Clément, R., & Vallerand, R. J. (2003). Why are you learning a second language? motivational orientations and self-determination theory. *Language Learning*, *53*(S1), 33–64. doi:10.1111/1467-9922.53223

Onwuegbuzie, A. J. (2016). *Seven steps to a comprehensive literature review. A multimodal and cultural approach*. SAGE Publications.

Paré, G., & Kitsiou, S. (2017). *Methods for literature reviews. In Handbook of eHealth Evaluation: An Evidence-based Approach*. University of Victoria.

Park, H., Burke, J. D., Blin, V., & Chrysanthou, H. (2020). Improving memory recall and measuring user ability through gamified techniques with 'chatty': An E-learning application for foreign languages. *Cross-Cultural Design. Applications in Health, Learning, Communication, and Creativity*, 349–366. doi:10.1007/978-3-030-49913-6_30

Parrish, A., & Lanvers, U. (2018). Student motivation, school policy choices and Modern Language Study in England. *Language Learning Journal*, *47*(3), 281–298. doi:10.1080/09571736.2018.1508305

Petersen, G. B., Petkakis, G., & Makransky, G. (2022). A study of how immersion and Interactivity Drive VR Learning. *Computers & Education*, *179*, 104429. doi:10.1016/j.compedu.2021.104429

Pinto, R. D., Peixoto, B., Melo, M., Cabral, L., & Bessa, M. (2021). Foreign language learning gamification using virtual reality—A systematic review of empirical research. *Education Sciences*, *11*(5), 222. doi:10.3390/educsci11050222

Pitoyo, M. D., & Asib, A. (2019). Gamification Based assessment: A Test Anxiety Reduction through Game Elements in Quizizz Platform. *International Online Journal of Education & Teaching*, *6*(3), 456–471.

Popescu, C. N., Attie, E., & Chadouteau, L. (2022). Gamified learning. *Advances in Human and Social Aspects of Technology*, 97–131. doi:10.4018/978-1-7998-8089-9.ch006

Prados Sánchez, G., Cózar-Gutiérrez, R., del Olmo-Muñoz, J., & González-Calero, J. A. (2021). Impact of a gamified platform in the promotion of reading comprehension and attitudes towards reading in primary education. *Computer Assisted Language Learning*, 1–25. doi:10.1080/09588221.2021.1939388

Pratama, G. A. (2020). Students perception of gamification to promote classroom engagement and motivation in senior high school. *Language Research Society*, *1*(1). Advance online publication. doi:10.33021/lrs.v1i1.1040

Pujolà, J.-T., & Appel, C. (2022). Gamification for technology-enhanced language teaching and learning. *Research Anthology on Developments in Gamification and Game-Based Learning*, 992–1010. doi:10.4018/978-1-6684-3710-0.ch045

Purgina, M., Mozgovoy, M., & Blake, J. (2019). WordBricks: Mobile Technology and visual grammar formalism for gamification of Natural Language Grammar Acquisition. *Journal of Educational Computing Research*, *58*(1), 126–159. doi:10.1177/0735633119833010

Putri, E., & Sari, F. M. (2020). Indonesian EFL students' perspectives towards Learning Management System Software. *Journal of English Language Teaching and Learning*, *1*(1), 20–24. doi:10.33365/jeltl.v1i1.244

Rahmani, E. F. (2020). The benefits of gamification in the English Learning Context. *IJEE*, *7*(1), 32–47. doi:10.15408/ijee.v7i1.17054

Rajendran, T., Bin Naaim, N. A., & Yunus, M. M. (2019). Pupils motivation and perceptions towards learning English using quizvaganza. *International Journal of Scientific and Research Publications*, *9*(1), p8529. Advance online publication. doi:10.29322/IJSRP.9.01.2019.p8529

Reinders, H. (2017). Digital Games and Second language learning. *Language. Educational Technology*, 329–343. doi:10.1007/978-3-319-02237-6_26

Reinhardt, J. (2019). *Gameful second and foreign language teaching and learning: Theory, research, and Practice.* Palgrave Macmillan. doi:10.1007/978-3-030-04729-0

Reitz, L., Sohny, A., & Lochmann, G. (2019). VR-based gamification of Communication Training and Oral Examination in a Second language. *Computer Assisted Language Learning*, 811–828. doi:10.4018/978-1-5225-7663-1.ch038

Roshandel, J., Ghonsooly, B., & Ghanizadeh, A. (2018). L2 motivational self-system and self-efficacy: A quantitative survey-based study. *International Journal of Instruction*, *11*(1), 329–344. doi:10.12973/iji.2018.11123a

Rueckert, D., Pico, K., Kim, D., & Calero Sánchez, X. (2020). Gamifying the foreign language classroom for brain-friendly learning. *Foreign Language Annals*, *53*(4), 686–703. doi:10.1111/flan.12490

Ryan, E. L., & Deci, R. M. (2017). *Self-determination theory. In Basic psychological needs in motivation, development, and wellness.* Guilford Press. doi:10.1521/978.14625/28806

Šafranj, J., & Zivlak, J. (2019). Effects of big five personality traits and fear of negative evaluation on Foreign Language Anxiety. *Croatian Journal of Education - Hrvatski Časopis Za Odgoj i Obrazovanje, 21*(1). doi:10.15516/cje.v21i1.2942

Salemink, E., de Jong, S. R. C., Notebaert, L., MacLeod, C., & Van Bockstaele, B. (2022). Gamification of cognitive bias modification for interpretations in anxiety increases training engagement and enjoyment. *Journal of Behavior Therapy and Experimental Psychiatry*, *76*, 101727. doi:10.1016/j.jbtep.2022.101727 PMID:35217211

Sari, F. M. (2020). Exploring english learners' engagement and their roles in the online language course. *Journal of English Language Teaching and Linguistics*, *5*(3), 349. doi:10.21462/jeltl.v5i3.446

Schwartz, R. N., & Plass, J. L. (2020). *Types of engagement in learning with games. Handbook of game-based learning.* The MIT Press.

Shalizar, R., & Rezaei, A. (2022). Examining the differential effects of focused vs. unfocused ZPD and explicit feedback on Second language writing. *Language Learning Journal*, *51*(3), 359–375. doi:10.1080/09571736.2022.2042366

Shelton-Strong, S. J. (2020). Advising in language learning and the support of learners' basic psychological needs: A self-determination theory perspective. *Language Teaching Research*, *26*(5), 963–985. doi:10.1177/1362168820912355

Shortt, M., Tilak, S., Kuznetcova, I., Martens, B., & Akinkuolie, B. (2021). Gamification in mobile-assisted language learning: A systematic review of Duolingo Literature from public release of 2012 to early 2020. *Computer Assisted Language Learning*, *36*(3), 517–554. doi:10.1080/09588221.2021.1933540

Siemon, D., & Eckardt, L. (2016). Gamification of teaching in higher education. *Progress in IS*, 153–164. doi:10.1007/978-3-319-45557-0_11

Simões, J., Redondo, R. D., & Vilas, A. F. (2013). A Social Gamification Framework for a K-6 learning platform. *Computers in Human Behavior*, *29*(2), 345–353. doi:10.1016/j.chb.2012.06.007

Sun, J. C. Y., & Hsieh, P. H. (2018). Application of a gamified interactive response system to enhance the intrinsic and extrinsic motivation, student engagement, and attention of English learners. *Journal of Educational Technology & Society*, *21*(3), 104–116. https://www.jstor.org/stable/26458511

Sun, T., & Wang, C. (2020). College students' writing self-efficacy and writing self-regulated learning strategies in learning English as a foreign language. *System*, *90*, 102221. doi:10.1016/j.system.2020.102221

Tan, D. A., Lee, B. C., Ganapathy, M., & Kasuma, S. A. (2022). Language learning in the 21st Century. *Research Anthology on Developments in Gamification and Game-Based Learning*, 802–820. doi:10.4018/978-1-6684-3710-0.ch036

Teimouri, Y., Goetze, J., & Plonsky, L. (2019). Second language anxiety and achievement. *Studies in Second Language Acquisition*, *41*(2), 363–387. doi:10.1017/S0272263118000311

ThékesI.SzilvássyO. (2021). The impact of Xeropan an online application assisting language learning on the processes of foreign language learning. *TEM Journal*. https://doi.org/ doi:10.18421/tem102-19

Toda, A. M., Klock, A. C., Oliveira, W., Palomino, P. T., Rodrigues, L., Shi, L., Bittencourt, I., Gasparini, I., Isotani, S., & Cristea, A. I. (2019). Analysing gamification elements in educational environments using an existing gamification taxonomy. *Smart Learning Environments*, *6*(1), 16. Advance online publication. doi:10.118640561-019-0106-1

Tsourounis, S., & Demmans Epp, C. (2016). Learning dashboards and gamification in MALL: Design guidelines in practice. The international handbook of mobile-assisted language learning, 370-398.

Tulloch, R. (2014). Reconceptualising gamification: Play and pedagogy. *Digital Culture & Education*, *6*(4), 317–333.

Vallejo Balduque, B. (2018). *Gamification and the Affective Aspects EFL Students: Effects on Anxiety and Motivation*. Language Education and Emotions.

VanPatten, B., Keating, G. D., & Wulff, S. S. (2020). *Theories in Second language acquisition: An introduction*. Routledge. doi:10.4324/9780429503986

Veryaeva, K., & Solovyeva, O. (2021). The influence of gamification and platform affordances on user engagement in online learning. *International Journal of Distance Education Technologies*, *19*(1), 1–17. doi:10.4018/IJDET.2021010101

Weissheimer, J., Souza, J. G., Antunes, J. P., & Souza Filho, N. S. (2019). Gamification and L2 vocabulary learning: The vocabox experience in the languages without borders program. *Revista Linguagem & Ensino*, *22*(4), 1136. doi:10.15210/rle.v22i4.16453

Werbach, K., & Hunter, D. (2012). *For the win: How game thinking can revolutionize your business.* Wharton Digital Press.

Wilson, E. (2017). School-based research: A guide for education students. *School-based Research*, 1-416.

Yamasaki, A. (2016). The Effectiveness of Gamification on Students' Motivation in Writing Class. 工学教育研究; *KIT Progress, 24*, 233-240. Retrieved from https://cir.nii.ac.jp/crid/1050282814025789184

Yunus, M., & Azmanuddin bin Azman, M. (2019). Memory stay or stray? Irregular verbs learning using Kahoot! *Arab World English Journal*, (5), 206–219. doi:10.24093/awej/call5.15

Yürük, N. (2019). Edutainment: Using Kahoot! as a review activity in foreign language classrooms. *Journal of Educational Technology and Online Learning*, 89–101. doi:10.31681/jetol.557518

Zainuddin, Z., Chu, S. K., Shujahat, M., & Perera, C. J. (2020). The impact of gamification on learning and instruction: A systematic review of empirical evidence. *Educational Research Review*, *30*, 100326. doi:10.1016/j.edurev.2020.100326

Zhang, L., & Chen, Y. (2021). Examining the effects of gamification on Chinese College Students' Foreign Language Anxiety: A Preliminary Exploration. *2021 4th International Conference on Big Data and Education*. 10.1145/3451400.3451401

Zheng, C., Liang, J.-C., Li, M., & Tsai, C.-C. (2018). The relationship between English language learners' motivation and online self-regulation: A structural equation modelling approach. *System*, *76*, 144–157. doi:10.1016/j.system.2018.05.003

Zhihao, Z., & Zhonggen, Y. (2022). The impact of gamification on the time-limited writing performance of English majors. *Education Research International*, *2022*, 1–11. doi:10.1155/2022/4650166

Zhou, L., Yu, J., Liao, C., & Shi, Y. (2017). Learning as adventure: An app designed with gamification elements to facilitate language learning. *HCI in Business, Government and Organizations. Interacting with Information Systems*, 266–275. doi:10.1007/978-3-319-58481-2_21

Zichermann, G., & Cunningham, C. (2011). *Gamification by design: Implementing game mechanics in web and mobile apps*. Verlag nicht ermittelbar.

Zou, D. (2020). Gamified flipped EFL classroom for primary education: Student and teacher perceptions. *Journal of Computers in Education*, 7(2), 213–228. doi:10.100740692-020-00153-w

174

Chapter 8
Integration of Digital Picture Books Into Young Learners' Language Classrooms:
A Novel Way to Develop Vocabulary Knowledge

Zeynep Çetin Köroğlu
iD https://orcid.org/0000-0002-9456-8910
Aksaray University, Turkey

ABSTRACT

The world we live in now is more technological than in the past and continues to change and develop day by day. Our children, who are accepted as 'digital natives,' start to live a life intertwined with technology from the first years of their lives. To prepare them for the age they are in and the lives that await them in the future, digital picture books should be used effectively, especially in early childhood. This chapter discusses the use and importance of picture books in early childhood foreign language learning, the features and usage areas of digital picture books, the role and importance of digital picture books in vocabulary teaching, examples of well-designed digital picture books, websites and applications that offer these examples, and the effects of digital picture books on young learners' foreign language learning.

DOI: 10.4018/979-8-3693-0353-5.ch008

Copyright © 2024, IGI Global. Copying or distributing in print or electronic forms without written permission of IGI Global is prohibited.

Digital Picture Books in Young Learners' Language Classrooms

INTRODUCTION

The instruction of vocabulary is a very significant component of teaching a foreign language. Without an adequate grasp of vocabulary, it is nearly impossible to communicate successfully in this language, which is one of the primary roles of language. If a student of a foreign language is lacking in vocabulary knowledge, then he or she will not be able to use the language successfully even if they have a very excellent understanding of the rules of the language (Alqahtani, 2015). This is true even if the student has a very high understanding of the rules of the language. Within the parameters of this discussion, vocabulary is one of the fundamental parts that make up the primary branches of the language (Cameron, 2001). When it comes to teaching children a foreign language, teaching vocabulary is another very crucial aspect. Because it is possible for children who are exposed to foreign languages at a young age to grow up to be individuals who are bilingual or multilingual. If children start studying a foreign language from a young age, it will be feasible for them to be prepared to learn a foreign language in the years to come and for them to develop the skills necessary to become individuals who are proficient in a foreign language (Akhtar & Menjivar, 2012).

The use of technological instructional tools has been increasingly common in recent years, and as technology continues to advance, these tools are also becoming easier to access and more efficient (Çetin Köroğlu, 2021). One of these resources is a digital format for children's picture books. Picture books have been digitized, and the resulting products, digital picture books, are now available as audio in various virtual environments. The teaching of foreign languages at a variety of different levels can benefit from the usage of digital books, which are rich in both visuals and content. Both the pupils and the teachers in early childhood foreign language programs will benefit from the usage of digital picture books, which will be an innovative and successful teaching tool (Bus & Anstadt, 2021). Examining the related literature indicated that digital picture books are not used sufficiently in the initial stages of foreign language instruction, and their effects on the language proficiency development of young learners haven't been investigated deeply.

This chapter of the book discusses the characteristics of digital picture books, their role and significance in the instruction of foreign languages, as well as some practical applications for the use of digital picture books in preschool settings.

REVIEW OF LITERATURE

Stories are important elements in all cultures from the past to the present, both in written and verbal forms. These elements, which reflect the experiences, imagination, and knowledge of mankind, are as important to children as they are to adults. Stories support children's cognitive development and have a stimulating effect on their cognitive development (Li & Bus, 2023). Stories prepared for children and often read by children are picture books. Children who read picture books can combine the joy of reading with their imagination and access a rich knowledge network in the language in which the story is told. Picture books enable children to easily express their feelings and thoughts, give creative answers, and spend quality time (Dobakhti & Panahi, 2022). In this context, young children should be supported and encouraged in their ability to understand what they read, internalize what they are reading, socialize with their peers, and tell their own stories to others (Dobakhti & Panahi, 2022). Thus, it's not wrong to say that picture books are a combined version of art with literature, and even to say they develop literary knowledge and concept of children (Yokata & Teale, 2014). It is possible to mention the various characteristics of picture books. Primarily, picture books provide prompt access. The images on the pages of the book do not require translation, and as the pages change, the reader can test his thoughts or develop new ideas. Another feature of picture books is that the paintings on the pages contain art. Thanks to these images, the reader's attention can be drawn to the book for a long time. Another feature is that picture books contribute to developing a positive attitude towards reading and thinking. Images in picture books can develop readers' analytical thinking, rational thinking, visual processing, hypothesis development, and testing skills (Perkins, 1994). Another feature of picture books is their ability to develop the communicative and linguistic skills of readers. Finally, picture books can be associated with many fields (Perkins, 1994).

With today's evolving technologies, digital versions of graphic books can be found in many applications, websites, or learning environments. Digital books are available in formats such as e-books, storytelling apps, image book apps, and interactive books, with multimedia and interactivity features that are accessible via touchscreens. In this context, digital books are a broad umbrella term (Kucirkova, 2019). Digital picture books have features that make the reader feel the reality in a virtual environment that will allow interaction through various animations, movies, and sounds within them (Hoffman & Paciga, 2014). According to Oaklay and Jay (2008), today's students are positively influenced by the sound, animation and a variety of other dynamics offered by digital storybooks, as they spend a lot of time with simulation and video games. Recent research has also revealed that digital stories improve children's reading experiences and enhance parent-child communication (Bai et al., 2022). Even the age of reading digital books starts at such an early age that three-year-old children access these contents independently of their parents through smartphones or tablets (Furenes, Kucirkova & Bus, 2021). It's very important to find out which content and what content they're more interested in (Furenes, Kucirkova

Digital Picture Books in Young Learners' Language Classrooms

& Bus, 2021). In this context, picture books have begun to be replaced by digital picture books and have become more widespread and accessible to children with their rich content. Pre-school students who learn English as a foreign language can access to digital picture books independently from their parents or with their help of them. The purpose of this book section is to introduce the characteristics of digital story books, to address the role and importance of digital stories in early childhood foreign language teaching, to present concrete examples of how digital stories can be used in teaching English vocabulary, and to focus on the role and significance of the digital Picture books in vocabulary teaching.

Digital Picture Books

Learning with digital picture books is compatible with the multimedia learning theory since people learn faster and more permanently when they see information or words with images than when they only see them as words (Mayer, 2014). Another theory which digital storytelling books are theoretically compatible is the theory of multimedia cognitive learning. According to this theory, more durable learning occurs when information is presented both verbally and visually (Mayer, 2023). However, according to the theory of binary encoding (Paivio, 2007) visually and auditorily presented information is presented to learners through two different channels, and these two channels do not negatively affect each other. In this context, digital Picture books provide more intricate learning than traditional picture books (Takacs et al., 2015). In a study by Oakley and Jay (2008), various digital-speaking books were assigned as homework to students who were unwilling to read, with little or no desire to read. These students did not read digital picture books with their parents outside of school, as they did not read these books themselves. Students who participated in the study noted that they started to read digital-speaking books, reading them was fun and educational, and they spent a lot of time with them. The parents of the participants also noted that their children had developed a positive attitude towards reading and that they continued to learn not only by reading but also by listening to books or by engaging in visual content (Oakley & Jay, 2008). It can be said that digital Picture books boost the motivation to read. In a study conducted by Richter and Courage in 2017, it was observed that 3- and 4-year-old students were distracted while reading classical books, but their motivation for reading was higher and they were more interested in the pictures while reading digital picture books. This study reveals that digital storybooks are the most innovative and exciting tools in the existing literature (Yokata & Teale, 2014). Another important feature of digital storytellers is their accessibility. All students who want to study regardless of time or place can easily access these tools.

Digital picture books can be classified into four categories according to their characteristics. The first category is scanned versions of printed books. The second category is picture books turned into movies by adding visual and audio elements. The third category includes picture books with media features such as music and sound added to images. The fourth category is that, with the addition of interactive features, picture books are transformed into games (Yokota and Teale, 2014). What these four categories have in common is that they contain a complex story pattern that can lead the reader to later comprehend what they read, enjoy reading and become conscious readers. Thus, these digital books enrich children's imagination and motivate them to learn (Bai et al., 2022; Montag, 2019). The story, spoken input, and complex linguistic structures that digital picture books offer to children are not available to children by their parents, caregivers, or those who care for them. In this context, digital picture books can make significant contributions to children's cognitive and linguistic development (Montag, 2019). A study of 1,500 parents with children under the age of 8 in the UK found that children read at least one digital picture book a week without the support of a parent (Kucirkova & Littleton, 2016). It can be assumed that younger students who read digital picture books could have learning autonomy. Individuals who gain learner autonomy at an early age will be more conscious and willing to learn later in life. In addition, they will be able to take an active role in their learning processes and be responsible for their learning.

To be able to choose good digital picture books, certain aspects need to be taken into account. First and foremost, the story must be well-told and conform to literary standards. The second important issue is whether the language of the story is used properly or not. The third issue is whether the story's visual features, and media features, such as sound, background, or animation, are designed to cover the whole story (Yokata & Teale, 2014). Digital picture books contribute significantly to children's cognitive, linguistic, and social development, resulting in advances including enhanced understanding and application of multimedia, improvement of language skills, and increased autonomy and motivation for learning (Yokata & Teale, 2014) In this context, digital image books can be used to teach vocabulary in language classes for young learners who are learning English as a foreign language. Presenting words to students in a particular context, supported by images, sounds and media, will enable students to learn words in a foreign language more permanently. In addition, interactions between young learners on the digital picture books with peers in a social learning environment, contribute to their social development. Young learners, however, can develop a positive attitude towards reading as they read digital picture books and become good readers in their advancing years. Given all these effects of digital images, it is very important to include these digital tools in language classes for young learners who are learning English as a foreign language.

Vocabulary Learning Through Digital Books

Vocabulary is an important link between all language skills. A language learner who does not have sufficient vocabulary knowledge will face difficulties in using other language skills Wilkins state (1972) that "there is not much value in being able to produce grammatical sentences if one has not got the vocabulary that is needed to convey what one wishes to say ... While without grammar very little can be conveyed, without vocabulary nothing can be conveyed" (pp. 110-111). These language students will not be fluent and understandable in the production of written or spoken language. A child who does not have sufficient vocabulary knowledge may experience a decline in his or her ability to read and, as a result, develop a negative attitude and behaviour towards reading (Rahman & Tan, 2022). However, an individual with sufficient vocabulary knowledge can develop his or her reading skills, enjoy reading, and develop linguistically and socially as he continues to read. That is why children need to have sufficient vocabulary in the target language they learn. In a study, Marion (2008) found that vocabulary acquisition was vital in completing and understanding information in written and spoken texts in a second foreign language. In the current context, children's vocabulary learning processes have attracted researchers' attention (e.g., Hindman et al., 2012). Thus, books contain words that don't appear in everyday talks or dialogues (Montag et al., 2015). It also contributes significantly to vocabulary development by presenting situations beyond the context in which their children live (Santaro et al., 2008). Understanding the context is important for eliciting the meaning of the word from the context and learning it without the need for another source or person (Penno, Wilkinson, & Moore, 2002).

Today, children who learn a foreign language at an early age are rapidly changing in their interest in and use of picture books. At a time when technology was not as widespread as it is today, children often read picture books that their parents chose for them, again accompanied by their parents. However, with changing and transforming technology, picture books have become digital picture books. With this change, digital picture books have been equipped with features that will attract individuals in early childhood. With this change, digital picture books have been equipped with features that will attract the attention of early childhood individuals. New generation digital picture books with multimedia, interaction and game features have become an important tool for foreign language learning due to the increased cognitive level of parents and the books' accessibility (Choi et al., 2019). Since individuals who learn a foreign language at an early age cannot define words independently from their parents, it is an important research question whether digital picture books can meet this need of individuals (Furenes et al., 2021). If the digital features added to the digital picture books contain words that the reader is not familiar with, and they can search and learn the meaning of those words within the book while reading the children's book, these tools will serve that need. A Canadian study of children aged 17 to 27 months found that children who read digital picture books were more interested in new words, more involved in reading, and socially expected behaviours (Strouse & Ganea, 2017). In another study of Dutch children between the ages of 3 and 4, children in the experimental group were read digital picture books, and children in control groups were read traditional picture books. The study revealed that children in the experimental group had higher incidental word scores than those in the control group (Gremmen, Molenaar, & Teepe, 2016). In China, a study of early childhood students found that participants' receptive and expressive vocabulary knowledge increased with the use of storybooks (Yeung et al., 2016). Takacs et al., (2014) conducted a meta-analysis of printed picture books and digital picture books, films and television programmes, and found that participants benefited more from multimedia-enriched books. A study conducted by Verhallen and Bus (2010) found that animated digital books increased expressive vocabulary skills in bilingual children more than traditional picture books. The study found that children learned new words using the multimedia features added to the books. The results of this study were confirmed by Pearman and Lefever-Davis (2006). Pearman and Lefever-Davis (2006) highlighted the contribution of animation and graphics to word learning, noting that readers react to these multimedia features.

Research shows that listening to digital-supported stories over and over again contributes positively to students' incidental vocabulary learning (Li & Bus, 2023). In addition to learning words, digital storytelling supports the reading habits of students who read them (Barnyak & McNelly, 2016). It is an inevitable positive result that individuals who develop a reading habit learn words when they read books in a foreign language. Research also reveals that students who read digital image books have improved their mental visualization abilities. (Li & Bus, 2023). In this context, the inclusion of digital picture books in the classrooms of early childhood language learners is of great importance for their linguistic development. Language teachers need to know the features and benefits of these tools (Dobakhti & Panahi, 2022).

RELATED RESEARCH

In this section, related research on digital picture books is examined in a detailed way. Li and Bus (2023) carried out experimental research to investigate the effects of visual and auditory enhancements of digital Picture books on comprehension and incidental vocabulary acquisition. Totally 183 children participated in their research whose ages varied from 3 to 5 years old. Results of the study showed that visual and auditory enhancements improved children's story comprehension and vocabulary learning process. Another significant finding is that both digital books with visual and auditory enhancement are more effective that the books with single enhancement in terms of comprehension. Another research was conducted to investigate enhancements' effects on children's understanding of digital stories. The results revealed that children with low language proficiency can arrange their pace of information processing. Another research examined parent and child interaction and digital pen use during digital picture reading while child is learning English (Choi, Kang, & Sheoi, 2020). In total, 320 Korean mothers participated in the study. The study showed that children were more engaged in reading process when they used digital pens, and they were more active in parent and child interaction during English picture book reading. A meta-analysis examined 39 studies on children's story comprehension and vocabulary learning through digital books in which 1,812 children's cases presented (Furenes, Kucirkova, & Bus, 2021). The analysis of digital books versus paper books, with the only distinguishing factor being digitization, revealed that digital books were associated with worse comprehension ratings. The efficacy of adults' mediation during the reading of print books was found to surpass the effectiveness of upgrades in digital books when children read independently. Nevertheless, when including story-congruent upgrades, digital books exhibited superior performance compared to their paper counterparts. The inclusion of an embedded dictionary did not yield any significant impact or detriment to children's comprehension of stories. However, it did have a positive influence on children's acquisition of vocabulary. The discussion pertains to the cognitive load hypothesis and its practical design consequences. Dobakhti and Panahi (2021) carried out another study to look into the impact of digital picture books on young Iranian learners' speaking abilities. A total of 18 language teachers and 272 young language learners took part in the study. Results of the experimental study showed that the utilization of digital picture storytelling has been found to augment learners' speech-producing abilities. The utilization of semi-structured interviews elucidated the favorable impact on the learners' motivation and the teachers' experiences while using this approach in their instructional sessions. The results of this study have the potential to assist language educators in their decision-making process when it comes to choosing an instructional approach that effectively supports the development of oral communication skills among young students. Another qualitative study was carried out in the Malaysian context on the effectiveness of picture books to develop vocabulary knowledge (Rahman & Tan, 2022). The results show that using pictures, short sentences, and carefully chosen words in picture books helps students understand difficult and new words better. In addition, the utilization of picture books facilitates comprehension of the narrative structure for individuals who are inclined towards visual learning. Various forms of presentation in picture books serve as a valuable means to engage students and sustain their interest in reading. Another study by

Li (2020) investigated whether the effects of the enhancements in digital e-books vary with age groups. The results show that adding enhancements to stories helped younger children understand them better than stories without these additions. The implementation of modifications specifically aimed at older children (aged 5–6) proved to be advantageous in facilitating the learning of expressive language. Researchers found that using either animation or music and sounds separately was better at helping younger kids understand stories and improving all kids' listening and speaking vocabulary than using animation, music, and sounds together in one format (Li, 2020). In another study carried out by Zhou, Fei, and Chen (2021), online picture books were found to be useful in developing reading comprehension ability, increasing students' reading interest, and developing reading habits and strategies. Another study showed the presence of a greater number of books and games inside one's home was found to be positively correlated with the development of a more extensive vocabulary. The research emphasizes the significance of establishing a robust Home Literacy Environment (HLE) and advocating for the practice of frequent readings to enhance the vocabulary development of youngsters (Sucuoğlu, 2023).

Upon comprehensive evaluation, scholarly research has demonstrated that digital picture books have a significant impact on the comprehension of narratives among young learners. These books enhance the acquisition of vocabulary words that are infrequently utilized in daily life, particularly when accompanied by multimedia aids. Furthermore, the utilization of digital image books in early education fosters a favourable disposition towards reading and facilitates the cultivation of diverse reading strategies.

Young Learners and L2 Vocabulary Acquisition Through Digital Picture Books

Certain features distinguish young learners from other individuals. Young learners expect approval and attention from educators, have shorter attention spans than adults, are curious, and they like to talk about themselves (Harmer, 2003). The learning processes of young learners, who have quite different characteristics from adults, the teaching activities to be used in these processes, the materials to be used and the course contents should be carefully selected and planned by the emotional, physical, and cognitive development of these students. One of the methods widely used in learning environments for young learners is reading stories and telling stories. Stories present social and linguistic components for young learners, either verbal or written, in a carefully designed context and plot. Since young learners are familiar with their parents' story-reading activities, conducting these activities in the classroom environment contributes positively to their learning processes. Because young learners have low affective filters, the natural learning process

Digital Picture Books in Young Learners' Language Classrooms

occurs (Dabakhti & Pinahi, 2022). The integration of stories in the target language classroom environment of young learners enables children to learn the language in context (Dabakhti & Pinahi, 2022). When story reading and storytelling activities are supported by guided questions and comprehension questions, young learners become involved in the learning process. In the process, they can also develop other cognitive strategies for predicting the meaning, understanding the gist of the story, identifying contextual clues, and learning languages (Dobakhti & Pinahi, 2022).

The books used for teaching English as a foreign language in the classrooms of young learners should be suitable for students' reading habits. It is also important that the design used in the books arouse curiosity and interest among the students. Pre-school English teachers should first share digital image books for students to read images. Then s/he should explain the words in the book and wait for the students to put them into their minds with their imagination. This activity should consider the attentiveness periods of young learners and should be completed in a way that does not exceed their cognitive load. At the end of the activity, learning should be reinforced by directed questions and comprehension questions (Zhao et al. 2018). Digital picture books, enriched with multimedia features, will help young learners concretize abstract words in their minds, imagine the story, and learn new words. Because reading digital picture books is a multi-faceted activity for children, such as seeing, listening, imagining, and learning (Ma & Wei, 2016). It will also promote the social aspects of young learners' interaction and communication with peers and teachers, thereby positively influencing them.

Samples for Websites and Applications Provide Digital Picture Books

There are many websites and apps today that offer digital image books for young learners. Some websites offer their readers completely free books, while others offer them to readers by subscription for a certain amount of fee. Digital image books can be accessed through their websites as well as apps that can be downloaded to mobile phones or tablets. This section takes a detailed look at websites and practical examples that offer digital image books for young learners.

One of the websites that can access digital image books is Tumblebooklibrary. The link to this site is https://www.tumblebooklibrary.com/. There are many options on the site, such as story books, read-along books, e-books, puzzles, and games. Books are supported by multimedia such as audio, and video, depending on their categories.

The following is a digital image book from the Tumble Book library entitled "Bounce", written by Doreen Cronin and Scott Menchin.

Figure 1. The following visual is from a digital image book in the Tumble Book library entitled Chicken, Ping, Cow, written by Ruth Ohi

Figure 2. Another website that offers digital image books is Hoopladigital. Access link; https://www.hoopladigital.com/home. The website has many books for both children and adults.

Digital Picture Books in Young Learners' Language Classrooms

Figure 3. The visual below is taken from the Hoopladigital

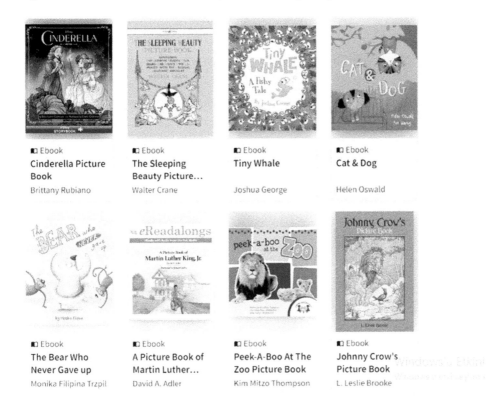

Another platform offering digital image books is barnesandnoble and the access link is https://www.barnesandNoble.com/b/free-ebooks/kids/_/N-ry0Ztu1. The site, which offers many digital image books, has quite rich content. This website, where books are classified according to the age or interest of the reader, is very interesting.

Figure 4. The following visual barnesandnoble site contains examples of books that might be of interest to the 0-2 age group.

Another website is kidlit.tv, access link; https://www.kidlit.TV/. KidLit TV is a winner of the Parent's Choice Gold Award and has been selected as an American Association of School Librarians Best Digital Tool for Teaching and Learning. There is a lot of content for children, such as audiobooks, drawing videos, storytelling and radio.

Another website is storylineonline, and the access link is https://storylineonline.net/. The SAG-AFTRA Foundation's Daytime Emmy®-nominated and award-winning children's literacy website, Storyline Online®, streams videos featuring celebrated actors reading children's books alongside creatively produced illustrations.

Digital Picture Books in Young Learners' Language Classrooms

Figure 5. The image below is from kidlit.tv

Another website is storyboxlibrary, access link; https://storylineonline.net/library/. The site contains audio digital books and offers users an extensive list of readings.

As a result, many websites and applications offer digital versions of printed picture books to early childhood students, enhanced with pictures, animations, and videos. The resources that can be used by parents who want to improve their children's skills such as reading, reading comprehension, critical thinking, and complex thinking, teachers who want to support the social, cognitive and linguistic development of students, and students who are conscious about their development and enjoy reading are accessible and easily usable on the above-mentioned websites. In foreign language programs, it is typically assumed that students possess a certain level of proficiency with technology tools when utilizing them for language skill instruction. In educational settings where students lack familiarity with electronic tools, a significant portion of their instructional time may be devoted to the exploration and acquisition of requisite skills, thereby bypassing the customary introduction phase. Regrettably, the duration dedicated to this exploration will exceed the allotted time for course content, perhaps impeding or omitting the learning opportunity. It is imperative to consider that assessing students' familiarity with the practical applications of electronic devices such as tablets or iPads before the class or providing further instruction during extracurricular periods for those lacking knowledge, may be adequate measures. In the context of utilizing digital stories as a means to enhance reading proficiency, it is plausible that certain students may have difficulties in accessing a digital book or comprehending the functionalities inherent within the application employed. In such instances, it would be advantageous to adhere to a set of procedural guidelines.

- The instructor ought to provide a demonstration to the pupils on the process of activating the electronic gadget and accessing the required applications.
- The teacher is required to provide instruction to the students regarding the appropriate positioning of the screen. The instructor ought to demonstrate the proper technique for accessing the contents of the book and turning its pages.
- It is recommended that educators provide clear criteria for students regarding the appropriate utilization of interactions, such as determining whether they should engage in them while reading, thereafter, or upon revisiting the text later.

It would be inappropriate to assume that students had a literal familiarity with programs or websites in educational settings when these tools are employed for skill instruction, notwithstanding the increasing prevalence of electronic tools among students. Another salient subject of discussion pertains to the interactive functionalities inherent in digital image books. It is imperative for language instructors to ensure that the interactive elements employed in language instruction do not serve as distractions for pupils, and to assess their ability to maintain focus on the text. The utilization of digital picture books in the instruction of foreign languages to young learners is a relatively recent pedagogical approach. In the present situation, there is a significant likelihood of heightened interest among children in digital picture books. In this domain, it has been observed that the aforementioned application is still in its nascent stage, hence indicating a dearth of established best practices.

CONCLUSION

In this book chapter, the contribution of picture books to young learners' development, the features of digital picture books and their effects on young learners' social, linguistic and cognitive development, the features of digital picture books, the use of digital picture books in young learner foreign language classrooms, examples of well-designed digital picture books and their applications, research on the use of digital picture books in foreign language teaching are discussed. With the changing and developing technology, the reading habits of young learners who open their eyes to a technological world and live in this world as well as adults are also changing. Today, accessible technologies continue to digitalize the reading habits of young learners. Digital picture books are one of the most important examples of this change. As discussed in detail in the existing book section, a well-designed technology-supported digital picture book can contribute to children's story comprehension and vocabulary learning with its visual and auditory features (Justice, Logan, & Damschroder, 2015). Digital picture books can improve children's interest in reading and books (Cjoi et al., 2020). In addition, digital picture books help children acquire skills that are very important for children by supporting cognitive engagement, critical thinking, and visualization (Agosto, 2016). Research has found that when a parent is present, there is no difference in children's story comprehension when reading traditional picture books and digital picture books (Takacs et al., 2014). However, in the absence of a parent or educator, multimedia supports will greatly contribute to the child's comprehension of what he/she reads, to visualize the story in his/her mind, to make sense of the newly learned vocabulary and to concretize it. The features of digital storybooks, their high-quality content and carefully designed multimedia features will contribute to children's academic success (Kucirkova, 2019). In this context, it is very important to integrate digital picture books into young learners' classrooms to contribute to vocabulary learning in a foreign language.

REFERENCES

Ab Rahman, F., & Tan, S. C. E. (2022). Can Picture Books In English Classroom Lead To Increase Vocabulary Learning? *International Journal of Education. Psychology and Counseling*, *7*(46), 286–301. doi:10.35631/IJEPC.746023

Agosto, D. E. (2016). Why storytelling matters: Unveiling the literacy benefits of storytelling. *Children & Libraries*, *14*(2), 21–26. doi:10.5860/cal.14n2.21

Akhtar, N., & Menjivar, J. A. (2012). Cognitive and linguistic correlates of early exposure to more than one language. In Benson, J.B. (ed) *Advances in child development and behavior.* Burlington: Academic. 10.1016/B978-0-12-394388-0.00002-2

Alqahtani, M. (2015). The importance of vocabulary in language learning and how to be taught. *International Journal of Teaching and Education*, *3*(3), 21–34. doi:10.20472/TE.2015.3.3.002

Barnyak, N. C., & McNelly, T. A. (2016). The literacy skills and motivation to read of children enrolled in Title I: A comparison of electronic and print nonfiction books. *Early Childhood Education Journal*, *44*(5), 527–536. doi:10.100710643-015-0735-0

Bus, G. A., & Anstadt, R. (2021). Toward Digital Picture Books for a New Generation of Emergent Readers. *AERA Open*, *7*(1), 1–15. doi:10.1177/23328584211063874

Cameron, L. (2001). *Teaching languages to young learners*. Cambridge University Press. doi:10.1017/CBO9780511733109

Choi, N., Kang, S., Cho, H. J., & Sheo, J. (2019). Promoting young children's interest in learning english in efl context: The role of mothers. *Education Sciences*, *9*(1), 46. doi:10.3390/educsci9010046

Choi, N., Kang, S. & Sheo, J. (2020). Children's Interest in Learning English Through Picture Books in an EFL Context: The Effects of Parent–Child Interaction and Digital Pen Use. *Education sciences, 2020* (10,40), 1-11. doi:10.3390/educsci10020040

Dobakhti, L., & Panahi, M. (2021). The Effect of Digital Picture Storytelling (PST) on Improving Young Iranian Learners' Foreign Language Oral Production. *Iranian Journal of English for Academic Purposes*, *11*(1), 40–56. 20.1001.1.24763187.2 022.11.1.4.5

Evans, M. A., Reynolds, K., Shaw, D., & Pursoo, T. (2011). Parental explanations of vocabulary during shared book reading: A missed opportunity. *First Language*, *31*(2), 195–213. doi:10.1177/0142723710393795

Furenes, I. M., Kucirkova, N., & Bus, A. G. (2021). A Comparison of Children's Reading on Paper Versus Screen: A Meta-Analysis. *Review of Educational Research*, *91*(4), 483–517. doi:10.3102/0034654321998074

Gremmen, M. C., Molenaar, I., & Teepe, R. (2016). Vocabulary development at home: A multimedia elaborated picture supporting parent– toddler interaction. *Journal of Computer Assisted Learning*, *32*(6), 548–560. doi:10.1111/jcal.12150

Harmer, J. (2003). *The practice of English language teaching*. Longman.

Hindman, A. H., Wasik, B. A., & Erhart, A. C. (2012). Shared book reading and Head Start preschoolers' vocabulary learning: The role of book-related discussion and curricular connections. *Early Education and Development*, *23*(4), 451–474. do i:10.1080/10409289.2010.537250

Hoffman, J. L., & Paciga, K. A. (2014). Click, Swipe, and Read: Sharing e-Books with Toddlers and Preschoolers. *Early Childhood Education Journal*, *42*(6), 379–388. doi:10.100710643-013-0622-5

Justice, L. M., Logan, J. R., & Damschroder, L. (2015). Designing caregiver-implemented shared-reading interventions to overcome implementation barriers. *Journal of Speech, Language, and Hearing Research: JSLHR, 58*(6), 1851–1863. doi:10.1044/2015_JSLHR-L-14-0344 PMID:26262941

Köroğlu, Z. Ç. (2021). Using Digital Formative Assessment to Evaluate EFL Learners' English Speaking Skills. *GIST–Education and Learning Research Journal*, (22), 103–123. doi:10.26817/16925777.1001

Kucirkova, N. (2019). Children's Reading with Digital Books: Past Moving Quickly to the Future. *Child Development Perspectives, 13*(4), 208–214. doi:10.1111/cdep.12339

Li, X. (2020). *The Effects of Enhanced E-Books on Young Children's Story Comprehension and Vocabulary Growth.* [Unpublished Doctoral Dissertation, University of Houston].

Li, X., & Bus, G. A. (2023). Efficacy of digital picture book enhancements grounded in multimedia learning principles: Dependent on age? *Learning and Instruction, 85*, 1–9. doi:10.1016/j.learninstruc.2023.101749

Marion, T. (2008). The effect of gestures on second language memorization by young children. *Gesture. John Benjamins Publishing, 8*(2), 219–235.

Mayer, R. E. (2003). The promise of multimedia learning: Using the same instructional design methods across different media. *Learning and Instruction, 13*(2), 125–139. doi:10.1016/S0959-4752(02)00016-6

Mayer, R. E. (2014). Principles for managing essential processing in multimedia learning: Segmenting, pretraining, and modality principles. In R. E. Mayer (Ed.), *The Cambridge handbook of multimedia learning* (pp. 169–182). Cambridge University. doi:10.1017/CBO9781139547369.016

Montag, J. L. (2019). Differences in sentence complexity in the text of children's picture books and child-directed speech. *First Language, 39*(5), 527–546. doi:10.1177/0142723719849996 PMID:31564759

Montag, J. L., Jones, M. N., & Smith, L. B. (2015). The words children hear: Picture books and the statistics for language learning. *Psychological Science, 26*(9), 1489–1496. doi:10.1177/0956797615594361 PMID:26243292

Oakley, G., & Jay, J. (2008). Making time for reading: Factors that influence the success of multimedia reading at home. *The Reading Teacher, 62*(3), 246–255. doi:10.1598/RT.62.3.6

Paivio, A. (2007). *Mind and its evolution: A dual coding theoretical approach. Mind and its evolution: A dual coding theoretical approach.* Lawrence Erlbaum Associates Publishers., doi:10.4324/9781315785233

Pearman, C. J., & Lefever-Davis, S. (2006). Supporting the essential elements with CD-ROM storybooks. *Reading Horizons, 46*(4), 301–313. doi:10.1598/RT.61.8.1

Penno, J. F., Wilkinson, I. A. G., & Moore, D. W. (2002). Vocabulary acquisition from teacher explanation and repeated listening to stories: Do they overcome the Matthew effect? *Journal of Educational Psychology, 94*(1), 23–33. doi:10.1037/0022-0663.94.1.23

Perkins, D. (1994). *The intelligent eye: learning to think by looking at art.* Harvard Graduate School of Education.

Richter, A., & Courage, M. L. (2017, January). Comparing electronic and paper storybooks for preschoolers: Attention, engagement, and recall. *Journal of Applied Developmental Psychology, 48,* 92–102. doi:10.1016/j.appdev.2017.01.002

Rubegni, E., Dore, R., Landoni, M., & Kan, L. (2021). "The girl who wants to fly": Exploring the role of digital technology in enhancing dialogic reading. *International Journal of Child-Computer Interaction, 30,* 100239. doi:10.1016/j.ijcci.2020.100239

Santoro, L. E., Chard, D. J., Howard, L., & Baker, S. K. (2008). Making the very most of classroom read-alouds to promote comprehension and vocabulary. *The Reading Teacher, 61*(5), 396–408. doi:10.1598/RT.61.5.4

Strouse, G. A., & Ganea, P. A. (2017). Parent–toddler behavior and language differ when reading electronic and print picture books. *Frontiers in Psychology, 8,* 677. doi:10.3389/fpsyg.2017.00677 PMID:28559858

Sucuoğlu, E. (2023). *Exploring Linguistic Transfer in Bilingual Children through Repeated Digital Picture Book Reading.* [Unpublished master's Thesis, University of Twente Student].

Takacs, Z. K., Swart, E. K., & Bus, A. G. (2014). Can the computer replace the adult for storybook reading? A meta-analysis on the effects of multimedia stories as compared to sharing print stories with an adult. *Frontiers in Psychology, 5,* 1366. doi:10.3389/fpsyg.2014.01366 PMID:25520684

Takacs, Z. K., Swart, E. K., & Bus, A. G. (2015). Benefits and Pitfalls of Multimedia and Interactive Features in Technology-Enhanced Storybooks: A Meta-Analysis. *Review of Educational Research, 85*(4), 698–739. doi:10.3102/0034654314566989 PMID:26640299

Verhallen, M. J. A. J., & Bus, A. G. (2010). Low-income immigrant pupils learning vocabulary through digital picture storybooks. *Journal of Educational Psychology*, *102*(1), 54–61. doi:10.1037/a0017133

Wilkins, D. A. (1981). *Second- language learning and teaching*. Edward Arnold.

Yeung, S. S., Ng, M., & King, R. B. (2016). English vocabulary instruction through storybook reading for Chinese EFL kindergarteners: Comparing rich, embedded, and incidental approaches. *Asian EFL J.*, *18*, 89–112.

Yokota, J., & Teale, W. H. (2014). Picture Books and the Digital World: Educators Making Informed Choices. *The Reading Teacher*, *67*(8), 577–585. doi:10.1002/trtr.1262

Zhao, J., Guo, L., Zheng, S., Li, S., & Zhu, J. (2018). In P. Zhao, Y. Ouyang, M. Xu, L. Yang, & Y. Ren (Eds.), *Design and Development of Mobile Interactive Picture Books* (pp. 353–360). Applied Sciences in Graphic Communication and Packaging., doi:10.1007/978-981-10-7629-9_43

Zhou, Y., Fei, T., & Chen, J. (2021). The Integration of Internet and Picture Book: Using Online Picture Book Reading Project to Promote Primary School Students' Reading Literacy. *SHS Web of Conferences* 123, 01025. 10.1051hsconf/202112301025

ADDITIONAL READING

Choi, N., Kang, S. & Sheo, J. (2020). Children's Interest in Learning English Through Picture Books in an EFL Context: The Effects of Parent–Child Interaction and Digital Pen Use. *Education sciences, 2020* (10,40), 1-11. doi:10.3390/educsci10020040

Li, X. (2020). *The Effects of Enhanced E-Books on Young Children's Story Comprehension and Vocabulary Growth*. University of Houston, Unpublished Doctoral Dissertation. Department of Curriculum and Instruction, College of Education.

Li, X., & Bus, G. A. (2023). Efficacy of digital picture book enhancements grounded in multimedia learning principles: Dependent on age? *Learning and Instruction*, *85*, 1–9. doi:10.1016/j.learninstruc.2023.101749

KEY TERMS AND DEFINITIONS

Digital Picture Book: Incorporates many elements such as illustrations, text, music, and occasionally movement, to enhance and complement one another, resulting in a multimedia textual experience.

Picture Book: A story intended for the youngest of readers, in which the illustrations and the text work together to tell the story.

Chapter 9
Human vs. AI:
The Use of ChatGPT in Writing Assessment

Betul Kınık
Inonu University, Turkey

Hande Çetin
ⓘ https://orcid.org/0000-0002-2710-4083
Tokat Gaziosmanpasa University, Turkey

ABSTRACT

The current study seeks to investigate whether ChatGPT 3.5 can be used as an aid to help diminish the teachers' workload in assessing writing. To this aim, a mixed-methods research design was employed for the study. Randomly selected, 20 descriptive essays written by freshman student teachers of English Language Teaching were scored by an experienced human rater and ChatGPT 3.5. An adapted 'descriptive essay rubric' by the researchers was used to assess the descriptive essays of the student teachers. The quantitative aspect of the study involved frequency and percentage analysis, while the qualitative dimension centered on analyzing the written feedback provided by both ChatGPT and the human rater. The findings showed that there is a disagreement between ChatGPT 3.5 and the human rater. Furthermore, there are some problems with the written feedback it provides. It is clear that it is rapid in terms of providing feedback. Thus, it is recommended that ChatGPT 3.5 can be employed as a tool under the supervision of teachers.

DOI: 10.4018/979-8-3693-0353-5.ch009

Copyright © 2024, IGI Global. Copying or distributing in print or electronic forms without written permission of IGI Global is prohibited.

Human vs. AI

INTRODUCTION

The literature consistently emphasizes the importance of students practicing writing extensively to enhance their ability to express themselves effectively. However, it is acknowledged that teachers often face time constraints, hindering their ability to provide timely feedback and evaluate student assignments. This challenge has led to the expansion of the Automated Writing Evaluation (AWE), also accentuated as Automated Essay Evaluation and Automated Essay Scoring (Huawei & Aryadoust, 2023) and its supporters. AWE leverages Artificial Intelligence (AI) technology to rapidly score written work (Cushing Weigle, 2010; Warschauer & Grimes, 2008). "The sheer number of hours commenting on student papers is reduced dramatically when instructors can rely on automated electronic feedback systems" (Ware & Warschauer, 2006, p. 108). Whereas the studies have shown that AWE can be used as an aid for teachers to score writing (Wilson & Roscoe, 2020), it is worth noting that there remain a number of concerns raised, especially among writing educators (Cushing Weigle, 2010).

AWE systems make use of AI (Steiss et al., 20223), which can be specified as "natural language processing (NLP) and machine learning techniques" (Uto, 2021), examine written texts, and promptly produce ratings based on the writing quality. Furthermore, they provide written feedback to improve overall and specific aspects of writing (Cushing Weigle, 2010). While the current functionalities of AWE systems are impressive, it's worth tracing their evolution over the decades.

It was 1960s when Page (1966) mentioned the possibility of scoring the essays in an automated way with their project called 'Project Essay Grade'. Three decades later, with the developments in computer and the Internet created possibilities for marketing globally (Warschauer & Grimes, 2008). Education Testing Service (ETS) developed a system which was called *e-rater* to score the essays written in TOEFL IBT (Cushing Weigle, 2010). Simultaneously, Intellimetric was developed by Vantage Learning. Another engine to score high-stake writing tasks was Intelligent Essay Assessor which was developed by a group of academics used a technique called latent semantic analysis. Pearson, a publishing company, later acquired this technology for their tests (Warschauer & Grimes, 2008). Apart from these, there are AWE tools which were designed for classroom use, including Writer's Workbench, MY Access!, WriteToLearn, Criterion, and RWT (Saricaoglu, 2015). AWE systems make use of natural language processing (NLP) (Wison & Roscoe, 2020).

AWE tools have been investigated from different aspects, such as the validity of the scoring in high-stakes tests (Attali & Burstein, 2006; Cushing Weigle, 2010); effectiveness of AWE (Stevenson & Phakiti, 2014; Wilson & Roscoe, 2020); AWE's reliability (Shermis, 2014). Furthermore, the researchers have started to examine how Chat Generative Pre-trained Transformer (ChatGPT) can be used for assessment

(Khademi, 2023). ChatGPT, which is one of the chatbots, was shared with the public in November, 2022. However, further research studies are needed to be conducted to be able to use these technologies more effectively. It has been exemplified how ChatGPT has been used as a mediator for learning. Different prompt examples have been shared so that learners can benefit from ChatGPT for their learning, however, integrating technology into the teaching part is also essential. Teachers can make use of ChatGPT for various purposes, such as designing their lessons and creating assignments and test questions (Trust et al., 2023). Teachers can also use ChatGPT for feedback purposes, but ChatGPT has not been designed specifically for giving feedback. Another issue with ChatGPT is that it may create information lacking accuracy but seeming perfectly reasonable (Borji, 2023). Therefore, the feedback features of it need to be explored. Considering the bulk of assessing writing and giving feedback to the students, the present study tries to unravel the potentials and constraints of ChatGPT-3.5 for writing assessment. The primary reasons for choosing ChatGPT-3.5 are its cost-effectiveness and widespread adoption. To this aim, the following research questions were asked:

1. What are the differences and similarities between the assessment scores of the human raters and ChatGPT-3.5 for the writing assignments of the students?
2. What are the positive aspects and limitations of ChatGPT-3.5 (2023) for assessing writing assignments?

By addressing these research questions, this study seeks to contribute to the existing body of knowledge on the use of AI in language education and writing assessment. In the following lines of this paper, the researchers use ChatGPT to refer to ChatGPT 3.5. To this aim, the following research questions were asked:

RELATED RESEARCH

Cushing Weigle's (2010) study focused on the validity of the e-rater and tried to understand what kind of a relationship there is between AWE and human scores in the grading process of independent writing tasks of TOEFL-IBT. For that purpose, the writer analyzed the correlations between both human and e-rater scores with some other criteria. Both human and e-rater scores and non-test indicators' correlation results showed moderate but consistent scores.

AWE tools used in the classroom have been widely investigated. In the study of Wilson and Roscoe (2020), they focused on the effectiveness of AWE and did by operationalizing efficacy in various aspects: "the effects of classroom AWE use on students' writing quality after instruction, students' writing self-efficacy, and students' performance on standardized state tests" (Wilson & Roscoe, 2020, p. 88). Furthermore, they investigated teachers' perceptions regarding AWE's effectiveness and usability. The findings revealed that students' self-efficacy level for writing and achievements in the high-stakes test was higher compared to the students who did not use AWE.

Incorporating AWE systems can increase the amount of feedback the teacher provides to the students as presented in a study by Wilson & Czik, 2016. The findings of their study showed that a group of teachers incorporated Project Essay Grade (PEG) Writing. Those teachers provided more feedback to the students on 'ideas', 'organization', and 'style' than the teachers who did not use any AWE system.

Chatbots have been investigated by scholars to see the effects of them on learners' language skills. Even though the studies mainly focused on the productive skills of the learners (Kim, 2016, Kim, 2018a, some studies investigated receptive skills (Kim, 2018b), as well.

ChatGPT, one of the popular chatbots, has been used for different functions. On its homepage, it suggests its users some prompts to write, such as "Design a database schema for an online merch store", or "Write a short email to my professor requesting a deadline extension for my project. I don't really have a good excuse, and I'm fine owning up to that – so please keep it real!".

As it can be seen from the prompts, one of the areas that ChatGPT has offered is writing. ChatGPT works differently compared to the AWE software tools. AWE tools have used corpora for different genres; however, ChatGPT does not function in that way. Unlike AWE tools, ChatGPT is affordable and can be easily reached (Steiss et al., 2023).

'ChatGPT has been widely used for essay writing, application drafting, email content generation, and research paper writing since its inception' (Sohail et al. 2023, p.11). Various studies have confirmed that ChatGPT is good at copying human writing. For example, in Bishop's study (2023), ChatGPT copied not only human style but also authors' styles.

Casal and Kessler's (2023) study focused on academic writing and using AI tools. They wanted to analyze whether the writings by AI tools can be differentiated by humans. Furthermore, they wanted to analyze its ethical dimensions from the perspective of editors. The findings revealed that reviewers were not successful in detecting AI writings. The editors' beliefs majorly centered on the idea that using AI tools does not compromise ethics.

An important feature of writing is to be able to be good at argumentation. Su et al. (2023) investigated whether ChatGPT had the potential to be used for the stages of argumentative writing when the students prepare their writing tasks. Their findings showed that students could get feedback about the organizational and mechanical dimensions of their essays from ChatGPT. Another positive aspect is that ChatGPT became the "virtual peer" (Su et al., 2023, p. 4) for the learners so that they could discuss with them and get some tips to develop their ideas and essays. Furthermore, ChatGPT can be seen in different roles like a teacher in the argumentative essay process. However, when it comes to logical reasoning, ChatGPT does not work efficiently. Another limitation, the authors highlighted was the concerns with the ethical issues.

Fang et al. (2023) revealed that ChatGPT's error correction is at the highest level. In parallel with that, it was seen that the fluency level was really high in the corrected sentences. Even though there are some problems with some corrections, scholars see the big potential of ChatGPT in reducing the burden on teachers.

The inquiries regarding ChatGPT's feedback capacity and quality have been increasing. It seems that different research studies have been searching for different aspects of feedback of ChatGPT: feedback quality comparison by ChatGPT and humans (Steiss et al., 2023); reliability of ChatGPT in giving feedback (Khademi, 2023). This research study aims to contribute to the feedback studies of ChatGPT.

METHODOLOGY

Procedure

For the research design, a mixed-methods design (Creswell, 2014) was adopted for the current study. In the research procedure, ChatGPT was shared with the descriptive writing rubric, which was adapted from the current study's researchers. One of the researchers, the instructor of the course, inserted the rubric into ChatGPT and asked it to assess randomly selected 20 essays one by one based on the rubric. The following prompt was used for ChatGPT: "Can you evaluate the following essay based on the rubric? Please share direct examples from the essay and your reasons why you scored in that way." While one researcher recorded the scores generated by ChatGPT in MS Excel, the other researcher, who is an experienced teacher educator in assessing writing, evaluated the writings independently without consulting ChatGPT's results and entered her scores into MS Excel. Even though the researchers wanted to see how teachers/instructors could use ChatGPT for their writing classes, they did not want to have any biases in assessing the essays. Thus, only one researcher graded the essays, however, the other researcher who was the instructor of the course completed the procedure with ChatGPT. Furthermore, ChatGPT's written feedback was copied into MS Word.

After the evaluation part was completed, the researchers compared the scores of the human rater and ChatGPT in MS Excel and tabulated them. They analyzed

Human vs. AI

the written feedback of both parties and realized the inconsistencies in ChatGPT's written evaluation.

Context

Even though only the writings of the student teachers and the feedback given to them by human rater and AI are the concerns of the study, it is worth mentioning the context and the students' profiles. The context of the study consists of an English Language Teaching department of a university located in the eastern part of Türkiye. The program offers a four-year education with a compulsory one-year of preparatory instruction, primarily dedicated to enhancing the English language proficiency of student teachers.

The student teachers in this study took Writing Skills 1, which was in English, in their first semester from a different instructor. They studied different types of paragraphs and learned how to create paragraphs. Additionally, they learned how to create an essay, but they did not have much chance to practice different genres. In the second semester, one of the researchers became their instructor; however, due to an earthquake in southeastern Turkey, all classes were conducted in an asynchronous online format. That means the instructor uploaded videos and gave assignments to student teachers regarding different genres.

Data Collection Instruments

Among 75 descriptive essays written by freshman student teachers of English, randomly selected 20 essays constituted the data collection instruments of the study. They were the assignments of the student teachers for the descriptive essay genre. They were given a prompt, which can be found in Appendix 1. It's worth noting that the students had information about the rubric they were going to be assessed. For the ethical integrity of the study, some measurements were taken. For example, the students' names and any other identifying information were removed from the essays. One of the researchers, who was the instructor of the Writing Skills 1 course, did not score the essays not to have any biases in the scoring even though the anonymity of the essays were ensured. The essays were stored in the shared folder of the researchers on Google Drive which can not be accessible by any other parties because of the 2-step verification was employed for the account of the mail holder.

Data Analysis

The data analysis of the study was conducted quantitatively and qualitatively. Firstly, the researchers used the "Descriptive Writing Rubric", which can be found in Appendix 2, in the assessment of the essays. For the quantitative analysis, a descriptive analysis of the scores of the ChatGPT and human raters was conducted. The researchers calculated the frequency of scores for each essay and performed frequency and percentage analyses for each aspect of the rubric. Additionally, they conducted the analyses to see the results of Cohen's Kappa. In the qualitative analysis, ChatGPT's reasons for the scores it shared were examined to identify the strengths and limitations of ChatGPT.

Reliability and Validity

While some scholars have expressed reservations about the use of rubrics (Balester, 2012), they have been widely embraced in language teaching and learning, receiving support from experts in the field of writing (Crusan, 2010; Crusan, 2015; Dempsey et al., 2009). The researchers align with the perspective of rubric advocates who assert that "...as a rubric can be seen as a regulatory device for scoring, it seems safe to say that scoring with a rubric is probably more reliable than scoring without one" (Jonsson & Svingby, 2007, p. 136). In our study, a rubric was employed to enhance the reliability of the assessment processes by human rater and ChatGPT. As mentioned before, a rubric was found online, and the researchers adapted it. Therefore, to ensure the content validity of the rubric, another expert with a PhD in language teaching was consulted.

Another reliability issue was related to the interrater reliability between the human rater and ChatGPT. Cohen's Kappa analysis on IBM SPSS Statistics was conducted.

FINDINGS and DISCUSSION

In this section, the findings regarding the research questions are presented. The first research question the researchers have tried to find an answer is:

1. What are the similarities and differences between the assessment scores of the human raters and ChatGPT for the writing assignments of the students?

To answer this question, first, writing assignments from two different perspectives were analyzed: human perspective and ChatGPT perspective. ChatGPT and the human rater were asked to analyze the 20 descriptive essays based on the rubric, which had seven dimensions. The ratings were from 4 (Excellent) to 1 (Needs Improvement). The total scores for each dimension of the rubric given by ChatGPT and the human rater are provided in Table 1. Based on these data, the researchers tried to find out

Human vs. AI

the similarities and differences between these two scorings. All the scores rated by ChatGPT and human rater can be seen in Table 1.

Table 1. Score ratings by human rater and ChatGPT

H/C	Ideas	Organization	Introduction	Word Choice	Sensory Detail	Sentence Fluency	Conventions	Total
Essay 1	4/3	4/3	4/3	3/2	2/2	4/3	3/2	24/18
Essay 2	4/4	4/3	3/3	4/4	3/4	4/3	4/3	26/24
Essay 3	4/4	4/3	2/4	3/4	4/4	3/4	3/3	23/26
Essay 4	2/3	2/3	2/3	3/3	1/2	3/3	3/3	16/20
Essay 5	4/4	4/3	2/3	4/3	3/2	3/3	4/3	24/21
Essay 6	4/4	4/3	3/3	4/3	3/3	3/3	4/3	25/22
Essay 7	4/4	4/3	4/3	4/3	4/3	4/3	4/3	28/22
Essay 8	2/3	3/3	2/3	4/3	2/3	4/3	3/3	20/21
Essay 9	3/3	3/3	2/3	4/3	1/3	4/3	3/3	20/21
Essay 10	3/3	2/3	2/3	3/3	2/3	3/3	3/3	18/21
Essay 11	2/3	2/3	3/3	3/3	3/2	3/4	3/3	19/21
Essay 12	4/4	4/3	4/3	3/3	2/4	4/3	4/3	25/23
Essay 13	2/2	2/2	2/3	2/2	2/2	3/3	3/3	16/17
Essay 14	3/3	3/3	2/2	2/3	2/3	3/3	3/3	18/20
Essay 15	3/4	2/3	3/3	2/3	3/4	3/3	3/3	19/23
Essay 16	4/4	4/4	4/4	4/4	3/4	3/3	4/4	26/27
Essay 17	3/3	4/3	2/3	2/3	3/3	3/3	3/3	20/21
Essay 18	4/3	4/3	4/3	3/3	3/3	2/3	3/3	23/21
Essay 19	2/2	3/2	2/2	2/2	2/2	2/2	2/2	15/14
Essay 20	3/3	3/3	2/3	2/2	2/2	2/3	3/3	17/19
	64/66	65/59	54/60	61/59	50/58	63/61	65/59	422/422

Table 1 shows each score given by both the human rater and ChatGPT for each dimension in the descriptive writing rubric. Additionally, with the help of Table 1, the total scores for each writing assignment and the total scores for each dimension of the 20 writing assignments altogether can be seen. The table provides us with a general impression of the scores given by both parties indicating an important inconsistency in each dimension. The similarities and differences in the total scores for each dimension between the human rater and ChatGPT are further illustrated below through the figures.

Figure 1. Total scores for each dimension by ChatGPT

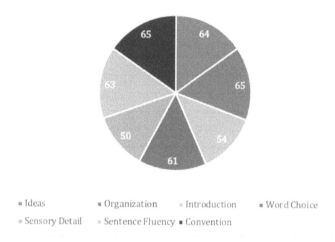

The figure shows the total scores for each dimension rated by Chat GPT. Whereas the 'Ideas' section was rated as the highest (f: 66) by ChatGPT, 'Sensory Detail' got the lowest (f: 58) score. As can be seen in Figure 1. The frequency values of 'Sentence Fluency' and 'Introduction' are 61 and 60 over 80 for 20 descriptive essays. Three dimensions: 'Organization', 'Word Choice', and 'Conventions' have the same frequency value, which is 59.

When the human rater's scores are examined, it is seen that 'Convention' and 'Organization' have the highest (f: 65) scores. Yet, 'Sensory Detail' has the lowest (f: 50) score. The frequency values of 'Ideas', 'Sentence Fluency', 'Word Choice', and 'Introduction' are 64, 63, 61, and 54, respectively.

To be able to analyze the similarities and differences, the scores given to each essay (N: 20) for each dimension (N: 7) were compared. The following table presents the scores for each dimension. While 'H' represents human rater, 'C' represents 'ChatGPT'.

Table 2 presents that the scores of human rater and ChatGPT differ for each dimension. However, interestingly, the total score for the 20 essays is 422 by both human rater and ChatGPT. As can be seen from the table, the scores of the human rater and ChatGPT are very close for "Sensory Detail", "Ideas", "Sentence Fluency", and "Word Choice". For the rest of the dimensions, it seems there is a four-digit difference.

Figure 2. Total scores for each dimension by human rater

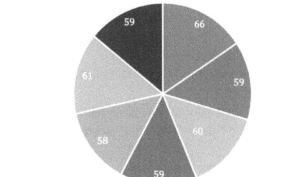

Table 2. Scores by human rater and ChatGPT

Ideas		Organization		Introduction		Word Choice		Sensory Detail		Sentence Fluency		Conventions		Total	
H	C	H	C	H	C	H	C	H	C	H	C	H	C	H	C
64	66	65	59	54	60	61	59	59	58	63	61	65	59	422	422

After calculating the scores for each dimension, the number of matches was calculated to see the level of the agreement as frequency and percentage between ChatGPT and the human rater.

Table 3. The number of matches in the scores for the dimensions of the rubric by human and ChatGPT

Ideas		Organization		Introduction		Word Choice		Sensory Detail		Sentence Fluency		Conventions		Total	
f	%	f	%	f	%	f	%	f	%	f	%	f	%	f	%
14	70	6	30	7	35	10	50	8	40	10	50	14	70	69	49.28

Table 3 clearly presents that scores by human raters and ChatGPT are the same in 14 essays out of 20 for the "Ideas" and "Conventions" dimension in the rubric. Human scores match with the ChatGPT scores 6 times in 20 essays for the "Organization" dimension in the rubric. The number of matches between human scores and chat scores for the item "Introduction" dimension is 7 out of 20. In terms of the dimension "Word choice", it is seen that the human scores and the ChatGPT scores match 10 times in the evaluation of 20 essays.

The "Sensory details" dimension is scored the same in 8 cases out of 20 by the human rater and ChatGPT.

Like the "Word choice" item scores, it is realized that there are 10 matching scores for the item "Sentence fluency" out of 20 scores in the evaluation by the human scorer and ChatGPT.

As a result, it can be said that the human scores and the scores of ChatGPT have the highest frequency for the aspects of "Ideas" and "Conventions" with a matching rate of 14 out of 20. Unlike these two dimensions in the rubric, the least consistent scores by human rater and ChatGPT are for the aspects of "Organization" (6 out of 20); "Introduction" (7 out of 20); and for "Sensory detail" (8 out of 20).

The researchers wanted to make sure of the agreement/disagreement level between the ChatGPT and human rater statistically. Therefore, they conducted Cohen's Kappa analysis on IBM SPSS Statistics to calculate the interrater reliability.

Table 4 presents how Cohen's Kappa should be interpreted (McHugh, 2012).

Table 4. Interpretation of Cohen's Kappa

Value of Kappa	Level of Agreement	% of Data that are Reliable
0-.20	None	0-4%
.21-.39	Minimal	4-15%
.40-.59	Weak	15-35%
.60-.79	Moderate	35-63%
.80-.90	Strong	64-81%
Above .90	Almost Perfect	82-100%

The rubric had a scale of 1 (Needs Improvement) to 4 (Excellent). Therefore, the researchers inserted the data from 1-4 for each dimension, however, the total scores were in the range of 20s. When the Kappa value for the total scores was calculated, a negative value was reached. The researchers decided to recode the total scores as in the dimensions so as not to have any biases in the results. Therefore, they recoded

Human vs. AI

the scores under 20 as 1, 20-25 as 2, and over 25 as 3. They reached the following results after recoding the total scores.

Table 5 shows that the agreement level of ChatGPT and human rater is weak for "Ideas", minimal for "Word Choice" and "Conventions", and the "Total Score". Even though the frequency of "Ideas" and "Word Choice" were the same in terms of the matched scores, their Cohen's Kappa values indicated different agreement levels.

Table 5. Results of Cohen's Kappa between the ChatGPT and human rater

Rubric Dimension	Kappa Value	Asymmetric Standard Error	Approximate T	Approximate Significance
Ideas	.535	.149	3.456	.001
Organization	.051	.100	.612	.541
Introduction	.145	.088	1.612	.107
Word Choice	.242	.162	1.726	.084
Sensory Detail	.111	.152	.772	.440
Sentence Fluency	-.010	.169	-.074	.941
Conventions	.298	.196	2.228	0.26
Total Score	.237	.174	1.546	.172

To the best of the knowledge of the researchers, the number of the studies comparing the agreement level between ChatGPT and human raters is not substantial (Khademi, 2023). Therefore, the researchers compared the findings of the present study with the findings of Khademi (2023) and those of AWE studies. However, the researchers kept in mind that there are differences in the working functions of AWE systems and ChatGPT.

When the results were compared with Khademi (2023), it was realized that it was reached similar findings in terms of the inconsistencies between the scores of humans and ChatGPT. However, the findings are different from the results of AWE softwares. For instance, the minimal agreement between the ChatGPT and human rater differs from the result of Cohen et al. (2003) in which they realized that the AWE software, in their case it was Intellimetric, had a correlation with a .82-.84 with a single human rater.

These findings should be discussed considering that all these software were developed for solely automated scoring, but the main development purpose of ChatGPT was not that. Another reason why there is a minimal agreement between the ChatGPT and human rater can be related to the low sample size of the essays (Covidence, 2023). "The human-computer interrater reliability is expected to be lower in classroom contexts, where the content of student writing is likely to be more important than for the standardized tests" (Warschauer & Grimes, 2008).

The second research question is:

2.   What are the positive aspects and limitations of ChatGPT-3.5 (2023) for assessing writing assignments?

Table 6 presents the positive aspects and the limitations of the use of ChatGPT for assessing writing assignments. These aspects are further illustrated with example extracts taken from the assessments of ChatGPT.

Table 6. Positive aspects and limitations of ChatGPT in writing assessment

Positive Aspects	Limitations
Generating any rubric	Taking long time to upload the rubric
Evaluating based on the rubric	Placing the wrong items under the dimension while generating the rubric
Suggesting items for the rubric's dimensions	Rewriting different items under the existing rubric
Providing written feedback	Inconsistency in the written feedback
Rapid feedback	Inconsistency with the human's ratings

Positive Aspects of ChatGPT

ChatGPT's rapid feedback, undoubtedly, is its most positive aspect in the assessment of descriptive writing. When it is given any prompt, it provides the response in only a few seconds. The other positive aspect is being able to use any rubric in ChatGPT that the teachers need depending on their writing course requirements. Although the whole rubric cannot be uploaded to ChatGPT as a table, it can be generated by providing ChatGPT with the prompts needed for the rubric. An example process adapted for the recent research is described below:

One researcher gave the prompt for the rubric and started with the following prompt: *"I need a table of the following. the left rows will be Ideas, Organization, Introduction, Word Choice, Sensory Detail, Sentence Fluency, and Conventions. The zupper rows will 4-Excellent, 3-Very Good, 2-Satisfactory, 1-Needs Improvement."*

Then, for each dimension, ChatGPT was given such a prompt: *"Can you add the following to the "Excellent" under the "Ideas" category: *"paints a picture" for the reader, *well-focused on the topic, *clear ideas are well- supported with interesting and vivid details"*

Human vs. AI

While generating the rubric, ChatGPT offers some suggestions. If the teachers do not have any rubric for descriptive writing analysis, ChatGPT's suggestions can be used to create their own rubric for assessment.

Besides these positive aspects, ChatGPT explains why the essay is scored in that way. In the first response, it did not provide any examples from the text. That's why, one researcher, who was responsible for ChatGPT's essay evaluation, wanted it to provide examples for each dimension. For example, for the descriptive essay about the painting "The Unequal Marriage" by Pukirev, ChatGPT shares the following for the "Word Choice". It uses the phrases from the Rubric's 'Excellent' rating, such as *precise and vivid word choices*. Lastly, it illustrates with examples.

Word Choice (4 - Excellent):

The author uses precise and vivid word choices throughout the essay to describe the painting and convey emotions.

Example: "The unhappiness and disappointment on the young woman's face carries over the picture in such a way that I feel her pain from this forced marriage in my heart."

The use of phrases like "miserable appearance," "exhausted from crying," and "great unhappiness" effectively conveys the emotions depicted in the painting.

Additionally, it offers some suggestions to develop the essay based on the rubric's items. For instance, for Essay #5, it is seen that it points to specific language flaws.

Conventions (3 - Very Good):

- The essay demonstrates strong grammar, punctuation, and usage for the most part.
- Example: "It's main point is you should live your life without worries because it is too short for that."
- While generally well-constructed, there are a few minor grammatical issues that could be addressed (e.g., "It's main point" could be "Its main point").

Limitations of ChatGPT in Assessing Writing

However, there are some limitations as presented in Table 6 regarding ChatGPT's feedback on writing assessment. First of all, uploading a rubric for ChatGPT 3.5, which is the free version, takes time. As it was explained above, it is not possible to upload a rubric as a whole table to the system in this version. Therefore, the teachers or instructors have to generate the table either in the form of codes or written prompts. Another limitation of ChatGPT is its misplacing the items under dimensions. While one of the researchers was forming the rubric, ChatGPT put the items given in the prompt under different dimensions. When the researcher realized it, ChatGPT was warned:

"It seems you wrote *Thesis statement is well-developed. under the "Very Good" category. However, *Thesis statement is well-developed should be under "Excellent" category for introduction"

Hence, it is necessary to be careful in the rubric generation process.

Another limitation is the inconsistencies between the scores of human rater and ChatGPT. Additionally, the explanations and the scores given by ChatGPT do not correlate with the score it gives. For example, for essay #3, ChatGPT presented the following feedback for the dimension of "Introduction". ChatGPT gave a full score for this dimension (4 out of 4) and provided the following feedback. To be noted, the explanation for the score 4 (Excellent) in the rubric for the dimension of "Introduction" was as follows:

Excellent: "Introductory paragraph clearly states subject of essay and captures reader's attention. Thesis statement is well-developed."

The introduction effectively grabs the reader's attention by immediately diving into the author's passion for cars and racing.

Example: "My biggest interest in this world is cars and anything related to them..."

The introduction sets the stage for the vivid description of the race experience that follows.

It can be seen that the numeric score and the explanation of ChatGPT do not match in this case. Its example for this dimension does not illustrate the explanation given by ChatGPT as well. The introduction of the essay #3 gives an idea about the essay itself but it cannot be said that it captures the reader's attention. Additionally, its score for this dimension is by far inconsistent with the score of human rater: 2 out of 4=satisfactory which is explained in the rubric as follows:

Satisfactory: Introductory paragraph attempts to state the subject of the essay but does not capture reader's attention. Thesis statement is not well enough.

Furthermore, it is realized the inconsistencies in the written feedback and the example that ChatGPT shares. For instance, for essay #13, both the human rater and

Human vs. AI

ChatGPT scored the "Word Choice" as 2 (Satisfactory). ChatGPT's explanation is consistent with its score but not the example taken from the essay.

Word Choice (Score: 2 - Satisfactory):

Example: "The outside of the large restaurant building housing Los Pollos Hermanos is sleek and contemporary."

While the essay provides descriptions of locations, it could benefit from more vivid and engaging word choices to create a stronger emotional impact and paint a clearer picture for the reader.

CONCLUSION

The current research aimed to answer the following research questions: RQ1: What are the differences and similarities between the assessment scores of the human raters and ChatGPT-3.5 for the writing assignments of the students? RQ2: What are the positive aspects and limitations of ChatGPT-3.5 (2023) for assessing writing assignments? A mixed methods design was adopted. In order to answer the first research question (RQ1), the researchers conducted a quantitative analysis and analyzed the scores of ChatGPT and the human rater which were given using the descriptive writing rubric which had seven dimensions as follows: ideas, organization, introduction, word choice, sensory detail, sentence fluency, and conventions. The researchers calculated the frequencies of each essay, and they carried out the frequency and percentage analyses for each dimension of the rubric. Cohen's Kappa was applied in order to see the match, that is to say consistency, between the scores of the human rater and ChatGPT. In light of the findings, it was seen that the scores given by ChatGPT and the human rater are mostly inconsistent. In order to find an answer to the second research question (RQ2), the researchers carried out a qualitative analysis and analyzed ChatGPT's descriptive evaluations, reasons for its scores, and its examples taking into consideration the numeric score it gave to each dimension of each essay to specify the strengths and limitations of the use of ChatGPT for the assessment of descriptive writing. Based on the qualitative analysis, the strengths, and limitations of the use of ChatGPT in descriptive writing assessment were identified and presented. It was seen that the findings from the qualitative analysis supported the results reached through quantitative analysis, both indicating some inconsistencies in the descriptive writing assessment between the human rater and ChatGPT. Despite the possible opportunities provided by the technology of AI in the name of ChatGPT in recent research, it can be seen that AI will not replace humans in the near future. It can be suggested that AI technology should be supported by humans, and more research is suggested to be able to gain in-depth insights into this significant subject.

REFERENCES

Attali, Y., & Burstein, J. (2006). Automated essay scoring with e-rater v. 2. *The Journal of Technology, Learning, and Assessment, 4*(3), 1–30.

Balester, V. (2012). How writing rubrics fail: Toward a multicultural model. In A. I. & M. P. (Eds.), Race and Writing Assessment, (pp. 63-77). Peter Lang.

Bishop, L. (2023). A computer wrote this paper: What ChatGPT means for education, research, and writing. *SSRN, 26.* doi:10.2139srn.4338981

Borji, A. (2023). A categorical archive of ChatGPT failures. *arXiv preprint. /* arXiv.2302.03494 doi:10.21203/rs.3.rs-2895792/v1

Casal, J. E., & Kessler, M. (2023). Can linguists distinguish between ChatGPT/AI and human writing?: A study of research ethics and academic publishing. *Research Methods in Applied Linguistics, 2*(3), 1–12. doi:10.1016/j.rmal.2023.100068

Cohen, Y., Ben-Simon, A., & Hovav, M. (2003, October). *The effect of specific language features on the complexity of systems for automated essay scoring.* Paper presented at the 29th Annual Conference of the International Association for Educational Assessment, Manchester, UK.

Covidence. (2023). *Why is my Cohen's kappa value low and what can I do to improve it?* Covidence. https://support.covidence.org/help/why-is-my-cohen-s-kappa-value-low-and-what-can-i-do-to-improve-it

Creswell, J. W. (2014). *Research design: Qualitative, quantitative, and mixed methods approaches* (4th ed.). Sage.

Crusan, D. (2010). *Assessment in the second language writing classroom.* University of Michigan Press. doi:10.3998/mpub.770334

Crusan, D. J. (2015). Dance, ten; looks, three: Why rubrics matter. *Assessing Writing, 26*(1), 1–4. Advance online publication. doi:10.1016/j.asw.2015.08.002

Cushing Weigle, S. (2010). Validation of automated scores of TOEFL iBT tasks against non-test indicators of writing ability. *Language Testing, 27*(3), 335–353. doi:10.1177/0265532210364406

Dempsey, M. S., PytlikZillig, L. M., & Bruning, R. H. (2009). Helping preservice teachers learn to assess writing: Practice and feedback in a Web-based environment. *Assessing Writing, 14*(1), 38–61. doi:10.1016/j.asw.2008.12.003

Fang, T., Yang, S., Lan, K., Wong, D. F., Hu, J., Chao, L. S., & Zhang, Y. (2023). Is ChatGPT a Highly Fluent Grammatical Error Correction System? A Comprehensive Evaluation. *arXiv (Cornell University).* https://doi.org//arxiv.2304.01746 doi:10.48550

Huawei, S., & Aryadoust, V. (2023). A systematic review of automated writing evaluation systems. *Education and Information Technologies, 28*(1), 771–795. doi:10.100710639-022-11200-7

Jonsson, A., & Svingby, G. (2007). The use of scoring rubrics: Reliability, validity and educational consequences. *Educational Research Review, 2*(2), 130–144. doi:10.1016/j.edurev.2007.05.002

Khademi, A. (2023). Can ChatGPT and bard generate aligned assessment items? A reliability analysis against human performance. *arXiv,* https://doi.org// arXiv.2304.05372 doi:10.48550

Kim, N. Y. (2016). Effects of voice chat on EFL learners' speaking ability according to proficiency levels. *Multimedia-Assisted Language Learning, 19*(4), 63–88. doi:10.15702/mall.2016.19.4.63

Kim, N. Y. (2018a). Chatbots and Korean EFL students' English vocabulary learning. *Journal of Digital Convergence, 16*(2), 1–7. doi:10.14400/JDC.2018.16.2.001

Kim, N.-Y. (2018b). A study on chatbots for developing Korean college students' English listening and reading skills. *Journal of Digital Convergence, 16*(8), 19–26. doi:10.14400/JDC.2018.16.8.019

Lin, M. P.-C., & Chang, D. (2020). Enhancing post-secondary writers' writing skills with a chatbot: A mixed-method classroom study. *Journal of Educational Technology & Society, 23*(1), 78–92. doi:10.30191/ETS.202001_23(1).0006

McHugh, M. L. (2012). Interrater reliability: The kappa statistic. *Biochemia Medica, 22*(3), 276–282. doi:10.11613/BM.2012.031 PMID:23092060

Page, E. B. (1966). The imminence of grading essays by computers. *Phi Delta Kappan, 47,* 238–243.

Saricaoglu, A. (2015). *A systemic functional perspective on automated writing evaluation: Formative feedback on causal discourse* (Publication No. 3728751) [Doctoral dissertation, Iowa State University]. ProQuest Dissertations Publishing.

Shermis, M. D. (2014). State-of-the-art automated essay scoring: Competition, results, and future directions from a United States demonstration. *Assessing Writing*, *20*, 53–76. doi:10.1016/j.asw.2013.04.001

Sohail, S. S., Farhat, F., Himeur, Y., Nadeem, M., Madsen, D. O., Singh, Y., Atalla, S., & Mansoor, W. (2023). Decoding ChatGPT: A taxonomy of existing research, current challenges, and possible future directions. *Journal of King Saud University. Computer and Information Sciences*, *35*(8), 1–23. doi:10.1016/j.jksuci.2023.101675

SteissJ.TateT.GrahamS.CruzJ.HebertM.WangJ.MoonY.TsengW.WarschauerM. (2023). Comparing the quality of human and ChatGPT feedback on students' writing. doi:10.35542/osf.io/ty3em

Stevenson, M., & Phakiti, A. (2014). The effects of computer-generated feedback on the quality of writing. *Assessing Writing*, *19*, 51–65. doi:10.1016/j.asw.2013.11.007

Su, Y., Lin, Y., & Lai, C. (2023). Collaborating with ChatGPT in argumentative writing classrooms. *Assessing Writing*, *57*, 1–11. doi:10.1016/j.asw.2023.100752

Trust, T., Whalen, J., & Mouza, C. (2023). Editorial: ChatGPT: Challenges, opportunities, and implications for teacher education. *Contemporary Issues in Technology & Teacher Education*, *23*(1), 1–23.

Uto, M. (2021). A review of deep-neural automated essay scoring models. *Behaviormetrika*, *48*(2), 459–484. doi:10.100741237-021-00142-y

Warschauer, M., & Grimes, D. (2008). Automated writing assessment in the classroom. *Pedagogies*, *3*(1), 22–36. doi:10.1080/15544800701771580

Warschauer, M., & Ware, P. (2006). Automated writing evaluation: Defining the classroom research agenda. *Language Teaching Research*, *10*(2), 157–180. doi:10.1191/1362168806lr190oa

Wilson, J., & Czik, A. (2016). Automated essay evaluation software in English language arts classrooms: Effects on teacher feedback, student motivation, and writing quality. *Computers & Education*, *100*, 94–109. doi:10.1016/j.compedu.2016.05.004

Wilson, J., & Roscoe, R. D. (2020). Automated writing evaluation and feedback: Multiple metrics of efficacy. *Journal of Educational Computing Research*, *58*(1), 87–125. doi:10.1177/0735633119830764

Yang, Y., Buckendahl, C. W., Jusziewicz, P. J., & Bhola, D. S. (2002). A review of strategies for validating computer-automated scoring. *Applied Measurement in Education*, *15*(4), 391–412. doi:10.1207/S15324818AME1504_04

Human vs. AI

APPENDIX

Prompt for Descriptive Writing

Choose ONE of the following topics, and write your essay about that topic.

1. Reflect on a significant personal experience that shaped your desire to become an English language teacher. Describe the events, interactions, or encounters that ignited your passion for language teaching and how they influenced your decision to pursue this profession. Discuss the impact this experience has had on your growth and development as an educator.

2. Art has the power to transport us to different worlds, evoke emotions, and spark our imagination. In this descriptive essay, you will embark on a visual journey through a painting of your choice. Select a painting that resonates with you personally and captivates your senses, allowing you to delve into its intricacies and unravel the artist's creative vision. Explore the emotions and feelings evoked by the painting. How does it make you feel and why? Does it elicit joy, melancholy, awe, or intrigue? Describe the ways in which the artist has conveyed these emotions through the choice of colors, facial expressions, or other visual elements.

3. Music has the power to stir emotions, transport us to different worlds, and unite people across cultures. Select a performance that resonates with you personally and captivates your senses, allowing you to delve into the captivating world of music. Immerse yourself in the sensory experience of the performance. Describe the sounds, melodies, and rhythms that fill the space. Explore the range of emotions evoked by the music. How does the music make you feel and why? Reflect on the ways in which the music resonates with your own personal experiences or memories.

4. If you have not liked any of the above topics for a descriptive essay, choose your own topic, and your descriptive essay about that topic.

In your essay, strive to create a vivid and sensory experience for your readers. Use descriptive language, figurative expressions, and storytelling techniques to engage your readers.

Your essay needs to have 5 paragraphs -Introduction, 3 body paragraphs, Conclusion-

The length of the essay should be around 500-550 words.

It's better to write your essays on Microsoft Word, but if you do not have that option, you can use the textbox option. You can also write your essay on a paper and take its picture, then upload its picture. All three ways are okay, but if you upload it as a Word document, please use Times New Roman, 12 Pts, and 1,5 line spacing. While evaluating your essays, I'm going to use this Rubric.

Table 7. Rubric for descriptive writing*

	4- Excellent	3- Very Good	2-Satisfactory	1-Needs Improvement-
Ideas	*"paints a picture" for the reader *well-focused on the topic *clear ideas are well-supported with interesting and vivid details	*creates some clear images for the reader *focused on the topic *ideas are well-supported with details	*sometimes strays from the topic *ideas are not well-developed *more details are needed	*poorly focused on the topic *ideas are unclear *few details are given
Organization	*well-focused on the topic *logical organization *excellent transitions *easy to follow	*generally focused on the topic *some lapses in organization *some transitions *usually easy to follow	*somewhat focused on the topic *poor organization *few transitions *difficult to follow	*not focused on the topic *no clear organization *no transitions *difficult to impossible to follow
Introduction	Introductory paragraph clearly states subject of essay and captures reader's attention. Thesis statement is well-developed.	Introductory paragraph states subject of essay but is not particularly inviting to the reader. Thesis statement is fairly developed.	Introductory paragraph attempts to state subject of essay but does not capture reader's attention. Thesis statement is not well enough.	No attempt is made to state the subject of the essay in an introductory paragraph. Thesis statement is vague or it does not exist.
Word Choice	*precise, vivid and interesting word choices *wide variety of word choices	*fairly precise, interesting and somewhat varied word choices *wording could be more specific	*vague, mundane word choices *wording is sometimes repetitive *more descriptive words are needed	*very limited word choices *wording is bland and not descriptive
Sensory Detail	Essay includes details that appeal to at least three of the five senses (taste, touch, sound, sight, smell).	Includes details that appeal to fewer than three of the five senses.	Includes details that appeal to only one of the five senses.	Includes no details that appeal to one of the five senses.
Sentence Fluency	*uses complete sentences *varying sentence structure and lengths	*uses complete sentences *generally simple sentence structures	*occasional sentence fragment or run-on sentences *simple sentence structure is used repeatedly	*frequent use of sentence fragments or run-on sentences *sentences are difficult to understand
Conventions	*proper grammar, usage *correct spelling *correct punctuation *correct capitalization	*few errors of grammar and usage *mostly correct spelling, punctuation and capitalization	*errors in grammar, usage and spelling sometimes make understanding difficult *some errors in punctuation and capitalization	*frequent errors in grammar, usage, spelling, capitalization and punctuation make understanding difficult or impossible

*

*Adapted from https://www.bvsd.k12.pa.us/site/handlers/filedownload.ashx?m
oduleinstanceid=1898&dataid=2403&FileName=Descriptive%20Writ
ing%20Rubric.doc

Chapter 10
Natural Language Processing Applications in Language Assessment:
The Use of Automated Speech Scoring

Tuğba Elif Toprak-Yıldız

iD https://orcid.org/0000-0003-0341-229X

Izmir Democracy University, Turkey & University of Hamburg, Germany

ABSTRACT

Natural language processing is a subfield of artificial intelligence investigating how computers can be utilised to understand and process natural language text or speech to accomplish useful things in various areas, and it draws on various disciplines, such as computer science, linguistics, and robotics. Natural language processing applications, including automated speech recognition and scoring, have several exciting prospects for language testing and assessment practices. These prospects include addressing practical constraints associated with test administration and scoring, securing standardisation in test delivery, ensuring objectiveness and reliability in scoring procedures, and providing personalised feedback for learning. This chapter focuses on automated speech scoring and its applications in language testing and assessment and discusses how these systems can be employed in assessment contexts. The chapter also discusses the potential benefits and drawbacks of automated speech scoring while focusing on construct-related and practical challenges surrounding such systems.

DOI: 10.4018/979-8-3693-0353-5.ch010

Copyright © 2024, IGI Global. Copying or distributing in print or electronic forms without written permission of IGI Global is prohibited.

INTRODUCTION

Artificial Intelligence has been considered one of the most significant technologies to transform any aspect of our lives, including but not limited to business, communication, education, and health. Artificial intelligence can be defined as "the integration of artificial (not a natural process, but one induced by machines) and intelligence (skills of learning, to extract concepts from data and to handle uncertainty in complex situations)" (González-Calatayud et al., 2021, p. 1). However, artificial intelligence cannot be considered a single technology and encompasses several methods and approaches, such as natural language processing, machine learning, and automated decision-making (Caspari-Sadeghi, 2023).

Natural language processing refers to a subfield of artificial intelligence that investigates the ways computers could be utilised to understand and process natural language text or speech to accomplish various tasks and activities in different areas. As a research and application area, natural language processing draws on several disciplines, such as computer science, linguistics, robotics, and electrical and electronic engineering (Chowdhury, 2003). Natural language processing applications entail obtaining knowledge about how people grasp and utilise language so that suitable means and methods can be generated to enable computer systems to understand and process natural languages to fulfil the functions or tasks of interest (Chowdhury, 2003). Machine translation, automated speech recognition, and language processing are among the widespread applications of natural language processing. Specifically, applications requiring text and speech processing (e.g., speech recognition, speech segmentation, sentence tokenisation) may offer new prospects for language testing and assessment (Chapelle & Chung, 2010).

In the context of language testing and assessment, automated essay scoring and automated speech scoring technologies have great potential for the assessment of written essays and spoken responses. Such natural language processing applications have provided many exciting prospects for language testing and assessment practices, such as addressing practical constraints associated with test administration and scoring, securing standardisation in test delivery, ensuring objectiveness and reliability in scoring procedures, providing personalised feedback for learning, and reporting assessment results to test takers in a timely manner (Enright & Quinlan, 2010; Xu et al., 2021; Van Moere & Downey, 2016). In close parallel to an increasing need for automated scoring systems and their apparently substantial benefits, a growing body of literature has been concentrating on how to utilise automated scoring technologies to assess particularly productive language skills (i.e., speaking and writing skills) (e.g., Latifi & Gierl, 2021; Shin & Gierl, 2021; Xu et al., 2021; Yoon & Bhat, 2018).

As such, this chapter focuses on automated speech scoring and its applications in the field of language testing and assessment. The rationale behind this decision is that automated speech scoring presents exciting prospects and implications for the field. However, there could be considerable hesitance or reluctance among practitioners to exploit the potential benefits of such systems due to a reliance on traditional means of assessment (Richard & Clasham, 2021) or a lack of knowledge about how these systems work to serve various assessment purposes since their use have been mainly confined to the commercial sector (Chapelle & Chung, 2010). Morever, to date, automated speech scoring has received relatively less attention than automated writing scoring (Chapelle & Chung, 2010). Thus, the chapter aims to provide a brief historical background to automated speech scoring and explain the fundamental working principles and components of automated speech scoring technology in an accessible manner. Furthermore, from a practical perspective, it showcases how these systems have been employed in various language testing and assessment contexts. The chapter also discusses the potential benefits and drawbacks of automated speech scoring, with a focus on construct-related and practical challenges surrounding such applications. Finally, the chapter emphasises several pedagogical consequences of using natural language processing tools in language assessment. These implications include interpreting test scores, supporting formative assessment practices, and fostering autonomous language learning experiences.

HISTORICAL BACKGROUND TO AUTOMATED SPEECH SCORING

The use of computers in language testing and assessment practices dates back to the 1930s when the IBM model 805 was first used in the US context to score objective tests and cut down the laborious and expensive task of grading millions of exams every year (Pathan, 2012). In a similar vein, audio-cassette tapes in the 1960s and video home system (VHS) tapes in the 1970s facilitated the standardisation of delivery in listening and speaking exams, enabled recording test takers' exam performances and allowed the evaluation of test takers' speaking performances at different times and locations by multiple raters (Van Moere & Downey, 2016). Another notable example would be the use of bubble-card readers in the early 1970s, which exerted a powerful impact on scoring processes and contributed to the popularity of multiple-choice item types. Furthermore, the integration of technology into language testing and assessment practices gained increased momentum in the 1980s and the 1990s, specifically fuelled by developments such as the availability of statistical programs, databases and language processing and recognition tools associated with Computer Assisted Language Learning (CALL) movement (Burstein et al., 1996; Chapelle & Voss, 2017). For instance, the LTRC (Language Testing Research Colloquium) conference in 1985 ignited the initial attempts associated with computer-assisted

Natural Language Processing Applications in Language Assessment

language testing (CALT) (Chalhoub-Deville, 2001) while many papers delivered at the 1985 LTRC dealt with computer-assisted language testing oriented topics, such as item-bank construction and computer adaptive testing (CAT). At that time, a significant number of computer-adaptive testing applications were based on an algorithm that use item response theory (IRT) to track adaptivity concerning a test taker's performance (Chapelle & Voss, 2016).

Automated scoring, mainly automated writing/essay scoring (AWE), was brought forward in the 1960s to expedite and ease the time-consuming process of written performance evaluation (Chapelle & Voss, 2016). Since these earlier times, the development of these automated systems has turned into an exciting and promising endeavour. Different forms of automated writing scoring systems (e.g., statistics-based, rule-based, and hybrid-based automated writing scoring systems) have been used in schemes such as Vantage Learning's IntelliMetric®, ETS' e-rater®, and Pearson's Intelligent Essay Assessor™ (IEA) (Hoang & Kunnan, 2016). Moreover, there has recently been a surge in artificial intelligence-based writing assistants that could be used for language testing and assessment purposes, including commercially available Grammarly, Ginger, ProWritingAid, and WhiteSmoke (Toprak-Yildiz, 2021). Even though automated writing scoring seems to attract more attention in comparison to automated speech scoring, with the developments taking place in natural language processing and speech recognition technologies, automated speech scoring has also turned into a viable alternative to human scoring (Xu et al., 2021).

The main driving force behind automated scoring has been the need to assess the performances of a large number of test takers and provide feedback on their performance in a timely manner (Van Moere & Downey, 2016). Along with this pressing need, several other factors, such as the standardisation of educational practices in the form of large-scale assessments (e.g., Common Core State Standards in the US) and increasing global workforce and immigration—which require language testing and assessment practices for admission and screening purposes (The International Research Foundation for English Language Education, TIRF, 2009) may have also contributed to the popularity of automated scoring technologies. This outcome is not surprising when considering that all the abovementioned conditions require language assessment practices conducted with efficient delivery, management, scoring, and reporting (Van Moere & Downey, 2016).

AUTOMATED SPEECH SCORING AND ITS COMPONENTS

Natural language processing can be defined as a field which explores the use of computers to understand natural language text and speech to accomplish various tasks. Natural language processing researchers and practitioners examine how human beings grasp and utilise language to devise tools and techniques that can help computers also grasp and use natural languages to accomplish tasks of interest (Chowdhury, 2003). Natural language processing, as a field of research and application, draws from various areas, including but not limited to computer science, linguistics, robotics, and electrical and electronic engineering. One of the most significant applications of natural language processing is automated scoring technologies, including automated scoring of speech and text. The chapter at hand focuses particularly on the former.

The earlier versions of automated speech scoring systems have long been available for the evaluation of pronunciation skills, yet, over time, these systems have grown into more sophisticated technologies that could be used to assess a broader range of skills needed for speaking performance (Franco et al., 2010; Van Moere & Downey, 2016). Along with assessing what has been said, these systems also focus on evaluating how speaking performance has been given. For instance, SRI International's (formerly known as the Stanford Research Institute) EduSpeak® is a software development toolkit which aids language education software developers in utilising the most recent speech and pronunciation recognition and scoring technology (Franco et al., 2010). The use of this technology makes it possible for the computer to yield feedback about the quality of individuals' pronunciation and to determine existing problems in the pronunciation process. The feedback on the quality of a given pronunciation is generated based on a set of predictor variables by making the use of databases of non-native speech and relevant human ratings at the sentence level. In addition, the EduSpeak includes a specific function which allows the detection of pronunciation mistakes at the phone level. This specific information is shared with relevant stakeholders in the form of performance feedback.

Technically speaking, automated speech recognition and scoring systems incorporate three critical components that are essential to effective automated speech scoring: the acoustic model, the language model, and the scoring model. The first associated model, the acoustic model, can be defined as speech recognisers, which identify each phoneme or sound (Young, 2001). Recognition can be expressed as a sequence of probabilities. The acoustic model determines the most probable phoneme or word from numerous possibilities (Van Moere & Downey, 2016). Every 10-millisecond speech frame has its spectral properties retrieved, and a model assigns a probability to each potential phoneme based on these features. The result, in the form of a transcript, is the most accurate statistical estimation of the words that were uttered. To illustrate, some facilities that we use daily on our smartphones, such as transferring oral speech into text or doing a voice search, are typically based on acoustic models (Richardson & Clasham, 2021). The acoustic model is trained using a set of speech data that are characterised by a broad scope of accents and pronunciation types. During the training, audio speech is paired with transcriptions.

Natural Language Processing Applications in Language Assessment

This way, it becomes possible for the model to establish links between sounds and orthographic representations.

The second component, the language model, is generated by training the artificial intelligence system on each spoken test/task item (Richardson & Clasham, 2021). The language model features spoken items that are probably included in the answer and is composed of frequencies for n-grams (Van Moere & Downey, 2016). Hence, if the task at hand requires a description of a picture featuring a boy using a computer, the bigram "a computer" and the trigram "using a computer" would frequently appear in test takers' answers.

The training of an automated speech recognition system is essential (Litman et al., 2018). Hence, the items are trialled on a broad representative population to ensure that an exemplary sample of answers is elicited. To illustrate, PTE Academic of Pearson uses test takers' performances to train automated scoring systems to ensure high levels of reliability. For the speaking component, around 400,000 responses are obtained from the participants, and these responses are marked by human raters and machines to yield a reliability measure (PTE, 2023). The information gathered from the test takers is used to feed the language model, which helps yield probabilities during word recognition. Previous research demonstrated that while reading aloud and repetition tasks usually yield higher recognition accuracy (Balogh et al., 2012), ensuring accuracy in spontaneous speech might be challenging (Ivanov et al., 2016).

The last component, the scoring model, stands for the method used for choosing the aspects of the speech recognition process and using them to predict human ratings. In the context of language assessment, test developers need to consider the features that are the most crucial predictors of human scores and the predictors that are relevant to human scores (Van Moere & Downey, 2016). In other words, if human raters and their rating scales do not consider fluency in evaluating test takers' performances, it would not be feasible and reasonable to include the fluency measure in the evaluation of vocabulary or grammar criteria. The Versant test by Pearson, which relies on the use of advanced AI to evaluate English communication skills in a business situation, aims to help employers identify which candidates will be successful in the role. These tests make use of different kinds of scoring models, such as pronunciation (e.g., rhythmic and segmental properties of speech), fluency (e.g., speech rate, words per time) and sentence mastery models (e.g., the number of word errors) (Bernstein et al., 2010). The Versant tests consider separate relevant properties in models to predict each trait individually; later, these subscores are combined to yield an overall score (Van Moere & Downey, 2016).

THE USE OF AUTOMATED SPEECH SCORING IN LANGUAGE TESTING AND ASSESSMENT

Even though the application of automated speech recognition and scoring systems seems to have lagged behind the application of automated writing scoring systems, there have also been several notable attempts which make use of the former, such as the Versant Tests, TOEFL iBT's SpeechRater[SM] (Chen et al., 2018; Xi et al., 2008), Elicited Oral Response (EOR) tests developed at Brigham Young University (Cox & Davies, 2012; Graham et al., 2008; Graham, 2011), and SRI International's EduSpeak system (Franco et al., 2010). Along with these initiatives, more recently, a growing number of commercial bodies and start-up companies have been generating online products that can be used for individual and classroom assessment purposes (Xu et al., 2021). So far, these applications have attempted to measure various language skills, including phonological awareness (Alwan et al., 2007), spoken language production (Cox & Davies, 2012), and oral reading fluency (Bolaños et al., 2013).

One of the most notable and earlier examples of speech recognition and processing systems is Pearson's Versant Tests, also initially known as PhonePassTM and commercially operated by Ordinate Corporation (Chapelle & Chung, 2010). The Versant Tests were the pioneer automated tests of speaking skills that employed state-of-the-art speech processing technology to evaluate the speaking performance of non-native individuals. The tests featured several languages, including English, Spanish, Dutch, French, and Arabic. The Versant tests can be taken online or over the phone and include assessment tasks which require reading aloud sentences, repeating sentences, saying opposite words, answering short response questions and open-ended free response questions (Chapelle & Chung, 2010). Test takers' overall scores are estimated by balancing five weighted subscores in these features: listening vocabulary, repeat accuracy, reciting and pronunciation, reading fluency, and repeat fluency. Test takers can receive feedback on their performance and obtain scores shortly after they submit their answers. The automated scoring system employed in the Versant Tests relies on numerous speech samples from native and non-native individuals. These speech samples are later transcribed to help train the automatic speech recognition system. The strengths of the Versant Tests can be listed as efficiency in test administration, availability of score feedback within minutes, reduction or elimination of human bias, 24/7 test availability on the website, mobile or desktop, and availability of detailed score reports. Nevertheless, the tests have also been criticised on the grounds that they do not fully address communicative competence and exclude the assessment of social skills and cultural or pragmatic elements that are essential to communicative competence (Bernstein, 1999).

Another significant example of automated speech scoring is SpeechRater, developed by the Educational Testing Service (ETS). SpeechRater employs

Natural Language Processing Applications in Language Assessment

sophisticated speech recognition and processing technology to yield feedback about the oral performances of individuals who speak English as a foreign language. The feedback, when compared to human raters, is provided in a short time. The SpeechRater service is also utilised in the TOEFL iBT test. The developers claim that the test provides a valid indicator of a test taker's given skill in the target language academic and work environment. According to Xi et al. (2008), the scoring process in SpeechRater is based on a program that obtains substantial properties of speech input to develop a multiple regression scoring model. In the development stage, 29 candidate features were reduced to render the regression model practically reasonable and characterise the construct of interest in the best and the most complete way by considering these dimensions: fluency, vocabulary, grammar, and pronunciation. In other words, various features pertaining to pronunciation, fluency, and vocabulary were included in a regression model to estimate the holistic scores on the given tasks (Van Moere & Downey, 2016). A committee appraised the final features by considering the construct representations of the features and the strength of the relationship with human ratings. In line with the data obtained, the committee recommended that fluency variables, which were the most powerful predictors, be overweight. At the same time, grammar and vocabulary were weaker predictors and, therefore, were underweight.

In addition to commercially available automated speech-scoring-based language assessments, there have also been academic or research-based initiatives in various contexts. One of the earlier and most notable examples that investigated the possibility of assessing speaking skills with automated speech scoring technology is the Elicited Oral Response (EOR) tests developed at Brigham Young University in the United States. These tests were generated to measure the second language (L2) oral language comprehension and production skills by using automatic speech recognition technology. Graham et al. (2008) explored the potential of automated speech-recognition-scored elicited oral response testing for the assessment of L2 (second language) English speaking skills. The authors chose the elicited imitation technique over other traditional assessment methods, maintaining that this technique enables the administration of the tests to many test takers at the same time in a standard computer lab without the help of a trained interviewer.

Accordingly, they validated the tool, which comprised 60 items featuring sentences varying between 5-23 syllables in several pilot and primary applications. Overall, it took around ten minutes for test takers to complete the task. First, test takers listened to the sentences using microphone headsets and recorded their answers by saving their sound files to a server. After taking the elicited oral response test, test takers also sat for several other speaking assessments, including an information placement interview (15 minutes), a simulated computer-administered oral proficiency test (30 minutes), a computer-elicited oral achievement test (30 minutes), and finally an oral proficiency interview (Graham et al., 2008). Responses to the developed elicited oral response test were scored by two human raters, while a set of reliability and correlation analyses were performed with the results of all assessments. It was found that the elicited response task results correlated with the results of other assessments. In another automated speech scoring-based elicited oral response assessment conducted at Brigham Young University, Cox and Davies (2012) used the test generated and developed by Graham et al. (2008). In this application, 179 test takers studying English as a second language were asked to repeat the sentence they heard. Test takers' oral responses were recorded and batch-scored, employing Sphinx, an open-source automated speech recognition software developed by Carnegie Mellon University. The Wall Street Journal corpus was used as the acoustic model, while the language model was limited to a dictionary merely featuring the words spoken in each elicited oral response sentence. Sphinx rated the responses by deciding if each word was repeated accurately. The overall score assigned to each test taker was specified as a proportion of the number of accurate words divided by the total number of words. The ratio for each item varied between 0 and 1. To illustrate, if a test taker was awarded 1 point, this indicated a 100% recognition of the repeated sentence, while 0 points indicated that the test taker failed to repeat the sentence accurately. The results of the study suggested that automated speech scoring-based elicited response assessments can be utilised as an alternative to speaking proficiency interviews (Cox & Davies, 2012). Furthermore, the study revealed that automated speech scoring assessments can yield reliable results, mainly unbiased by variations across gender or native languages. The authors concluded that automated speech scoring-based assessments provide obvious benefits and render themselves cost-effective alternatives to traditional face-to-face speaking assessments. However, they also suggested that including a listening component in such assessments might improve the assessment.

Regarding tasks that are usually utilised within an automated speaking assessment context, there are two fundamental task types: constrained and free speaking tasks (Xu, 2015; Xu et al., 2020). For the former, tasks which require test takers to read aloud sentences, repeat sentences, verbally indicate opposite words, provide short answers to questions, and construct a sentence by using phrases would be representative examples. These tasks constitute the basis for the Versant Tests and the Duolingo English Test (Wagner & Kunnan, 2015). There are several advantages and disadvantages associated with constrained tasks. One obviously significant benefit is the ease of training automated scoring systems since test-taker responses are quite predictable. Nevertheless, this convenience can be dwarfed by the lack of authenticity in this type of task (Wagner & Kunnan, 2015). Another major drawback that these tasks suffer from would be the issue of construct under-representation, leading to concerns about whether the speaking performance given on a task aligns

Natural Language Processing Applications in Language Assessment

with the behaviours exhibited in real life or whether the task fails to address a wide range of cognitive and linguistic processes (Xu et al., 2020). Contrary to constrained speaking tasks, free speaking tasks usually elicit open-ended answers from test takers. Typical tasks would include describing a picture, reading a text, responding to a text, and speaking about a specific topic. Due to their nature, free-speaking tasks can be used to address a more communicative oral construct and may yield more authentic responses (Chun, 2006). For instance, the Test of English as a Foreign Language (TOEFL) has incorporated free-speaking tasks to assess test takers' oral performances (Xu et al., 2020).

Even though free-speaking tasks would allow for authenticity to a considerable extent, these tasks are also limited in eliciting co-constructed responses or engaging interactional competence. The effective use of interactional resources (e.g., turn-taking and repair strategies) can help speakers respond to interactional troubles in a speaking context and identify boundaries (e.g., the opening and closing acts of a speech event). These properties have been shown to be quite vital for an effective spoken interaction (Young, 2011). On the one hand, the limited inclusion of interactional competence in automated speaking assessments has resulted in ongoing discussions concerning the validity and the use of such assessments for different purposes (Vinther, 2002; Xu, 2015). On the other hand, even when such difficulties are faced, automated scoring systems continue to expand their scope and strength to provide valuable information in line with the developments in artificial intelligence (Chen et al., 2018).

IMPLICATIONS OF AUTOMATED SPEECH SCORING FOR LANGUAGE TESTING AND ASSESSMENT

Automated scoring technologies have become vital, notably in formative and summative assessment practices. These technologies have considerably sped up the marking and scoring processes, helped reduce the impact of human judgement—which can introduce bias in assessments, and increased accuracy and reliability in assessment reports (Bernstein et al., 2010). In particular, during the global pandemic, when individuals were not able to take exams due to quarantine regulations and restrictions, the availability of online examinations in which test takers were able to have their language skills assessed in the comfort of their homes proved to be a great convenience. However, considering the existing and potential benefits that automated scoring systems could offer, it is quite surprising that most people keep questioning how the systems work rather than focusing on how they work to serve our purposes (Richardson & Clasham, 2021).

This situation might have to do with the hesitancy in acknowledging the new natural language processing-driven tools, especially in contexts where assessments are still conducted by means of traditional paper-based assessments. Another plausible explanation could be that since most of the developments and practices in this field take place in the commercial sector, relatively few language assessment researchers and practitioners have adequate information about how these automated processing technologies work (Chapelle & Chung, 2010). Nevertheless, automated scoring systems have long been used in large-scale summative assessments, and they can bear crucial implications for other types of assessment, most notably for formative and diagnostic language assessments where test takers would benefit from fine-grained individualised and pedagogically meaningful feedback. Since performance feedback can be given in a relatively short time, this feedback can be used to identify weaknesses, strengths, misconceptions and knowledge gaps in language learners' skills and knowledgebase. As a result, both test takers and language educators can use this formative feedback to tailor language teaching and learning practices in the learning contexts. Moreover, language educators can employ these systems to enhance opportunities for autonomous learning and carry out personal formative evaluations with their students (Richardson & Clasham, 2021).

Amid the confusion mentioned above and potential suspicions surrounding particularly the validity of inferences arising from automated speech-scoring systems, language assessment researchers, practitioners, and test takers might consider several issues to fully exploit the potential of these automated systems. To begin with, as pointed out previously, automated speech scoring systems may offer a wide range of opportunities but are not without drawbacks. These drawbacks usually have to do with construct representation. For instance, there is a risk that automated speech processing might not necessarily capture the multifaceted features of speaking performance when compared to more communicatively directed face-to-face oral assessments, which consider interactional elements of language and communication (Khabbazbashi et al., 2021). Moreover, there might be a mismatch between the criteria employed by human raters and the features that are automatically extracted by the systems.

Another significant issue would be the susceptibility of the automated systems to test-taker cheating behaviour (Xu et al., 2021). In such cases, one possible solution could be the inclusion of content relevance and topic development aspects in the extracted features so that the potential for cheating behaviour can be predicted and reduced to a considerable degree (Khabbazbashi et al., 2021). Overall, an essential takeaway from the existing approaches and debates is that, despite its various obvious benefits, automated evaluation should not be the only factor taken into account when specifically making high-stakes decisions depending upon test takers' performances, considering each test is valid for a given objective. Finally, it would be safe to say

Natural Language Processing Applications in Language Assessment

that more validation research is needed to help inform the use of automated language scoring in language assessment.

CONCLUSION

Developments in the field of natural language processing provide novel and exciting prospects for language testing and assessment practices (Chapelle & Chung, 2010). One notable technological development which has exerted a drastic impact on language testing and assessment is the automated scoring technology. This technology particularly has proved effective in the assessment of writing and speaking skills. Automated speech scoring, which has been the main focus of the present chapter, may be regarded as an artificial intelligence task in which test takers' digitised spoken performance in a language assessment task is assigned a score (Chen et al., 2018). In principle, a mapping function from the speech signal to the speaking score is created, while scores assigned by human raters are utilised as benchmarks to train the model (Chen et al., 2018). To date, in line with developments taking place in the field of natural language processing and speech recognition technologies, automated speech scoring has been turning into a feasible alternative to human scoring (Xu et al., 2021).

Historically, there have been various factors that contributed to the inception and popularity of those technologies. For instance, the need for assessing a significant number of people in quite a short time, the standardisation of educational and assessment-related practices, the popularity of large-scale assessments, and the increasing need for language testing and assessment practices for screening and admission purposes—particularly at the workplace –have influenced the adoption of these technologies (Van Moere & Downey, 2016). Given that all these conditions call for language testing and assessment practices that should be carried out with considerable efficiency in delivery, administration, scoring, and reporting, this increasing interest in such technologies is not surprising. In addition, these technologies have also proved to be efficient in eliminating or reducing the impact of human judgements, ensuring fairness and equality, and improving the accuracy, objectivity, and reliability of assessment results (Bernstein et al., 2010; Van Moere & Downey, 2016). Even though existing applications have mainly been commercially driven, there are now various automated scoring technologies with different working principles (e.g., statistics-based, rule-based, and hybrid-based automated writing scoring systems) implemented in various assessment settings (e.g., high, medium, low stakes language assessment settings and research settings).

In the simplest technical sense, these systems can be characterised as comprising three vital components: the acoustic model, the language model, and the scoring model. The acoustic model helps recognise phonemes or sounds (Young, 2001). The language model is developed by training the artificial intelligence system on each spoken test/task item and includes spoken items that might be uttered in an answer (Richardson & Clasham, 2021). The scoring model stands for the method used for choosing the aspects of the speech recognition process and employing these aspects to predict human ratings (Van Moere & Downey, 2016). Even though technical issues surrounding the automated speech scoring systems and the working principles of these systems might not always be accessible to every language testing and assessment specialist, researcher, or practitioner, these technologies have been used in language assessment schemes such as the Versant Tests, SpeechRater, Elicited Oral Response (EOR) tests developed by Brigham Young University (Chen et al., 2018; Cox & Davies, 2012; Graham et al., 2008), SRI International's EduSpeak system (Franco et al., 2010), and the Duolingo English Test (Wagner & Kunnan, 2015). These assessments have usually incorporated two main task types: constrained and free-speaking tasks. Constrained speaking tasks such as reading aloud, or repeating sentences are primarily associated with an ease of application. Nevertheless, they seemingly lack authenticity and may suffer from the issue of construct under-representation. Free speaking tasks, on the other hand, may not be as practical as their constrained counterparts, yet they are more authentic in nature and can better address communicative constructs.

In line with these considerations, there is a pending issue of addressing interactional competence in automated speaking assessments, and this issue has caused subsequent debates about the validity and the use of such assessments for different purposes (Xu, 2015). According to these ongoing debates, it is possible that automated speech processing might not essentially address and measure the multifaceted dimensions of speaking construct contrary to more communicatively driven face-to-face oral assessments, which pay more attention to interactional elements of language and communication (Khabbazbashi et al., 2021). Apparently, more research is needed in this domain to help language testers deal with the issue of construct representation in automated speech scoring-based language assessments. However, a note of caution is also needed. Automated speech scoring systems are constantly evolving in line with the developments taking place in natural language processing. For instance, the two versions of SpeechRater (i.e., Version 1 and Version 5) were released in 2006 and 2016, respectively. There have been various distinctions between these two versions, such as an improved automated speech recognition, a considerable expansion in the linguistic features that are employed to assess test takers' speaking performance, and a set of upgraded methods that could be utilised for selecting linguistic features, building models, and indicating nonscorable answers (Chen et al., 2018). In line with these improvements, the feature set was expanded from less than 50 in Version 1 to more than 100 features in Version 5. Moreover, the coverage of the speaking

Natural Language Processing Applications in Language Assessment

construct has been considerably extended, thereby addressing almost all the aspects featured in TOEFL IBT's speaking construct. Thus, it is safe to assume that even though automated speech scoring systems have several shortcomings, such as being prone to construct underrepresentation or overlooking more fine-grained aspects of language competence and performance, there is also a great promise and room for improvement, which could solve these central problems in the future.

REFERENCES

Alwan, A., Yijian, B., Black, M., Casey, L., Gerosa, M., Heritage, M., Iseli, M., Jones, B., Kazemzadeh, A., Lee, S., Narayanan, S., Price, P., Tepperman, J., & Wang, S. (2007). A system for technology-based assessment of language and literacy in young children: The role of multiple information sources. In *Proceedings of IEEE 9th Workshop on Multimedia Signal Processing*. Institute of Electrical and Electronics Engineers. 10.1109/MMSP.2007.4412810

Balogh, J., Bernstein, J., Cheng, J., Van Moere, A., & Suzuki, M. (2012). Validation of automated scoring of oral reading. *Educational and Psychological Measurement*, *72*(3), 435–452. doi:10.1177/0013164411412590

Bernstein, J. (1999). *PhonePassTM testing: Structure and construct*. Ordinate.

Bernstein, J., Van Moere, A., & Cheng, J. (2010). Validating automated speaking tests. *Language Testing*, *27*(3), 355–377. doi:10.1177/0265532210364404

Bolaños, D., Cole, R. A., Ward, W. H., Tindal, G. A., Hasbrouck, J., & Schwanenflugel, P. J. (2013). Human and automated assessment of oral reading fluency. *Journal of Educational Psychology*, *105*(4), 1142–1151. doi:10.1037/a0031479

Burstein, J., Frase, L., Ginther, A., & Grant, L. (1996). Technologies for language assessment. *Annual Review of Applied Linguistics*, *16*, 240–260. doi:10.1017/S0267190500001537

Caspari-Sadeghi, S. (2023). Artificial intelligence in technology-enhanced assessment: A survey of machine learning. *Journal of Educational Technology Systems*, *51*(3), 372–386. doi:10.1177/00472395221138791

Chalhoub-Deville, M. (2001). Language testing and technology: Past and future. *Language Learning & Technology*, *5*(2), 95–98.

Chapelle, C. A., & Chung, Y. R. (2010). The promise of NLP and speech processing technologies in language assessment. *Language Testing*, *27*(3), 301–315. doi:10.1177/0265532210364405

Chapelle, C. A., & Voss, E. (2016). 20 years of technology and language assessment in language learning & technology. *Language Learning & Technology*, *20*(2), 116–128.

Chapelle, C. A., & Voss, E. (2017). Utilizing technology in language assessment. In E. Shohamy & I. G. Or (Eds.), Language testing and assessment (pp. 149–161). Cham, Switzerland: Springer. doi:10.1007/978-3-319-02261-1_10

Chen, L., Zechner, K., Yoon, S., Evanini, K., Wang, X., Loukina, A., Tao, J., Davis, L., Chong, M. L., Ma, M., Mundkowsky, R., Lu, C., Leong, C. L., & Gyawali, B. (2018). Automated scoring of non-native speech using the SpeechRaterSM v. 5.0 engine. *ETS Research Report Series*, *2018*(1), 1–31. doi:10.1002/ets2.12198

Chowdhury, G. (2003). Natural language processing. *Annual Review of Information Science & Technology*, *37*(1), 51–89. doi:10.1002/aris.1440370103

Chun, C. W. (2006). Commentary: An analysis of a language test for employment: The authenticity of the PhonePass test. *Language Assessment Quarterly*, *3*(3), 295–306. doi:10.120715434311laq0303_4

Cox, T., & Davies, R. S. (2012). Using automatic speech recognition technology with elicited oral response testing. *CALICO Journal*, *29*(4), 601–618. doi:10.11139/cj.29.4.601-618

Enright, M. K., & Quinlan, T. (2010). Complementing human judgment of essays written by English language learners with e-rater® scoring. *Language Testing*, *27*(3), 317–334. doi:10.1177/0265532210363144

Franco, H., Bratt, H., Rossier, R., Rao Gadde, V., Shriberg, E., Abrash, V., & Precoda, K. (2010). EduSpeak®: A speech recognition and pronunciation scoring toolkit for computer-aided language learning applications. *Language Testing*, *27*(3), 401–418. doi:10.1177/0265532210364408

González-Calatayud, V., Prendes-Espinosa, P., & Roig-Vila, R. (2021). Artificial intelligence for student assessment: A systematic review. *Applied Sciences (Basel, Switzerland)*, *11*(12), 5467. doi:10.3390/app11125467

Graham, C. R. (2011). *Examining the validity of an elicited imitation instrument to test oral language in Spanish.* Presentation at *33rd Annual Convention of the Language Testing Research Colloquium (LTRC 2011)*. Ann Arbor, MI, USA.

Graham, C. R., Lonsdale, D., Kennington, C., Johnson, A., & McGhee, J. (2008). Elicited imitation as an oral proficiency measure with ASR scoring. In *Proceedings of the Sixth International Conference on Language Resources and Evaluation (LREC 2008)* (pp. 1604–1610). European Language Resources Association.

Hoang, G. T. L., & Kunnan, A. J. (2016). Automated essay evaluation for English language learners: A case study of MY Access. *Language Assessment Quarterly*, *13*(4), 359–376. doi:10.1080/15434303.2016.1230121

Ivanov, A. V., Lange, P. L., Suendermann-Oeft, D., Ramanarayanan, V., & Yu, Z., Y. K., & Tao, J. (2016). *Speed vs. accuracy: Designing an optimal ASR system for spontaneous non-native speech in a real-time application.* Proceedings of the 7th International Workshop on Spoken Dialogue Systems, IWSDS 2016, Saariselkä, Finland.

Khabbazbashi, N., Xu, J., & Galaczi, E. D. (2021). Opening the Black box: Exploring automated speaking evaluation. In B. Lanteigne, C. Coombe, & J. D. Brown (Eds.), *Challenges in language testing around the world* (pp. 333–343). Springer. doi:10.1007/978-981-33-4232-3_25

Latifi, S., & Gierl, M. (2021). Automated scoring of junior and senior high essays using Coh-Metrix features: Implications for large-scale language testing. *Language Testing*, *38*(1), 62–85. doi:10.1177/0265532220929918

Litman, D., Strik, H., & Lim, G. S. (2018). Speech technologies and the assessment of second language speaking: Approaches, challenges, and opportunities. *Language Assessment Quarterly*, *15*(3), 294–309. doi:10.1080/15434303.2018.1472265

Pathan, M. M. (2012). Computer Assisted Language Testing [CALT]: Advantages, implications and limitations. *Research Vistas*, *1*, 30–45.

Richardson, M., & Clesham, R. (2021). Rise of the machines? The evolving role of AI technologies in high-stakes assessment. *London Review of Education*, *19*(1), 1–13. doi:10.14324/LRE.19.1.09

Shin, J., & Gierl, M. J. (2021). More efficient processes for creating automated essay scoring frameworks: A demonstration of two algorithms. *Language Testing*, *38*(2), 247–272. doi:10.1177/0265532220937830

TIRF. (2009). *The impact of English and plurilingualism in global corporations.* The International Research Foundation for English Language Education. https://www.tirfonline.org/wp-content/uploads/2010/09/TIRF_KeyQuestionsWorkforcePaper_Final_25March2009.pdf

Toprak-Yildiz, T. E. (2021). *Current practices in technology-based language testing and assessment.* In *Proceedings of the Izmir Democracy University International Humanities Congress (IDU-IHC)*, Izmir, Turkiye.

Van Moere, A., & Downey, R. (2016). Technology and artificial intelligence in language assessment. In D. Tsagari & J. Banerjee (Eds.), *Handbook of second language assessment* (pp. 341–357). De Gruyter Mouton., doi:10.1515/9781614513827-023

Vinther, T. (2002). Elicited imitation: A brief overview. *International Journal of Applied Linguistics*, *12*(1), 54–73. doi:10.1111/1473-4192.00024

Wagner, E., & Kunnan, A. J. (2015). The Duolingo English test. *Language Assessment Quarterly*, *12*(3), 320–331. doi:10.1080/15434303.2015.1061530

Xi, X., Higgins, D., Zechner, K., & Williamson, D. M. (2008). Automated scoring of spontaneous speech using SpeechRater v1.0. ETS Research report RR-08-62. Princeton, NJ: ETS. https://doi.org/ doi:10.1002/j.2333-8504.2008.tb02148.x

Xu, J. (2015). *Predicting ESL learners' oral proficiency by measuring the collocations in their spontaneous speech* [Doctoral dissertation, Iowa State University]. Iowa State University Digital Repository. doi:10.31274/etd-180810-4474

Xu, J., Brenchley, J., Jones, E., Pinnington, A., Benjamin, T., Knill, K., Seal-Coon, G., Robinson, M., & Geranpayeh, A. (2020). *Linguaskill: Building a validity argument for the Speaking test*. Cambridge Assessment English.

Xu, J., Jones, E., Laxton, V., & Galaczi, E. (2021). Assessing L2 English speaking using automated scoring technology: Examining automarker reliability. *Assessment in Education: Principles, Policy & Practice*, *28*(4), 411–436. doi:10.1080/096959 4X.2021.1979467

Yoon, S. Y., & Bhat, S. (2018). A comparison of grammatical proficiency measures in the automated assessment of spontaneous speech. *Speech Communication*, *99*, 221–230. doi:10.1016/j.specom.2018.04.003

Young, R. (2011). Interactional competence in language learning, teaching, and testing. In E. Hinkel (Ed.), *Handbook of research in language learning and teaching* (pp. 426–443). Routledge. doi:10.4324/9780203836507.ch26

Young, S. (2001). Statistical modeling in continuous speech recognition (CSR). *Proceedings of the Seventeenth Conference on Uncertainty in Artificial Intelligence*. San Francisco: Morgan Kaufman.

ADDITIONAL READING

Benzeghiba, M., De Mori, R., Deroo, O., Dupont, S., Erbes, T., Jouvet, D., Fissore, L., Laface, P., Mertins, A., Ris, C., Rose, R., Tyagi, V., & Wellekens, C. (2007). Automatic speech recognition and speech variability: A review. *Speech Communication*, *49*(10), 763–786. doi:10.1016/j.specom.2007.02.006

Chapelle, C. A., & Douglas, D. (2006). *Assessing language through computer technology*. Cambridge University Press. doi:10.1017/CBO9780511733116

Higgins, D., Xi, X., Zechner, K., & Williamson, D. M. (2011). A three-stage approach to the automated scoring of spontaneous spoken responses. *Computer Speech & Language*, *25*(2), 282–306. doi:10.1016/j.csl.2010.06.001

Jurafsky, D., & Martin, J. H. (2000). *Speech and language processing: An introduction to natural language processing, computational linguistics, and speech recognition*. Prentice Hall.

Kane, M. T., Crooks, T., & Cohen, A. (1999). Validating measures of performance. *Educational Measurement: Issues and Practice*, *18*(2), 5–17. doi:10.1111/j.1745-3992.1999.tb00010.x

O'Brien, M. G., Derwing, T. M., Cucchiarini, C., Hardison, D. M., Mixdorff, H., Thomson, R. I., Strik, H., Levis, J. M., Munro, M. J., Foote, J. A., & Muller Levis, G. (2018). Directions for the future of technology in pronunciation research and teaching. *Journal of Second Language Pronunciation*, *4*(2), 182–207. doi:10.1075/jslp.17001.obr

Renals, S., Morgan, N., Bourlard, H., Cohen, M., & Franco, H. (1994). Connectionist probability estimators in HMM speech recognition. *IEEE Transactions on Speech and Audio Processing*, *2*(1), 161–174. doi:10.1109/89.260359

Whitely, S. E. (1983). Construct validity: Construct representation versus nomothetic span. *Psychological Bulletin*, *93*(1), 179–197. doi:10.1037/0033-2909.93.1.179

Williamson, D. M., Xi, X., & Breyer, F. J. (2012). A framework for evaluation and use of automated scoring. *Educational Measurement: Issues and Practice*, *31*(1), 2–13. doi:10.1111/j.1745-3992.2011.00223.x

Xi, X. (2010). Automated scoring and feedback systems: Where are we and where are we heading? *Language Testing*, *27*(3), 291–300. doi:10.1177/0265532210364643

KEY TERMS AND DEFINITIONS

Artificial Intelligence: Artificial intelligence (AI) can be defined as the ability of a digital computer or robot to carry out actions that are commonly performed by intelligent beings.

Automated Speech Scoring: Automatic speech scoring refers to the computer assisted assessment of a test taker's speaking performance.

Interactional Competence: Interactional competence stands for the ability to use linguistic resources to express communicative intents in real-world situational circumstances through the use of interactional resources (e.g., turn-taking, repair, speech acts, etc.).

Natural Language Processing: NLP can be defined as a multidisciplinary field of research and application that uses computational techniques for the analysis and synthesis of human language.

N-Gram: n-gram refers to a series of n adjacent letters and syllables that exist in a language dataset or adjacent phonemes obtained from a speech-recording dataset.

Speech Processing: Speech processing refers to the study of speech signals and the processing methods of signals.

Speech Recognition: Speech recognition refers to an interdisciplinary subfield of computer science and computational linguistics that creates technologies helping the recognition and translation of spoken language into text by computers.

Chapter 11

Hybrid Flexible (HyFlex) Teaching in Foreign Language Education:
Enhancing Equity, Inclusion, and Accessibility Through an Innovative Digital Pedagogy

Gülşah Öz
Aksaray University, Turkey

ABSTRACT

Hybrid flexible (HyFlex) teaching, which is assumed as a much more flexible and learner-centered instruction mode, has received great attention from educators and researchers in recent years. In HyFlex learning and teaching environment, learners can make decisions on how they attend lessons i.e., face-to-face in a real classroom, online synchronously, or asynchronously after the allotted real lesson time. The present chapter aims to introduce HyFlex teaching as a new digital pedagogical and technological approach to the mode of instruction in relation to the foreign language learning and teaching field. In addition, this chapter discusses the benefits of EFL teaching in HyFlex classroom environments along with some challenges and possible solutions proposed by instructors in the light of the current relevant literature and empirical research. Furthermore, HyFlex teaching can promote equal, inclusive, and accessible learning conditions for all students regardless of their diverse backgrounds are addressed, in turn fostering foreign language learning and teaching processes.

DOI: 10.4018/979-8-3693-0353-5.ch011

Copyright © 2024, IGI Global. Copying or distributing in print or electronic forms without written permission of IGI Global is prohibited.

INTRODUCTION

A variety of instruction modes of education have emerged with the support of recent technological developments. Many institutions now offer some or all of their undergraduate, graduate, and doctoral courses online through the use of online education, blended learning, or flipped instruction as a result of the growth and improvement of technology (Köroğlu et al., 2022). Within this concern, such innovative educational models as online learning, blended learning, and hybrid learning have started to be implemented as a delivery mode of foreign language teaching in the last decades, especially since the outbreak of the Covid-19 pandemic and other natural disasters, for instance, deadly earthquakes that hinder face-to-face learning and teaching process around the world. Thus, digital instruction has become a crucial component of education all over the world (Köroğlu & Öz, 2023). Providing more flexibility and agency to learners in the process of learning, Hybrid Flexible (HyFlex) teaching has become more popular at all levels of education. In HyFlex teaching, instructors adopt not only face-to-face but also online learning platforms, including both synchronous and asynchronous conditions; therefore, learners feel free to attend lessons in their preferred mode of instruction. As Kelly (2020) advocated, the core principle of this type of teaching lies in the fact that all students are equal, and educational conditions need to be equal for each one regardless of their way of attendance to the course. Unlike and beyond blended learning, in which teachers themselves are decision-makers in the choice of instruction mode, students are the agents and decision makers of their preferred way of course delivery mode in the HyFlex teaching context, enhancing learner autonomy and agency by providing flexibility to the students in how to attend the class. HyFlex combines blended learning features with more flexibility (Abdelmalak & Parra, 2016). That is, traditional blended or flipped classroom training, in which the online and in-person components of a course complement one another but often do not overlap, does not provide this kind of flexibility (Garrison & Kanuka, 2004; Hill, 2012; McGee & Reis, 2012; Singh, 2003). In this regard, HyFlex teaching as a new digital pedagogical approach refers to an innovative course format that is learner-directed and learner-centered as well as a multimodal education environment in which learners have the opportunity of participating in lessons regardless of their current physical locations, all of which in turn promote equity and inclusion by increasing accessibility to teaching context for every participant learner of that class. In addition to learners, instructors can also benefit from HyFlex teaching in that they deliver each lecture once rather than teaching the same course both in-person and in online platforms separately (Kohnke & Moorhouse, 2021). As for EFL teaching, HyFlex approach also provides similar opportunities and contributions into foreign language learning and teaching process in a positive way with its primary concern that education is for all so let every learner attend classes no matter where they are during the allotted real course time. With this in mind, this chapter discusses the current literature of HyFlex teaching in relation to foreign language learning and teaching field. Beginning with the introduction of HyFlex teaching as a new digital pedagogical approach, this chapter presents the benefits of EFL teaching in HyFlex classroom environments along with some challenges and possible solutions proposed by instructors in the light of the current relevant literature and empirical research. More specifically, how HyFlex teaching can enhance equity, inclusion, and accessibility in education for all students regardless of their diverse backgrounds as well as fostering foreign language learning and teaching process.

BACKGROUND

HyFlex Teaching

In higher education, blended learning can be implemented in three different ways (MacDonald, 2006). Student meetings and asynchronous online activities take place on campus in the first method. In order to structure a course, the second method combines synchronous meetings, social network tools, and possible in-person meetings with asynchronous work. The third strategy combines students who are physically apart but located on a campus with those who are online. The HyFlex is a prime example of the third blended learning strategy, which takes into account both in-person and online learners when designing courses. HyFlex additionally enrolls all students in a single portion of the course rather than dividing sections based on the method of distribution.

HyFlex is a term coined with the combination of the following two words: 'hybrid' and 'flexible'. As an innovative approach to delivery mode of education, HyFlex teaching, designed at San Francisco State University, intends to give learners the switch option of attending course sessions between in-person and online platforms from synchronous to asynchronous learning. In other words, HyFlex classroom structure (see Figure 1) involves three different instruction types, i.e., synchronous, face-to-face, synchronous virtual, and asynchronous online, all in a single course session (Wilson & Alexander, 2021).

Figure 1. HyFlex classroom structure

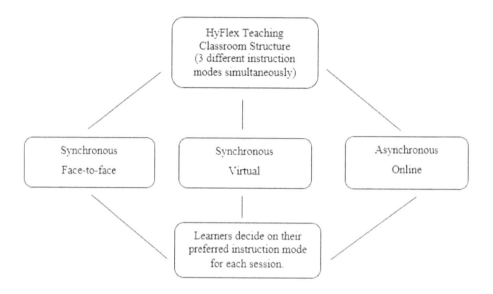

The HyFlex course design employs a hybrid approach to education to incorporate in-person contacts, online interactions, and physical surroundings. Within this flexible educational approach, all students in a HyFlex course have an equal chance to connect with the teacher and their fellow students; however, the nature of this interaction (i.e., whether it takes place in person or online) can change depending on the preference and needs of the individual student (Miller et al., 2013). Therefore, higher education's HyFlex learning environment takes into account a number of factors, including course designs and student preferences. Miller et al. (2021) assert that teachers' adaptation to curriculum design and instructional practices takes place in literary form. In addition, no student should ever be at a disadvantage, which is a key aspect of the hybrid teaching-learning paradigm (Chirițescu, Păunescu, 2021). That is why, equal opportunities for accomplishing learning goals must be provided by learning experiences in face-to-face and online classes, whether they are synchronous or asynchronous, and by how they are set up. Students are free to choose how they will participate, allowing them to be flexible and easily integrated into the learning process. Compared to traditional, face-to-face, or solely online models, a well-designed hybrid learning model produces higher educational results (Bărbuceanu, 2022).

In the implementation of a HyFlex course, more specifically, an instructor delivers the digital content and selects the best methods and exercises to meet the needs of both online and physically enrolled students. This enables all students, regardless of learning preferences, to improve their emotional intelligence and internalize the ideas they will later deal with when developing new models (Buşu, 2020). Regardless of the format selected, teaching and learning activities should ideally communicate digital content effectively and practically, involve students in worthwhile educational activities, and use authentic evaluation to evaluate student learning. All students are not given identical assignments in each teaching mode; rather, they are all supposed to produce comparable educational outcomes. (Bărbuceanu, 2022). As a result of this, in order to attain educational goals for a subject taught in a HyFlex class, thorough planning with different versions of activities unique to each learning environment is required (Bărbuceanu, 2022). Furthermore, a HyFlex course should guarantee that students have the technological know-how required to access the participation options (Miller et al., 2013).

Based on the nature and its integration to classes, HyFlex teaching can be a new challenge for educators and teachers on the ground. Thus, instructor training is important for effective HyFlex implementation (Beatty, 2014; Romero et al., 2016; Taylor & Newton, 2013), as is the use of the right technology (Abdelmalak & Parra, 2016; Liu et al., 2014; Miller et al., 2013; Taylor & Newton, 2013). Students should receive information about their attendance options as well as advice (Abdelmalak & Parra, 2016; Gounari & Koutropoulos, 2015; Inglis et al., 2011; Taylor & Newton, 2013). This is because HyFlex's flexibility places the responsibility for choosing the "right" attendance choice on the students.

In order for a HyFlex teaching process to achieve its ultimate goal, Beatty (2019) proposes four core principles that a HyFlex teaching environment needs to possess. These four fundamental principles of HyFlex teaching are namely, *learner choice*, *equivalency*, *reusability*, and *accessibility*.

1. *Learner Choice*: Learners are agents and decision makers in the option of how they participate and complete course sessions.
2. *Equivalency*: Equivalent instructional activities are provided in each mode.
3. *Reusability*: Course materials and activities can be utilized by all learners in each mode of instruction.
4. *Accessibility*: Learners need to be equipped with appropriate and sufficient technological tools and skills to access education equally, no matter how their preferred instruction modes are.

HyFlex EFL Teaching

Despite the fact that computer-assisted language learning and technologically enhanced language learning have been employed in the teaching of English, they are still used in traditional classrooms for some of the classes; however, English language teachers were compelled to transition to entirely online instruction and evaluation as a result of the Covid-19 pandemic (Öz & Köroğlu, 2023). Because of the development and use of technology, many universities now offer some or all of their undergraduate, graduate, and doctorate courses online using online education, blended learning, or flipped instruction (Köroğlu et al., 2022). As in other fields of education, foreign language learning and teaching process should also encourage inclusive educational environments for all students through practical applications (Köroğlu et al., 2023). From this point of view, HyFlex teaching plays a crucial role in providing a positive and inclusive classroom environment where all learners are valued and educated with equal opportunities. In this sense, the usefulness of HyFlex in teaching languages is already the focus of some research investigations (Jaime & Kateryna, 2022; Karpava, 2022; Kohnke & Moorhouse, 2021; Sheerah & Yadav, 2022; Taylor, 2020; Tolosa-Casadont, 2022) though the number of the relevant studies are limited specifically regarding implications and integration of it to foreign language teaching context.

To illustrate, in order to improve the speaking abilities of EFL students, Sheerah and Yadav (2022) looked into the flipped classroom method (FCM), which uses hybrid-flexible and hyflex models based on tri-model teaching approaches. Within the purpose of the research, the students were sent two sets of opinion and satisfaction questionnaires to get their thoughts on learning how to talk, as well as the teacher's observations of the approach and the tools used to access speaking during the study. In order to determine the students' happiness and uniform competency level in achieving the goals of adopting the flipped classroom strategy, the researchers conducted a focused group interview. The results of the study, which lasted for one semester (13 weeks), showed that the FCM was effective in helping the students become more fluent, self-assured, and competent in their production classes. In a small-scale exploratory study, Kohnke and Moorhouse (2021) interviewed with nine post-graduate students who took a six-week course through HyFlex about their experiences and opinions. Despite communication difficulties between students who attended through various modalities, individuals did value the flexibility it provided, according to the findings. Moreover, the use of several aspects of video conferencing software and other digital tools was considered crucial to HyFlex's effectiveness.

Karpava (2022) looked into a variety of topics in a course on teaching methodology and teaching practicum, including student engagement in a hybrid learning environment, attitudes toward online and in-person teaching and learning, the use of information and communication technology (ICT), the development of students' cognitive, social, and self-directed learning skills, and potential EFL teaching. The examination of the data revealed that both positive and negative views of online and hybrid teaching and learning were held by the students who would go on to become EFL teachers. Furthermore, the students agreed that online and hybrid learning were flexible and practical teaching and learning approaches and that synchronous and asynchronous learning could be completed without leaving the comfort of home. On the other hand, they believed that face-to-face instruction was more effective because they were able to interact directly with their teachers and peers, ask questions, and engage in productive class discussions that might raise the students' motivation and engagement. On the other hand, Jaime and Kateryna (2022) conducted research on students' perceptions of Hyflex teaching based on English language learning courses. More specifically, the researchers examined the views that students have toward online learning in their study, as well as how they might react in a hypothetical HyFlex course setting. In this sense, the researchers acknowledge the constraints this places on the research's findings when considering the hypothetical HyFlex circumstance. That is, a language learning course built on the HyFlex learning paradigm, for example, can look appealing in the beginning, but after a semester of use, it might be seen in a much less favorable light. However, as Beatty (2020) a key figure in the development of the HyFlex learning paradigm, notes, "A well-designed HyFlex class, with effective alternative participation modes that all lead to the same learning outcomes, can provide meaningful learning opportunities for all students." Within this concern, more students may be able to complete their education goals with the help of a HyFlex model, but it must guarantee equal access to course material and learning engagement.

The review of the relevant literature on the studies of HyFlex teaching in the field of foreign language learning and teaching reveals that more studies are needed to shed light on educators in respect to how to implement HyFlex language-based courses by which types of methods and techniques to ensure equity, accessibility, and inclusion in classroom environment for all language learners.

Benefits of HyFlex EFL Teaching

Considering that learning a foreign language is a highly complex process that has physical, cognitive, and emotional impacts on individuals while they are learning the language (Öz & Şahinkarakaş, 2023), it is essential to take into account the beneficial effects of pedagogical instructions utilized in the process of foreign language teaching. When the related studies are reviewed, it is clear that HyFlex teaching offers a variety of benefits on the sides of students, teachers, and institutions. In this sense, some researchers categorized these benefits. For instance, according to Howell (2022), the benefits of HyFlex teaching can be thematized as institutional benefits and learning outcomes. Students' greater learning flexibility, increased autonomy, and better accessibility to learning resources were detected as the advantages after implementing a hybrid flexible mode in language teaching (Hodges et al., 2022). Additionally, the improved flexibility (Binnewies & Wang, 2019) without affecting student grades (Binnewies & Wang, 2019; Calafiore & Giudici, 2021; Miller et al., 2013) and student completion rate (Wigal, 2021) are other benefits to students covered in the relevant literature. In addition, it can guarantee everyone has access to school, no matter where they live, resulting in more inclusive education and equal learning outcomes (Bower et al., 2015; Weitze et al., 2013). Furthermore, HyFlex teaching model increases both student enrollment and retention (Samuel et al., 2019), encourages greater levels of student engagement than traditional face-to-face courses (Malczyk, 2020), increases levels of student satisfaction with their learning experience and assists students in achieving desired learning outcomes (Bower et al., 2015; Kyei-Blankson & Godwyll, 2010). On the other hand, research has also shown that HYFlex teaching may benefit colleges and universities by increasing student enrollment, requiring less investment in equipment and staff, and consolidating expenses (Lakhal et al., 2017; Wang et al., 2017).

In a similar vein, Beatty (2019) explicates advantages of HyFlex teaching categorizing in respect to students, teachers, and administrations. To illustrate, the primary advantage of HyFlex for students is typically reported as the flexible participation requirement, which allows them to make personal choices regarding the best way to take part and fulfill class requirements, often contrary to their own preferences (ibid.). Furthermore, according to Beatty (2019, p.25), benefits of HyFlex teaching to students are linked to increased access to lessons, schedule control, and more learning resources, which are delineated below:

Benefits to students
- *Increased access to courses*: when taking lessons in person is difficult, or when your preferred classes are being offered at the same time.
- *Schedule control*: more control over day-to-day schedules associated with attending class.
- *More learning resources*: Various ways of participation frequently necessitate enhanced educational resources, allowing for deeper education and more opportunities to learn.

In addition to the three benefits listed below, teachers value the opportunity to carry out their instructional research on HyFlex and the potential for further presentation of their work in their own discipline of study (Beatty, 2019, p. 25).

Benefits to teachers
- Able to provide more pupils with similar resources (time, instructional materials) as before.
- Gain knowledge and expertise in online teaching without giving up the classroom environment.

Hybrid Flexible (HyFlex) Teaching in Foreign Language Education

- Offer an integrated alternative when learning in class is not possible due to time constraints.

On the other hand, benefits of HyFlex teaching to administrations or institutions are presented below (Beatty, 2019, p. 25)

Benefits to Administration
- Boost overall educational enrollment by providing students with more scheduling and location flexibility. When implemented on a large scale, HyFlex may result in an increased per unit course load and shorter time to graduation.
- Boost person class section (a single instance of a course) participation beyond an actual classroom's seat capacity. When executed on a large scale, HyFlex could minimize the need for additional space while increasing the availability of bottleneck courses.
- Encourage novel approaches to education that, when carried out effectively, should lead to increased achievement among pupils. This can result in enhanced learning for students, opportunities for faculty research and publication as well as opportunities for institutional marketing to other stakeholders.

Likewise, Raes et al. (2019) summarize the overall benefits of HyFlex teaching from the perspectives of teachers and students below in Figure 2.

Figure 2. Overall benefits of HyFlex teaching from the perspectives of teachers and students

Benefits for teachers	Benefits for students
• Teachers don't have to sit behind a screen, but can teach as they normally do: standing or walking around.	• Based on students' personal situation, they can choose to come to campus or follow the session remotely.
• Teachers can naturally interact with on-site and remote students as both are visible.	• Remote students are projected on the screens in the back of the classroom as they are the last row in the classroom. This makes them part of the classroom.
• The teachers do not have to bother about his/her position, as the virtual room director follows the teacher.	• Remote students can select different viewpoints.
• Multiple options for interaction make it easier to know if your students are still engaged.	• Multiple options for interaction make it easier to stay motivated during lessons.
	• Interaction between onsite and remote students is possible.

Research has shown that HyFlex teaching provides a variety of benefits to educational field in general, as delineated above in light of the relevant literature. Overall, these benefits can be associated with foreign language learning and teaching process in HyFlex classroom contexts. As Raes et al. (2019) advocate, for instance on the side of students, students' motivation can be kept at high level thanks to multiple options for interaction provided in Hyflex classroom context. Similarly, as for the benefits to teachers, multiple options for interaction help teachers understand easier whether students are still motivated or not. Based on the review of the studies indicating advantages and benefits of Hyflex teaching, it is evident that such an innovative mode of teaching enhances learning and teaching process in the field of education, including foreign language learning and teaching as well.

HyFlex EFL Teaching Challenges and Possible Solutions

Besides a number of advantages and benefits of HyFlex teaching, there are some challenges that educators come across while delivering their courses in HyFlex classroom contexts in almost every field of education, as well as foreign language teaching. In this regard, despite the advantages of more flexibility that it offers, HyFlex teaching has two particular challenges according to Binnewies and Wang (2019). First and foremost, students should be given equal opportunities to study in all modes and not be disadvantaged for preferring one over the other. Students should have equal access to learning materials, tools for completing assignments, and learning support. Second, applying active learning strategies for student engagement in a face-to-face situation frequently differs from doing so in an online setting. These strategies include feedback, classroom response systems, and collaborative activities. As a result, each distribution option requires a different set of student engagement metrics. In a similar vein, Romero-Hall and Ripine (2021) advocate that HyFlex teaching provides students with a mix of in-person and online sessions, providing flexibility. However, as Bashir et al. (2021) assert that teaching face-to-face and online groups of students at the same time or at different times can be difficult for teachers because they may not be able to adequately support the students or meet all of their needs, in turn teaching students in two different groups can cause a disparity in their experiences and sense of belonging to one class. In addition, some researchers touch upon the following issues as challenges that the lack of motivation and engagement among students is one of the drawbacks of online and hybrid teaching, as well as technical issues like malfunctioning cameras and microphones, slow or inconsistent internet connections at home (Goodyear, 2020; Hod & Katz, 2020; Hwang, 2018; Leoste et al., 2019; Simpson, 2018; Traxler, 2018); and the challenge of ensuring effective interactions between in-person and remote students are stressed in the relevant literature (Hodges et al., 2022; Park & Bonk,

2007; Stewart et al., 2011). In other words, teachers are supposed to overcome such challenges; therefore, being able to equally monitor all of the in-person and remote groups presents another difficult barrier for them. To illustrate, when remote students choose not to turn on their webcams due to student preference or internet issues, ensuring equal interaction among students becomes even more difficult. Broadly speaking, as Howell (2022) claims, differentiated instruction, student digital literacy, learner agency, social interaction, attendance, and self-regulation are some of the challenging areas that need to be addressed, and social interaction, which appears to be the biggest challenge highlighted in HyFlex related research.

In response to such challenges faced in HyFlex teaching classes, the relevant literature also shows some possible solutions that teacher can take into consideration to overcome technical, digital, methodological, and pedagogical difficulties in their HyFlex classroom practices. Within this consideration, Hodges et al. (2022) delineate the challenges faced by teachers and possible solutions that can be utilized in detail. According to the researchers, their study revealed that it was frequently difficult for online and in-person students to communicate with one another outside of the synchronous class times because of the different time zones they were in. As possible solutions to such challenges, researchers discovered that interactions and communication through videoconferencing technologies facilitated dynamic group collaboration. The course learning materials, which were available on CourseLink and contained course summaries, weekly learning contents, PowerPoint presentations in class, descriptions of tasks and assessments, and learning resources, allowed for a higher level of accessibility for all students (Hodges et al., 2022). Furthermore, the results of their study showed that there were additional significant issues while using and interacting with in-person student laptop microphones and speakers and remote student laptop microphones and speakers. For instance, it was difficult to maintain the proper volume levels since the sounds coming from the classroom speakers occasionally had distortion. The quality and placement of the laptop microphones used by the in-person students were also crucial in this regard to ensure that the voices of the students and the teacher could be heard by students online (Hodges et al., 2022).

Another important point raised by the researchers is that, even if students are physically present in class, the HyFlex learning mode necessitates that they be willing and accepting of working part of the time online with the distant students (Hodges et al., 2022). In order to establish a collaborative and participatory learning environment, it is therefore necessary for the instructors to properly prepare before class and multitask numerous pieces of equipment while in class. The teachers can find it difficult to make the learning process interesting and equal for all pupils as a result of the multitasking. Thus, in HyFlex classes, teachers need to learn rapidly how to use a variety of technology, including the laptop, projector, document camera, microphone, and webcam, as well as how to arrange the seats in the best possible way; and student self-efficacy is a crucial factor to take into account when designing this teaching method because students required to have or gain the confidence to solve technological difficulties in order to succeed (Hodges et al., 2022).

All of these aforementioned challenges stressed in the related literature are the ones that all educators from every branch of education, as well as foreign language teaching, can come across while delivering courses in HyFlex teaching environments; therefore, it is paramount to be aware of the fact that the digitalization of education not only benefits students' learning but also improves the knowledge and abilities of teachers in the use of digital technologies in foreign language instruction (Cabaroğlu & Öz, 2023). In this regard, a teacher using the HyFlex model must be able to interact with all the various places while still being able to communicate. When establishing a design and installing new equipment, it is important to take into account the teacher's movement throughout the classroom as well as the various teaching philosophies (Detyna et al., 2023). In this regard, as Mantooth et al. (2021) advocate, any novel technology must be used in conjunction with effective pedagogy in order to create effective learning settings. As delineated in Figure 3, competing requirements and challenges in implementing HyFlex teaching are summarized under four domains namely, student experience, student and environmental limitations, academic and security requirements, and external limitations (Detyna et al., 2023).

In sum, research has shown that HyFlex teaching brings new challenges to educators besides providing a variety of benefits to students, institutions, learning and teaching process in the field of foreign language education and in general. Therefore, it is crucial for foreign language teachers to ensure efficient learning experiences in their teaching contexts enhancing equity, accessibility, and inclusion believing the power of education is for all. Within this perspective, there are some important factors that are necessary to consider in designing and implementing the teaching process in HyFlex classrooms. In this sense, some key points for consideration while teaching language in HyFlex classes are addressed as follows. First, the efficient delivery of course information is greatly aided by the instructors' knowledge of the technologies accessible in the classroom and online and their proficiency with those technologies. Second, the degree of student participation is determined by their readiness to adopt this teaching approach. The third crucial factor to take into account is how to make group work in class flexible in order to lessen the pressure students felt while trying to arrange meetings outside of class with classmates who were in various time zones (Hodges et al., 2022).

Figure 3. Competing requirements and challenges in implementing HyFlex teaching

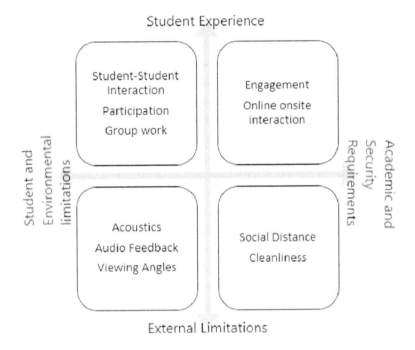

Enhancing Equity, Inclusion, and Accessibility (EIA) in HyFlex EFL Classes

To ensure that all students, regardless of their backgrounds or abilities, have equal opportunities for learning and involvement, it is imperative to improve equity, inclusion, and accessibility in HyFlex EFL programs. Access, which in education typically refers to the ability to interact with people, appears to be associated with flexibility in the HyFlex mode, which is a defining feature of this approach (Howell, 2022). Students should not be restricted to a single option in this flexibility because this access is regarded as having an enhanced need due to demands outside of the classroom learning environment (Malczyk, 2020; Miller et al., 2013). Components of HyFlex also supported equity, or the capability to obtain comparable learning results, as it established parity by focusing on the concept of reusability, allowing students like English language learners to review asynchronous content while reinforcing synchronous content (Abdelmalak & Parra, 2016; Raes et al., 2020).

Research has shown that, particularly in online modes, decreased engagement with instructors and a lack of student self-regulation skills may result in lower course performance or even unenrollment (Deimann & Bastiaens, 2010; Guglielmino &

Guglielmino, 2002; Shedletsky & Aitken, 2001). Since there may be drawbacks when students pick one mode over another, the design of HyFlex courses should put a strong emphasis on equity between online and face-to-face modes (Beatty, 2007). HyFlex mode gives learning an even greater degree of flexibility, but it is still difficult to ensure that online students are not disadvantaged in terms of social interaction and knowledge acquisition (Binnewies & Wang, 2019). Within this concern, Stone (2017)'s ten recommendation for enhancing the outcomes of online learning based on the best practices of online delivery design can be benefited to increase students' engagement and academic performance in online mode of teaching so that equity can be ensured among online and face-to-face classroom environment. Specifically created short videos with captions, tasks that promote communication and collaboration, the use of online tools to provide synchronous and asynchronous activities, the ability for students to move at their own pace, and assessments that are designed using a variety of approaches and are relevant to and relatable to the learning content are just a few examples of content that is designed to encourage online engagement and interactivity. On the other hand, mini lectures, as opposed to lengthy recordings of the entire face-to-face lectures, should be created for online students, according to CarrChellman and Duchastel (2000). Furthermore, research has shown that in online classes, video conferencing and discussion boards can be helpful tools to improve synchronous and asynchronous interaction between students and instructors as well as among students (Carr-Chellman & Duchastel, 2000; Luo & Clifton, 2017).

Ensuring a fair way to respond to queries from both online and in-person students on the lecture's substance is another barrier for equity in HyFlex classrooms. During the face-to-face lectures, any queries raised by students can be answered right away while there may be some late responses for online learners. In this sense, Binnewies and Wang (2019) recommend that despite the fact that conversations are recorded with lectures, it is still necessary to simulate the ability for online students to submit their own questions, and as a strategy, instructors can create forums for course discussion, in which students could ask questions and get responses from instructors as well as other course participants. Finding appropriate software for workout assignments is another challenge for equity considering practical content in HyFlex teaching environments, that is to provide online students equal access to practice. To this end, practical exercises can be created on a more user-friendly platform that can imitate the topics taught in the course to engage students in language learning process in HyFlex classes (Binnewies & Wang, 2019). Additionally, how to give students timely support in both cohorts is a second equity challenge for practical content, like the delivery of concepts. As a strategy recommended by Binnewies and Wang (2019) instructors can create detailed, step-by-step instructions with plenty of screenshots for each week to help students master the practical components. According to the researchers, equity in assessment is also essential, and this entails offering assessment tools that are equally accessible to students who study online and those in person. Therefore, they recommend instructors to allow online submission of all assessment items, so that online students would not be disadvantaged (Binnewies & Wang, 2019). Furthermore, Heilporn and Lakhal (2021) propose main strategies that are beneficial to students' physical, emotional, and cognitive engagement in HyFlex teaching environment. More specifically, the researchers recommend open and trustful interactions for student physical engagement while advocating the significance of links with practice and learning support to ensure emotional engagement of students; moreover, they advocate links with practice, learning support and instructor's facilitation role to increase students' cognitive engagement in HyFlex learning and teaching context.

Based on the literature, it can be stressed that some strategies need to be utilized to ensure equal, accessible, and inclusive language learning environment. In this sense, teachers can establish a diverse learning environment in the classroom that considers all student requirements and preferences. Moreover, according to students' circumstances and comfort level, teachers can let them select their preferred way of involvement, whether it be in-person, online, or a combination of both in addition to providing choices for tasks and tests that take into account various learning modalities and capacities. Putting into practice variety of equity and engagement strategies to help students in their learning in a HyFlex course, teachers can contribute to students' engagement, satisfaction, motivation, and academic achievement performance, which in turn enhance foreign language learning and teaching process in HyFlex mode of teaching environments.

IMPLICATIONS

HyFlex teaching has a lot of implications for active learning initiatives in language classrooms and can offer a solid basis for raising student language learning outcomes. HyFlex teaching can encourage learner autonomy and make it easier to create individualized instruction based on the requirements of the students. HyFlex classroom teaching also takes into account the various learning styles and preferences of language learners by promoting student-centered, reflective, and creative language learning practices. By enhancing engagement, fulfillment, and performance among learners, such an innovative active learning program as HyFlex teaching can raise the overall value of language learning and teaching process.

Language course material can be personalized to each student's unique requirements and preferences using HyFlex teaching. Through the use of technology, distance instruction, and multimedia content in HyFlex classroom contexts, teachers can promote collaboration between students and themselves in addition to strengthen student engagement, facilitate active learning, and enrich the language learning and teaching process. More specifically, regarding classroom practices, HyFlex teaching facilitates the accessibility, student-centeredness, and adaptability of technology-based learning in the field of foreign language learning and teaching, which can be accomplished utilizing online resources to help with assessment, cooperation, and communication. Instructors can meet the specific needs of each student while guaranteeing that they cover a common set of topics or skills by using a range of learning activities. Additionally, teachers can improve students' learning experiences by giving prompt feedback and assistance via digital tools and resources, in turn foreign language learning motivation, engagement, and outcomes may all be enhanced.

Furthermore, fairness and equity for all students must be ensured in HyFlex teaching like in any mode of teaching, and it is essential to give all students an experience they believe is helpful and just. Student equity may suffer if participants who attend in person believe they are receiving a better education than those who attend online, or vice versa. In this sense, teachers can benefit from strategies utilized and suggested in the relevant literature to enhance equity, inclusion, and accessibility in HyFlex mode of teaching process. To illustrate, student equity in HyFlex teaching and useful recommendations and strategies are addressed in depth by Binnewies and Wang (2019). Therefore, the researchers' valuable recommendations on enhancing student equity in HyFlex context can shed light on teachers in the field of foreign language learning and teaching. Ensuring that all students—online and on campus—raise their hands before speaking and providing in-person students with a device to interact with online students might be another two implications on how equity may be embedded in instruction (Detyna et al., 2023).

In this regard, this chapter provides detailed review of the current literature of HyFlex teaching in relation to foreign language learning and teaching field by presenting the benefits of EFL teaching in HyFlex classroom environments along with some challenges and possible solutions proposed by instructors in the light of the current relevant literature and empirical research. In addition, how HyFlex teaching can enhance equity, inclusion, and accessibility in education for all students regardless of their diverse backgrounds as well as fostering foreign language learning and teaching process are delineated in the light of the relevant literature as well as offering some useful strategies and providing abovementioned implications for the benefit of foreign language learning and teaching field.

CONCLUSION

The literature on HyFlex teaching as it relates to the study and teaching of foreign languages is discussed in this chapter. This chapter begins with the introduction of HyFlex teaching as a new digital pedagogical approach before presenting the advantages of teaching EFL in HyFlex classroom settings, as well as some difficulties and potential solutions put forth by teachers in light of recent relevant literature and empirical research. More particularly, it discusses how HyFlex teaching may promote the acquisition and teaching of foreign languages while improving equality, inclusion, and accessibility in education for all students, regardless of their varied backgrounds. Based on the review of related studies in the literature, the following concluding remarks and recommendations can be presented below.

As an educational strategy, it is clear that hybrid flexible (HyFlex) teaching combines aspects of in-person instruction and online learning to give students freedom in how they interact with the course materials and take part in class activities. HyFlex teaching is designed to take into account each student's unique learning preferences, schedule, and circumstances. For each class period, students in a HyFlex model can select the method of involvement that best meets their needs. In-person attendance, remote participation in synchronous online sessions, and asynchronous access to recorded lectures and course materials are all options available to participants. With this flexibility, students can tailor their educational experience to suit their needs and those of their environment, among other things.

Numerous advantages can come from HyFlex EFL education, including more adaptability, individualized learning opportunities, improved accessibility, and the incorporation of technology. For all students, regardless of their preferred mode of involvement, it also demands careful preparation, a strong technological foundation, and pedagogical considerations to maintain engagement and guarantee learning outcomes. Overall, HyFlex EFL teaching creates a flexible and adjustable learning environment by combining the advantages of in-person instruction and online learning. It empowers students, encourages participation, and improves accessibility, which ultimately helps with efficient language learning and skill development.

HyFlex EFL teaching gives flexibility and advantages, but it also has certain challenges related to technology, student engagement and interaction, learning environment, assessment and feedback, classroom management, and inclusion and equity. However, it's crucial to keep in mind that putting a HyFlex Teaching model into practice calls for thorough planning and consideration of technology setup, instructional design, and student support services. While preserving fairness and inclusion for all students, instructors need to establish techniques to manage and encourage learning across various modes of involvement. All of these challenges require that teachers need to gain new knowledge and skills to enhance foreign language learning and teaching process in HyFlex classrooms. Moreover, it seems essential for not only teachers but also students to have adequate knowledge and skills, and self-efficacy in utilizing digital tools for effective interaction in HyFlex environments. Apart from the technological and methodological responsibilities that teachers need to gain while delivering their courses in HyFlex teaching contexts, they should also consider the issues of equity, inclusion, and accessibility of their teaching process for all students. In other words, every teacher needs to consider and learn how to provide equal opportunities to their students and how to make HyFlex teaching process more accessible and inclusive for all in the class. However, in the relevant literature, the studies related to EFL teaching in HyFlex environments, especially empirical ones that offer best practices and implications for foreign language teachers, are limited in both number and contexts. That is why, more research is needed to shed light on foreign language teachers and researchers in implementing sustainable EFL teaching in HyFlex classes effectively in order to promote equity, accessibility, and inclusion for all learners throughout the world.

REFERENCES

Abdelmalak, M. M. M., & Parra, J. L. (2016). Expanding learning opportunities for graduate students with HyFlex course design. [IJOPCD]. *International Journal of Online Pedagogy and Course Design, 6*(4), 19–37. doi:10.4018/IJOPCD.2016100102

Bărbuceanu, C. D. (2022). HyFlex-Rethinking courses in online teaching. *Revista de Științe Politice. Revue des Sciences Politiques*, (73), 241–247.

Bashir, A., Bashir, S., Rana, K., Lambert, P., & Vernallis, A. (2021). Post-COVID-19 adaptations; the shifts towards online learning, hybrid course delivery and the implications for biosciences courses in the higher education setting. *Frontiers in Education, 6*(711619), 711619. doi:10.3389/feduc.2021.711619

Beatty, B. (2014). *Hybrid courses with flexible participation: The HyFlex course design*. IGI Global. doi:10.4018/978-1-4666-4912-5.ch011

Beatty, B. (2019). *Hybrid-flexible course design*. EdTech Books. doi:10.59668/33

Beatty, B. J. (2007, October). *Hybrid classes with fexible participation options—If you build it, how will they come?* In Paper presented at the 2007 association for educational communications and technology annual convention, Anaheim, CA.

Beatty, B. J. (2020). Can HyFlex options support students in the midst of uncertainty. *Educause Review.* https://er.educause.edu/blogs/2020/5/can-hyflex-options-support-students-in-the-midst-of-uncertainty

Binnewies, S., & Wang, Z. (2019). *Challenges of student equity and engagement in a HyFlex course*. Springer. doi:10.1007/978-981-13-6982-7_12

Bower, M., Dalgarno, B., Kennedy, G. E., Lee, M. J., & Kenney, J. (2015). Design and implementation factors in blended synchronous learning environments: Outcomes from a cross-case analysis. *Computers & Education*, *86*, 1–17. doi:10.1016/j.compedu.2015.03.006

Bozkurt, A. (2019). *From distance education to open and distance learning: a holistic evaluation of history, definitions, and theories*. IGI Global. doi:10.4018/978-1-5225-8431-5.ch016

Buşu, A.-F. (2020). Emotional intelligence as a type of cognitive ability. *Revista de Ştiinţe Politice. Revue des Sciences Politiques*, (66), 204–215.

Cabaroğlu, N., & Öz, G. (2023). Practicum in ELT: a systematic review of 2010–2020 research on ELT practicum. *European Journal of Teacher Education*. https://doi.org/https://doi.org/10.1080/02619768.2023.2242577

Calafiore, P., & Giudici, E. (2021). Hybrid Versus HyFlex Instruction in an introductory finance course. *International Journal of Education and Research*, *16*(1), 40–52.

Carr-Chellman, A., & Duchastel, P. (2000). The ideal online course. *British Journal of Educational Technology*, *31*(3), 229–241. doi:10.1111/1467-8535.00154

Deimann, M., & Bastiaens, T. (2010). The role of volition in distance education: An exploration of its capacities. *International Review of Research in Open and Distance Learning*, *11*(1), 1–16. doi:10.19173/irrodl.v11i1.778

Detyna, M., Sanchez-Pizani, R., Giampietro, V., Dommett, E. J., & Dyer, K. (2023). Hybrid flexible (HyFlex) teaching and learning: Climbing the mountain of implementation challenges for synchronous online and face-to-face seminars during a pandemic. *Learning Environments Research*, *26*(1), 145–159. doi:10.100710984-022-09408-y PMID:35399562

Garrison, D. R., & Kanuka, H. (2004). Blended learning: Uncovering its transformative potential in higher education. *The Internet and Higher Education*, *7*(2), 95–105. doi:10.1016/j.iheduc.2004.02.001

Goodyear, P. (2020). Design and co-configuration for hybrid learning: Theorising the practices of learning space design. *British Journal of Educational Technology*, *51*(4), 1045–1060. doi:10.1111/bjet.12925

Gounari, P., & Koutropoulos, A. (2015). *Using blended principles to bridge the gap between online and on-campus courses*. IGI Global. doi:10.4018/978-1-4666-8246-7.ch065

Guglielmino, P. J., & Guglielmino, L. M. (2001). *Learner characteristics affecting success in electronic distance learning*. Motorola University Press.

Heilporn, G., & Lakhal, S. (2021). Converting a graduate-level course into a HyFlex modality: What are effective engagement strategies? *International Journal of Management Education, 19*(1), 100454. doi:10.1016/j.ijme.2021.100454

Henriksen, D., Creely, E., & Henderson, M. (2020). Folk pedagogies for teacher transitions: Approaches to synchronous online learning in the wake of Covid-19. *Journal of Technology and Teacher Education, 28*(2), 201–209.

Hill, P. (2012). Online educational delivery models: A descriptive view. *EDUCAUSE Review, 47*(6), 84–86.

Hod, Y., & Katz, S. (2020). Fostering highly engaged knowledge building communities in socioemotional and sociocognitive hybrid learning spaces. *British Journal of Educational Technology, 51*(4), 1117–1135. doi:10.1111/bjet.12910

Hodges, B., Hu, L., & Siefker, D. (2022, August). Benefits and challenges of a hybrid flexible EAP Program. *TESL Ontario: Contact magazine*, 15-26.

Howell, E. (2022). HyFlex model of higher education: Understanding the promise of flexibility. *On the Horizon, 30*(4), 173–181. doi:10.1108/OTH-04-2022-0019

Hwang, A. (2018). Online and hybrid learning. *Journal of Management Education, 42*(4), 557–563. doi:10.1177/1052562918777550

Inglis, M., Palipana, A., Trenholm, S., & Ward, J. (2011). Individual differences in students' use of optional learning resources. *Journal of Computer Assisted Learning, 27*(6), 490–502. doi:10.1111/j.1365-2729.2011.00417.x

Jaime, S., & Kateryna, N. (2022). Students' perceptions of the hyflex learning model from Ukraine and Japan: A realistic future for university language learning? *Hiroshima Studies in Language and Language Education, 25*, 45–59. doi:10.15027/51960

Karpava, S. (2022, January). *The challenge of change: hybrid teaching and learning during the pandemic*. Trends in Language Teaching 2022 Conference Post-Conference Proceedings, Okinawa.

Kohnke, L., & Moorhouse, B. L. (2021). Adopting HyFlex in higher education in response to covid-19: Students' perspectives. *Open Learning*, *36*(3), 231–244. doi :10.1080/02680513.2021.1906641

Köroğlu, Ç. Z., Öz, G., & Yüce, E. (2022). *Enhancing EFL learners' self-regulatory skill and autonomy in digital learning environments*. Nobel Publishing.

Köroğlu, Z. Ç., & Öz, G. (2023). Preservice English teachers' speaking skills assessment literacy: Transformation to digital assessment. *The Reading Matrix: An International Online Journal*, *23*(1), 1–17.

Kyei-Blankson, L., & Godwyll, F. (2010). *An examination of learning outcomes in Hyflex learning environments*. In J. Sanchez & K. Zhang (Eds.), Proceedings of E-Learn 2010--World Conference on E-Learning in Corporate, Government, Healthcare, and Higher Education. Orlando, Florida.

Lakhal, S., Bateman, D., & Bédard, J. (2017). Blended synchronous delivery mode in graduate programs: A literature review and its implementation in the master teacher program. *Collected Essays on Learning and Teaching*, *10*, 47–60. doi:10.22329/ celt.v10i0.4747

Leoste, J., Tammets, K., & Ley, T. (2019). Co-creating learning designs in professional teacher education: knowledge appropriation in the teacher's innovation laboratory. *Adopting and Sustaining Technological Innovations in Teachers' Classroom Practices–The Case of Integrating Educational Robots into Math Classes*, 89.

Leoste, J., Tammets, K., & Ley, T. (2019). Co-creating learning designs in professional teacher education: Knowledge appropriation in the teacher's innovation laboratory. Interaction Deisgn and Architecture(s). *Journal*, *42*, 131–163.

Libasin, Z., Azudin, R. A., Idris, M. A., Rahman, M. S. A., & Umar, N. (2021). Comparison of students' academic performance in mathematics course with synchronous and asynchronous online learning environments during Covid-19 crisis. *International Journal of Academic Research in Progressive Education and Development*, *10*(2), 492–501. doi:10.6007/IJARPED/v10-i2/10131

Liu, M., McKelroy, E., Winzeler, E., Adams, D., Davis, P., Ziai, K., & Roberts, R. (2014). *Exploration of best practices to support active learning in a synchronous multi-site learning environment*. In T. Bastiaens (Ed.), *Proceedings of World Conference on E-Learning*. New Orleans, LA, USA.

Luo, T., & Clifton, L. (2017). Examining collaborative knowledge construction in microblogging-based learning environments. *Journal of Information Technology Education*, *16*, 365–390. doi:10.28945/3869

MacDonald, J. (2006). *Blended learning and online tutoring: a good practice guide*. Gower.

Malczyk, B. R. (2020). *Introducing social work to HyFlex blended learning: a student-centered approach*. Routledge.

Mantooth, R., Usher, E. L., & Love, A. M. (2021). Changing classrooms bring new questions: Environmental influences, self-efficacy, and academic achievement. *Learning Environments Research, 24*(3), 519–535. doi:10.100710984-020-09341-y

McGee, P., & Reis, A. (2012). Blended course design: A synthesis of best practices. *Online Learning : the Official Journal of the Online Learning Consortium, 16*(4), 7–22. doi:10.24059/olj.v16i4.239

Miller, A. N., Sellnow, D. D., & Strawser, M. G. (2021). Pandemic pedagogy challenges and opportunities: Instruction communication in remote, HyFlex, and BlendFlex courses. *Communication Education, 70*(2), 202–204. doi:10.1080/036 34523.2020.1857418

Miller, J., Risser, M., & Griffiths, R. (2013). Student choice, instructor flexibility: moving beyond the blended instructional model. *Issues and trends in educational technology, 1*(1), 8-24.

Öz, G., & Köroğlu, Ç. Z. (2023). English language teachers' assessment procedure during covid19 pandemic: challenges and solutions. *i-manager's Journal on English Language Teaching, 13*(1), 42-53. doi:10.26634/jelt.13.1.19058

Öz, G., & Şahinkarakaş, Ş. (2023). The relationship between Turkish EFL learners' academic resilience and English language achievement. *The Reading Matrix: An International Online Journal, 23*(1), 80–91.

Park, Y. J., & Bonk, C. J. (2007). Is online life a breeze? A case study for promoting synchronous learning. *Journal of Online Learning and Teaching, 3*(3), 307–323.

Raes, A., Detienne, L., Windey, I., & Depaepe, F. (2020). A systematic literature review on synchronous hybrid learning: Gaps identified. *Learning Environments Research, 23*(3), 269–290. doi:10.100710984-019-09303-z

Raes, A., Pieters, M., & Bonte, P. (2019). *Hyflex Learning within the Master of Teaching Program@ KU Leuven*. EdTech Books.

Romero, H. Y., Chávez, N. V., & Gutiérrez, I. M. (2016). *HyFlex, hybrid and flexible model for university education: case study: Universidad Técnica Particular de Loja—Ecuador. 11th Iberian Conference on Information Systems and Technologies (CISTI)*, Gran Canaria, Spain. 10.1109/CISTI.2016.7521455

Romero-Hall, E., & Ripine, C. (2021). Hybrid flexible instruction: Exploring faculty preparedness. *Online Learning : the Official Journal of the Online Learning Consortium, 25*(3), 289–312. doi:10.24059/olj.v25i3.2426

Samuel, J. C., Rosenzweig, A. H., McLean, M., & Cintrón, R. (2019). *One size fits none. Beatty BJ. Hybrid-Flexible Course Design: Implementing Student-Directed Hybrid Classes.* EdTech Books.

Shedletsky, L. J., & Aitken, J. E. (2001). The paradoxes of online academic work. *Communication Education, 50*(3), 206–217. doi:10.1080/03634520109379248

Sheera, H., & Yadav, M. (2022). An analytical investigation of flipped classroom to improve Saudi EFL learners' speaking skills: A case study at Applied College. *Arab World English Journal. Special Issue on CALL., 8*(8), 274–298. doi:10.24093/awej/call8.19

Simpson, O. (2018). *Supporting students in online, open and distance learning.* Routledge.

Singh, H. (2003). Building effective blended learning programs. *Educational Technology, 43*(6), 51–54.

Singh, H. (2021). *Building effective blended learning programs.* IGI Global. doi:10.4018/978-1-7998-7607-6.ch002

Stewart, A. R., Harlow, D. B., & DeBacco, K. (2011). Students' experience of synchronous learning in distributed environments. *Distance Education, 32*(3), 357–381. doi:10.1080/01587919.2011.610289

Stone, C. (2017). *Opportunity through online learning: improving student access, participation and success in higher education.* NCSHEHE. https://www.ncsehe.edu.au/publications/opportunity-online learningimproving-student-access-participation-success-higher-education/

Taylor, J. A., & Newton, D. (2013). Beyond blended learning: A case study of institutional change at an Australian regional university. *The Internet and Higher Education, 18*, 54–60. doi:10.1016/j.iheduc.2012.10.003

Taylor, L. (2020). Teaching and learning languages under covid-19. *Conference Proceedings. Innovation in Language Learning, 2020.*

Tolosa-Casadont, L. (2022). *Using multimodal pedagogy to teach languages online: Reimagining language teaching with elementary school children.* IGI Global.

Traxler, J. (2018). Distance learning—Predictions and possibilities. *Education Sciences*, *8*(1), 35. doi:10.3390/educsci8010035

Wang, Q., Quek, C. L., & Hu, X. (2017). Designing and improving a blended synchronous learning environment: An educational design research. *International Review of Research in Open and Distance Learning*, *18*(3). doi:10.19173/irrodl. v18i3.3034

Weitze, C. L., Ørngreen, R., & Levinsen, K. (2013, October). The global classroom video conferencing model and first evaluations. *Proceedings of the 12th European Conference on E-Learning*. SKEMA Business School.

Wigal, C. M. (2021). Teaching the design process in a HyFlex environment. *Journal of Higher Education Theory and Practice*, *21*(10), 226–235.

Wilson, T. J., & Alexander, M. (2021). HyFlex course delivery: Addressing the change in course modality brought on by the pandemic. *Journal of the International Society for Teacher Education*, *25*(2), 41–58. doi:10.26522/jiste.v25i2.3668

ADDITIONAL READING

Aldosemani, T. (2023). Adopting HyFlex Course Design: Actions for Policymakers, Researchers, and Practitioners. *Active and Transformative Learning in STEAM Disciplines*, 197-227. doi:10.1108/978-1-83753-618-420231010

Beatty, B. J. (2019). *Hybrid-flexible course design*. EdTech Books. doi:10.59668/33

Bergstrom, M. (2020). *Teaching HyFlex: It's a Genre Problem*. Faculty Focus.

KEY TERMS AND DEFINITIONS

Asynchronous Online Learning: This refers to instruction in which teachers and pupils interact only intermittently. This online learning approach has a time lag, indicating that the actual time involvement of students or teachers is not needed (Libasin et al., 2021).

Blended Learning: A teaching approach that incorporates the advantages of traditional classrooms as well as ICT-supported educational activities such as both online and offline learning (Singh, 2021).

Distance Learning: A method of instruction that allows students to participate in learning without having to attend traditional classroom sessions (Bozkurt, 2019).

HyFlex Teaching: Defined as a course that allows students to participate in a flexible manner. Students may participate in synchronous in person classes or complete course tasks online without actually being in class (Beatty, 2019).

Synchronous Online Learning: This refers to a real-time instructor-led approach in which participants must be logged on at the same time and communicate directly with one another. (Henriksen et al., 2020).

Chapter 12
EFL Learners' Digitalized Practices in Promoting Vocabulary Learning at the Higher Education Level

Fatma Kimsesiz
https://orcid.org/0000-0001-6758-7393
Kırşehir Ahi Evran University, Turkey

ABSTRACT

Technology has become an integral part of education; and language instruction, which is communicative in nature, has a share in the whole unit. The widespread use of portable devices has also transformed language learning through diverse accessible facilities that can alternatively be evaluated in an out-of-school context. This paved the way for self-directed learning practices that enable learners to advance their language skills and vocabulary. This study aimed to investigate these self-directed practices for learning vocabulary in English. 120 EFL learners at diverse departments at a state university in Turkiye participated in the study. For data collection, a survey was employed that interrogated the self-directed vocabulary learning practices of the participants in digital contexts. The results of the study showed that learners use mobile technology for English language practices and adopt different strategies in vocabulary learning supplied by a variety of digital applications and facilities. The results are discussed and related implications are addressed based on the findings.

DOI: 10.4018/979-8-3693-0353-5.ch012

Copyright © 2024, IGI Global. Copying or distributing in print or electronic forms without written permission of IGI Global is prohibited.

INTRODUCTION

The tendency to remote learning has been prevalent among learners with the expansion of online education facilities. The incorporation of digital tools and resources that have been designed for specific purposes in education has also become widespread for more efficient learning and teaching outcomes (González-Lloret, 2017). An increase in the use of technology for self-directed learning was documented in the previous years (Plews, 2017), yet the integration of remote learning has peaked specifically after the COVID-19 pandemic (Bozkurt and Sharma, 2020). Hence, it became significant to examine the self-directed practices of learners and also teachers for a better understanding and evaluation of the practices. Within this respect, technology-mediated learning and teaching are at the center of remote learning on behalf of both learners and teachers (Sung et al., 2015). Within this scope, language instruction also benefits from the opportunities provided by computer-assisted or mobile-assisted learning practices. In this context, it is worthwhile to consider the significance of learner strategies that direct individual learning practices in the mastery of a target language. According to Oxford (2011), selected among alternatives by the learners, these self-directed strategies are "deliberate goal-directed attempts to manage and control efforts to learn the L2" (p. 12). Referring to this situation, the importance of learner-initiated practices is recognized, and this caused a need for the discovery of these practices that are commonly conducted in out-of-class contexts (Lai et al., 2022). Effective strategies in self-directed foreign language learning may guide other learners who want to follow autonomous tracks in learning. Furthermore, it is essential for language teachers to guide learners at the higher education level for self-directed learning practices through digital tools (Kimsesiz, 2023). As suggested by Xodabande and Atai (2022), receptive and productive vocabulary development through digital tools should be focused. According to Çetin Köroğlu et al. (2022), as online learning has a direct connection with autonomy, self-directed learning is essential for learners "to have agency in their own learning actions as well as for an effective language learning process and progress" (p. 103). Hence, the investigation of these strategies is essential to provide alternatives to foreign language learners and to understand the most applicable and efficient ways of learning. For these reasons, this study aimed to investigate the self-directed vocabulary learning practices of English as a foreign language (EFL) learners at the higher education level through computer-assisted learning facilities. The research questions that motivated the study are:

1- What is the level of EFL learners' access to and preference for digital devices, digital programs, and translation programs?
2- Which digital platforms do EFL learners use for vocabulary learning?

3- Which activities do EFL learners use for vocabulary learning on digital platforms?

4- What strategies do EFL learners adopt for learning vocabulary in digital platforms?

LITERATURE REVIEW

Learner Autonomy and Self-Directed Learning

Recent research has implicated the promising impact of self-directed learning practices on learner achievement in education (Little, 2007; Shapely, 2000; Viberg, et al., 2020). Relatedly, learner autonomy has been a popular conception for proficiency in language skills and vocabulary knowledge in second/foreign language (L2) learning. Learner autonomy is closely related to self-directed or in other words self-regulated learning in education (Zimmerman, 1989). As reflected by Ciekanski (2007), autonomous learners tend to follow a self-directed learning path. According to the definition provided by Little (2007), learner autonomy is "the ability to take charge of one's own learning" (p.15). Benson (2011) connected the same concept to individuals' capacity to control their own learning. Little (2007) argues that learner autonomy is attained through a process during which language teachers help learners enlarge their scope of learning and undertake control of their own learning. Since interaction is a key factor in language development, improving communicative proficiency and learner autonomy is essential to devising interaction. Little (2007) implies that the autonomy of a learner is advocated by the autonomy of teachers who will use their professional skills in an autonomous way in the classroom, and "to produce and manage the many varieties of target language discourse required by the autonomous classroom" (p. 27). According to Wenden (1991), learners who have grasped the best ways to learn succeed easily since they know and use the best models to learn, access, and use information which eventually causes them to become autonomous learners. Similarly, if a language learner is autonomous, s/he is more likely to reflect positive behaviors and attitudes toward self-directed language learning with a willingness and consciousness to control their learning process (Curry et al., 2017). Learner autonomy has a direct association with learners' efforts to control their self-directed learning practices in foreign language education (Benson, 2011; Curry et al., 2017). This process also helps learners gain proficiency in language learning (Little, 2007; Wenden, 1991), particularly when assisted by online learning facilities in out-of-class contexts (Shapely, 2000). As suggested by Yosintha and Yunianti (2021), learner autonomy has a positive impact on the outcomes of EFL online learning.

Considering the effect of autonomous learning, it is essential to clarify that self-regulated and self-directed learning refers to the same process of learning and practice (Sert and Boynueğri, 2017; Thomas and Rose, 2019). Conde Gafaro (2019) explained self-regulated learning as the processes through which learners "plan, monitor, and reflect their performance" to attain their goal (p. 1). Zimmerman (1989) explained self-regulated learning as "the degree to which students are metacognitively, motivationally, and behaviorally active participants in their own learning processes" (p. 329). Zimmerman (2000) illustrated a self-regulated model that represents the process through the direction of three phases "forethought", "performance", and "self-reflection". In this process, learners are expected to set goals for learning and to monitor and evaluate the strategies used for goal attainment. Each phase has sub-areas which determine the processes that will be followed by learners for self-regulation till the end.

On the other hand, self-directed learning can be handled based on two main perspectives: process and personal attributes (Plews, 2017). The continuum revolves around the organization of instruction and goals to models that promote interaction and learning (Plews, 2017). As framed by Curry et al. (2017), self-directed language learning covers identifying goals for learning, planning the process and implementing the plan, utilizing proper materials and strategies, and finally evaluating the learning process. As addressed by Lai et al. (2022), learners may tend to maintain a self-directed language learning process to augment their foreign language learning practices by using a variety of technology-assisted facilities. At this point, learners will be able to regulate their learning process in a much more efficient way by the leadership of their teachers (Gan, 2004). Upon the same issue, Du (2013) offered that, teachers should help students attain discipline-specific knowledge and improve their competencies in self-directed learning.

Digital Practices in Language Learning

In recent years, technology has been integrated into the educational context through computers, mobile technology, and the Internet (Nada, 2021). The prevalence of computer-assisted learning has paved the way for learners to enable interaction, process information, and reach resources provided by multiple facilities in a large domain of digital sources (Gündüz, 2005). Through computers, learners are able to increase personal focus and practice to gain proficiency in language learning. Yet, digital innovations have caused an increase in demand for portable devices and now language learning can also be maintained by mobile-assisted devices such as mobile phones and tablets, and downloadable applications on them (Lai et al., 2022). These tools also supply an autonomous function of language learning studies (Kukulska-Hulme et al., 2017). Learners are supported to have access to online language courses, individual practice, and focus on language skills and knowledge (Viberg et al., 2020) and to foster learner engagement in an informal context of learning (Botero et al., 2019).

The field closely follows the paradigm of functions provided by technological platforms. Although the terms "online learning", "distance education", "virtual learning", and "e-learning" are often used interchangeably in form and variation, the common ground represented by all versions is the delivery of instruction through technology (Plews, 2017). This context has brought another point on how to teach and learn effectively through technology for both teachers and learners. According to Plews (2017), through online learning, learners may reach a variety of resources that enable them to benefit from meaningful learning. Communication and time management are two crucial factors in managing the process of learning in an online context. Yet, communication is in written form contrary to environments that are in person and this situation is open to misinterpretation (Plews, 2017). Scheduling participation and response are also essential for both learners and educators in the online context. According to Smaldino et al. (2008), learners are active in the online learning process in which they can take control over their own learning, whereas they tend to be passive in a receptive mode in traditional learning conditions. Moreover, the equipment system plays a crucial role in accessing to the interactive practices during online learning, which can be affected by a number of factors such as the internet connection and the access to the data reflected on the screen of the digital devices (Dolgunsöz and Yıldırım, 2021). The internet speed is another promoter for qualified access to the data. As implicated by Dolgunsöz and Yıldırım (2021), using notebooks rather than mobile phones provide learners with more effective practices especially when multitasking during an online course or practice.

Another substantial aspect of online learning is that it enables learners through "anytime, anywhere" feasibility that learners can access the same content at any convenient time (Plews, 2017). Based on this feature, convenience and flexibility are two central profits of remote learning (Song and Hill, 2007). The main advantage is a simplified pattern of access to the sources of information when individuals are available at best. de Marcos et al. (2014) highlighted the use of games in information and communication technology since games endow players with instant feedback and connection with other players. Promoting creativity and productivity, video games also appear as attractive alternatives in gamification (Chatfield, 2010). Wang et al. (2020) also found that mobile-assisted vocabulary learning was more effective compared to traditional learning strategies for learning target words.

The impact of a digitalized form of information is not definitely without changes or adaptations. Karakas and Manisalıgil (2012) designated five transformations to describe the shift in the learning environment in a digital context. These are "virtual collaboration, technological convergence, global connectivity, online communities,

EFL Learners' Digitalized Practices in Promoting Vocabulary

and digital creativity" (p.715). Virtual collaboration enables members to collaborate and share ideas and documents through diverse facilities of digital platforms in an easy, cheap, and fast way of collaboration. People can connect and actively participate in innovation to improve their understanding and experience in art, culture, science, and education. Although people used to benefit from autonomous learning conditions in isolation, self-directed learning is now transformed into a collaborative nature of interaction through access to different learning networks, and support and feedback from other participants. In this sense, Karakas and Manisalıgil (2012) propose that the focal tenet of virtual collaboration is the social and networked process of self-directed learning through which people can collaborate worldwide. The second transformation concerns the technological convergence that combines several media resources such as TV, radio, mobile devices, and the internet to constitute a "global information channel" (p. 717). It is evident in technological convergence since it enables a context for social, communicative, and interpersonal interaction for learners to share their experiences and exchange ideas and feedback. Within this context, it is implicated that the utilization of these tools has a significant role in maintaining continuous learning. Learners are also supported for self-directed learning through a number of communication channels and access to information presented in a digital context. As the third transformation, global connectivity refers to the facility to connect to the internet since it enables users to gain access to information resources that are available worldwide. Global connectivity helps individuals to feel global citizenship, to be part of a larger social community, and to have a global understanding. This paves the way for an association between self-directed learning and global connectivity. Since self-directed learners are part of a web of connections and networks in the digital environment, they possess the tools to be engaged in a highly interconnected world. The next transformation occurs in internet platforms and social media that enable users to educate, communicate, share information, and increase social awareness. This kind of environment can also reflect itself to cover "the world cafe´ method, project wikis, idea contests, or a virtual town hall meeting" (p. 719). In this sense, the use of technology in education enables access to multiple materials and resources and provides learners with chances to fulfill their needs and preferences to advance the conditions for self-directed learning. The final transformation that was introduced by Karakas and Manisalıgil (2012) deals with digital creativity which is considered to be significant for professional competency. Within the context of digital creativity, individuals need to be directed to think creatively, improve their skills, and self-actualize their ideals. Through this paradigm, learners are able to customize their learning in relation to their needs, interest, and skills; advance their abilities and strengths, and plan and implement their own works in an autonomous way.

Learning Vocabulary in a Digitalized Context

Vocabulary learning has gradually gained significance and recognition, and scholarly attention has been directed to vocabulary learning and instruction since the 1980s). Empirical research on vocabulary learning in an L2 has shown that vocabulary knowledge is a key factor for overall language ability and performance. Vocabulary knowledge is a core element in language learning and teaching and has a crucial role in language proficiency (Nation, 2001). The extent of vocabulary acquisition impacts the precision and efficacy of linguistic interaction encompassing both comprehension and language production.

According to Nation (2001), in learning vocabulary, implicit learning provides more effective outcomes than explicit learning. Within this scope, attention and noticing are two essential factors that promote learning (Laufer and Hulstjin, 2001). However, knowing a word does not exactly mean knowing its equivalent in the target language. According to Cook (2008), knowing a word is associated with recalling information about the meaning, lexical properties, pronunciation, spelling, and structural and pragmatic use of a specific word or lexical item. From a similar viewpoint, Cameron (2001) claimed that knowing a word also covers recalling it when needed and using it with proper meaning, collocation, connotation, orthography, pragmatics, and cultural context. More importantly, knowing a word is not an end, but a process to be fulfilled.

Schmitt and Schmitt (1995), offer several principles that should be followed for effective vocabulary learning. They suggest that it will be more effective to incorporate words into the language that is already known and to recycle the words to be learned. They also suggest that words should be learnt in an organized way such as word pairs, and similar words should not be taught at the same time. Furthermore, it is better to consider vocabulary learning which entails the operation of a deeper mental process and the generation of different individual learning styles. Related implications on learning vocabulary are also accordingly provided for learner strategies. Within this context, it is essential to consider that the process of foreign language learning is ultimately affected by learner strategies. In its broadest sense, learner strategies refer to the conscious actions controlled by the learners to attain their goals of learning a specific topic and assuming responsibility for their own learning. Diyono (2009) described learner strategies as certain ways followed to enhance comprehension, learning, or retention of information. In vocabulary learning, using a variety of strategies contributes to vocabulary retention (Li, 2009). Chamot (1990) categorized learning strategies as metacognitive strategies that involve "self-regulation, cognitive strategies, and finally social-affective strategies" that involve interaction with others for learning (p.497). Regarding these dimensions, learner strategies are multifaceted and formed through the combination of distinct elements.

The research that focuses on vocabulary learning in the technology-enhanced environment is organized around direct and indirect vocabulary learning strategies in a target language which eventually implicate the benefits of learning language proficiency and vocabulary building utilizing technology-enhanced facilities directed by autonomous learning strategies (Du, 2013; Gan, 2004; Kimsesiz, 2023; Li, 2009; Wu, 2015; Xodabande and Atai, 2022; Zhang and Perez-Paredes, 2021).

Gan (2004) conducted a study to address the attitudes and strategies used by Chinese learners. A questionnaire that was developed by the author was applied to 357 learners of EFL at higher education levels in China. The results showed that strategies used in self-directed language learning were directly implicated in language proficiency. Although attitudes in self-directed language learning do not seem to have a direct effect on proficiency, major attitude components were found to be linked to all strategy components in self-directed language learning. The results showed that attitudes and strategies used in self-directed learning were determined by the constraints of the particular learning and teaching context.

Applying focus group interviews to 13 students, Du (2013) investigated the perspectives of Chinese students learning EFL on the benefits of engaging in self-directed learning, the role of teachers, and the potential factors that accounted for variances in the performance of participants within the context of self-directed learning. The results confirmed that self-directed learning was promising and beneficial in foreign language learning. It was also found that participants had high expectations from the teachers on feedback which was important for the evaluation of their learning outcomes. Findings also suggested that learners' initial comfort with self-directed learning was affected by their prior experience and self-efficacy. The study implicated that learners should be given orientations, specifically with the help of their teachers on the basis of actualizing their competencies in self-directed learning. To gain greater insight into the outer factors, Du (2013) also elicited that it is essential to consider key attributes such as learners' previous experiences and readiness levels, the skills, and attitudes of teachers toward self-directed learning, and the reasons lying behind adopting a self-directed learning strategy.

In a study administered by Wu (2015), the application of computer technology was tested in enhancing vocabulary learning strategies and improving self-directed vocabulary learning of 61 freshman students learning EFL at two different universities in China. A questionnaire for judgmental analysis and three vocabulary tests for empirical analysis based on a computerized system were applied for data collection. To process self-directed vocabulary learning, "Learning Vocabulary in Domain" was developed as a system that facilitates the composition of diverse tasks which focus on different vocabulary learning strategies. The results of the survey demonstrated that the system was superior compared to the printed material which involved almost the same tasks for enhancing strategies for vocabulary building. Furthermore, the application of computer technology helped learners enhance their use of strategies and retain vocabulary knowledge of the target words.

In an attempt to understand the uses and motivation behind language learners' preferences for mobile-assisted language learning resources, Zhang and Perez-Paredes (2021) conducted a mixed-method study employing a questionnaire and an interview. The quantitative data was collected from 95 post-graduate students and the qualitative data were gathered from some of the participants in the same sample (N=8) from four different universities in China. The results revealed that participants used mobile-assisted language learning tools for a variety of reasons such as passing exams and expanding their vocabulary knowledge in English. The results also showed that few students could select suitable practices for their learning needs and they elicited that they are not actively involved in mobile resources for learning English. The participants also revealed that they mostly rely on recommendations provided by social media and education experts. Among the resources, the learners mostly used mobile dictionaries and vocabulary learning applications based on their perception that vocabulary learning is significant in learning an L2. It was also implicated that learners' needs and motivations should be considered when designing and selecting mobile-assisted resources. Moreover, teachers need to help learners discover and maximize the use of these resources.

In a more recent study, Xodabande and Atai (2022) examined the effect of a mobile application for academic vocabulary in an autonomous process directed by 38 EFL learners at the university level in Iran. The learners in the experimental group used a mobile application whereas the learners in the control group used traditional materials during a semester. Throughout the study, the receptive vocabulary knowledge of the participants was tested three times. The results displayed that vocabulary knowledge improved in both groups. Yet, participants in the experimental group statistically performed better than the control group. In addition, the time factor proved to hold a significant effect on mobile-assisted vocabulary learning. The study implicated that integrating diverse materials covering technology-assisted devices or applications for learning vocabulary may yield gain and retention in vocabulary knowledge.

Kimsesiz (2023) examined 182 tertiary-level EFL learners' digital practices for enhancing their language skills in English. Through a mixed method design, the data was collected through an online survey and was analyzed through descriptive and content analysis. The results showed that most of the learners used portable devices. Yet, the frequency of using these devices for language learning practices was low. The results also showed that learners used different language learning practices supported by mobile-assisted applications and platforms. The study implicated that self-directed language learning practices should be regulated in a more conscious way for more efficient learning outcomes in order to improve target language skills.

METHODOLOGY

Research Design

This study employs a quantitative design involving a survey that investigates the digitalized practices of EFL learners in practicing vocabulary learning.

Participants

The participants in this study were selected through convenience sampling which involves respondents who are convenient for the research purposes (Galloway, 2005). Totally 120 EFL learners (F=81; M=39) with an age range of 18-34 (M=19.7) from diverse departments at a state university in Turkiye voluntarily participated in this study. All of the participants were 1st-grade university students at the A2 level of EFL and had been taking English courses through a remote learning program affiliated with the same university. All of the participants had a native Turkish language background.

Instrument

An online survey was designed in a research tool of a database that permits data collection for scientific research. The survey investigated EFL learners' self-directed practices in learning vocabulary through digital tools. The survey consisted of 8 items, four of which were related to demographic information such as gender, age, department, and native language background. The items between 5-10 covered survey items that focused on learners' preferences in using digital tools for language learning and practicing vocabulary through self-directed learning. The items between 7- 10 were designed in a multiple-fashion for the selection of participants in the related items. The items in each question were designed in consideration of the most popular activities and strategies for vocabulary learning practices in online platforms (Ji and Aziz, 2021). To refrain from misapprehension of the items, the survey was available in Turkish language. The instrument was inspired by Grover et al. (2014) to discover learners' self-directed learning practices for improving vocabulary in English. The items in each question were formed based on a literature review of self-directed learning practices in vocabulary learning (Diyono, 2009; Nation, 2001; Schmitt and Schmitt, 1995; Wodabande and Atai, 2022; Wu, 2015), which was also pilot and field tested. The items in each question were also checked by a lecturer to confirm the reliability of the items.

Data Collection

The data was collected through an online form that was sent to the volunteer participants. In each item, the participants were asked to click on the best answer(s) that suit(s) their preference based on the questions and reflect other practices and digital programs they use. The data were collected between May-July 2023.

Data analysis

The data analysis of the survey results involves the descriptive analysis of demographic information about the learners and learners' preferences for self-directed practices in vocabulary learning through mobile-assisted platforms or programs. Total number of answers were calculated based on each item in the given questions. The results cover the frequency distribution of the records by the participants presented in horizontal bar charts.

RESULTS

R. Q. 1- What is the level of learners' access to and preference for digital devices, digital programs, and translation programs?

According to the results, nearly all of the participants (n=109; 91%) revealed that they use smartphones for language practice. The majority of the participants revealed (n=92; 77%) that they use digital programs for vocabulary learning. The frequency level of using digital programs for vocabulary learning was moderate (M=2.9). As demonstrated by the results, nearly all of the participants (n=106; 88%) revealed that they use translation platforms. The level of frequency in using translation platforms was also moderate (M=3.3). Some of the participants (n=45; 37.5%) often use translation platforms and some others (n =48; 40%) sometimes use translation platforms to search for word meaning. Nearly half of the learners (n =57; 47.5%) revealed that they use digital applications specifically for vocabulary learning. Most of the participants (n =94; 78%) reflected that they would like to get training on effective strategies for vocabulary learning in digital platforms. A great majority of the learners (*n* =94; 73%) commented that they would like to be introduced to effective strategies for vocabulary learning in digital platforms.

R.Q. 2- Which digital platforms do EFL learners use for vocabulary learning?

To discover learners' self-directed learning practices through digital tools, learners were asked to identify their practices for expanding their vocabulary in English. The results are shown in the horizontal bar chart below.

Figure 1. Digital platforms used for vocabulary learning

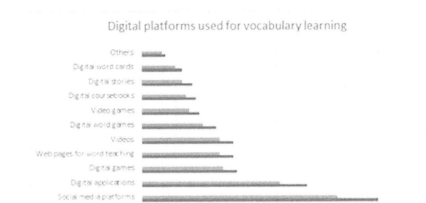

As shown in the bar chart, most of the participants use social media platforms (*n*=70; 58%) and digital applications (*n*=49; 41%). Some of the participants revealed that they play digital games (*n*=28; 24%), and digital word games (*n*=22; 18%), visit web pages designed for vocabulary instruction (*n*=27; 23%) and watch videos for their vocabulary growth (*n*=27; 23%). Few of the participants play video games (*n*=17; 14%), benefit from digital coursebooks (*n*=16; 13%), digital stories (*n*=15; 12%), and digital word cards (*n*=12; 10%) for vocabulary learning.

R. Q. 3- Which activities do EFL learners use for vocabulary learning on digital platforms?

Participants were asked to identify the digital activities they were engaged in for vocabulary learning. The results are illustrated in Figure 2 below.

Figure 2. Digital activities used by the participants for vocabulary learning

As shown in Figure 2 above, more than half of the participants (*n*=65; 54%) revealed that they preferred the "guess the meaning of the word" activity. Nearly half of the participants stated that they use visual word match (*n*=52; 43%) and practice pronunciation (*n*=49; 41%). Some of the participants selected that they play word games (*n*=36; 30%), word completion (*n*=28; 23%), and word puzzle (*n*=25; 21%). Few of the learners revealed that they play word challenges (*n*=19; 16%) and spelling games (*n*=10; 8%).

Figure 3. The vocabulary learning strategies used by EFL learners in digital contexts

R. Q. 4. What strategies do EFL learners adopt for learning vocabulary in digital platforms?

The vocabulary learning strategies used by the participants were examined. The results are displayed in Figure 3 below.

As seen in the bar chart above, most of the learners preferred to learn daily expressions in English ($n=68$; 57%). Some of the participants revealed that they prefer learning vocabulary through word lists ($n=46$; 38%), using words in a sentence ($n=43$; 36%), word categories ($n=38$; 31%), and learning the synonyms and the antonyms of the words ($n=29$; 24%). Few of the participants opted that they tend to search for the meaning of the words from digital dictionaries ($n=22$; 18%), from words in a context ($n=21$; 17%), and word pairs ($n=21$; 17%). Other opted strategies were learning vocabulary through proverbs or idioms ($n=11$; 9%), and homonyms ($n=9$; 8%).

DISCUSSION

Regarding the level of learners' access to and preferences for digital devices, digital programs, and translation programs, results were examined. The findings showed that most of the participants use smartphones for L2 practice. Within this framework, learners elicited that they mostly use digital programs, translation programs, and digital applications to expand their vocabulary in English. Most of the participants also favored the notion to be introduced effective strategies for vocabulary learning practices in digital platforms. Thanks to the advances in technology, mobile-assisted language learning evolved out of computer-assisted language learning. Hence, mobile devices enable new ways of learning supplied by continuous and spontaneous access across a variety of contexts (Kukulska-Hulme and Shields, 2008). In line with the findings, an increase in demand for portable devices is evident due to digital innovations and individuals may benefit from mobile-assisted tools such as smartphones, tablets, or applications on these tools (Kimsesiz, 2023; Lai et al., 2022). As described in the literature, self-directed learning practices and language achievement have a direct association (Little, 2007; Shapely, 2000; Viberg et al., 2020). Lai et al. (2022) proposed that to augment their language learning, learners may tend to exert control over self-directed learning practices through using divergent computer-based facilities. The process of self-directed language learning involves setting goals, planning, implementing, using appropriate materials and strategies, and evaluating the process (Curry et al., 2017). In this sense, it is significant to follow a well-organized track for more efficient outcomes for vocabulary growth through self-directed learning practices.

With reference to digital platforms used by the learners for vocabulary building, the results indicated that participants use a variety of platforms and deal with diverse practices for vocabulary learning. Among these practices, playing digital games, video games, and digital word games and word cards, watching digital stories and videos, using the applications for digital coursebooks, and visiting web pages specifically designed for vocabulary teaching were mentioned. Since technology has become an important part of educational implementations (Nada, 2021), learners and teachers also benefit from the advantages of technology-enhanced applications. Learners use technology for interaction, and access to information and resources supplied by numerous facilities in a large domain (Gonzalez-Lloret, 2017; Gündüz, 2005). Learners can also use this domain for attending online courses and individual practices to improve their language skills and vocabulary knowledge (Viberg et al., 2020). As framed by Karakas and Manisalıgil (2012), a radical change was observable for learning in the digital context that bolstered virtual collaboration, technological convergence, global connectivity, online communities, and digital creativity. Within this framework, it is indispensable for both learners and teachers to keep pace with the drift toward new applications facilitated by technological innovations.

Pertaining to digital activities in which learners are engaged in expanding vocabulary in the digital context, the findings showed that participants commonly played word games that cover word completion, word puzzles, visual word matches, spelling games, and word challenges. The findings also drew attention to learners' interest in pronunciation practice through digital activities. Parallel to these findings, some studies also yielded results in favor of using vocabulary learning strategies and retaining vocabulary knowledge of the L2 by using a computer-based system for vocabulary teaching (Lai et al., 2022; Plews, 2017; Wu, 2015). The role of gamification was also emphasized by de-Marcos et al. (2014) advocating academic achievement for practical tasks. Similarly, Xodabande and Atai (2022) found that the integration of different materials involving software-based devices or applications may promote vocabulary gain and retention. Learners may benefit from social media and education experts providing information and recommendations on the internet for improving vocabulary in English (Zhang and Perez-Paredes, 2021). Related studies promote the integration of technology in L2 instruction using digital learning resources with the design and development of interactive content (Saputro et al., 2020).

Regarding vocabulary learning strategies used by learners in digital contexts, the results displayed that learning daily expressions in English, learning vocabulary through word lists and word categories, and using words in a sentence were among the most preferred strategies for improving vocabulary. Learners also mentioned learning the synonyms/ antonyms of the words, learning proverbs/ idioms, and homonyms in English, looking up word meanings from a digital dictionary, and learning words through word pairs and from context. Considering the effect of learner strategies, it is crucial to benefit from diverse vocabulary learning techniques and principles. Learning a vocabulary means not only knowing the equivalence of a word, but also knowing the lexical, pragmatic, structural, and cultural properties of that word (Nation, 2001) and also other related elements associated with the word such as the information about its orthography, collocation, pronunciation, etc. (Cameron, 2001; Cook, 2008). As promoted by Schmitt and Schmitt (1995), for effective vocabulary learning, several strategies can be employed. The research that analyses self-directed vocabulary learning strategies in a digital environment implicates promising results in terms of learner achievement (Du, 2013; Gan, 2004; Li, 2009; Wu, 2015; Xodabande and Atai, 2022; Zhang and Perez-Paredes, 2021). Taking all them into account, it is essential to keep track of comprehensive and facilitating vocabulary learning strategies that can be utilized for L2 vocabulary learning through digital tools and applications.

CONCLUSION AND PEDAGOGICAL IMPLICATIONS

This study aimed to investigate self-directed vocabulary learning practices of EFL learners through technology-assisted learning facilities. The results demonstrated that participants mostly used mobile phones for language practices and they used digital programs and applications for vocabulary learning. The practices for vocabulary learning in digital contexts were diversified and they commonly involved digital games, videos, digital stories, and digital applications designed for vocabulary instruction. The results also demonstrated that digital activities were also varied involving different types of word games and pronunciation practice. Finally, the findings also revealed that learners used different strategies for vocabulary learning. These strategies covered learning words based on their linguistic and pragmatic features.

In this digital century, technology grants multifunctional options for digital learning resources, materials, and practices. This increased the integration of technological tools and applications in different fields of education. Each day, innovative or updated programs are introduced for more effective results in instruction and learning. In this sense, following a proper way is essential for obtaining the learning goals in language practices. We all know that the internet bestows users with multiple options for access to information. However, the individuals need to be directed by suitable applications and platforms. Language learners may reach countless websites or specifically designed programs for language instruction. It is of great importance to have specific and clear goals in learning a target language. Whether the students will improve their language skills, or whether expanding their vocabulary will deeply change the direction of the route in language learning practices and strategies used. Hence, teacher support and direction are crucial to drawing a straight line in self-directed language learning endeavors in terms of learner achievement. The process of self-directed learning entails planning, monitoring, and reflecting to attain learning goals (Conde Gafaro, 2019; Zimmerman, 1990). Insights drawn from scholarly literature show that self-directed learning practices yield favorable results in terms of learning (Little, 2007; Shapely, 2000; Viberg, et al., 2020). Related implications were also provided for the significance of learner autonomy (Curry et al., 2017; Little, 2007; Wenden, 1991). The advantage and practicability of autonomous learning manifest itself in the positive attitudes and behaviors of learners in constructing knowledge and learning practices (Wenden, 1991). Upon the same issue, teacher autonomy regulates the production and management of different varieties of target language discourse in the classroom (Little, 2007). A well-designed self-directed learning route will result in proficiency in language learning, especially when accompanied by digital resources and practices (Shapely, 2000).

LIMITATIONS AND FURTHER RESEARCH

This study was limited to 120 A2 level EFL learners at higher education level at a state university in Turkiye. With a larger sample of the participants, the results would be more varied, comprehensive, and satisfactory. In addition, this study investigated the digital practices of the participants in learning English vocabulary. However, for more comprehensive outcomes, learners' preferences in improving language skills and performance in using digital tools, and their attitudes toward using digital applications can also be examined. Moreover, individuals from different age ranges have access to mobile devices and the Internet. Further research can focus on the impact of using technology in language instruction involving learners from diverse levels of language and from different grades of learners.

REFERENCES

Benson, P. (2011). *Teaching and researching autonomy in language learning.* Pearson.

Botero, G. G., Questier, F., & Zhu, C. (2019). Self-directed language learning in a mobile-assisted, out-of-class context: Do students walk the talk? *Computer Assisted Language Learning, 32*(1-2), 71–97. doi:10.1080/09588221.2018.1485707

Bozkurt, A., & Sharma, R. C. (2020). Emergency remote teaching in a time of global crisis due to CoronaVirus pandemic. *Asian Journal of Distance Education, 15*(1), i–vi. doi:10.5281/zenodo.3778083

Cameron, L. (2001). *Teaching languages to young learners*. Ernst Klett Sprachen. doi:10.1017/CBO9780511733109

Çetin Köroğlu, Z., Öz, G., & Yüce, E. (2022). Enhancing EFL Learners' Self-regulatory skill and autonomy in digital learning environments. In F. N. Ekizer & Ş. Sarı Yıldırım, (Eds.), A Contemporary Perspective on English Language Teaching. Nobel Publishing.

Chamot, A. U. (1990). Cognitive instruction in the second language classroom: The role of learning strategies. In Alatis, James, E. (Ed.), Linguistics, language teaching and language acquisition: The interdependence of theory, practice and research. Georgetown University Press.

Chatfield, T. (2010). *Fun Inc: Why Games are the Twenty-first Century's Most Serious Business*. Random House.

Ciekanski, M. (2007). Fostering learner autonomy: Power and reciprocity in the relationship between language learner and language learning adviser. *Cambridge Journal of Education*, *37*(1), 111–127. doi:10.1080/03057640601179442

Conde Gafaro, B. (2019). Exploring Self-Regulated Language Learning with MOOCs. *Journal of Interactive Media in Education*, *14*(1), 1–5. doi:10.5334/jime.527

Cook, V. (2008). *Second language learning and language teaching* (4th ed.). Routledge.

Curry, N., Mynard, J., Noguchi, J., & Watkis, S. (2017). Evaluating a self-directed language learning course in a Japanese University. *International Journal of Self-Directed Learning*, *14*(1), 17–36.

de-Marcos, L., Domínguez, A., Saenz-de-Navarrete, J., & Pagés, C. (2014). Am empirical study comparing gamification and social networking on e-learning. *Computers & Education*, *75*, 82–91. doi:10.1016/j.compedu.2014.01.012

Diyono, Y. L. (2009). Learning Strategies for EFL students in Developing their Vocabulary Mastery. *Universitas Semarang: LITE*, *5*(1), 1–12. doi:10.33633/lite.v5i1.1342

Dolgunsöz, E., & Yıldırım, G. (2021). The Role of Mobile Devices on Online EFL Skill Courses During Covid-19 Emergency Remote Education. *JELPEDLIC*, *6*(2), 118–131. doi:10.35974/acuity.v6i2.2486

Du, F. (2013). Student Perspectives of Self-Directed Language Learning: Implications for Teaching and Research. *International Journal for the Scholarship of Teaching and Learning*, *7*(2), 1–16. doi:10.20429/ijsotl.2013.070224

Galloway, A. (2005). Non-probability sampling. In K. Kempf-Leonard (Ed.), *Encyclopedia of Social Measurement* (pp. 859–864). Elsevier. doi:10.1016/B0-12-369398-5/00382-0

Gan, Z. (2004). Attitudes and strategies as predictors of self-directed language learning in an EFL context. *International Journal of Applied Linguistics*, *14*(3), 389–411. doi:10.1111/j.1473-4192.2004.00071.x

González-Lloret, M. (2017). Technology for Task-based language teaching. In C. A. Chapelle & S. Sauro (Eds.), *The handbook of technology and second language teaching and learning* (pp. 234–247). John Wiley & Sons, Inc. doi:10.1002/9781118914069.ch16

Grover, K. S., Miller, M. T., Swearingen, B., & Wood, N. (2014). An Examination of the Self-Directed Learning Practices of ESL Adult Language Learners. *Journal of Adult Education*, *43*(2), 12–19.

Gündüz, N. (2005). Computer Assisted Language Learning. *Journal of Language and Linguistic Studies*, *1*(2), 193–214. doi:10.17263/jlls.24391

Ji, P. W., & Aziz, A. A. (2021). A Systematic Review of Vocabulary Learning with MobileAssisted Learning Platforms. *International Journal of Academic Research in Business & Social Sciences*, *11*(11), 1503–1521.

Karakas, F., & Manisaligil, A. (2012). Reorienting self-directed learning for the creative digital era. *European Journal of Training and Development*, *36*(7), 712–731. doi:10.1108/03090591211255557

Kimsesiz, F. (2023). An Examination of Digitalized Self-directed Language Learning Practices of Tertiary Level EFL learners in Turkey. *Journal of Educational Technology and Online Learning*, *6*(3), 683–701. doi:10.31681/jetol.1276105

Kukulska- Hulme. A., Lee, H., & Norris, L. (2017). Mobile Learning Revolution: Implications for Language Pedagogy. In Carol A. Chapelle & Shannon Sauro (Eds.), The handbook of technology and second language teaching and learning. John Wiley & Sons, Inc.

Kukulska-Hulme, A., & Shield, L. (2008). An overview of mobile-assisted language learning: From content delivery to supported collaboration and interaction. *ReCALL*, *20*(3), 271–289. doi:10.1017/S0958344008000335

Lai, Y., Saab, N., & Admiraal, W. (2022). Learning Strategies in Self-directed Language Learning Using Mobile Technology in Higher Education: A Systematic Scoping Review. *Education and Information Technologies*, *27*(6), 7749–7780. doi:10.100710639-022-10945-5

Laufer, B., & Hulstijn, J. (2001). Incidental vocabulary acquisition in a second language: The construct of task-induced involvement. *Applied Linguistics*, *22*(1), 1–26. doi:10.1093/applin/22.1.1

Li, J. (2009). The Evolution of Vocabulary Learning Strategies in a Computer-Mediated Reading Environment. *CALICO Journal*, *27*(1), 118–146. doi:10.11139/cj.27.1.118-146

Little, D. (2007). Language Learner Autonomy: Some Fundamental Considerations Revisited. *Innovation in Language Learning and Teaching*, *1*(1), 14–29. doi:10.2167/illt040.0

Nada, M. A. L. (2021). Vlogging towards improving students' speaking skills. [IJRD]. *EPRA International Journal of Research and Development*, *6*(7), 711–722. doi:10.36713/epra2016

Nation, I. S. (2001). *Learning vocabulary in another language*. Ernst Klett Sprachen. doi:10.1017/CBO9781139524759

Oxford, R. L. (2011). *Teaching and researching language learning strategies*. Pearson Longman.

Plews, R. C. (2017). Self-direction in online learning: The student experience. *International Journal of Self-Directed Learning*, *14*(1), 37–57.

Saputro, T. H., Tafsidurun, I. C., & Farah, R. R. (2020). The use of Vlog in improving students' oral language production: A case study. *English Education: Jurnal Tadris Bahasa Inggris 13*(1), 135-158. https://ejournal.radenintan.ac.id/index.php/ENGEDU

Schmitt, N., & Schmitt, D. (1995). Vocabulary notebooks: Theoretical underpinnings and practical suggestions. *ELT Journal*, *49*(2), 133–143. doi:10.1093/elt/49.2.133

Sert, N., & Boynuegri, E. (2017). Digital technology use by the students and english teachers and self-directed language learning. *World Journal on Educational Technology: Current Issues.*, *9*(1), 24–34. doi:10.18844/wjet.v9i1.993

Shapely, P. (2000). On-line education to develop complex reasoning skills in organic chemistry. *Journal of Asynchronous Learning Networks*, *4*(2), 43–52.

Smaldino, S., Lowther, D., & Russell, J. (2008). *Instructional technology and media for learning*. Pearson Prentice Hall.

Song, L., & Hill, J. R. (2007). A conceptual model for understanding self-directed learning in online environments. *Journal of Interactive Online Learning*, *6*(1), 27–41.

Sung, Y. T., Chang, K. E., & Yang, J. M. (2015). How effective are mobile devices for language learning? A meta-analysis. *Educational Research Review*, *16*, 68–84. doi:10.1016/j.edurev.2015.09.001

Thomas, N., & Rose, H. (2019). Do Language Learning Strategies Need to Be Self-Directed? Disentangling Strategies from Self-Regulated Learning. *TESOL Quarterly*, *53*(1), 248–257. doi:10.1002/tesq.473

Viberg, O., Wasson, B., & Kukulska-Hulme, A. (2020). Mobile-assisted language learning through learning analytics for self-regulated learning (MALLAS): A conceptual framework. *Australasian Journal of Educational Technology*, *36*(6), 34–52. doi:10.14742/ajet.6494

Wang, Z., Hweng, G. J., Yin, Z., & Ma, Y. (2020). A contribution-oriented self-directed mobile learning ecology approach to improving ELF students' vocabulary retention and second language motivation. *Journal of Educational Technology & Society*, *23*(1), 16–29. https://www.jstor.org/stable/10.2307/26915404

Wenden, A. L. (1991). *Learner strategies for learner autonomy*. Prentice Hall.

Wu, J. (2015). Effects of CALL on self-directed FL vocabulary learning. *Studies in Self-Access Learning Journal*, *6*(2), 191–215. doi:10.37237/060204

Xodabande, İ., & Atai, M. R. (2022). Using mobile applications for self-directed learning of academic vocabulary among university students. *Open Learning*, *37*(4), 330–347. doi:10.1080/02680513.2020.1847061

Yosintha, R., & Yunianti, S. S. (2021). Learner autonomy in EFL online classes in Indonesia: Students'voices. *Langkawi:Journal of the Association for Arabic and English*, *7*(1), 119–133. doi:10.31332/lkw.v7i1.2637

Zhang, D., & Perez Paredes, P. (2021). Chinese postgraduate EFL learners' self-directed use of mobile English learning resources. *Computer Assisted Language Learning*, *34*(8), 1128–1153. doi:10.1080/09588221.2019.1662455

Zimmerman, B. J. (1989). A Social Cognitive View of Self-Regulated Academic Learning. *Journal of Educational Psychology*, *81*(3), 329–339. doi:10.1037/0022-0663.81.3.329

Zimmerman, B. J. (1990). Self-regulated learning and academic achievement: An overview. *Educational Psychologist*, *25*(1), 3–17. doi:10.120715326985ep2501_2

Zimmerman, B. J. (2000). Attaining Self-Regulation. A Social Cognitive Perspective. In M. Boekaerts, P. Pintrich, & M. Zeidner (Eds.), *Handbook of Self-Regulation* (pp. 13–39). Academic Press. doi:10.1016/B978-012109890-2/50031-7

Compilation of References

Aaronson, D., Barrow, L., & Sander, W. (2007). Teachers and student achievement in the Chicago public high schools. *Journal of Labor Economics*, *25*(1), 95–135. doi:10.1086/508733

Ab Rahman, F., & Tan, S. C. E. (2022). Can Picture Books In English Classroom Lead To Increase Vocabulary Learning? *International Journal of Education. Psychology and Counseling*, *7*(46), 286–301. doi:10.35631/IJEPC.746023

Abdelmalak, M. M. M., & Parra, J. L. (2016). Expanding learning opportunities for graduate students with HyFlex course design. [IJOPCD]. *International Journal of Online Pedagogy and Course Design*, *6*(4), 19–37. doi:10.4018/IJOPCD.2016100102

Abouhashem, A., Abdou, R. M., Bhadra, J., Siby, N., Ahmad, Z., & Al-Thani, N. J. (2021). Covid-19 inspired a stem-based virtual learning model for middle schools—A case study of Qatar. *Sustainability (Basel)*, *13*(5), 2799. doi:10.3390u13052799

Açıkgöz, K. Ü. (2007). *Aktif öğrenme*. İzmir: Eğitim Dünyası.

Adesso, G. (2023). Towards the ultimate brain: Exploring scientific discovery with ChatGPT AI. *AI Magazine*, *44*(3), 328–342. Advance online publication. doi:10.1002/aaai.12113

Adıgüzel, T., Kaya, M. H., & Cansu, F. K. (2023). Revolutionizing education with AI: Exploring the transformative potential of ChatGPT. *Contemporary Educational Technology*, *15*(3), ep429. doi:10.30935/cedtech/13152

Aditya, D. (2020). The effect of gamification based on Balinese local story. *ACITYA Journal of Teaching & Education*, *2*(2), 115–128. doi:10.30650/ajte.v2i2.1368

Admiraal, W., Louws, M., Lockhorst, D., Paas, T., Buynsters, M., Cviko, A., Janssen, C., de Jonge, M., Nouwens, S., Post, L., van der Ven, F., & Kester, L. (2017). Teachers in school-based technology innovations: A typology of their beliefs on teaching and technology. *Computers & Education*, *114*, 57–68. doi:10.1016/j.compedu.2017.06.013

Agosto, D. E. (2016). Why storytelling matters: Unveiling the literacy benefits of storytelling. *Children & Libraries*, *14*(2), 21–26. doi:10.5860/cal.14n2.21

Agyei, D., & Voogt, J. (2011). Exploring the potential of the Will, Skill, Tool model in Ghana: Predicting prospective and practicing teachers' use of technology. *Computers & Education*, *56*(1), 91–100. doi:10.1016/j.compedu.2010.08.017

Ahmed, S. T. S., Qasem, B. T. A., & Pawar, S. V. (2020). Computer-assisted language instruction in South Yemeni context: A study of teachers' attitudes, ICT uses and challenges. *International Journal of Language Education*, *4*(1), 59–73. doi:10.26858/ijole.v4i2.10106

Akhtar, N., & Menjivar, J. A. (2012). Cognitive and linguistic correlates of early exposure to more than one language. In Benson, J.B. (ed) *Advances in child development and behavior.* Burlington: Academic. 10.1016/B978-0-12-394388-0.00002-2

Alam, A. (2022). Employing adaptive learning and intelligent tutoring robots for virtual classrooms and smart campuses: Reforming education in the age of artificial intelligence. *Advanced Computing and Intelligent Technologies Proceedings of ICACIT*, *2022*, 395–406.

Alamer, A. (2021). Basic psychological needs, motivational orientations, effort, and vocabulary knowledge. *Studies in Second Language Acquisition*, *44*(1), 164–184. doi:10.1017/S027226312100005X

Alamer, A., & Al Khateeb, A. (2021). Effects of using the WhatsApp application on Language learners motivation: A controlled investigation using structural equation modelling. *Computer Assisted Language Learning*, *36*(1-2), 149–175. doi:10.1080/09588221.2021.1903042

Alavi, S. M., & Esmaeilifard, F. (2021). The effect of emotional scaffolding on language achievement and willingness to communicate by providing recast. *Cogent Psychology*, *8*(1), 1911093. Advance online publication. doi:10.1080/23311908.2021.1911093

Aldemir, T., Ataş, A. H., & Celik, B. (2022). A systematic design model for gamified learning environments. *Research Anthology on Developments in Gamification and Game-Based Learning*, 214–234. doi:10.4018/978-1-6684-3710-0.ch011

Aljraiwi, S. (2019). Effectiveness of gamification of web-based learning in improving academic achievement and creative thinking among primary school students. *International Journal of Education and Practice*, *7*(3), 242–257. doi:10.18488/journal.61.2019.73.242.257

Almusharraf, N. (2021). Incorporation of a game-based approach into the EFL online classrooms: Students' perceptions. *Interactive Learning Environments*, 1–14. doi:10.1080/10494820.2021.1969953

Alobaid, A. (2021). ICT multimedia learning affordances: Role and impact on ESL learners' writing accuracy development. *Heliyon*, *7*(7), e07517. Advance online publication. doi:10.1016/j.heliyon.2021.e07517 PMID:34307944

Alqahtani, M. (2015). The importance of vocabulary in language learning and how to be taught. *International Journal of Teaching and Education*, *3*(3), 21–34. doi:10.20472/TE.2015.3.3.002

Compilation of References

Alwan, A., Yijian, B., Black, M., Casey, L., Gerosa, M., Heritage, M., Iseli, M., Jones, B., Kazemzadeh, A., Lee, S., Narayanan, S., Price, P., Tepperman, J., & Wang, S. (2007). A system for technology-based assessment of language and literacy in young children: The role of multiple information sources. In *Proceedings of IEEE 9th Workshop on Multimedia Signal Processing.* Institute of Electrical and Electronics Engineers. 10.1109/MMSP.2007.4412810

Anderson, A. (2019). *Virtual reality, augmented reality and artificial intelligence in special education: a practical guide to supporting students with learning differences.* Routledge. doi:10.4324/9780429399503

Anderson, T., Rourke, L., Garrison, D. R., & Archer, W. (2001). Assessing teaching presence in a computer conferencing context. *Journal of Asynchronous Learning Networks, 5*(2), 1–17.

Andrade, F. R., Mizoguchi, R., & Isotani, S. (2016). The bright and dark sides of Gamification. *Intelligent Tutoring Systems,* 176–186. doi:10.1007/978-3-319-39583-8_17

An, Y., & Mindrila, D. (2020). Strategies and tools used for learner-centered instruction. *International Journal of Technology in Education and Science, 4*(2), 133–143. doi:10.46328/ijtes.v4i2.74

Arce, N. H., & Valdivia, A. C. (2020). Adapting competitiveness and gamification to a digital platform for foreign language learning. *International Journal of Emerging Technologies in Learning, 15*(20), 194–209. doi:10.3991/ijet.v15i20.16135

Ary, D., Jacobs, L. C., & Sorensen, C. (2010). *Introduction to research in education* (8th ed.). Wadsworth.

Aslantaş, T. (2014). *Uzaktan eğitim, uzaktan eğitim teknolojileri ve Türkiye'de bir uygulama.* Gazi Üniversitesi Fen Bilimleri Enstitüsü. Retrieved from https://www.tankutaslantas.com/wp-content/uploads/2014/04/Uzaktan-E%C4%9Fitim-Uzaktan-E%C4%9Fitim-Teknolojileri-ve-T%C3%BCrkiyede-bir-Uygulama.pdf

Athugala, R. M. V. (2020). *Developing a computer-based interactive system that creates a sense of deep engagement* [Doctoral dissertation]. Faculty of Fine Arts and Music, University of Melbourne.

Atlas, S. (2023). *ChatGPT for higher education and professional development: A guide to conversational AI.* Retrieved from https://digitalcommons.uri.edu/cba_facpubs/548

Attali, Y., & Burstein, J. (2006). Automated essay scoring with e-rater v. 2. *The Journal of Technology, Learning, and Assessment, 4*(3), 1–30.

Aydın, S. M., & Çakır, N. A. (2022). The effects of a game-enhanced learning intervention on Foreign Language Learning. *Educational Technology Research and Development, 70*(5), 1809–1841. doi:10.100711423-022-10141-9

Azouz, O., & Lefdaoui, Y. (2018). Gamification design frameworks: A systematic mapping study. *2018 6th International Conference on Multimedia Computing and Systems (ICMCS).* 10.1109/ICMCS.2018.8525900

Azzouz Boudadi, N., & Gutiérrez-Colón, M. (2020). Effect of gamification on students' motivation and learning achievement in Second language acquisition within higher education: A literature review 2011-2019. *The EuroCALL Review, 28*(1), 40. doi:10.4995/eurocall.2020.12974

Bachman, L. F. (2000). Modern language testing at the turn of the century: Assuring that what we count counts. *Language Testing, 17*(1), 1–42. doi:10.1177/026553220001700101

Bachman, L., & Palmer, A. (2022). *Language assessment in practice: Developing language assessments and justifying their use in the real world.* Oxford University.

Bagunaid, W. A., Meccawy, M., Allinjawi, A., & Meccawy, Z. (2019). The Impact of Gamification on Self-Assessment for English Language Learners in Saudi Arabia. *International Journal of Educational and Pedagogical Sciences, 13*(2), 129–134. doi:10.5281/zenodo.2571829

Bai, L., & Wang, Y. X. (2020). Pre-departure English language preparation of students on joint 2+2 programs. *System, 90,* 102219. doi:10.1016/j.system.2020.102219

Balester, V. (2012). How writing rubrics fail: Toward a multicultural model. In A. I. & M. P. (Eds.), Race and Writing Assessment, (pp. 63-77). Peter Lang.

Balogh, J., Bernstein, J., Cheng, J., Van Moere, A., & Suzuki, M. (2012). Validation of automated scoring of oral reading. *Educational and Psychological Measurement, 72*(3), 435–452. doi:10.1177/0013164411412590

Bărbuceanu, C. D. (2022). HyFlex-Rethinking courses in online teaching. *Revista de Ştiinţe Politice. Revue des Sciences Politiques,* (73), 241–247.

Barnyak, N. C., & McNelly, T. A. (2016). The literacy skills and motivation to read of children enrolled in Title I: A comparison of electronic and print nonfiction books. *Early Childhood Education Journal, 44*(5), 527–536. doi:10.100710643-015-0735-0

Barrot, J. S. (2023). Using ChatGPT for second language writing: Pitfalls and potentials. *Assessing Writing, 57,* 100745. doi:10.1016/j.asw.2023.100745

Barut Tuğtekin, E. (2022). Açık ve Uzaktan Öğrenme Kuramlarının Öğrenenler, Öğrenme Ortamları ve Etkileşim Açısından İncelenmesi. *Eğitim Bilim ve Araştırma Dergisi, 3*(1), 118–137. doi:10.54637/ebad.1059890

Bashir, A., Bashir, S., Rana, K., Lambert, P., & Vernallis, A. (2021). Post-COVID-19 adaptations; the shifts towards online learning, hybrid course delivery and the implications for biosciences courses in the higher education setting. *Frontiers in Education, 6*(711619), 711619. doi:10.3389/feduc.2021.711619

Basuki, Y., & Hidayati, Y. (2019, April). Kahoot! or Quizizz: the Students' Perspectives. In *Proceedings of the 3rd English Language and Literature International Conference (ELLiC)* (pp. 202-211). Academic Press.

Baxter, P., & Jack, S. (2008). Qualitative case study methodology: Study design and implementation for novice researchers. *The Qualitative Report, 13*(4), 544–559.

Compilation of References

Beatty, B. J. (2007, October). *Hybrid classes with fexible participation options—If you build it, how will they come?* In Paper presented at the 2007 association for educational communications and technology annual convention, Anaheim, CA.

Beatty, B. J. (2020). Can HyFlex options support students in the midst of uncertainty. *Educause Review.* https://er.educause.edu/blogs/2020/5/can-hyflex-options-support-students-in-the-midst-of-uncertainty

Beatty, B. (2014). *Hybrid courses with flexible participation: The HyFlex course design.* IGI Global. doi:10.4018/978-1-4666-4912-5.ch011

Beatty, B. (2019). *Hybrid-flexible course design.* EdTech Books. doi:10.59668/33

Belda-Medina, J. (2022). Using augmented reality (AR) as an authoring tool in EFL through mobile computer-supported collaborative learning. *Teaching English with Technology, 22*(2), 115–135.

Benson, P. (1997). The philosophy and politics of learner autonomy. In Autonomy & Independence in language learning. Longman.

Benson, P. (2001). *Teaching and Researching Autonomy in Language Learning.* Longman.

Benson, P. (2006). Autonomy in language teaching and learning. *Language Teaching, 40*(1), 21–40. doi:10.1017/S0261444806003958

Benson, P. (2011). *Teaching and researching autonomy in language learning.* Pearson.

Benson, P., & Voller, P. (1997). *Autonomy and Independence in Language Learning.* Longman.

Bernius, J. P., Krusche, S., & Bruegge, B. (2022). Machine learning based feedback on textual student answers in large courses. *Computers and Education: Artificial Intelligence, 3,* 100081. doi:10.1016/j.caeai.2022.100081

Bernstein, J. (1999). *PhonePassTM testing: Structure and construct.* Ordinate.

Bernstein, J., Van Moere, A., & Cheng, J. (2010). Validating automated speaking tests. *Language Testing, 27*(3), 355–377. doi:10.1177/0265532210364404

Binnewies, S., & Wang, Z. (2019). *Challenges of student equity and engagement in a HyFlex course.* Springer. doi:10.1007/978-981-13-6982-7_12

Bishop, L. (2023). A computer wrote this paper: What ChatGPT means for education, research, and writing. *SSRN, 26.* doi:10.2139srn.4338981

Bitchener, J. (2008). Evidence in support of written corrective feedback. *Journal of Second Language Writing, 17*(2), 102–118. doi:10.1016/j.jslw.2007.11.004

Black, P. (2009). Formative assessment issues across the curriculum: The theory and the practice. *TESOL Quarterly, 43*(3), 519–524. doi:10.1002/j.1545-7249.2009.tb00248.x

Bolaños, D., Cole, R. A., Ward, W. H., Tindal, G. A., Hasbrouck, J., & Schwanenflugel, P. J. (2013). Human and automated assessment of oral reading fluency. *Journal of Educational Psychology, 105*(4), 1142–1151. doi:10.1037/a0031479

Bonham, S. W., Beichner, R. J., Titus, A., & Martin, L. (2000). Education research using Web-based assessment systems. *Journal of Research on Computing in Education, 33*(1), 28–45. doi:10.1080/08886504.2000.10782298

Booton, S. A., Hodgkiss, A., & Murphy, V. A. (2023). The impact of mobile application features on children's language and literacy learning: A systematic review. *Computer Assisted Language Learning, 36*(3), 400–429. doi:10.1080/09588221.2021.1930057

Borg, S. (2009). Language teacher cognition. *The Cambridge guide to second language teacher education,* 163-171. doi:10.1017/9781139042710.022

Borg, S. (2015). *Professional development for English language teachers: Perspectives from higher education in Turkey.* British Council.

Borji, A. (2023). A categorical archive of ChatGPT failures. *arXiv preprint.* /arXiv.2302.03494 doi:10.21203/rs.3.rs-2895792/v1

Botero, G. G., Questier, F., & Zhu, C. (2019). Self-directed language learning in a mobile-assisted, out-of-class context: Do students walk the talk? *Computer Assisted Language Learning, 32*(1-2), 71–97. doi:10.1080/09588221.2018.1485707

Botes, E., Dewaele, J.-M., & Greiff, S. (2020). The foreign language classroom anxiety scale and academic achievement: An overview of the prevailing literature and a meta-analysis. *Journal for the Psychology of Language Learning, 2*(1), 26–56. doi:10.52598/jpll/2/1/3

Bower, M., Dalgarno, B., Kennedy, G. E., Lee, M. J., & Kenney, J. (2015). Design and implementation factors in blended synchronous learning environments: Outcomes from a cross-case analysis. *Computers & Education, 86,* 1–17. doi:10.1016/j.compedu.2015.03.006

Bozkurt, A. (2019). *From distance education to open and distance learning: a holistic evaluation of history, definitions, and theories.* IGI Global. doi:10.4018/978-1-5225-8431-5.ch016

Bozkurt, A., & Sharma, R. C. (2020). Emergency remote teaching in a time of global crisis due to CoronaVirus pandemic. *Asian Journal of Distance Education, 15*(1), i–vi. doi:10.5281/zenodo.3778083

Brandtzaeg, P. B., & Følstad, A. (2017). *Why people use chatbots.* Paper presented at the International Conference on Internet Science, Thessaloniki, Greece. 10.1007/978-3-319-70284-1_30

Breen, M. P., & Mann, S. J. (1997). Shooting arrows at the sun: Perspectives on a pedagogy for autonomy (Vol. 132-149). Longman.

Breen, M. P., & Mann, S. J. (1997). Shooting Arrows at the Sun: Perspectives on a Pedagogy for Autonomy' in Benson and Voller. In P. Benson & P. Voller (Eds.), *Autonomy and Independence in Language Learning* (pp. 132–149). Longman.

Compilation of References

Brown, T. B., Mann, B., Ryder, N., Subbiah, M., Kaplan, J., Dhariwal, P., Neelakantan, A., Shyam, P., Sastry, G., Askell, A., Agarwal, S., Herbert-Voss, A., Krueger, G., Henighan, T., Child, R., Ramesh, A., Ziegler, D. M., Wu, J., Winter, C., & Amodei, D. (2020). Language models are few-shot learners. *Advances in Neural Information Processing Systems, 33,* 1877–1901. https://proceedings.neurips.cc/paper/2020

Brown, D. (2001). *Teaching by principles: An interactive approach to language pedagogy.* Pearson Education.

Brown, H. D., & Abeywickrama, P. (2010). *Language assessment: Principles and classroom practices.* Pearson Education.

Bueno, M., Perez, F., Valerio, R., & Areola, E. M. Q. (2022). A usability study on Google site and Wordwall.net: Online instructional tools for learning basic integration amid pandemic. *Journal of Global Business and Social Entrepreneurship, 7*(23), 61–71.

Burns, A., & Richards, J. C. (2009). *Second language teacher education.* Cambridge University., doi:10.1017/9781139042710

Burns, A., & Richards, J. C. (2018). *The Cambridge Guide to learning English as a second language.* Cambridge University Press. doi:10.1017/9781009024761

Burstein, J., Frase, L., Ginther, A., & Grant, L. (1996). Technologies for language assessment. *Annual Review of Applied Linguistics, 16,* 240–260. doi:10.1017/S0267190500001537

Burton, R. (2019). A review of Nearpod – an interactive tool for student engagement. *Journal of Applied Learning & Teaching, 2*(2), 95–97. doi:10.37074/jalt.2019.2.2.13

Bus, G. A., & Anstadt, R. (2021). Toward Digital Picture Books for a New Generation of Emergent Readers. *AERA Open, 7*(1), 1–15. doi:10.1177/23328584211063874

Buşu, A.-F. (2020). Emotional intelligence as a type of cognitive ability. *Revista de Ştiinţe Politice. Revue des Sciences Politiques,* (66), 204–215.

Cabaroğlu, N., & Öz, G. (2023). Practicum in ELT: a systematic review of 2010–2020 research on ELT practicum. *European Journal of Teacher Education.* https://doi.org/https://doi.org/10.1080/02619768.2023.2242577

Çakmak, F. (2022). Chatbot-human interaction and its effects on EFL students' L2 speaking performance and anxiety. *Novitas-ROYAL, 16*(2), 113–131.

Calafiore, P., & Giudici, E. (2021). Hybrid Versus HyFlex Instruction in an introductory finance course. *International Journal of Education and Research, 16*(1), 40–52.

Cameron, L. (2001). *Teaching languages to young learners.* Cambridge University Press. doi:10.1017/CBO9780511733109

Candy, P. C. (1991). *Self-direction for lifelong learning.* Jossey Bass.

Carr-Chellman, A., & Duchastel, P. (2000). The ideal online course. *British Journal of Educational Technology*, *31*(3), 229–241. doi:10.1111/1467-8535.00154

Carr, N. (2008). Is Google making us stupid? *Teachers College Record*, *110*(14), 89–94. doi:10.1177/016146810811001427

Casal, J. E., & Kessler, M. (2023). Can linguists distinguish between ChatGPT/AI and human writing?: A study of research ethics and academic publishing. *Research Methods in Applied Linguistics*, *2*(3), 1–12. doi:10.1016/j.rmal.2023.100068

Cascella, M., Montomoli, J., Bellini, V., & Bignami, E. (2023). Evaluating the feasibility of ChatGPT in healthcare: An analysis of multiple clinical and research scenarios. *Journal of Medical Systems*, *47*(1), 1–5. doi:10.100710916-023-01925-4 PMID:36869927

Caspari-Sadeghi, S. (2023). Artificial intelligence in technology-enhanced assessment: A survey of machine learning. *Journal of Educational Technology Systems*, *51*(3), 372–386. doi:10.1177/00472395221138791

Çetin Köroğlu, Z., Öz, G., & Yüce, E. (2022). Enhancing EFL Learners' Self-regulatory skill and autonomy in digital learning environments. In F. N. Ekizer & Ş. Sarı Yıldırım, (Eds.), A Contemporary Perspective on English Language Teaching. Nobel Publishing.

Chalhoub-Deville, M. (2001). Language testing and technology: Past and future. *Language Learning & Technology*, *5*(2), 95–98.

Chalhoub-Deville, M., & Deville, C. (1999). Computer adaptive testing in second language contexts. *Annual Review of Applied Linguistics*, *19*, 273–299. doi:10.1017/S0267190599190147

Challenor, J., & Ma, M. (2019). A review of augmented reality applications for history education and heritage isualization. *Multimodal Technologies and Interaction*, *3*(2), 39. doi:10.3390/mti3020039

Chamot, A. U. (1990). Cognitive instruction in the second language classroom: The role of learning strategies. In Alatis, James, E. (Ed.), Linguistics, language teaching and language acquisition: The interdependence of theory, practice and research. Georgetown University Press.

Chapelle, C. A., & Voss, E. (2017). Utilizing technology in language assessment. In E. Shohamy & I. G. Or (Eds.), Language testing and assessment (pp. 149–161). Cham, Switzerland: Springer. doi:10.1007/978-3-319-02261-1_10

Chapelle, C. A., & Chung, Y. R. (2010). The promise of NLP and speech processing technologies in language assessment. *Language Testing*, *27*(3), 301–315. doi:10.1177/0265532210364405

Chapelle, C. A., & Voss, E. (2016). 20 years of technology and language assessment in language learning & technology. *Language Learning & Technology*, *20*(2), 116–128.

Chatfield, T. (2010). *Fun Inc: Why Games are the Twenty-first Century's Most Serious Business.* Random House.

Compilation of References

Chatterjee, S., & Bhattacharjee, K. K. (2020). Adoption of artificial intelligence in higher education: A quantitative analysis using structural equation modelling. *Education and Information Technologies*, 25(5), 3443–3463. doi:10.100710639-020-10159-7

Cheng, L., Rogers, T., & Hu, H. (2004). ESL/EFL instructors' classroom assessment practices: Purposes, methods and procedures. *Language Testing*, 21(3), 360–389. doi:10.1191/0265532204lt288oa

Chen, L., Zechner, K., Yoon, S., Evanini, K., Wang, X., Loukina, A., Tao, J., Davis, L., Chong, M. L., Ma, M., Mundkowsky, R., Lu, C., Leong, C. L., & Gyawali, B. (2018). Automated scoring of non-native speech using the SpeechRaterSM v. 5.0 engine. *ETS Research Report Series*, 2018(1), 1–31. doi:10.1002/ets2.12198

Chen, S., Nassaji, H., & Liu, Q. (2016). EFL learners' perceptions and preferences of written corrective feedback: A case study of university students from Mainland China. *Asian-Pacific Journal of Second and Foreign Language Education*, 1(1), 5. doi:10.118640862-016-0010-y

Chen, X., Zou, D., Xie, H., & Cheng, G. (2021). Twenty years of personalized language learning. *Journal of Educational Technology & Society*, 24(1), 205–222.

Chen, X., Zou, D., Xie, H., Cheng, G., & Liu, C. (2022). Two decades of artificial intelligence in education. *Journal of Educational Technology & Society*, 25(1), 28–47.

Chiu, T. K. (2021). Applying the self-determination theory (SDT) to explain student engagement in online learning during the COVID-19 pandemic. *Journal of Research on Technology in Education, 54*(sup1). doi:10.1080/15391523.2021.1891998

Chiu, T. K. F., Moorhouse, B. L., Chai, C. S., & Ismailov, M. (2023). Teacher support and student motivation to learn with Artificial Intelligence (AI) based chatbot. *Interactive Learning Environments*, 1–17. Advance online publication. doi:10.1080/10494820.2023.2172044

Choi, N., Kang, S. & Sheo, J. (2020). Children's Interest in Learning English Through Picture Books in an EFL Context: The Effects of Parent–Child Interaction and Digital Pen Use. *Education sciences, 2020* (10,40), 1-11. doi:10.3390/educsci10020040

Choi, H., & Lee, C. H. (2020). Learner autonomy in EFL reading with digital technology at secondary school level. *The Journal of AsiaTEFL*, 17(2), 463–478. doi:10.18823/asiatefl.2020.17.4.11.1323

Choi, N., Kang, S., Cho, H. J., & Sheo, J. (2019). Promoting young children's interest in learning english in efl context: The role of mothers. *Education Sciences*, 9(1), 46. doi:10.3390/educsci9010046

Chowdhury, G. (2003). Natural language processing. *Annual Review of Information Science & Technology*, 37(1), 51–89. doi:10.1002/aris.1440370103

Christensen, R., & Knezek, G. (2008). Self-report measures and findings for information technology attitudes and competencies. In J. Voogt & G. Knezek (Eds.), *International handbook of information technology in primary and secondary education* (pp. 349–365). Springer. doi:10.1007/978-0-387-73315-9_21

Christensen, R., & Knezek, G. (2009). Construct validity for the teachers' attitudes toward computers questionnaire. *Journal of Computing in Teacher Education*, *25*(4), 143–155.

Chuah, K. M., & Kabilan, M. K. (2021). Teachers' Views on the Use of Chatbots to Support. *International Journal of Emerging Technologies in Learning*, *16*(20), 223–237. doi:10.3991/ijet.v16i20.24917

Chun, C. W. (2006). Commentary: An analysis of a language test for employment: The authenticity of the PhonePass test. *Language Assessment Quarterly*, *3*(3), 295–306. doi:10.120715434311laq0303_4

Ciekanski, M. (2007). Fostering learner autonomy: Power and reciprocity in the relationship between language learner and language learning adviser. *Cambridge Journal of Education*, *37*(1), 111–127. doi:10.1080/03057640601179442

Çil, E. (2021). The effect of using Wordwall.net in increasing vocabulary knowledge of 5th grade EFL students. *Language Education & Technology*, *1*(1), 21–28.

Clapham, C. (2000). Assessment and testing. *Annual Review of Applied Linguistics*, *20*, 147–161. doi:10.1017/S0267190500200093

Clarizia, F., Colace, F., Lombardi, M., Pascale, F., & Santaniello, D. (2018). *Chatbot: An education support system for student. International symposium on cyberspace safety and security.* Springer.

Cohen, Y., Ben-Simon, A., & Hovav, M. (2003, October). *The effect of specific language features on the complexity of systems for automated essay scoring.* Paper presented at the 29th Annual Conference of the International Association for Educational Assessment, Manchester, UK.

Cohen, A. D. (2007). Becoming a strategic language learner in CALL. *Applied Language Learning*, *17*(1-2), 57–71.

Conde Gafaro, B. (2019). Exploring Self-Regulated Language Learning with MOOCs. *Journal of Interactive Media in Education*, *14*(1), 1–5. doi:10.5334/jime.527

Cook, V. (2008). *Second language learning and language teaching* (4th ed.). Routledge.

Cotterall, S. (2000). Promoting learner autonomy through the curriculum: Principles for designing language courses. *ELT Journal*, *54*(2), 109–117. doi:10.1093/elt/54.2.109

Cotton, D. R., Cotton, P. A., & Shipway, J. R. (2023). Chatting and cheating: Ensuring academic integrity in the era of ChatGPT. *Innovations in Education and Teaching International*, 1–12. doi:10.1080/14703297.2023.2190148

Covidence. (2023). *Why is my Cohen's kappa value low and what can I do to improve it?* Covidence. https://support.covidence.org/help/why-is-my-cohen-s-kappa-value-low-and-what-can-i-do-to-improve-it

Cox, T., & Davies, R. S. (2012). Using automatic speech recognition technology with elicited oral response testing. *CALICO Journal*, *29*(4), 601–618. doi:10.11139/cj.29.4.601-618

Compilation of References

Creswell, J. W. (2014). *Research design: Qualitative, quantitative and mixed methods approaches* (4th ed.). Sage.

Creswell, J. W. (2014). *Research design: Qualitative, quantitative, and mixed methods approaches* (4th ed.). Sage.

Creswell, J. W., & Poth, C. N. (2016). Qualitative inquiry and research design: Choosing among five approaches. *Sage (Atlanta, Ga.)*.

Cripps, T. (2020). We are mobile magicians but digital refugees: Helping prospective English teachers explore technology and ubiquitous learning. *Electronic Journal of Foreign Language Teaching*, *17*(S1), 168–189. doi:10.56040/tncp171a

Crusan, D. (2010). *Assessment in the second language writing classroom*. University of Michigan Press. doi:10.3998/mpub.770334

Crusan, D. J. (2015). Dance, ten; looks, three: Why rubrics matter. *Assessing Writing*, *26*(1), 1–4. Advance online publication. doi:10.1016/j.asw.2015.08.002

Csizér, K. (2017). Motivation in the L2 classroom. The Routledge Handbook of Instructed Second Language Acquisition, 418–432. doi:10.4324/9781315676968-23

Curry, N., Mynard, J., Noguchi, J., & Watkis, S. (2017). Evaluating a self-directed language learning course in a Japanese University. *International Journal of Self-Directed Learning*, *14*(1), 17–36.

Cushing Weigle, S. (2010). Validation of automated scores of TOEFL iBT tasks against non-test indicators of writing ability. *Language Testing*, *27*(3), 335–353. doi:10.1177/0265532210364406

Dai, J., Wang, L., & He, Y. (2023). Exploring the effect of wiki-based writing instruction on writing skills and writing self-efficacy of Chinese English-as-a-foreign language learners. *Frontiers in Psychology*, *13*, 1069832. Advance online publication. doi:10.3389/fpsyg.2022.1069832 PMID:36704680

Darling-Hammond, L. (2010). Teacher education and the American future, *Journal of Teacher Education*, *61*(1–2), 35–47. doi:10.1177/0022487109348024

Darling-Hammond, L. (2017). Teacher education around the world: What can we learn from international practice? *European Journal of Teacher Education*, *40*(3), 291–309. doi:10.1080/02619768.2017.1315399

De La Cruz, K. M., Gebera, O. W., & Copaja, S. J. (2021). Application of gamification in higher education in the teaching of English as a foreign language. *Perspectives and Trends in Education and Technology*, 323–341. doi:10.1007/978-981-16-5063-5_27

Dehganzadeh, H., & Dehganzadeh, H. (2020). Investigating effects of digital gamification-based language learning: A systematic review. *Two Quarterly Journal of English Language Teaching and Learning University of Tabriz*, *12*(25), 53–93. doi:10.22034/ELT.2020.10676

Dehghanzadeh, H., Fardanesh, H., Hatami, J., Talaee, E., & Noroozi, O. (2019). Using gamification to support learning English as a Second language: A systematic review. *Computer Assisted Language Learning, 34*(7), 934–957. doi:10.1080/09588221.2019.1648298

Dehouche, N. (2021). Plagiarism in the age of massive generative pre-trained transformers (GPT-3). *Ethics in Science and Environmental Politics, 2,* 17–23. doi:10.3354/esep00195

Deimann, M., & Bastiaens, T. (2010). The role of volition in distance education: An exploration of its capacities. *International Review of Research in Open and Distance Learning, 11*(1), 1–16. doi:10.19173/irrodl.v11i1.778

Delacruz, S. (2014). Using Nearpod in elementary guided reading groups. *TechTrends, 58*(5), 63–70. doi:10.100711528-014-0787-9

Dellos, R. (2015). Kahoot! A digital game resource for learning. *International Journal of Instructional Technology and Distance Learning, 12*(4), 49–52.

de-Marcos, L., Domínguez, A., Saenz-de-Navarrete, J., & Pagés, C. (2014). Am empirical study comparing gamification and social networking on e-learning. *Computers & Education, 75,* 82–91. doi:10.1016/j.compedu.2014.01.012

Demirel, E. T., & Aksu, M. G. (2019). The application of technology to feedback in academic writing classes: The use of screencasting feedback and student attitudes. *Ufuk University Journal of Social Sciences Institute, 8*(16), 183–203. doi:10.4018/978-1-4666-9577-1.ch019

Demirel, Ö. (1998). *Eğitimde yeni yönelimler.* Pegem Yayıncılık.

Dempsey, M. S., PytlikZillig, L. M., & Bruning, R. H. (2009). Helping preservice teachers learn to assess writing: Practice and feedback in a Web-based environment. *Assessing Writing, 14*(1), 38–61. doi:10.1016/j.asw.2008.12.003

Deng, J., & Lin, Y. (2023). The cenefits and challenges of ChatGPT: An overview. *Frontiers in Computing and Intelligent Systems.* doi:10.54097/fcis.v2i2.4465

Desimone, L. M. (2009). Improving impact studies of teachers' professional development: Toward better conceptualizations and measures. *Educational Researcher, 38*(3), 181–199. doi:10.3102/0013189X08331140

Deterding, S., Sicart, M., Nacke, L., O'Hara, K., & Dixon, D. (2011). Gamification. using game-design elements in non-gaming contexts. *CHI '11 Extended Abstracts on Human Factors in Computing Systems.* doi:10.1145/1979742.1979575

Detyna, M., Sanchez-Pizani, R., Giampietro, V., Dommett, E. J., & Dyer, K. (2023). Hybrid flexible (HyFlex) teaching and learning: Climbing the mountain of implementation challenges for synchronous online and face-to-face seminars during a pandemic. *Learning Environments Research, 26*(1), 145–159. doi:10.100710984-022-09408-y PMID:35399562

Compilation of References

Deutsch, T., Herrmann, K., Frese, T., & Sandholzer, H. (2012). Implementing computer-based assessment – A web-based mock examination changes attitudes. *Computers & Education*, *58*(4), 1068–1075. doi:10.1016/j.compedu.2011.11.013

Dewaele, J.-M. (2017). Psychological dimensions and foreign language anxiety. The Routledge Handbook of Instructed Second Language Acquisition, 433–450. doi:10.4324/9781315676968-24

Dicheva, D., Dichev, C., Agre, G., & Angelova, G. (2015). Gamification in education: A systematic mapping study. *Journal of Educational Technology & Society*, *18*(3), 75–88.

Dichev, C., & Dicheva, D. (2017). Gamifying education: What is known, what is believed and what remains uncertain: A critical review. *International Journal of Educational Technology in Higher Education*, *14*(1), 9. Advance online publication. doi:10.118641239-017-0042-5

Dickinson, L. (1992). *Learning autonomy 2: Learner training for language learning*. Authentik.

Dickinson, L. (1995). Autonomy and motivation: A literature review. *System*, *23*(2), 165–174. doi:10.1016/0346-251X(95)00005-5

Dincer, A. (2020). Understanding the characteristics of English language learners' out-of-class language learning through digital practices. *IAFOR Journal of Education*, *8*(2), 47–65. doi:10.22492/ije.8.2.03

Dindar, M., Ren, L., & Järvenoja, H. (2020). An experimental study on the effects of gamified cooperation and competition on English vocabulary learning. *British Journal of Educational Technology*, *52*(1), 142–159. doi:10.1111/bjet.12977

Ding, L., Er, E., & Orey, M. (2018). An exploratory study of student engagement in gamified online discussions. *Computers & Education*, *120*, 213–226. doi:10.1016/j.compedu.2018.02.007

Diyono, Y. L. (2009). Learning Strategies for EFL students in Developing their Vocabulary Mastery. *Universitas Semarang: LITE*, *5*(1), 1–12. doi:10.33633/lite.v5i1.1342

Dobakhti, L., & Panahi, M. (2021). The Effect of Digital Picture Storytelling (PST) on Improving Young Iranian Learners' Foreign Language Oral Production. *Iranian Journal of English for Academic Purposes*, *11*(1), 40–56. 20.1001.1.24763187.2022.11.1.4.5

Dolgunsöz, E., & Yıldırım, G. (2021). The Role of Mobile Devices on Online EFL Skill Courses During Covid-19 Emergency Remote Education. *JELPEDLIC*, *6*(2), 118–131. doi:10.35974/acuity.v6i2.2486

Dörnyei Zoltán. (2005). *The psychology of the language learner: Individual differences in Second language acquisition*. Routledge.

Dowling, M., & Lucey, B. (2023). ChatGPT for (Finance) research: The bananarama conjecture. *Finance Research Letters*, *53*, 103662. doi:10.1016/j.frl.2023.103662

Drent, M., & Meelissen, M. (2008). Which factors obstruct or stimulate teacher educators to use ICT innovatively? *Computers & Education*, *51*(1), 187–199. doi:10.1016/j.compedu.2007.05.001

Dubin, F.E.O. (1986). Course Design: Developing programs and materials for language learning. *New Directions in Language Teaching, 15*(3).

Du, F. (2013). Student Perspectives of Self-Directed Language Learning: Implications for Teaching and Research. *International Journal for the Scholarship of Teaching and Learning, 7*(2), 1–16. doi:10.20429/ijsotl.2013.070224

Dunn, J. (2016). Computational learning of construction grammars. *Language and Cognition, 9*(2), 254–292. doi:10.1017/langcog.2016.7

Education. *Artificial Intelligence*. Advance online publication. doi:10.1016/j.caeai.2022.100119

Efron, S. E., & Ravid, R. (2020). *Action research in education: A practical guide*. The Guilford Press.

Ellis, G., & Sinclair, B. (1989). *Learning to Learn English a Course in Learner Training Teacher's Book*. Cambridge University Press.

Ellis, R. (2009). A typology of written corrective feedback types. *ELT Journal, 63*(2), 97–107. doi:10.1093/elt/ccn023

Ellis, R. (2014). Principles of instructed second language learning. In M. Celce-Murcia, D. Brinton, & M. Snow (Eds.), *Teaching English as a second or foreign language* (4th ed., pp. 31–45). Cengage Learning.

Ellis, R. (2019). *Understanding second language acquisition*. Oxford University Press.

Enright, M. K., & Quinlan, T. (2010). Complementing human judgment of essays written by English language learners with e-rater® scoring. *Language Testing, 27*(3), 317–334. doi:10.1177/0265532210363144

Ertmer, P., Ottenbreit-Leftwich, A., Sadik, O., Sendurur, E., & Sendurur, P. (2012). Teacher beliefs and technology integration practices: A critical relationship. *Computers & Education, 59*(2), 423–435. doi:10.1016/j.compedu.2012.02.001

Esch, E. (1997). Learner training for autonomous language learning. In Autonomy and independence in language learning (pp. 164- 176). Longman.

Esch, K., Schalkwijk, E., Elsen, A., & Setz, W. (2000). *Autonomous Learning in Foreign Language Teacher Training*. https://lc.ust.hk/ailasc/lapi2000.html

Esch, E. (1996). *Promoting learner autonomy: Criteria for the selection of appropriate methods*. Hong Kong University.

Evans, M. A., Reynolds, K., Shaw, D., & Pursoo, T. (2011). Parental explanations of vocabulary during shared book reading: A missed opportunity. *First Language, 31*(2), 195–213. doi:10.1177/0142723710393795

Compilation of References

Falloon, G. (2011). Making the connection: Moore's theory of transactional distance and its relevance to the use of a virtual classroom in postgraduate online teacher education. *Journal of Research on Technology in Education*, *43*(3), 187–209. doi:10.1080/15391523.2011.10782569

Farazouli, A., Cerratto-Pargman, T., Bolander-Laksov, K., & McGrath, C. (2023). Hello GPT! Goodbye home examination? An exploratory study of AI chatbots impact on university teachers' assessment practices. *Assessment & Evaluation in Higher Education*, 1–13. Advance online publication. doi:10.1080/02602938.2023.2241676

Farjon, D., Smits, A., & Voogt, J. (2019). Technology integration of pre-service teachers explained by attitudes and beliefs, competency, access, and experience. *Computers & Education*, *130*, 81–93. doi:10.1016/j.compedu.2018.11.010

Farrokhnia, M., Banihashem, S. K., Noroozi, O., & Wals, A. (2023). A SWOT analysis of ChatGPT: Implications for educational practice and research. *Innovations in Education and Teaching International*, 1–15. Advance online publication. doi:10.1080/14703297.2023.2195846

Fendji, J. L. K. E., Tala, D. C., Yenke, B. O., & Atemkeng, M. (2022). Automatic speech recognition using limited vocabulary: A survey. *Applied Artificial Intelligence*, *36*(1), 2095039. doi:10.1080/08839514.2022.2095039

Feng, L., & Sass, T. R. (2018). The impact of incentives to recruit and retain teachers in "hard-to-staff" subjects. *Journal of Policy Analysis and Management*, *37*(1), 112–135. doi:10.1002/pam.22037

Ferris, D. R., Liu, H., Sinha, A., & Senna, M. (2013). Written corrective feedback for individual L2 writers. *Journal of Second Language Writing*, *22*(3), 307–329. doi:10.1016/j.jslw.2012.09.009

Flanagan, J. L. (2008). *Technology: The positive and negative effects on student achievement*. University of New York.

Fogolin, A. (2012). *Bildungsberatung im Fernlernen*. Beiträge aus Wissenschaft und Praxis.

Franco, H., Bratt, H., Rossier, R., Rao Gadde, V., Shriberg, E., Abrash, V., & Precoda, K. (2010). EduSpeak®: A speech recognition and pronunciation scoring toolkit for computer-aided language learning applications. *Language Testing*, *27*(3), 401–418. doi:10.1177/0265532210364408

Fried, C. B. (2008). In-class laptop use and its effects on student learning. *Computers & Education*, *50*(3), 906–914. doi:10.1016/j.compedu.2006.09.006

Fryer, L. K., Ainley, M., Thompson, A., Gibson, A., & Sherlock, Z. (2017). Stimulating and sustaining interest in a language course: An experimental comparison of Chatbot and Human task partners. *Computers in Human Behavior*, *75*, 461–468. doi:10.1016/j.chb.2017.05.045

Fryer, L. K., & Carpenter, R. (2006). Bots as language learning tools. *Language Learning & Technology*, *10*, 8–14. http://llt.msu.edu/vol10num3/emerging/default.html

Fryer, L. K., Coniam, D., Carpenter, R., & Lăpușneanu, D. (2020). Bots for language learning now: Current and future directions. *Language Learning & Technology*, *24*(2), 8–22.

Fryer, L. K., Nakao, K., & Thompson, A. (2019). Chatbot learning partners: Connecting learning experiences, interest and competence. *Computers in Human Behavior*, *93*, 279–289. doi:10.1016/j. chb.2018.12.023

Fulcher, G. (2012). Assessment literacy for the language classroom. *Language Assessment Quarterly*, *9*(2), 113–132. doi:10.1080/15434303.2011.642041

Furenes, I. M., Kucirkova, N., & Bus, A. G. (2021). A Comparison of Children's Reading on Paper Versus Screen: A Meta-Analysis. *Review of Educational Research*, *91*(4), 483–517. doi:10.3102/0034654321998074

Fu, S., Gu, H., & Yang, B. (2020). The affordances of AI-enabled automatic scoring applications on learners' continuous learning intention: An empirical study in China. *British Journal of Educational Technology*, *51*(5), 1674–1692. doi:10.1111/bjet.12995

Gallegos, C., & Nakashima, H. (2018). Mobile devices: A distraction, or a useful tool to engage nursing students? *The Journal of Nursing Education*, *57*(3), 170–173. doi:10.3928/01484834-20180221-09 PMID:29505077

Galloway, A. (2005). Non-probability sampling. In K. Kempf-Leonard (Ed.), *Encyclopedia of Social Measurement* (pp. 859–864). Elsevier. doi:10.1016/B0-12-369398-5/00382-0

Gan, Z. (2004). Attitudes and strategies as predictors of self-directed language learning in an EFL context. *International Journal of Applied Linguistics*, *14*(3), 389–411. doi:10.1111/j.1473-4192.2004.00071.x

García-Sánchez, S., & Luján-García, C. (2016). Ubiquitous knowledge and experiences to foster EFL learning affordances. *Computer Assisted Language Learning*, *29*(7), 1169–1180. doi:10.1080/09588221.2016.1176047

Gardner, D., & Miller, L. (1996). *Tasks for independent language learning*. TESOL.

Gardner, D., & Miller, L. (1999). *Establishing Self Access: From Theory to Practice*. Cambridge University.

Gardner, D., & Miller, L. (2011). Managing self-access language learning: Principles and practice. *System*, *39*(1), 78–89. doi:10.1016/j.system.2011.01.010

Gardner, R. C., & Macintyre, P. D. (1993). A student's contributions to second language learning: Part II: Affective variables. *Language Teaching*, *26*(1), 1–11. doi:10.1017/S0261444800000045

Garrison, D. R. (2003). Self-directed learning and distance education. In Handbook of Distance Education. Lawrence Erlbaum Associates.

Garrison, D. R., Anderson, T., & Archer, W. (2000). Critical inquiry in a text-based environment: Computer conferencing in higher education. *The Internet and Higher Education*, *2*(2), 87–105.

Compilation of References

Garrison, D. R., & Arbaugh, J. B. (2007). Researching the community of inquiry framework: Review, issues, and future directions. *The Internet and Higher Education*, *10*(3), 157–172. doi:10.1016/j.iheduc.2007.04.001

Garrison, D. R., Cleveland-Innes, M., & Fung, T. S. (2010). Exploring causal relationships among teaching, cognitive and social presence: Student perceptions of the community of inquiry framework. *The Internet and Higher Education*, *13*(1), 31–36. doi:10.1016/j.iheduc.2009.10.002

Garrison, D. R., & Kanuka, H. (2004). Blended learning: Uncovering its transformative potential in higher education. *The Internet and Higher Education*, *7*(2), 95–105. doi:10.1016/j.iheduc.2004.02.001

Gašević, D., Siemens, G., & Sadiq, S. (2023). Empowering learners for the age of artificial intelligence. *Computers and Education: Artificial Intelligence*, *100130*, 100130. Advance online publication. doi:10.1016/j.caeai.2023.100130

George, A. S., & George, A. H. (2023). A review of ChatGPT AI's impact on several business sectors. *Partners Universal International Innovation Journal*, *1*(1), 9–23.

Ghaith, G. (2003). Effects of the learning together model of cooperative learning on English as foreign language reading achievement, academic self-esteem, and feelings of school alienation. *Bilingual Research Journal*, *27*(3), 451–474. doi:10.1080/15235882.2003.10162603

Ghonsooly, B., & Shalchy, S. (2013). Cultural intelligence and writing ability: Delving into fluency, accuracy and complexity. [Research on Youth and Language]. *Novitas-ROYAL*, *7*(2), 147–159.

Giossos, Y., Koutsouba, M., Lionarakis, A., & Skavantzos, K. (2009). Reconsidering Moore's transactional distance theory. *European Journal of Open Distance and ELearning*, *2009*(2), 1–6. https://files.eric.ed.gov/fulltext/EJ911768.pdf

Goethe, O. (2019). *Gamification mindset*. Springer. doi:10.1007/978-3-030-11078-9

Gökmen, Ö. F., Duman, İ., & Horzum, M. B. (2016). Uzaktan eğitimde kuramlar, değişimler ve yeni yönelimler. *AUAd, 2*(3), 29-51. http://auad.anadolu.edu.tr/yonetim/icerik/makaleler/167-published.pdf

González-Calatayud, V., Prendes-Espinosa, P., & Roig-Vila, R. (2021). Artificial intelligence for student assessment: A systematic review. *Applied Sciences (Basel, Switzerland)*, *11*(12), 5467. doi:10.3390/app11125467

González-Lloret, M. (2017). Technology for Task-based language teaching. In C. A. Chapelle & S. Sauro (Eds.), *The handbook of technology and second language teaching and learning* (pp. 234–247). John Wiley & Sons, Inc. doi:10.1002/9781118914069.ch16

Goodyear, P. (2020). Design and co-configuration for hybrid learning: Theorising the practices of learning space design. *British Journal of Educational Technology*, *51*(4), 1045–1060. doi:10.1111/bjet.12925

Gorin, J. S. (2007). Cognitive diagnostic assessment for education. In J. P. Leighton & M. J. Gierl (Eds.), *Test construction and diagnostic testing* (pp. 173–204). Cambridge University.

Gounari, P., & Koutropoulos, A. (2015). *Using blended principles to bridge the gap between online and on-campus courses*. IGI Global. doi:10.4018/978-1-4666-8246-7.ch065

Govender, T., & Arnedo-Moreno, J. (2021). An analysis of game design elements used in digital game-based language learning. *Sustainability (Basel)*, *13*(12), 6679. doi:10.3390u13126679

Graham, C. R. (2011). *Examining the validity of an elicited imitation instrument to test oral language in Spanish*. Presentation at *33rd Annual Convention of the Language Testing Research Colloquium (LTRC 2011)*. Ann Arbor, MI, USA.

Graham, C. R. (2011). Theoretical considerations for understanding technological pedagogical content knowledge (TPACK). *Computers & Education*, *57*(3), 1953–1960. doi:10.1016/j.compedu.2011.04.010

Graham, C. R., Lonsdale, D., Kennington, C., Johnson, A., & McGhee, J. (2008). Elicited imitation as an oral proficiency measure with ASR scoring. In *Proceedings of the Sixth International Conference on Language Resources and Evaluation (LREC 2008)* (pp. 1604–1610). European Language Resources Association.

Graham, F. (2022). Daily briefing: Will ChatGPT kill the essay assignment? *Nature*. Advance online publication. doi:10.1038/d41586-022-04437-2 PMID:36517680

Granata, K. (2019). Tech may be to blame for decline in students' reading for pleasure. *Education World*. Retrieved from https://www.educationworld.com/a_news/technology-proves-negatively-effect-reading-skills

Gremmen, M. C., Molenaar, I., & Teepe, R. (2016). Vocabulary development at home: A multimedia elaborated picture supporting parent– toddler interaction. *Journal of Computer Assisted Learning*, *32*(6), 548–560. doi:10.1111/jcal.12150

Griffiths, C., & Soruç Adem. (2020). *Individual differences in language learning: A complex systems theory perspective*. Palgrave Macmillan.

Gronlund, N. E. (1998). *Assessment of student achievement*. Allyn and Bacon.

Grover, K. S., Miller, M. T., Swearingen, B., & Wood, N. (2014). An Examination of the Self-Directed Learning Practices of ESL Adult Language Learners. *Journal of Adult Education*, *43*(2), 12–19.

Guglielmino, P. J., & Guglielmino, L. M. (2001). *Learner characteristics affecting success in electronic distance learning*. Motorola University Press.

Gunawan, S., & Shieh, C. (2020). Effects of the application of STEM curriculum integration model to living technology teaching on business school students' learning effectiveness. *Contemporary Educational Technology*, *12*(2), ep279. Advance online publication. doi:10.30935/cedtech/8583

Compilation of References

Gündüz, N. (2005). Computer Assisted Language Learning. *Journal of Language and Linguistic Studies*, *1*(2), 193–214. doi:10.17263/jlls.24391

Guodong, Z., Huanhuan, Y., & Yuanzhong, X. (2021). *Metaverse. Beijing Book Co.* Inc.

Hakami, M. (2020). Using Nearpod as a tool to promote active learning in higher education in a BYOD learning environment. *Journal of Education and Learning*, *9*(1), 119–126. doi:10.5539/jel.v9n1p119

Han, S. (2023). The contribution of blog-based writing instruction to enhancing writing performance and writing motivation of Chinese EFL learners. *Frontiers in Psychology*, *13*, 1069585. Advance online publication. doi:10.3389/fpsyg.2022.1069585 PMID:36743589

Harmer, J. (2001). *The Practice of English Language Teaching*. Longman.

Harmer, J. (2003). *The practice of English language teaching*. Longman.

Harris, J., Mishra, P., & Koehler, M. (2009). Teachers' technological pedagogical content knowledge and learning activity types. *Journal of Research on Technology in Education*, *41*(4), 393–416. doi:10.1080/15391523.2009.10782536

Healey, D., Hegelheimer, V., Hubbard, P., Ioannou-Georgiou, S., Kessler, G., & Ware, P. (2008). *TESOL technology standards framework*. TESOL. Retrieved from https://www.tesol.org

Hedjazi Moghari, M., & Marandi, S. S. (2017). Triumph through texting: Restoring Learners' interest in grammar. *ReCALL*, *29*(3), 357–372. doi:10.1017/S0958344017000167

Heilporn, G., & Lakhal, S. (2021). Converting a graduate-level course into a HyFlex modality: What are effective engagement strategies? *International Journal of Management Education*, *19*(1), 100454. doi:10.1016/j.ijme.2021.100454

Henriksen, D., Creely, E., & Henderson, M. (2020). Folk pedagogies for teacher transitions: Approaches to synchronous online learning in the wake of Covid-19. *Journal of Technology and Teacher Education*, *28*(2), 201–209.

Hernández-Prados, M. Á., Belmonte, M. L., & Manzanares-Ruiz, J. C. (2021). How to run your own online business: A gamification experience in ESL. *Education Sciences*, *11*(11), 697. doi:10.3390/educsci11110697

Hill, P. (2012). Online educational delivery models: A descriptive view. *EDUCAUSE Review*, *47*(6), 84–86.

Hindman, A. H., Wasik, B. A., & Erhart, A. C. (2012). Shared book reading and Head Start preschoolers' vocabulary learning: The role of book-related discussion and curricular connections. *Early Education and Development*, *23*(4), 451–474. doi:10.1080/10409289.2010.537250

Hoang, G. T. L., & Kunnan, A. J. (2016). Automated essay evaluation for English language learners: A case study of MY Access. *Language Assessment Quarterly*, *13*(4), 359–376. doi:10.1080/15434303.2016.1230121

Hodges, B., Hu, L., & Siefker, D. (2022, August). Benefits and challenges of a hybrid flexible EAP Program. *TESL Ontario: Contact magazine*, 15-26.

Hod, Y., & Katz, S. (2020). Fostering highly engaged knowledge building communities in socioemotional and sociocognitive hybrid learning spaces. *British Journal of Educational Technology*, *51*(4), 1117–1135. doi:10.1111/bjet.12910

Hoffman, J. L., & Paciga, K. A. (2014). Click, Swipe, and Read: Sharing e-Books with Toddlers and Preschoolers. *Early Childhood Education Journal*, *42*(6), 379–388. doi:10.100710643-013-0622-5

Holec, H. (1985). On Autonomy: some elementary concepts. In P. Riley (Ed.), Discourse and Learning (pp. 173–190). Academic Press.

Holec, H. (1981). *Autonomy in foreign language learning*. Pergamon.

Holmberg, B. (2000). *Theory and practice of distance education* (2nd ed.). Routledge, Tylor&Francis Group.

Hong, W. C. H. (2023). The impact of ChatGPT on foreign language teaching and learning. *Journal of Educational Technology and Innovation, 1*(1).

Hong, J.-C., Hwang, M.-Y., Liu, Y.-H., & Tai, K.-H. (2020). Effects of gamifying questions on English grammar learning mediated by epistemic curiosity and language anxiety. *Computer Assisted Language Learning*, *35*(7), 1458–1482. doi:10.1080/09588221.2020.1803361

Horzum, M. B. (2011). Transaksiyonel Uzaklık Algısı Ölçeğinin Geliştirilmesi ve Karma Öğrenme Öğrencilerinin Transaksiyonel Uzaklık Algılarının Çeşitli Değişkenler Açısından İncelenmesi. *Kuram ve Uygulamada Eğitim Bilimleri*, 1571-1587. http://toad.edam.com.tr/sites/default/files/pdf/transaksiyonel-uzaklik-algisi-olcegi-toad.pdf

Horzum, M. B. (2007). *İnternet tabanlı eğitimde transaksiyonel uzaklığın öğrenci başarısı, doyumu ve özyeterlilik algısına etkisi*. Yayınlanmamış Doktora Tezi, Ankara Üniversitesi, Eğitimi Bilimleri Enstitüsü.

Houston, A. B., & Corrado, E. M. (2023). Embracing ChatGPT: Implications of Emergent Language Models for Academia and Libraries. *Technical Services Quarterly*, *40*(2), 76–91. doi:10.1080/07317131.2023.2187110

Howell, E. (2022). HyFlex model of higher education: Understanding the promise of flexibility. *On the Horizon*, *30*(4), 173–181. doi:10.1108/OTH-04-2022-0019

Hsu, H. C. (2019). Wiki-mediated collaboration and its association with L2 writing development: An exploratory study. *Computer Assisted Language Learning*, *32*(8), 945–967. doi:10.1080/09588221.2018.1542407

Hsu, H. T. (2018). *L2 learning motivation from the perspective of self-determination theory: A qualitative case study of hospitality and tourism students in Taiwan. In ELT in Asia in the Digital Era: Global Citizenship and Identity*. Routledge.

Compilation of References

Hu, K. (2023). *ChatGPT sets record for fastest-growing user base - analyst note.* Reuters. https://www.reuters.com/technology/chatgpt-sets-record-fastest-growing-user-base-analyst-note-2023-02-01

Huang, B., Hew, K. F., & Lo, C. K. (2019). Investigating the effects of gamification-enhanced flipped learning on undergraduate students' behavioral and cognitive engagement. *Interactive Learning Environments, 27*(8), 1106–1126. doi:10.1080/10494820.2018.1495653

Huang, R., Ritzhaupt, A. D., Sommer, M., Zhu, J., Stephen, A., Valle, N., Hampton, J., & Li, J. (2020). The impact of gamification in educational settings on student learning outcomes: A meta-analysis. *Educational Technology Research and Development, 68*(4), 1875–1901. doi:10.100711423-020-09807-z

Huang, W. H. Y., & Soman, D. (2013). Gamification of education. *Report Series: Behavioural Economics in Action, 29*(4), 37.

Huang, W., Hew, K. F., & Fryer, L. K. (2022). Chatbots for language learning – are they really useful? A systematic review of chatbot-supported language learning. *Journal of Computer Assisted Learning, 38*(1), 237–257. doi:10.1111/jcal.12610

Huang, X. (2021). Aims for cultivating students' key competencies based on artificial intelligence education in China. *Education and Information Technologies, 26*(5), 5127–5147. doi:10.100710639-021-10530-2

Huang, X., Zou, D., Cheng, G., & Xie, H. (2021). A systematic review of AR and VR enhanced language learning. *Sustainability (Basel), 13*(9), 4639. doi:10.3390u13094639

Huawei, S., & Aryadoust, V. (2023). A systematic review of automated writing evaluation systems. *Education and Information Technologies, 28*(1), 771–795. doi:10.100710639-022-11200-7

Hughes, A. (2003). *Testing for language teachers.* Cambridge University.

Hunicke, R., LeBlanc, M., & Zubek, R. (2004, July). MDA: A formal approach to game design and game research. In *Proceedings of the AAAI Workshop on Challenges in Game AI (Vol. 4,* No. 1, p. 1722). AAAI.

Huotari, K., & Hamari, J. (2012). Defining gamification. *Proceeding of the 16th International Academic MindTrek Conference.* 10.1145/2393132.2393137

Hwang, A. (2018). Online and hybrid learning. *Journal of Management Education, 42*(4), 557–563. doi:10.1177/1052562918777550

Hwang, G. J., & Chien, S. Y. (2022). Definition, roles, and potential research issues of the metaverse in education: An artificial intelligence perspective. *Computers and Education: Artificial Intelligence, 3,* 100082. doi:10.1016/j.caeai.2022.100082

Idris, M. I., Said, N. E., & Tan, K. H. (2020). Game-based learning platform and its effects on present tense mastery: Evidence from an ESL classroom. *International Journal of Learning. Teaching and Educational Research, 19*(5), 13–26. doi:10.26803/ijlter.19.5.2

Inglis, M., Palipana, A., Trenholm, S., & Ward, J. (2011). Individual differences in students' use of optional learning resources. *Journal of Computer Assisted Learning*, *27*(6), 490–502. doi:10.1111/j.1365-2729.2011.00417.x

Ishaq, K., Mat Zin, N. A., Rosdi, F., Jehanghir, M., Ishaq, S., & Abid, A. (2021). Mobile-assisted and gamification-based Language Learning: A Systematic Literature Review. *PeerJ. Computer Science*, *7*, e496. Advance online publication. doi:10.7717/peerj-cs.496 PMID:34084920

Ivanov, A. V., Lange, P. L., Suendermann-Oeft, D., Ramanarayanan, V., & Yu, Z., Y. K., & Tao, J. (2016). *Speed vs. accuracy: Designing an optimal ASR system for spontaneous non-native speech in a real-time application.* Proceedings of the 7th International Workshop on Spoken Dialogue Systems, IWSDS 2016, Saariselkä, Finland.

Jaime, S., & Kateryna, N. (2022). Students' perceptions of the hyflex learning model from Ukraine and Japan: A realistic future for university language learning? *Hiroshima Studies in Language and Language Education*, *25*, 45–59. doi:10.15027/51960

Jamieson, J. (2005). Trends in computer-based second language assessment. *Annual Review of Applied Linguistics*, *25*, 228–242. doi:10.1017/S0267190505000127

Jannah, M., & Syafryadin, S. (2022). EFL students' perspectives on the use of Wordwall.net as vocabulary learning media. *Journal of English Language Teaching*, *11*(2), 115–124. doi:10.15294/elt.v11i2.57120

Jenkins, J. R., & Pany, D. (1978). Standardized achievement tests: How useful for special education? *Exceptional Children*, *44*(6), 448–453. doi:10.1177/001440297804400606

Jia, F., Sun, D., Ma, Q., & Looi, C.-K. (2022). Developing an AI-Based learning system for L2 learners' authentic and ubiquitous learning in English language. *Sustainability (Basel)*, *14*(23), 15527. doi:10.3390u142315527

Ji, P. W., & Aziz, A. A. (2021). A Systematic Review of Vocabulary Learning with Mobile Assisted Learning Platforms. *International Journal of Academic Research in Business & Social Sciences*, *11*(11), 1503–1521.

Johns, K. (2015). Engaging and assessing students with technology: A review of Kahoot! *Delta Kappa Gamma Bulletin*, *81*(4), 89–91.

Johnson, D. W., & Johnson, R. T. (2003). Student motivation in co-operative groups: Social interdependence theory. RoutledgeFalmer.

Johnson, D. W., & Johnson, R. T. (2009). An educational psychology success story: Social interdependence theory and cooperative learning. *Educational Researcher*, *38*(5), 365–379. doi:10.3102/0013189X09339057

Jonsson, A., & Svingby, G. (2007). The use of scoring rubrics: Reliability, validity and educational consequences. *Educational Research Review*, *2*(2), 130–144. doi:10.1016/j.edurev.2007.05.002

Compilation of References

Justice, L. M., Logan, J. R., & Damschroder, L. (2015). Designing caregiver-implemented shared-reading interventions to overcome implementation barriers. *Journal of Speech, Language, and Hearing Research: JSLHR*, *58*(6), 1851–1863. doi:10.1044/2015_JSLHR-L-14-0344 PMID:26262941

Kaban, A. L. (2021). Gamified e-reading experiences and their impact on reading comprehension and attitude in EFL classes. *International Journal of Mobile and Blended Learning*, *13*(3), 71–90. doi:10.4018/IJMBL.2021070105

Kahn, P. H. Jr. (2011). *Technological nature: Adaptation and the future of human life*. MIT. doi:10.7551/mitpress/7983.001.0001

Kaplan, A. (2023). *Business Schools Post-COVID-19: A Blueprint for Survival*. Taylor & Francis. doi:10.4324/9781003343509

Karakas, F., & Manisaligil, A. (2012). Reorienting self-directed learning for the creative digital era. *European Journal of Training and Development*, *36*(7), 712–731. doi:10.1108/03090591211255557

Karataş, S. (2005). *Deneyim eşitliğine dayalı internet temelli ve yüz yüz öğrenme sistemlerinin öğrenen başarısı ve doyumu açısından karşılaştırılması*. Yayınlanmamış Doktora Tezi, Ankara Üniversitesi.

Karpava, S. (2022, January). *The challenge of change: hybrid teaching and learning during the pandemic*. Trends in Language Teaching 2022 Conference Post-Conference Proceedings, Okinawa.

Kartal, G. (2023). Contemporary language teaching and learning with ChatGPT. *Contemporary Research in Language and Linguistics*, *1*(1), 59–70.

Kashive, N., Powale, L., & Kashive, K. (2020). Understanding user perception toward artificial intelligence (AI) enabled e-learning. *The International Journal of Information and Learning Technology*, *38*(1), 1–19. doi:10.1108/IJILT-05-2020-0090

Kasneci, E., Seßler, K., Küchemann, S., Bannert, M., Dementieva, D., Fischer, F., Gasser, U., Groh, G., Günnemann, S., Hüllermeier, E., Krusche, S., Kutyniok, G., Michaeli, T., Nerdel, C., Pfeffer, J., Poquet, O., Sailer, M., Schmidt, A., Seidel, T., ... Kasneci, G. (2023). ChatGPT for good? On opportunities and challenges of large language models for education. *Learning and Individual Differences*, *103*, 102274. doi:10.1016/j.lindif.2023.102274

Keegan, D. (1996). *Foundations of distance education*. Routledge.

Keegan, D. J. (1983). *On defining distance education*. St. Martin's.

Kerly, A., Hall, P., & Bull, S. (2007). Bringing chatbots into education: Towards natural language negotiation of open learner models. *Knowledge-Based Systems*, *20*(2), 177–185. doi:10.1016/j.knosys.2006.11.014

Keshavarz, H., Esmaeili Givi, M., & Vafaeian, A. (2016). Students' sense of self-efficacy in searching information from the web: A PLS approach. *Webology*, *13*(2), 16–31.

Kessler, G. (2018). Technology and the future of language teaching. *Foreign Language Annals*, *51*(1), 205–218. doi:10.1111/flan.12318

Khabbazbashi, N., Xu, J., & Galaczi, E. D. (2021). Opening the Black box: Exploring automated speaking evaluation. In B. Lanteigne, C. Coombe, & J. D. Brown (Eds.), *Challenges in language testing around the world* (pp. 333–343). Springer. doi:10.1007/978-981-33-4232-3_25

Khalilian, B., Hosseini, H., & Ghabanchi, Z. (2021). On the Effect of Employing the Online Kahoot Game-Based App on Iranian EFL Learners' Structural Ability and their Motivation. *Journal of Language Teaching and Learning*, *11*(2), 42–60. https://www.jltl.com.tr/index.php/jltl/article/view/330

Khany, R., & Amiri, M. (2016). Action control, L2 motivational self system, and motivated learning behavior in a foreign language learning context. *European Journal of Psychology of Education*, *33*(2), 337–353. doi:10.100710212-016-0325-6

Kılıçkaya, F., & Kic-Drgas, J. (2023). Misuse of AI (Artificial Intelligence) in assignments: Can AI-written content be detected? In R. E. Ferdig, R. Hartshorne, E. Baumgartner, R. Kaplan-Rakowski, & C. Mouza (Ed.), What PreK-12 teachers should know about educational technology in 2023: A research-to-practice anthology, (pp. 145-152). AACE2023.

Kim, H.-S., Cha, Y., & Kim, N. Y. (2021). Effects of AI chatbots on EFL students' communication skills. *Korean Journal of English Language and Linguistics*, *21*, 712–734. doi:10.15738/kjell.21.202108.712

Kim, M. K., Kim, N. J., & Heidari, A. (2022). Learner experience in artificial intelligence-scaffolded argumentation. *Assessment & Evaluation in Higher Education*, *47*(8), 1301–1316. doi:10.1080/02602938.2022.2042792

Kim, N. Y. (2016). Effects of voice chat on EFL learners' speaking ability according to proficiency levels. *Multimedia-Assisted Language Learning*, *19*(4), 63–88. doi:10.15702/mall.2016.19.4.63

Kim, N. Y. (2018a). Chatbots and Korean EFL students' English vocabulary learning. *Journal of Digital Convergence*, *16*(2), 1–7. doi:10.14400/JDC.2018.16.2.001

Kim, N. Y. (2019). A study on the use of artificial intelligence chatbots for improving English grammar skills. *Journal of Digital Convergence*, *17*(8), 37–46.

Kim, N. Y., Cha, Y., & Kim, H.-S. (2019). Future English learning: Chatbots and artificial intelligence. *Multimedia Assisted Language Learning*, *22*(3), 32–53. doi:10.15702/mall.2019.22.3.32

Kim, N.-Y. (2018b). A study on chatbots for developing Korean college students' English listening and reading skills. *Journal of Digital Convergence*, *16*(8), 19–26. doi:10.14400/JDC.2018.16.8.019

Kimsesiz, F. (2023). An Examination of Digitalized Self-directed Language Learning Practices of Tertiary Level EFL learners in Turkey. *Journal of Educational Technology and Online Learning*, *6*(3), 683–701. doi:10.31681/jetol.1276105

Compilation of References

Kiptonui, B. P., Too, J. K., & Mukwa, C. W. (2018). teacher attitude towards use of chatbots in routine teaching. *Universal Journal of Educational Research*, 6(7), 1586–1597. doi:10.13189/ujer.2018.060719

Klímová, B., & Ibna Seraj, P. M. (2023). The use of chatbots in university EFL settings: Research trends and pedagogical implications. *Frontiers in Psychology*, 14, 1131506. Advance online publication. doi:10.3389/fpsyg.2023.1131506 PMID:37034959

Knezek, G., & Christensen, R. (2008). The importance of information technology attitudes and competencies in primary and secondary education. In J. Voogt & G. Knezek (Eds.), *International handbook of information technology in primary and secondary education* (pp. 321–331). Springer. doi:10.1007/978-0-387-73315-9_19

Knowles, M. (1995). *Designs for Adult Learning: Practical Resources, Exercises, and Course Outlines from the Father of Adult Learning*. American Society for Training and Development.

Knowles, M. S. (1975). *Self-directed learning: A guide for learners and teachers*. Association.

Koehler, M., & Mishra, P. (2009). What is technological pedagogical content knowledge (TPACK)? *Contemporary Issues in Technology & Teacher Education*, 9(1), 60–70. doi:10.1177/002205741319300303

Kohnke, L. (2020). Exploring learner perception, experience and motivation of using a mobile app in L2 vocabulary acquisition. *International Journal of Computer-Assisted Language Learning and Teaching*, 10(1), 15–26. doi:10.4018/IJCALLT.2020010102

Kohnke, L. (2022). A qualitative exploration of student perspectives of chatbot use during emergency remote teaching. *International Journal of Mobile Learning and Organization*, 16(4), 475–488. doi:10.1504/IJMLO.2022.125966

Kohnke, L. (2023). L2 learners' perceptions of a chatbot as a potential independent language learning tool. *International Journal of Mobile Learning and Organisation*, 17(1-2), 214–226. doi:10.1504/IJMLO.2023.128339

Kohnke, L., & Moorhouse, B. L. (2021). Adopting HyFlex in higher education in response to covid-19: Students' perspectives. *Open Learning*, 36(3), 231–244. doi:10.1080/02680513.2021.1906641

Kohnke, L., Moorhouse, B. L., & Zou, D. (2023). ChatGPT for language teaching and learning. *RELC Journal*, 1–14. doi:10.1177/00336882231162

Kohnke, L., Moorhouse, B. L., & Zou, D. (2023). ChatGPT for Language Teaching and Learning. *RELC Journal*, 54(2), 537–550. doi:10.1177/00336882231162868

Kohnke, L., & Ting, A. (2021). ESL Students' Perceptions of Mobile Applications for Discipline-Specific Vocabulary Acquisition for Academic Purposes. *Knowledge Management & E-Learning*, 13(1), 102–117. doi:10.34105/j.kmel.2021.13.006

Kohonen, V. (2001). Experiential language learning: Second language learning as cooperative learner education. In Collaborative language learning and teaching (pp. 14-39). Cambridge University.

Kohonen, V. (2012). Developing autonomy through ELP-oriented pedagogy: Exploring the interplay of the shallow and deep structures in a major change within language education. In B. Kühn & M. L. Pérez Cavana (Eds.), *Perspectives from the European Language Portfolio: Learner autonomy and self-assessment içinde* (pp. 22–42). Routledge.

Koraishi, O. (2023). Teaching English in the age of AI: Embracing ChatGPT to optimize EFL materials and assessment. *Language Education and Technology, 3*(1).

Köroğlu, Ç. Z., Öz, G., & Yüce, E. (2022). *Enhancing EFL learners' self-regulatory skill and autonomy in digital learning environments.* Nobel Publishing.

Köroğlu, Z. Ç. (2021). Using Digital Formative Assessment to Evaluate EFL Learners' English Speaking Skills. *GIST–Education and Learning Research Journal*, (22), 103–123. doi:10.26817/16925777.1001

Köroğlu, Z. Ç., & Öz, G. (2023). Preservice English teachers' speaking skills assessment literacy: Transformation to digital assessment. *The Reading Matrix: An International Online Journal, 23*(1), 1–17.

Korosidou, E., & Bratitsis, T. (2019). Infusing multimodal tools and digital storytelling in developing vocabulary and intercultural communicative awareness of young EFL learners. *Lecture Notes in Computer Science, 11899*, 191–200. doi:10.1007/978-3-030-34350-7_19

Krashen, S. (1985). *The Input Hypothesis Issues and Implications.* Longman.

Kruk, M. A. R. I. U. S. Z. (2022). *Investigating dynamic relationships among individual difference variables in learning... English as a foreign language in a virtual world.* SPRINGER.

Kucirkova, N. (2019). Children's Reading with Digital Books: Past Moving Quickly to the Future. *Child Development Perspectives, 13*(4), 208–214. doi:10.1111/cdep.12339

Kuhail, M. A., Alturki, N., Alramlawi, S., & Alhejori, K. (2023). Interacting with educational chatbots: A systematic review. *Education and Information Technologies, 28*(1), 973–1018. doi:10.100710639-022-11177-3

Kukulska-Hulme. A., Lee, H., & Norris, L. (2017). Mobile Learning Revolution: Implications for Language Pedagogy. In Carol A. Chapelle & Shannon Sauro (Eds.), The handbook of technology and second language teaching and learning. John Wiley & Sons, Inc.

Kukulska-Hulme, A., & Shield, L. (2008). An overview of mobile-assisted language learning: From content delivery to supported collaboration and interaction. *ReCALL, 20*(3), 271–289. doi:10.1017/S0958344008000335

Compilation of References

Kuleto, V., Ilić, M., Dumangiu, M., Ranković, M., Martins, O. M., Păun, D., & Mihoreanu, L. (2021). Exploring opportunities and challenges of artificial intelligence and machine learning in higher education institutions. *Sustainability (Basel)*, *13*(18), 10424. doi:10.3390u131810424

Kulikowski, K., Przytuła, S., & Sułkowski, Ł. (2022). E-learning? Never again! On the unintended consequences of COVID-19 forced e-learning on academic teacher motivational job characteristics. *Higher Education Quarterly*, *76*(1), 174–189. doi:10.1111/hequ.12314

Kumar, A. H. (2023). Analysis of ChatGPT tool to assess the potential of its utility for academic writing in biomedical domain. *Biology, Engineering, Medicine and Science Reports*, *9*(1), 24–30. doi:10.5530/bems.9.1.5

Kushmar, L. V., Vornachev, A. O., Korobova, I. O., & Kaida, N. O. (2022). Artificial intelligence in language learning: What are we afraid of. *Arab World English Journal (AWEJ)*, (8), 262–273. doi:10.24093/awej/call8.18

Kwangsawad, T. (2016). Examining EFL pre-service teachers' TPACK trough self-report, lesson plans and actual practice. *Journal of Education and Learning*, *10*(2), 103–108. doi:10.11591/edulearn.v10i2.3575

Kyei-Blankson, L., & Godwyll, F. (2010). *An examination of learning outcomes in Hyflex learning environments*. In J. Sanchez & K. Zhang (Eds.), Proceedings of E-Learn 2010--World Conference on E-Learning in Corporate, Government, Healthcare, and Higher Education. Orlando, Florida.

Lai, Y., Saab, N., & Admiraal, W. (2022). Learning Strategies in Self-directed Language Learning Using Mobile Technology in Higher Education: A Systematic Scoping Review. *Education and Information Technologies*, *27*(6), 7749–7780. doi:10.100710639-022-10945-5

Lakhal, S., Bateman, D., & Bédard, J. (2017). Blended synchronous delivery mode in graduate programs: A literature review and its implementation in the master teacher program. *Collected Essays on Learning and Teaching*, *10*, 47–60. doi:10.22329/celt.v10i0.4747

Lancaster, T. (2023). Artificial intelligence, text generation tools and ChatGPT – does digital watermarking offer a solution? *International Journal for Educational Integrity*, *19*(10), 10. Advance online publication. doi:10.100740979-023-00131-6

Latifi, S., & Gierl, M. (2021). Automated scoring of junior and senior high essays using Coh-Metrix features: Implications for large-scale language testing. *Language Testing*, *38*(1), 62–85. doi:10.1177/0265532220929918

Laufer, B., & Hulstijn, J. (2001). Incidental vocabulary acquisition in a second language: The construct of task-induced involvement. *Applied Linguistics*, *22*(1), 1–26. doi:10.1093/applin/22.1.1

Lavidas, K., Achriani, A., Athanassopoulos, S., Messinis, I., & Kotsiantis, S. (2020). University students' intention to use search engines for research purposes: A structural equation modeling approach. *Education and Information Technologies*, *25*(4), 2463–2479. doi:10.100710639-019-10071-9

Lee, F. L. M., Yeung, A. S., Tracey, D., & Barker, K. (2015). Inclusion of children with special needs in early childhood education: What teacher characteristics matter. *Topics in Early Childhood Special Education, 35*(2), 79–88. doi:10.1177/0271121414566014

Lee, H., & Hwang, Y. (2022). Technology-enhanced education through VR-making and metaverse-linking to foster teacher readiness and sustainable learning. *Sustainability (Basel), 14*(8), 4786. doi:10.3390u14084786

Lee, J. J., & Hammer, J. (2011). Gamification in education: What, how, why bother? *Academic Exchange Quarterly, 15*(2), 146. https://www.researchgate.net/publication/258697764_Gamification_in_Education_What_How_Why_Bother

Lee, J. S., & Lee, K. (2020). The role of informal digital learning of English and L2 motivational self system in foreign language enjoyment. *British Journal of Educational Technology, 52*(1), 358–373. doi:10.1111/bjet.12955

Leighton, J. P., & Gierl, M. J. (2007). Cognitive diagnostic assessment for education. In J. P. Leighton & M. J. Gierl (Eds.), *Why cognitive diagnostic assessment?* (pp. 3–18). Cambridge University. doi:10.1017/CBO9780511611186.001

Leoste, J., Tammets, K., & Ley, T. (2019). Co-creating learning designs in professional teacher education: knowledge appropriation in the teacher's innovation laboratory. *Adopting and Sustaining Technological Innovations in Teachers' Classroom Practices–The Case of Integrating Educational Robots into Math Classes, 89.*

Leoste, J., Tammets, K., & Ley, T. (2019). Co-creating learning designs in professional teacher education: Knowledge appropriation in the teacher's innovation laboratory. Interaction Deisgn and Architecture(s). *Journal, 42*, 131–163.

Li, L., Ma, Z., Fan, L., Lee, S., Yu, L., & Hemphill, L. (2023). *ChatGPT in education: A discourse analysis of worries and concerns on social media.* arXiv, https://doi.org//arXiv.2305.02201 doi:10.48550

Li, X. (2020). *The Effects of Enhanced E-Books on Young Children's Story Comprehension and Vocabulary Growth.* [Unpublished Doctoral Dissertation, University of Houston].

Libasin, Z., Azudin, R. A., Idris, M. A., Rahman, M. S. A., & Umar, N. (2021). Comparison of students' academic performance in mathematics course with synchronous and asynchronous online learning environments during Covid-19 crisis. *International Journal of Academic Research in Progressive Education and Development, 10*(2), 492–501. doi:10.6007/IJARPED/v10-i2/10131

Liebrenz, M., Schleifer, R., Buadze, A., Bhugra, D., & Smith, A. (2023). Generating scholarly content with ChatGPT: Ethical challenges for medical publishing. *The Lancet. Digital Health, 5*(3), 105–106. doi:10.1016/S2589-7500(23)00019-5 PMID:36754725

Compilation of References

Li, H. H., & Zhang, L. J. (2021). Effects of structured small-group student talk as collaborative prewriting discussions on Chinese University EFL students' individual writing: A quasi-experimental study. *PLoS One*, *16*(5), e0251569. Advance online publication. doi:10.1371/journal.pone.0251569 PMID:34048435

Li, J. (2009). The Evolution of Vocabulary Learning Strategies in a Computer-Mediated Reading Environment. *CALICO Journal*, *27*(1), 118–146. doi:10.11139/cj.27.1.118-146

Li, M., Wang, Y., & Xu, Y. Q. (2022). Computing for Chinese cultural heritage. *Visual Informatics*, *6*(1), 1–13. doi:10.1016/j.visinf.2021.12.006 PMID:36312746

Lincoln, Y. S., & Guba, E. G. (1985). Naturalistic inquiry. *Sage (Atlanta, Ga.)*.

Ling V. Sotnikova L. Rodionova I. Vasilets I. Zavjalova O. Fedorovskaya V. Datkova E. (2020). Online educational resources for students and digital barrier. *TEM Journal, 9*(1), 373-379. doi:10.18421/TEM91-51

Lin, M. P.-C., & Chang, D. (2020). Enhancing post-secondary writers' writing skills with a chatbot: A mixed-method classroom study. *Journal of Educational Technology & Society*, *23*(1), 78–92. doi:10.30191/ETS.202001_23(1).0006

Lin, P., Wooders, A., Wang, J., & Yuan, W. (2018). Artificial intelligence, the missing piece of online education? *IEEE Engineering Management Review*, *46*(3), 25–28. doi:10.1109/EMR.2018.2868068

Lister, M. (2015). Gamification: The effect on student motivation and performance at the post-secondary level. *Issues and Trends in Educational Technology*, *3*(2). Advance online publication. doi:10.2458/azu_itet_v3i2_lister

Li, T., & Liu, Z. (2021). Exploring effects of the Second Language Motivational Self System on chinese EFL learners' willingness to communicate in English and implications for L2 education. *Journal of Higher Education Research*, *2*(4). Advance online publication. doi:10.32629/jher.v2i4.404

Litman, D., Strik, H., & Lim, G. S. (2018). Speech technologies and the assessment of second language speaking: Approaches, challenges, and opportunities. *Language Assessment Quarterly*, *15*(3), 294–309. doi:10.1080/15434303.2018.1472265

Little, D. (2007). Reconstructing learner and teacher autonomy in language education. In Reconstructing autonomy in language education: Inquiry and Innovation (pp. 1-13). Palgrave Macmillan.

Little, D. (1991). *Learner autonomy 1: Definitions, issues and problems*. Authentik.

Little, D. (1994). Learner autonomy: A theoretical construct and its practical application. *Die Neuere Sprache*, *93*(5), 430–442.

Little, D. (1995). Learning as dialogue: The dependence of learner autonomy on teacher autonomy. *System*, *23*(2), 175–182. doi:10.1016/0346-251X(95)00006-6

Little, D. (1996). Learner autonomy: Some steps in the evolution of theory and practice. *Irish Association for Applied Linguistics, 16*, 1–13.

Little, D. (2007). Language Learner Autonomy: Some Fundamental Considerations Revisited. *Innovation in Language Learning and Teaching, 1*(1), 14–29. doi:10.2167/illt040.0

Little, D. (2009). Language learner autonomy and the European Language Portfolio: Two L2 English examples. *Language Teaching, 42*(2), 222–233. doi:10.1017/S0261444808005636

Littlewood, W. (1997). Self-access: Why do we want it and what can it do? In P. Benson & P. Voller (Eds.), *Autonomy and independence in language learning içinde* (pp. 79–92). Longman.

Liu, M. (2022). Exploring the motivation-engagement link: The moderating role of positive emotion. *Journal for the Psychology of Language Learning, 4*(1), 1–18. doi:10.52598/jpll/4/1/3

Liu, M., McKelroy, E., Winzeler, E., Adams, D., Davis, P., Ziai, K., & Roberts, R. (2014). *Exploration of best practices to support active learning in a synchronous multi-site learning environment.* In T. Bastiaens (Ed.), *Proceedings of World Conference on E-Learning.* New Orleans, LA, USA.

Liu, Z. Y., Lomovtseva, N., & Korobeynikova, E. (2020). Online learning platforms: Reconstructing modern higher education. *International Journal of Emerging Technologies in Learning, 15*(13), 4–21. doi:10.3991/ijet.v15i13.14645

Li, X., & Bus, G. A. (2023). Efficacy of digital picture book enhancements grounded in multimedia learning principles: Dependent on age? *Learning and Instruction, 85*, 1–9. doi:10.1016/j.learninstruc.2023.101749

Lo, C. K. (2023). What is the impact of ChatGPT on education? A rapid review of the literature. *Education Sciences, 13*(4), 410. doi:10.3390/educsci13040410

Luckin, R., Holmes, W., Griffiths, M., & Forcier, L. B. (2016). *Intelligence unleashed: An argument for AI in education.* Pearson London.

Luo, T., & Clifton, L. (2017). Examining collaborative knowledge construction in microblogging-based learning environments. *Journal of Information Technology Education, 16*, 365–390. doi:10.28945/3869

Lyu, Y. (2019). *Using Gamification and Augmented Reality to Encourage Japanese Second Language Students to Speak English.* Retrieved from https://www.diva-portal.org/smash/record.jsf?pid=diva2%3A1416017&dswid=2225

MacDonald, J. (2006). *Blended learning and online tutoring: a good practice guide.* Gower.

Mackey, A. (2012). *Input, interaction, and corrective feedback in L2 learning.* Oxford University Press.

Madsen, H. (1986). Evaluating a computer-adaptive ESL placement test. *CALICO Journal, 4*(2), 41–50. doi:10.1558/cj.v4i2.41-50

Compilation of References

Mageira, K., Pittou, D., Papasalouros, A., Kotis, K., Zangogianni, P., & Daradoumis, A. (2022). Educational AI chatbots for content and language integrated learning. *Applied Sciences (Basel, Switzerland)*, *12*(7), 3239. Advance online publication. doi:10.3390/app12073239

Mahmud, M. M. (2018). Technology and language–what works and what does not: A meta-analysis of blended learning research. *The Journal of AsiaTEFL, 15*(2), 365-382. https://doi.org/.365 doi:10.18823/asiatefl.2018.15.2.1

Malczyk, B. R. (2020). *Introducing social work to HyFlex blended learning: a student-centered approach*. Routledge.

Mallik, S., & Gangopadhyay, A. (2023). Proactive and reactive engagement of artificial intelligence methods for education: A review. *Frontiers in Artificial Intelligence*, *6*, 1151391. doi:10.3389/frai.2023.1151391 PMID:37215064

Mantooth, R., Usher, E. L., & Love, A. M. (2021). Changing classrooms bring new questions: Environmental influences, self-efficacy, and academic achievement. *Learning Environments Research*, *24*(3), 519–535. doi:10.100710984-020-09341-y

Marion, T. (2008). The effect of gestures on second language memorization by young children. *Gesture. John Benjamins Publishing*, *8*(2), 219–235.

Marshall, G., & Cox, M. (2008). Research methods: Their design, applicability and reliability. In J. Voogt & G. Knezek (Eds.), *International handbook of information technology in primary and secondary education* (pp. 983–987). Springer. doi:10.1007/978-0-387-73315-9_62

Mayer, R. E. (2003). The promise of multimedia learning: Using the same instructional design methods across different media. *Learning and Instruction*, *13*(2), 125–139. doi:10.1016/S0959-4752(02)00016-6

Mayer, R. E. (2014). Principles for managing essential processing in multimedia learning: Segmenting, pretraining, and modality principles. In R. E. Mayer (Ed.), *The Cambridge handbook of multimedia learning* (pp. 169–182). Cambridge University. doi:10.1017/CBO9781139547369.016

Mazhar, B. A. L. (2019). Use of digital games in writing education: An action research on gamification. *Contemporary Educational Technology*, *10*(3), 246–271. doi:10.30935/cet.590005

McClean, S., & Crowe, W. (2017). Making room for interactivity: Using the cloud-based audience response system Nearpod to enhance engagement in lectures. *FEMS Microbiology Letters*, *364*(6), 1–7. doi:10.1093/femsle/fnx052 PMID:28333274

McGee, P., & Reis, A. (2012). Blended course design: A synthesis of best practices. *Online Learning : the Official Journal of the Online Learning Consortium*, *16*(4), 7–22. doi:10.24059/olj.v16i4.239

McHugh, M. L. (2012). Interrater reliability: The kappa statistic. *Biochemia Medica*, *22*(3), 276–282. doi:10.11613/BM.2012.031 PMID:23092060

McKnight, L., & Hicks, T. (2023). Generative AI writing tools: How they work, what they do, and why they matter. In R. E. Ferdig, R. Hartshorne, E. Baumgartner, R. Kaplan-Rakowski, & C. Mouza (Eds.), What PreK-12 teachers should know about educational technology in 2023: A research-to-practice anthology, (pp. 117-121). AACE2023.

Meishar-Tal, H. (2015). Teachers' use of Wikipedia with their Students. *The Australian Journal of Teacher Education*, *40*(12), 126–140. doi:10.14221/ajte.2015v40n12.9

Mhlanga, D. (2023). Open AI in education, the responsible and ethical use of ChatGPT towards lifelong learning. SSRN *Electronic Journal*. https://doi.org/ doi:10.2139/SSRN.4354422

Miles, M. B., & Huberman, A. M. (1994). Qualitative tata analysis: An expanded sourcebook. *Sage (Atlanta, Ga.)*.

Miller, J., Risser, M., & Griffiths, R. (2013). Student choice, instructor flexibility: moving beyond the blended instructional model. *Issues and trends in educational technology, 1*(1), 8-24.

Miller, A. N., Sellnow, D. D., & Strawser, M. G. (2021). Pandemic pedagogy challenges and opportunities: Instruction communication in remote, HyFlex, and BlendFlex courses. *Communication Education*, *70*(2), 202–204. doi:10.1080/03634523.2020.1857418

Mishra, P., & Koehler, M. J. (2006). Technological pedagogical content knowledge: A new framework for teacher knowledge. *Teachers College Record*, *108*(6), 1017–1054. doi:10.1111/j.1467-9620.2006.00684.x

Mitchell, K. M., McMillan, D. E., & Rabbani, R. (2019). An exploration of writing self-efficacy and writing self-regulatory behaviours in undergraduate writing. *The Canadian Journal for the Scholarship of Teaching and Learning*, *10*(2), 1–25. doi:10.5206/cjsotl-rcacea.2019.2.8175

Mitchell, T., & Shachter, J. (2021). The Effects of Gamified Instruction on Japanese English Language Learner Vocabulary Recall. *Language Education and Research Center Journal*, *16*, 54–75.

Montag, J. L. (2019). Differences in sentence complexity in the text of children's picture books and child-directed speech. *First Language*, *39*(5), 527–546. doi:10.1177/0142723719849996 PMID:31564759

Montag, J. L., Jones, M. N., & Smith, L. B. (2015). The words children hear: Picture books and the statistics for language learning. *Psychological Science*, *26*(9), 1489–1496. doi:10.1177/0956797615594361 PMID:26243292

Moore, M. G. (1993). Theory of transactional distance. In Theoretical Principle of Distance Education. Routledge.

Moore, M. (1997). *Theoretical Principles of Distance Education*. Routledge. http://www.c3l.uni-oldenburg.de/cde/found/moore93.pdf

Moore, M. G. (1972). Learner autonomy: The second dimension of independent learning. *Convergence (Toronto)*, *5*(2), 76–88.

Moore, M. G. (1986). Self-directed learning and distance education. *Journal of Distance Education, 1*(1), 7–24.

Moore, M. G. (1994). Autonomy and interdependence. *American Journal of Distance Education, 8*(2), 1–5. doi:10.1080/08923649409526851

Moore, M., & Greg, K. (1996). *Distance education: A systems view.* Wadsworth Publishing Company.

Morera, L. S., Antonio, A. A., & Laura, G. H. (2012). Analysis of Online Quizzes as a Teaching and assessment tool. *Journal of Technology and Science Education, 2*(1), 39–45.

Morrow, K. (1977). Authentic texts in ESP. *English for Specific Purposes,* 13–17.

Mouza, C., Karchmer-Klein, R., Nandakumar, R., Yilmaz Ozden, S., & Hu, L. (2014). Investigating the impact of an integrated approach to the development of preservice teachers' technological pedagogical content knowledge (TPACK). *Computers & Education, 71,* 206–221. doi:10.1016/j.compedu.2013.09.020

Mylnikova, S. (2022). A unity of obucheniye and vospitaniye: An unexplored unity in Vygotskian Zone of Proximal Development. *Pakistan Social Sciences Review, 2*(6). Advance online publication. doi:10.35484/pssr.2022(6-II)70

Nada, M. A. L. (2021). Vlogging towards improving students' speaking skills. [IJRD]. *EPRA International Journal of Research and Development, 6*(7), 711–722. doi:10.36713/epra2016

Nah, F. F. H., Zeng, Q., Telaprolu, V. R., Ayyappa, A. P., & Eschenbrenner, B. (2014). Gamification of education: a review of literature. In *HCI in Business: First International Conference, HCIB 2014, Held as Part of HCI International 2014, Heraklion, Crete, Greece, June 22-27, 2014. Proceedings I* (pp. 401-409). Springer International Publishing. 10.1007/978-3-319-07293-7_39

Nahmod, D. M. (2017). *Vocabulary gamification vs traditional learning instruction in an inclusive high school classroom.* Rowan University.

Nation, I. S. (2001). *Learning vocabulary in another language.* Ernst Klett Sprachen. doi:10.1017/CBO9781139524759

Navarrate, C. (1990). *Informal assessment in educational evaluation: Implications for bilingual education programs.* Educational Resources Information Center.

Neri, A., Mich, O., Gerosa, M., & Giuliani, D. (2008). The effectiveness of computer assisted pronunciation training for foreign language learning by children. *Computer Assisted Language Learning, 21*(5), 393–408. doi:10.1080/09588220802447651

Ngah, E., Fauzi, W. J., Radzuan, N. R. M., Abdullah, H., Ali, A. Z. M., Abidin, N. A. Z., & Fadzillah, F. I. M. (2022). Snapticon: Developing Effective Listening Skills for Group Oral Discussion. *Asian Journal of University Education, 18*(2), 361–374. doi:10.24191/ajue.v18i2.17991

Nguyen, T. T. H. (2023). EFL teachers' perspectives toward the use of ChatGPT in writing classes: A case study at Van Lang University. *International Journal of Language Instruction*, 2(3), 1–47. doi:10.54855/ijli.23231

Nicholson, S. (2015). A recipe for meaningful gamification. *Gamification in Education and Business*, 1–20. doi:10.1007/978-3-319-10208-5_1

Niess, M. L. (2005). Preparing teachers to teach science and mathematics with technology: Developing a technology pedagogical content knowledge. *Teaching and Teacher Education*, 21(5), 509–523. doi:10.1016/j.tate.2005.03.006

Noels, K. A., Pelletier, L. G., Clément, R., & Vallerand, R. J. (2003). Why are you learning a second language? motivational orientations and self-determination theory. *Language Learning*, 53(S1), 33–64. doi:10.1111/1467-9922.53223

Nunan, D. (1997). Designing and adapting materials to encourage learner autonomy. In Autonomy and independence in language learning içinde (pp. 192-203). Longman.

Nunan, D. (2000). *Seven hypotheses about language teaching and learning*. Plenary presentation, TESOL Convention, Vancouver, Canada.

Nunan, D. (2004). *Nine steps to learner autonomy: Plenary speech*. Shantou University. 13Mart2004.www.nunan.info/presentations/steps_learner_autonomy_files/frame.htm

Nunan, D., & Carter, R. (2001). *The Cambridge guide to teaching English to speakers of other languages*. Ernst Klett Sprachen.

Nye, B. D. (2015). Intelligent tutoring systems by and for the developing world: A review of trends and approaches for educational technology in a global context. *International Journal of Artificial Intelligence in Education*, 25(2), 177–203. doi:10.100740593-014-0028-6

Oakley, G., & Jay, J. (2008). Making time for reading: Factors that influence the success of multimedia reading at home. *The Reading Teacher*, 62(3), 246–255. doi:10.1598/RT.62.3.6

Oda Abunamous, M., Boudouaia, A., Jebril, M., Diafi, S., & Zreik, M. (2022). The decay of traditional education: A case study under covid-19. *Cogent Education*, 9(1), 2082116. doi:10.1 080/2331186X.2022.2082116

OECD. (2005). *Teachers matter: Attracting, developing and retaining effective teachers*. https://www.oecd.org/education/school/34990905.pdf

Oh, M. K. (2002). *Four Korean adult learners' ESL learning beliefs and learner autonomy* [Unpublished doctoral dissertation]. Faculty of the Graduate School of State University of New York at Buffalo.

Onwuegbuzie, A. J. (2016). *Seven steps to a comprehensive literature review. A multimodal and cultural approach*. SAGE Publications.

Compilation of References

Ottenbreit-Leftwich, A., Glazewski, K., Newby, T., & Ermer, P. (2010). Teacher value beliefs associated with using technology: Addressing professional and student needs. *Computers & Education*, 55(3), 1321–1335. doi:10.1016/j.compedu.2010.06.002

Oxford, R. L. (2001). Language learning strategies. In The Cambridge guide to teaching English to speakers of other languages (pp. 166-172). Cambridge University.

Oxford, R. L. (1990). *Language learning strategies: What every teacher should know*. Heinle & Heinle.

Oxford, R. L. (2011). *Teaching and researching language learning strategies*. Pearson Longman.

Öz, G., & Köroğlu, Ç. Z. (2023). English language teachers' assessment procedure during covid19 pandemic: challenges and solutions. *i-manager's Journal on English Language Teaching, 13*(1), 42-53. doi:10.26634/jelt.13.1.19058

Özçelik, A. E., & Gündüz, Z. E. (2023). Embracing ChatGPT in foreign language writing classes: Potentials and challenges. In R. E. Ferdig, R. Hartshorne, E. Baumgartner, R. Kaplan-Rakowski, & C. Mouza (Eds.), What PreK-12 teachers should know about educational technology in 2023: A research-to-practice anthology (pp. 133-143). AACE2023.

Öz, G., & Şahinkarakaş, Ş. (2023). The relationship between Turkish EFL learners' academic resilience and English language achievement. *The Reading Matrix: An International Online Journal*, 23(1), 80–91.

Page, E. B. (1966). The imminence of grading essays by computers. *Phi Delta Kappan, 47*, 238–243.

Paivio, A. (2007). *Mind and its evolution: A dual coding theoretical approach. Mind and its evolution: A dual coding theoretical approach*. Lawrence Erlbaum Associates Publishers., doi:10.4324/9781315785233

Panigrahi, C., & Joshi, V. (2020). Use of artificial intelligence in education. *The Management Accountant Journal*, 55(5), 64–67. doi:10.33516/maj.v55i5.64-67p

Paré, G., & Kitsiou, S. (2017). *Methods for literature reviews. In Handbook of eHealth Evaluation: An Evidence-based Approach*. University of Victoria.

Park, H., Burke, J. D., Blin, V., & Chrysanthou, H. (2020). Improving memory recall and measuring user ability through gamified techniques with 'chatty': An E-learning application for foreign languages. *Cross-Cultural Design. Applications in Health, Learning, Communication, and Creativity*, 349–366. doi:10.1007/978-3-030-49913-6_30

Park, Y. J., & Bonk, C. J. (2007). Is online life a breeze? A case study for promoting synchronous learning. *Journal of Online Learning and Teaching*, 3(3), 307–323.

Parrish, A., & Lanvers, U. (2018). Student motivation, school policy choices and Modern Language Study in England. *Language Learning Journal*, 47(3), 281–298. doi:10.1080/09571 736.2018.1508305

Pathan, M. M. (2012). Computer Assisted Language Testing [CALT]: Advantages, implications and limitations. *Research Vistas*, *1*, 30–45.

Pearman, C. J., & Lefever-Davis, S. (2006). Supporting the essential elements with CD-ROM storybooks. *Reading Horizons*, *46*(4), 301–313. doi:10.1598/RT.61.8.1

Pemberton, R., Toogood, S., & Barfield, A. (2009). *Maintaining control: Autonomy and language learning*. Hong Kong University. doi:10.5790/hongkong/9789622099234.001.0001

Penno, J. F., Wilkinson, I. A. G., & Moore, D. W. (2002). Vocabulary acquisition from teacher explanation and repeated listening to stories: Do they overcome the Matthew effect? *Journal of Educational Psychology*, *94*(1), 23–33. doi:10.1037/0022-0663.94.1.23

Perkins, D. (1994). *The intelligent eye: learning to think by looking at art*. Harvard Graduate School of Education.

Petersen, G. B., Petkakis, G., & Makransky, G. (2022). A study of how immersion and Interactivity Drive VR Learning. *Computers & Education*, *179*, 104429. doi:10.1016/j.compedu.2021.104429

Petrović, J., & Jovanović, M. (2021). The role of chatbots in foreign language learning: the present situation and the future outlook. In E. Pap (Ed.), *Artificial Intelligence: Theory and Applications. Studies in Computational Intelligence, 973*. Springer. doi:10.1007/978-3-030-72711-6_17

Pinto, R. D., Peixoto, B., Melo, M., Cabral, L., & Bessa, M. (2021). Foreign language learning gamification using virtual reality—A systematic review of empirical research. *Education Sciences*, *11*(5), 222. doi:10.3390/educsci11050222

Pitoyo, M. D., & Asib, A. (2019). Gamification Based assessment: A Test Anxiety Reduction through Game Elements in Quizizz Platform. *International Online Journal of Education & Teaching*, *6*(3), 456–471.

Plews, R. C. (2017). Self-direction in online learning: The student experience. *International Journal of Self-Directed Learning*, *14*(1), 37–57.

Pokrivcakova, S. (2019). Preparing teachers for the application of AI-powered technologies in foreign language education. *Journal of Language and Cultural Education*, *7*(3), 135–153. doi:10.2478/jolace-2019-0025

Popescu, C. N., Attie, E., & Chadouteau, L. (2022). Gamified learning. *Advances in Human and Social Aspects of Technology*, 97–131. doi:10.4018/978-1-7998-8089-9.ch006

Prados Sánchez, G., Cózar-Gutiérrez, R., del Olmo-Muñoz, J., & González-Calero, J. A. (2021). Impact of a gamified platform in the promotion of reading comprehension and attitudes towards reading in primary education. *Computer Assisted Language Learning*, 1–25. doi:10.1080/0958 8221.2021.1939388

Pratama, G. A. (2020). Students perception of gamification to promote classroom engagement and motivation in senior high school. *Language Research Society*, *1*(1). Advance online publication. doi:10.33021/lrs.v1i1.1040

Compilation of References

Pratiwi, D. I., & Ubaedillah, U. (2021). Digital vocabulary class in English for railway mechanical technology. *Teaching English with Technology*, *21*(3), 67–88.

Prestridge, S. (2012). The beliefs behind the teacher that influences their ICT practices. *Computers & Education*, *58*(1), 449–458. doi:10.1016/j.compedu.2011.08.028

Pujolà, J.-T., & Appel, C. (2022). Gamification for technology-enhanced language teaching and learning. *Research Anthology on Developments in Gamification and Game-Based Learning*, 992–1010. doi:10.4018/978-1-6684-3710-0.ch045

Purgina, M., Mozgovoy, M., & Blake, J. (2019). WordBricks: Mobile Technology and visual grammar formalism for gamification of Natural Language Grammar Acquisition. *Journal of Educational Computing Research*, *58*(1), 126–159. doi:10.1177/0735633119833010

Putra, F. W., Rangka, I. B., Aminah, S., & Aditama, M. H. R. (2023). ChatGPT in the higher education environment: Perspectives from the theory of high order thinking skills. *Journal of Public Health (Oxford, England)*, *45*(4), fdad120. Advance online publication. doi:10.1093/pubmed/fdad120 PMID:37455540

Putri, E., & Sari, F. M. (2020). Indonesian EFL students' perspectives towards Learning Management System Software. *Journal of English Language Teaching and Learning*, *1*(1), 20–24. doi:10.33365/jeltl.v1i1.244

Qian, K., Owen, N., & Bax, S. (2018). Researching mobile-assisted Chinese-character learning strategies among adult distance learners. *Innovation in Language Learning and Teaching*, *12*(1), 56–71. doi:10.1080/17501229.2018.1418633

Raes, A., Detienne, L., Windey, I., & Depaepe, F. (2020). A systematic literature review on synchronous hybrid learning: Gaps identified. *Learning Environments Research*, *23*(3), 269–290. doi:10.100710984-019-09303-z

Raes, A., Pieters, M., & Bonte, P. (2019). *Hyflex Learning within the Master of Teaching Program@ KU Leuven*. EdTech Books.

Rahmani, E. F. (2020). The benefits of gamification in the English Learning Context. *IJEE*, *7*(1), 32–47. doi:10.15408/ijee.v7i1.17054

Rajendran, T., Bin Naaim, N. A., & Yunus, M. M. (2019). Pupils motivation and perceptions towards learning English using quizvaganza. *International Journal of Scientific and Research Publications*, *9*(1), p8529. Advance online publication. doi:10.29322/IJSRP.9.01.2019.p8529

Reinders, H. (2017). Digital Games and Second language learning. *Language. Educational Technology*, 329–343. doi:10.1007/978-3-319-02237-6_26

Reinhardt, J. (2019). *Gameful second and foreign language teaching and learning: Theory, research, and Practice*. Palgrave Macmillan. doi:10.1007/978-3-030-04729-0

Reitz, L., Sohny, A., & Lochmann, G. (2019). VR-based gamification of Communication Training and Oral Examination in a Second language. *Computer Assisted Language Learning*, 811–828. doi:10.4018/978-1-5225-7663-1.ch038

Richards, J., & Farrell, T. (2009). *Professional development for language teachers.* Cambridge University.

Richardson, M., & Clesham, R. (2021). Rise of the machines? The evolving role of AI technologies in high-stakes assessment. *London Review of Education*, *19*(1), 1–13. doi:10.14324/LRE.19.1.09

Richardson, V. (2003). Preservice teachers' beliefs. In J. Rath & A. C. McAninch (Eds.), *Advances in Teacher Education Series* (Vol. 6, pp. 1–22). Information Age.

Richter, A., & Courage, M. L. (2017, January). Comparing electronic and paper storybooks for preschoolers: Attention, engagement, and recall. *Journal of Applied Developmental Psychology*, *48*, 92–102. doi:10.1016/j.appdev.2017.01.002

Rofiah, N. L., & Waluyo, B. (2020). Using socrative for vocabulary tests: Thai EFL learner acceptance and perceived risk of cheating. *Journal of Asia TEFL*, *17*(3), 966–982. doi:10.18823/asiatefl.2020.17.3.14.966

Roll, I., & Wylie, R. (2016). Evolution and revolution in artificial intelligence in education. *International Journal of Artificial Intelligence in Education*, *26*(2), 582–599. doi:10.100740593-016-0110-3

Romero, H. Y., Chávez, N. V., & Gutiérrez, I. M. (2016). *HyFlex, hybrid and flexible model for university education: case study: Universidad Técnica Particular de Loja—Ecuador. 11th Iberian Conference on Information Systems and Technologies (CISTI)*, Gran Canaria, Spain. 10.1109/CISTI.2016.7521455

Romero-Hall, E., & Ripine, C. (2021). Hybrid flexible instruction: Exploring faculty preparedness. *Online Learning : the Official Journal of the Online Learning Consortium*, *25*(3), 289–312. doi:10.24059/olj.v25i3.2426

Ronfeldt, M., Farmer, S. O., McQueen, K., & Grissom, J. A. (2015). Teacher collaboration in instructional teams and student achievement. *American Educational Research Journal*, *52*(3), 475–514. doi:10.3102/0002831215585562

Roshandel, J., Ghonsooly, B., & Ghanizadeh, A. (2018). L2 motivational self-system and self-efficacy: A quantitative survey-based study. *International Journal of Instruction*, *11*(1), 329–344. doi:10.12973/iji.2018.11123a

Rospigliosi, P. (2023). Artificial intelligence in teaching and learning: What questions should we ask of ChatGPT? *Interactive Learning Environments*, *31*(1), 1–3. doi:10.1080/10494820.2023.2180191

Rubegni, E., Dore, R., Landoni, M., & Kan, L. (2021). "The girl who wants to fly": Exploring the role of digital technology in enhancing dialogic reading. *International Journal of Child-Computer Interaction*, *30*, 100239. doi:10.1016/j.ijcci.2020.100239

Compilation of References

Rudolph, J., Tan, S., & Tan, S. (2023). ChatGPT: Bullshit spewer or the end of traditional assessments in higher education? *Journal of Applied Learning and Teaching*, *6*(1). Advance online publication. doi:10.37074/jalt.2023.6.1.9

Rueckert, D., Pico, K., Kim, D., & Calero Sánchez, X. (2020). Gamifying the foreign language classroom for brain-friendly learning. *Foreign Language Annals*, *53*(4), 686–703. doi:10.1111/flan.12490

Rusandi, M. A., Ipah Saripah, A., Yunika, D., & Mutmainnah, K. (2023). No worries with ChatGPT: Building bridges between artificial intelligence and education with critical thinking soft skills. *Journal of Public Health (Oxford, England)*, *45*(3), e602–e603. doi:10.1093/pubmed/fdad049 PMID:37099761

Ryan, E. L., & Deci, R. M. (2017). *Self-determination theory. In Basic psychological needs in motivation, development, and wellness*. Guilford Press. doi:10.1521/978.14625/28806

Sadaghian, S., & Marandi, S. (2021). Fostering language learner autonomy through interdependence: The power of Wikis. *Turkish Online Journal of Distance Education*, *22*(1), 194–208. doi:10.17718/tojde.849907

Šafranj, J., & Zivlak, J. (2019). Effects of big five personality traits and fear of negative evaluation on Foreign Language Anxiety. *Croatian Journal of Education - Hrvatski Časopis Za Odgoj i Obrazovanje, 21*(1). doi:10.15516/cje.v21i1.2942

Salehi, S., Du, J. T., & Ashman, H. (2018). Use of Web search engines and personalization in information searching for educational purposes. *Information Research*, *23*(2), 1–13.

Salemink, E., de Jong, S. R. C., Notebaert, L., MacLeod, C., & Van Bockstaele, B. (2022). Gamification of cognitive bias modification for interpretations in anxiety increases training engagement and enjoyment. *Journal of Behavior Therapy and Experimental Psychiatry*, *76*, 101727. doi:10.1016/j.jbtep.2022.101727 PMID:35217211

Samuel, J. C., Rosenzweig, A. H., McLean, M., & Cintrón, R. (2019). *One size fits none. Beatty BJ. Hybrid-Flexible Course Design: Implementing Student-Directed Hybrid Classes*. EdTech Books.

Santoro, L. E., Chard, D. J., Howard, L., & Baker, S. K. (2008). Making the very most of classroom read-alouds to promote comprehension and vocabulary. *The Reading Teacher*, *61*(5), 396–408. doi:10.1598/RT.61.5.4

Santos, M. E. C., Lübke, A. I. W., Taketomi, T., Yamamoto, G., Rodrigo, M. M. T., Sandor, C., & Kato, H. (2016). Augmented reality as multimedia: The case for situated vocabulary learning. *Research and Practice in Technology Enhanced Learning*, *11*(1), 1–23. doi:10.118641039-016-0028-2 PMID:30613237

Saputro, T. H., Tafsidurun, I. C., & Farah, R. R. (2020). The use of Vlog in improving students' oral language production: A case study. *English Education: Jurnal Tadris Bahasa Inggris 13*(1), 135-158. https://ejournal.radenintan.ac.id/index.php/ENGEDU

Saragih, N. A., Madya, S., Siregar, R. A., & Saragih, W. (2021). Written corrective feedback: Students' perception and preferences. *International Online Journal of Education & Teaching*, *8*(2), 676–690.

Saricaoglu, A. (2015). *A systemic functional perspective on automated writing evaluation: Formative feedback on causal discourse* (Publication No. 3728751) [Doctoral dissertation, Iowa State University]. ProQuest Dissertations Publishing.

Sari, F. M. (2020). Exploring english learners' engagement and their roles in the online language course. *Journal of English Language Teaching and Linguistics*, *5*(3), 349. doi:10.21462/jeltl.v5i3.446

Schmidt, D., Baran, E., Thompson, A., Mishra, P., Koehler, M., & Shin, T. (2009). Technological Pedagogical Content Knowledge (TPACK): The development and validation of an assessment instrument for preservice teachers. *Journal of Research on Technology in Education*, *42*(2), 123–149. doi:10.1080/15391523.2009.10782544

Schmitt, N., & Schmitt, D. (1995). Vocabulary notebooks: Theoretical underpinnings and practical suggestions. *ELT Journal*, *49*(2), 133–143. doi:10.1093/elt/49.2.133

Schulman, L. S. (1987). Knowledge and teaching: Foundations of the new form. *Harvard Educational Review*, *57*(1), 1–23. doi:10.17763/haer.57.1.j463w79r56455411

Schwartz, R. N., & Plass, J. L. (2020). *Types of engagement in learning with games. Handbook of game-based learning*. The MIT Press.

Selwyn, N. (2011). *Education and technology: Key issues and debates*. Continuum International.

Sepasgozar, S. M. (2020). Digital twin and web-based virtual gaming technologies for online education: A case of construction management and engineering. *Applied Sciences (Basel, Switzerland)*, *10*(13), 4678. doi:10.3390/app10134678

Serrano, D. R., Dea-Ayuela, M. A., Gonzalez-Burgos, E., Serrano-Gil, A., & Lalatsa, A. (2019). Technology-enhanced learning in higher education: How to enhance student engagement through blended learning. *European Journal of Education*, *54*(2), 273–286. doi:10.1111/ejed.12330

Sert, N., & Boynuegri, E. (2017). Digital technology use by the students and english teachers and self-directed language learning. *World Journal on Educational Technology: Current Issues.*, *9*(1), 24–34. doi:10.18844/wjet.v9i1.993

Shalizar, R., & Rezaei, A. (2022). Examining the differential effects of focused vs. unfocused ZPD and explicit feedback on Second language writing. *Language Learning Journal*, *51*(3), 359–375. doi:10.1080/09571736.2022.2042366

Shapely, P. (2000). On-line education to develop complex reasoning skills in organic chemistry. *Journal of Asynchronous Learning Networks*, *4*(2), 43–52.

Sharma, R. C. (2022). Reshaping teaching and learning engineering through next-gen learning technologies. *Journal of Online Learning Studies*, *1*(1), 1–8.

Compilation of References

Shedletsky, L. J., & Aitken, J. E. (2001). The paradoxes of online academic work. *Communication Education*, *50*(3), 206–217. doi:10.1080/03634520109379248

Sheera, H., & Yadav, M. (2022). An analytical investigation of flipped classroom to improve Saudi EFL learners' speaking skills: A case study at Applied College. *Arab World English Journal. Special Issue on CALL.*, *8*(8), 274–298. doi:10.24093/awej/call8.19

Sheerin, S. (1997). An exploration of the relationship between self- access and independent learning. In P. Benson & P. Voller (Eds.), *Autonomy and independence in language learning* (pp. 54–65). Longman.

Shelton-Strong, S. J. (2020). Advising in language learning and the support of learners' basic psychological needs: A self-determination theory perspective. *Language Teaching Research*, *26*(5), 963–985. doi:10.1177/1362168820912355

Shermis, M. D. (2014). State-of-the-art automated essay scoring: Competition, results, and future directions from a United States demonstration. *Assessing Writing*, *20*, 53–76. doi:10.1016/j.asw.2013.04.001

Shin, J., & Gierl, M. J. (2021). More efficient processes for creating automated essay scoring frameworks: A demonstration of two algorithms. *Language Testing*, *38*(2), 247–272. doi:10.1177/0265532220937830

Shintani, N., Ellis, R., & Suzuki, W. (2014). Effects of written feedback and revision on learners' accuracy in using two english grammatical structures. *Language Learning*, *64*(1), 103–131. doi:10.1111/lang.12029

Shiri, A. (2023). ChatGPT and academic integrity. SSRN *Electronic Journal.* / doi:10.2139/ssrn.4360052

Shortt, M., Tilak, S., Kuznetcova, I., Martens, B., & Akinkuolie, B. (2021). Gamification in mobile-assisted language learning: A systematic review of Duolingo Literature from public release of 2012 to early 2020. *Computer Assisted Language Learning*, *36*(3), 517–554. doi:10.1080/09588221.2021.1933540

Siemon, D., & Eckardt, L. (2016). Gamification of teaching in higher education. *Progress in IS*, 153–164. doi:10.1007/978-3-319-45557-0_11

Simões, J., Redondo, R. D., & Vilas, A. F. (2013). A Social Gamification Framework for a K-6 learning platform. *Computers in Human Behavior*, *29*(2), 345–353. doi:10.1016/j.chb.2012.06.007

Simonson, M., Smaldino, S., Albright, M., & Zvacek, S. (2006). Teaching and Learning at a Distance (3rd ed.). Pearson Prentice Hall.

Simonson, M. (1999). Equivalency theory and distance education. *TechTrends*, *43*(5), 5–8. doi:10.1007/BF02818157

Simonson, M., & Schlosser, C. (2002). *Distance education: Definition and glossary of terms*. Nova Southeastern University Fischler School of Education and Human Services.

Simpson, O. (2018). *Supporting students in online, open and distance learning*. Routledge.

Singh, H. (2003). Building effective blended learning programs. *Educational Technology, 43*(6), 51–54.

Singh, H. (2021). *Building effective blended learning programs*. IGI Global. doi:10.4018/978-1-7998-7607-6.ch002

Smaldino, S., Lowther, D., & Russell, J. (2008). *Instructional technology and media for learning*. Pearson Prentice Hall.

Smutny, P., & Schreiberova, P. (2020). Chatbot for learning: A review of educational chatbots for the Facebook messenger. *Computers & Education, 151*, 1–11. doi:10.1016/j.compedu.2020.103862

Socrative. (2023). Retrieved from https://www.socrative.com/

Sohail, S. S., Farhat, F., Himeur, Y., Nadeem, M., Madsen, D. O., Singh, Y., Atalla, S., & Mansoor, W. (2023). Decoding ChatGPT: A taxonomy of existing research, current challenges, and possible future directions. *Journal of King Saud University. Computer and Information Sciences, 35*(8), 1–23. doi:10.1016/j.jksuci.2023.101675

Song, L., & Hill, J. R. (2007). A conceptual model for understanding self-directed learning in online environments. *Journal of Interactive Online Learning, 6*(1), 27–41.

Srinivasa, K. G., Kurni, M., & Saritha, K. (2022). Harnessing the Power of AI to Education. In *Learning, Teaching, and Assessment Methods for Contemporary Learners: Pedagogy for the Digital Generation* (pp. 311–342). Springer Nature Singapore. doi:10.1007/978-981-19-6734-4_13

SteissJ.TateT.GrahamS.CruzJ.HebertM.WangJ.MoonY.TsengW.WarschauerM. (2023). Comparing the quality of human and ChatGPT feedback on students' writing. doi:10.35542/osf.io/ty3em

Stevenson, M., & Phakiti, A. (2014). The effects of computer-generated feedback on the quality of writing. *Assessing Writing, 19*, 51–65. doi:10.1016/j.asw.2013.11.007

Stewart, A. R., Harlow, D. B., & DeBacco, K. (2011). Students' experience of synchronous learning in distributed environments. *Distance Education, 32*(3), 357–381. doi:10.1080/0158 7919.2011.610289

Stone, C. (2017). *Opportunity through online learning: improving student access, participation and success in higher education*. NCSHEHE. https://www.ncsehe.edu.au/publications/opportunity-online learningimproving-student-access-participation-success-higher-education/

Strouse, G. A., & Ganea, P. A. (2017). Parent–toddler behavior and language differ when reading electronic and print picture books. *Frontiers in Psychology, 8*, 677. doi:10.3389/fpsyg.2017.00677 PMID:28559858

Sucuoğlu, E. (2023). *Exploring Linguistic Transfer in Bilingual Children through Repeated Digital Picture Book Reading*. [Unpublished master's Thesis, University of Twente Student].

Compilation of References

Sung, Y. T., Chang, K. E., & Yang, J. M. (2015). How effective are mobile devices for language learning? A meta-analysis. *Educational Research Review*, *16*, 68–84. doi:10.1016/j.edurev.2015.09.001

Sun, J. C. Y., & Hsieh, P. H. (2018). Application of a gamified interactive response system to enhance the intrinsic and extrinsic motivation, student engagement, and attention of English learners. *Journal of Educational Technology & Society*, *21*(3), 104–116. https://www.jstor.org/stable/26458511

Sun, T., & Wang, C. (2020). College students' writing self-efficacy and writing self-regulated learning strategies in learning English as a foreign language. *System*, *90*, 102221. doi:10.1016/j.system.2020.102221

Su, Y., Lin, Y., & Lai, C. (2023). Collaborating with ChatGPT in argumentative writing classrooms. *Assessing Writing*, *57*, 1–11. doi:10.1016/j.asw.2023.100752

Swan, K., Garrison, D. R., & Richardson, J. (2009). A constructivist approach to online learning: The community of inquiry framework. In C. R. Payne (Ed.), *Information technology and constructivism in higher education: Progressive learning frameworks*. IGI Global. doi:10.4018/978-1-60566-654-9.ch004

Takacs, Z. K., Swart, E. K., & Bus, A. G. (2014). Can the computer replace the adult for storybook reading? A meta-analysis on the effects of multimedia stories as compared to sharing print stories with an adult. *Frontiers in Psychology*, *5*, 1366. doi:10.3389/fpsyg.2014.01366 PMID:25520684

Takacs, Z. K., Swart, E. K., & Bus, A. G. (2015). Benefits and Pitfalls of Multimedia and Interactive Features in Technology-Enhanced Storybooks: A Meta-Analysis. *Review of Educational Research*, *85*(4), 698–739. doi:10.3102/0034654314566989 PMID:26640299

Tan, D. A., Lee, B. C., Ganapathy, M., & Kasuma, S. A. (2022). Language learning in the 21st Century. *Research Anthology on Developments in Gamification and Game-Based Learning*, 802–820. doi:10.4018/978-1-6684-3710-0.ch036

Tan, D. A. L., Ganapathy, M., & Kaur, M. (2018). Kahoot! It: Gamification in Higher Education. *Pertanika Journal of Social Science & Humanities*, *26*(1), 565–582.

Taylor, L. (2020). Teaching and learning languages under covid-19. *Conference Proceedings. Innovation in Language Learning, 2020*.

Taylor, J. A., & Newton, D. (2013). Beyond blended learning: A case study of institutional change at an Australian regional university. *The Internet and Higher Education*, *18*, 54–60. doi:10.1016/j.iheduc.2012.10.003

Teimouri, Y., Goetze, J., & Plonsky, L. (2019). Second language anxiety and achievement. *Studies in Second Language Acquisition*, *41*(2), 363–387. doi:10.1017/S0272263118000311

The Council of Europe's Modern Languge Project. (2002). https://www.ecml.at/efsz/files/Trim.pdf

ThékesI.SzilvássyO. (2021). The impact of Xeropan an online application assisting language learning on the processes of foreign language learning. *TEM Journal*. https://doi.org/ doi:10.18421/ tem102-19

Thomas, N., & Rose, H. (2019). Do Language Learning Strategies Need to Be Self-Directed? Disentangling Strategies from Self-Regulated Learning. *TESOL Quarterly*, *53*(1), 248–257. doi:10.1002/tesq.473

TIRF. (2009). *The impact of English and plurilingualism in global corporations*. The International Research Foundation for English Language Education. https://www.tirfonline.org/wp-content/ uploads/2010/09/TIRF_KeyQuestionsWorkforcePaper_Final_25March2009.pdf

Tlili, A., Shehata, B., Adarkwah, M. A., Bozkurt, A., Hickey, D. T., Huang, R., & Agyemang, B. (2023). What if the devil is my guardian angel: ChatGPT as a case study of using chatbots in education. *Smart Learning Environments*, *10*(1), 15. doi:10.118640561-023-00237-x

Toda, A. M., Klock, A. C., Oliveira, W., Palomino, P. T., Rodrigues, L., Shi, L., Bittencourt, I., Gasparini, I., Isotani, S., & Cristea, A. I. (2019). Analysing gamification elements in educational environments using an existing gamification taxonomy. *Smart Learning Environments*, *6*(1), 16. Advance online publication. doi:10.118640561-019-0106-1

Tolosa-Casadont, L. (2022). *Using multimodal pedagogy to teach languages online: Reimagining language teaching with elementary school children*. IGI Global.

Tondeur, J., van Braak, J., Siddiq, F., & Scherer, R. (2016). Time for a new approach to prepare future teachers for educational technology use: Its meaning and measurement. *Computers & Education*, *94*, 134–150. doi:10.1016/j.compedu.2015.11.009

Toprak-Yildiz, T. E. (2021). *Current practices in technology-based language testing and assessment.* In *Proceedings of the Izmir Democracy University International Humanities Congress (IDU-IHC)*, Izmir, Turkiye.

Traxler, J. (2018). Distance learning—Predictions and possibilities. *Education Sciences*, *8*(1), 35. doi:10.3390/educsci8010035

Trust, T., Whalen, J., & Mouza, C. (2023). Editorial: ChatGPT: Challenges, Opportunities, and Implications for Teacher Education. *Contemporary Issues in Technology and Teacher Education*, *23*(1), 1-23. Retrieved August 15, 2023 from https://www.learntechlib.org/primary/p/222408/

Trust, T., Whalen, J., & Mouza, C. (2023). Editorial: ChatGPT: Challenges, opportunities, and implications for teacher education. *Contemporary Issues in Technology & Teacher Education*, *23*(1), 1–23.

Tsang, S. L., Katz, A., & Stack, J. (2008). Achievement testing for English language learners, ready or not? *Education Policy Analysis Archives*, *16*(1), 1–29. doi:10.14507/epaa.v16n1.2008

Tsourounis, S., & Demmans Epp, C. (2016). Learning dashboards and gamification in MALL: Design guidelines in practice. The international handbook of mobile-assisted language learning, 370-398.

Compilation of References

Tudor, I. (1993). Teacher roles in the learner-centered classroom. *ELT Journal, 47*(1), 23–24. doi:10.1093/elt/47.1.22

Tulloch, R. (2014). Reconceptualising gamification: Play and pedagogy. *Digital Culture & Education, 6*(4), 317–333.

Ubaedillah, U., & Pratiwi, D. I. (2021). Utilization of information technology during the COVID-19 pandemic: Student's perception of online lectures. *Edukatif: Jurnal Ilmu Pendidikan, 3*(2), 447-455. doi:10.31004/edukatif.v3i2.320

Uto, M. (2021). A review of deep-neural automated essay scoring models. *Behaviormetrika, 48*(2), 459–484. doi:10.100741237-021-00142-y

Vall, R., & Araya, F. (2023). Exploring the benefits and challenges of AI-language learning tools. *International Journal of Social Sciences and Humanities Invention.* doi:10.18535/ijsshi/v10i01.02

Vallejo Balduque, B. (2018). *Gamification and the Affective Aspects EFL Students: Effects on Anxiety and Motivation.* Language Education and Emotions.

Van der Mars, H., Timken, G., & McNamee, J. B. (2018). Systematic observation of formal assessment of students by teachers (SOFAST). *Physical Educator, 75*(3), 341–373. doi:10.18666/TPE-2018-V75-I3-8113

van Dis, E. A. M., Bollen, J., Zuidema, W., van Rooij, R., & Bockting, C. L. (2023). ChatGPT: Five priorities for research. *Nature, 614*(7947), 224–226. doi:10.1038/d41586-023-00288-7 PMID:36737653

Van Moere, A., & Downey, R. (2016). Technology and artificial intelligence in language assessment. In D. Tsagari & J. Banerjee (Eds.), *Handbook of second language assessment* (pp. 341–357). De Gruyter Mouton., doi:10.1515/9781614513827-023

VanPatten, B., Keating, G. D., & Wulff, S. S. (2020). *Theories in Second language acquisition: An introduction.* Routledge. doi:10.4324/9780429503986

Varatharaj, A. (2020). *Developing Automated Audio Assessment Tools for a Chinese Language Course* [Doctoral dissertation]. Worcester Polytechnic Institute.

Verhallen, M. J. A. J., & Bus, A. G. (2010). Low-income immigrant pupils learning vocabulary through digital picture storybooks. *Journal of Educational Psychology, 102*(1), 54–61. doi:10.1037/a0017133

Veryaeva, K., & Solovyeva, O. (2021). The influence of gamification and platform affordances on user engagement in online learning. *International Journal of Distance Education Technologies, 19*(1), 1–17. doi:10.4018/IJDET.2021010101

Viberg, O., Wasson, B., & Kukulska-Hulme, A. (2020). Mobile-assisted language learning through learning analytics for self-regulated learning (MALLAS): A conceptual framework. *Australasian Journal of Educational Technology, 36*(6), 34–52. doi:10.14742/ajet.6494

Vincent, T. (2015). *Class Quiz Games with Quizizz (an Alternative to Kahoot)*. Retrieved from https://learninginhand.com/blog/quiziz

Vinther, T. (2002). Elicited imitation: A brief overview. *International Journal of Applied Linguistics*, *12*(1), 54–73. doi:10.1111/1473-4192.00024

Voogt, J., Fisser, P., Pareja Roblin, N., Tondeur, J., & Van Braak, J. (2013b). Technological Pedagogical Content Knowledge (TPACK) - a review of the literature. *Journal of Computer Assisted Learning*, *29*(2), 109–121. doi:10.1111/j.1365-2729.2012.00487.x

Voogt, J., Knezek, G., Cox, M., Knezek, D., & Ten Brummelhuis, A. (2013a). Under which conditions does ICT have a positive effect on teaching and learning? A Call to Action. *Journal of Computer Assisted Learning*, *29*(1), 4–14. doi:10.1111/j.1365-2729.2011.00453.x

Wagner, E., & Kunnan, A. J. (2015). The Duolingo English test. *Language Assessment Quarterly*, *12*(3), 320–331. doi:10.1080/15434303.2015.1061530

Wang, A. I. (2015). The wear out effect of a game-based student response system. *Computers & Education*, *82*, 217–227. doi:10.1016/j.compedu.2014.11.004

Wang, A. I., & Tahir, R. (2020). The effect of using Kahoot! for learning – a literature review. *Computers & Education*, *149*, 1–22. doi:10.1016/j.compedu.2020.103818

Wang, M., Callaghan, V., Bernhardt, J., White, K., & Peña-Rios, A. (2018). Augmented reality in education and training: Pedagogical approaches and illustrative case studies. *Journal of Ambient Intelligence and Humanized Computing*, *9*(5), 1391–1402. doi:10.100712652-017-0547-8

Wang, Q., Quek, C. L., & Hu, X. (2017). Designing and improving a blended synchronous learning environment: An educational design research. *International Review of Research in Open and Distance Learning*, *18*(3). doi:10.19173/irrodl.v18i3.3034

Wang, Y. H. (2017). Exploring the effectiveness of integrating augmented reality-based materials to support writing activities. *Computers & Education*, *113*, 162–176. doi:10.1016/j.compedu.2017.04.013

Wang, Z., Hweng, G. J., Yin, Z., & Ma, Y. (2020). A contribution-oriented self-directed mobile learning ecology approach to improving ELF students' vocabulary retention and second language motivation. *Journal of Educational Technology & Society*, *23*(1), 16–29. https://www.jstor.org/stable/10.2307/26915404

Warschauer, M., & Grimes, D. (2008). Automated writing assessment in the classroom. *Pedagogies*, *3*(1), 22–36. doi:10.1080/15544800701771580

WarschauerM.TsengW.YimS.WebsterT.JacobS.DuQ.TateT. (2023). *The affordances and contradictions of AI-generated text for second language writers*. doi:10.2139/ssrn.4404380

Warschauer, M., & Ware, P. (2006). Automated writing evaluation: Defining the classroom research agenda. *Language Teaching Research*, *10*(2), 157–180. doi:10.1191/1362168806lr190oa

Compilation of References

Wedemeyer, C. A. (1977). Independent study. In A. S. Knowles (Ed.), *The International Encyclopedia of Higher Education*. Northeastern University.

Weissheimer, J., Souza, J. G., Antunes, J. P., & Souza Filho, N. S. (2019). Gamification and L2 vocabulary learning: The vocabox experience in the languages without borders program. *Revista Linguagem & Ensino*, *22*(4), 1136. doi:10.15210/rle.v22i4.16453

Weitze, C. L., Ørngreen, R., & Levinsen, K. (2013, October). The global classroom video conferencing model and first evaluations. *Proceedings of the 12th European Conference on E-Learning*. SKEMA Business School.

Wei, X., Weng, D., Liu, Y., & Wang, Y. (2015). Teaching based on augmented reality for a technical creative design course. *Computers & Education*, *81*, 221–234. doi:10.1016/j.compedu.2014.10.017

Wenden, A. L. (1991). *Learner strategies for learner autonomy*. Prentice Hall.

Wentworth, D. K., & Middleton, J. H. (2014). Technology Use and Academic Performance. *Computers & Education*, *78*, 306–311. doi:10.1016/j.compedu.2014.06.012

Werbach, K., & Hunter, D. (2012). *For the win: How game thinking can revolutionize your business*. Wharton Digital Press.

White, C. (2006). Distance learning of foreign languages. *Language Teaching*, *39*(4), 247–264. doi:10.1017/S0261444806003727

Wigal, C. M. (2021). Teaching the design process in a HyFlex environment. *Journal of Higher Education Theory and Practice*, *21*(10), 226–235.

Wilkins, D. A. (1981). *Second- language learning and teaching*. Edward Arnold.

Wilson, E. (2017). School-based research: A guide for education students. *School-based Research*, 1-416.

Wilson, J., & Czik, A. (2016). Automated essay evaluation software in English language arts classrooms: Effects on teacher feedback, student motivation, and writing quality. *Computers & Education*, *100*, 94–109. doi:10.1016/j.compedu.2016.05.004

Wilson, J., & Roscoe, R. D. (2020). Automated writing evaluation and feedback: Multiple metrics of efficacy. *Journal of Educational Computing Research*, *58*(1), 87–125. doi:10.1177/0735633119830764

Wilson, K., Boyd, C., Chen, L., & Jamal, S. (2011). Improving student performance in a first year geography course: Examining the importance of computer-assisted formative assessment. *Computers & Education*, *57*(2), 1493–1500. doi:10.1016/j.compedu.2011.02.011

Wilson, T. J., & Alexander, M. (2021). HyFlex course delivery: Addressing the change in course modality brought on by the pandemic. *Journal of the International Society for Teacher Education*, *25*(2), 41–58. doi:10.26522/jiste.v25i2.3668

Wu, J. (2015). Effects of CALL on self-directed FL vocabulary learning. *Studies in Self-Access Learning Journal*, *6*(2), 191–215. doi:10.37237/060204

Xi, X., Higgins, D., Zechner, K., & Williamson, D. M. (2008). Automated scoring of spontaneous speech using SpeechRater v1.0. ETS Research report RR-08-62. Princeton, NJ: ETS. https://doi.org/ doi:10.1002/j.2333-8504.2008.tb02148.x

Xodabande, İ., & Atai, M. R. (2022). Using mobile applications for self-directed learning of academic vocabulary among university students. *Open Learning*, *37*(4), 330–347. doi:10.1080/02680513.2020.1847061

Xu, J. (2015). *Predicting ESL learners' oral proficiency by measuring the collocations in their spontaneous speech* [Doctoral dissertation, Iowa State University]. Iowa State University Digital Repository. doi:10.31274/etd-180810-4474

Xue, V. W., Lei, P., & Cho, W. C. (2023, March). medicine. *Clinical and Translational Medicine*, *13*(3), e1216. Advance online publication. doi:10.1002/ctm2.1216

Xu, J., Brenchley, J., Jones, E., Pinnington, A., Benjamin, T., Knill, K., Seal-Coon, G., Robinson, M., & Geranpayeh, A. (2020). *Linguaskill: Building a validity argument for the Speaking test*. Cambridge Assessment English.

Xu, J., Jones, E., Laxton, V., & Galaczi, E. (2021). Assessing L2 English speaking using automated scoring technology: Examining automarker reliability. *Assessment in Education: Principles, Policy & Practice*, *28*(4), 411–436. doi:10.1080/0969594X.2021.1979467

Yaman, S., Bal-İncebacak, B., & Sarışan-Tungaç, A. (2022). Öğretmen niteliklerinin belirlenmesinde paydaşların görüşleri. *Ahmet Keleşoğlu Eğitim Fakültesi Dergisi (AKEF)*, *4*(2), 376–397. doi:10.38151/akef.2022.24

Yamasaki, A. (2016). The Effectiveness of Gamification on Students' Motivation in Writing Class. 工学教育研究; *KIT Progress, 24*, 233-240. Retrieved from https://cir.nii.ac.jp/crid/1050282814025789184

YanD. (2023). *How ChatGPT's automatic text generation impact on learners in a L2 writing practicum: an exploratory investigation*. https://doi.org/ doi:10.35542/osf.io/s4nfz

Yang, Y., Buckendahl, C. W., Jusziewicz, P. J., & Bhola, D. S. (2002). A review of strategies for validating computer-automated scoring. *Applied Measurement in Education*, *15*(4), 391–412. doi:10.1207/S15324818AME1504_04

Yeung, S. S., Ng, M., & King, R. B. (2016). English vocabulary instruction through storybook reading for Chinese EFL kindergarteners: Comparing rich, embedded, and incidental approaches. *Asian EFL J.*, *18*, 89–112.

Yıldırım, A., & Şimşek, H. (2006). *Sosyal bilimlerde nitel araştırma yöntemleri*. Seçkin.

Yin, Q., & Satar, M. (2020). English as a foreign language learner interaction with chatbots: Negotiation for meaning. *International Online Journal of Education & Teaching*, *7*(2), 390–410.

Compilation of References

Yokota, J., & Teale, W. H. (2014). Picture Books and the Digital World: Educators Making Informed Choices. *The Reading Teacher*, *67*(8), 577–585. doi:10.1002/trtr.1262

Yoon, S. Y., & Bhat, S. (2018). A comparison of grammatical proficiency measures in the automated assessment of spontaneous speech. *Speech Communication*, *99*, 221–230. doi:10.1016/j.specom.2018.04.003

Yosintha, R., & Yunianti, S. S. (2021). Learner autonomy in EFL online classes in Indonesia: Students' voices. *Langkawi: Journal of the Association for Arabic and English*, *7*(1), 119–133. doi:10.31332/lkw.v7i1.2637

Young, S. (2001). Statistical modeling in continuous speech recognition (CSR). *Proceedings of the Seventeenth Conference on Uncertainty in Artificial Intelligence*. San Francisco: Morgan Kaufman.

Young, R. (1986). *Personal autonomy: beyond negative and positive liberty*. Croom Helm.

Young, R. (2011). Interactional competence in language learning, teaching, and testing. In E. Hinkel (Ed.), *Handbook of research in language learning and teaching* (pp. 426–443). Routledge. doi:10.4324/9780203836507.ch26

Yuan, Y. (2022). Quantitative analysis of Chinese classroom teaching activity under the background of artificial intelligence. *Education and Information Technologies*, *27*(8), 11161–11177. doi:10.100710639-022-11080-x

Yunus, M., & Azmanuddin bin Azman, M. (2019). Memory stay or stray? Irregular verbs learning using Kahoot! *Arab World English Journal*, (5), 206–219. doi:10.24093/awej/call5.15

Yürük, N. (2019). Edutainment: Using Kahoot! as a review activity in foreign language classrooms. *Journal of Educational Technology and Online Learning*, 89–101. doi:10.31681/jetol.557518

Zainuddin, Z., Chu, S. K., Shujahat, M., & Perera, C. J. (2020). The impact of gamification on learning and instruction: A systematic review of empirical evidence. *Educational Research Review*, *30*, 100326. doi:10.1016/j.edurev.2020.100326

Zawacki-Richter, O., Marín, V. I., Bond, M., & Gouverneur, F. (2019). Systematic review of research on artificial intelligence applications in higher education–where are the educators? *International Journal of Educational Technology in Higher Education*, *16*(1), 1–27. doi:10.118641239-019-0171-0

Zhai, X., Chu, X., Chai, C. S., Jong, M. S. Y., Istenic, A., Spector, M., Liu, J.-B., Yuan, J., & Li, Y. (2021). A Review of Artificial Intelligence (AI) in Education from 2010 to 2020. *Complexity*, *2021*, 1–18. doi:10.1155/2021/8812542

Zhang, L., & Chen, Y. (2021). Examining the effects of gamification on Chinese College Students' Foreign Language Anxiety: A Preliminary Exploration. *2021 4th International Conference on Big Data and Education*. 10.1145/3451400.3451401

Zhang, D., & Perez Paredes, P. (2021). Chinese postgraduate EFL learners' self-directed use of mobile English learning resources. *Computer Assisted Language Learning*, *34*(8), 1128–1153. doi:10.1080/09588221.2019.1662455

Zhang, K., & Aslan, A. B. (2021). AI technologies for education: Recent research & future directions. *Computers and Education: Artificial Intelligence*, *2*, 100025. doi:10.1016/j.caeai.2021.100025

Zhang, Q. (2023). Secure Preschool Education Using Machine Learning and Metaverse Technologies. *Applied Artificial Intelligence*, *37*(1), 2222496. doi:10.1080/08839514.2023.2 222496

Zhang, T., Chen, X., Hu, J., & Ketwan, P. (2021). EFL students' preferences for written corrective feedback: Do error types, language proficiency, and foreign language enjoyment matter? *Frontiers in Psychology*, *12*, 660564. doi:10.3389/fpsyg.2021.660564 PMID:33897570

Zhao, J., Guo, L., Zheng, S., Li, S., & Zhu, J. (2018). In P. Zhao, Y. Ouyang, M. Xu, L. Yang, & Y. Ren (Eds.), *Design and Development of Mobile Interactive Picture Books* (pp. 353–360). Applied Sciences in Graphic Communication and Packaging., doi:10.1007/978-981-10-7629-9_43

Zheng, C., & Henning, G. (1985). Linguistic and cultural bias in language proficiency tests. *Language Testing*, *2*(2), 155–163. doi:10.1177/026553228500200204

Zheng, C., Liang, J.-C., Li, M., & Tsai, C.-C. (2018). The relationship between English language learners' motivation and online self-regulation: A structural equation modelling approach. *System*, *76*, 144–157. doi:10.1016/j.system.2018.05.003

Zhihao, Z., & Zhonggen, Y. (2022). The impact of gamification on the time-limited writing performance of English majors. *Education Research International*, *2022*, 1–11. doi:10.1155/2022/4650166

Zhou, L., Yu, J., Liao, C., & Shi, Y. (2017). Learning as adventure: An app designed with gamification elements to facilitate language learning. *HCI in Business, Government and Organizations. Interacting with Information Systems*, 266–275. doi:10.1007/978-3-319-58481-2_21

Zhou, Y., Fei, T., & Chen, J. (2021). The Integration of Internet and Picture Book: Using Online Picture Book Reading Project to Promote Primary School Students' Reading Literacy. *SHS Web of Conferences* 123, 01025. 10.1051hsconf/202112301025

Zichermann, G., & Cunningham, C. (2011). *Gamification by design: Implementing game mechanics in web and mobile apps*. Verlag nicht ermittelbar.

Zimmerman, B. J. (1989). A Social Cognitive View of Self-Regulated Academic Learning. *Journal of Educational Psychology*, *81*(3), 329–339. doi:10.1037/0022-0663.81.3.329

Zimmerman, B. J. (1990). Self-regulated learning and academic achievement: An overview. *Educational Psychologist*, *25*(1), 3–17. doi:10.120715326985ep2501_2

Compilation of References

Zimmerman, B. J. (2000). Attaining Self-Regulation. A Social Cognitive Perspective. In M. Boekaerts, P. Pintrich, & M. Zeidner (Eds.), *Handbook of Self-Regulation* (pp. 13–39). Academic Press. doi:10.1016/B978-012109890-2/50031-7

Zou, D. (2020). Gamified flipped EFL classroom for primary education: Student and teacher perceptions. *Journal of Computers in Education*, 7(2), 213–228. doi:10.100740692-020-00153-w

Zreik, M. (2023). Navigating the Dragon: China's Ascent as a Global Power Through Public Diplomacy. In Global Perspectives on the Emerging Trends in Public Diplomacy (pp. 50-74). IGI Global.

Zreik, M. (2021). Academic Exchange Programs between China and the Arab Region: A Means of Cultural Harmony or Indirect Chinese Influence? *Arab Studies Quarterly*, 43(2), 172–188. doi:10.13169/arabstudquar.43.2.0172

Zreik, M., & Abunamous, M. O. (2020). Human thinking at the time of Covid-19 and the role of swot analysis: A case study on the Chinese and Palestinian societies. *Psychology Research on Education and Social Sciences*, 2(1), 31–40.

About the Contributors

Zeynep Çetin Köroğlu has been working as an Associate Professor Doctor at the English Language Teaching Department of Aksaray University. She got her MA and Ph.D. degrees from Gazi University, Türkiye. Her academic background mainly consists of English Language Teaching. She acts as a reviewer at various international academic journals. She is a technology enthusiast, established researcher, and international conference presenter. Her areas of expertise include intercultural communication, language teachers' education, ICT implementations in language pedagogy, and language assessment. She published numerous book chapters and articles related to her research interests.

Abdulvahit Çakır has been working as a Professor Doctor at the English Language Teaching Department of Ufuk University. He got his MA degree from Edinburg College of Art in 1982. He got his Ph.D degree from Gazi University, Türkiye. His academic background mainly consists of English Language Teaching. He acts as a reviewer at various international academic journals. His research areas include intercultural communication, language teachers' education, psycholinguistic, and language assessment. He published several book chapters and articles related to his research interests.

***

Hande Çetin currently works as an Assistant Professor in the English Language Teaching Department, Faculty of Education of Tokat Gaziosmanpaşa University. Her research interests include pragmatics, continuing professional development, learner autonomy, and integration of technology into language learning and teaching.

Farzaneh Dehghan has got her BA, MA and PhD in TEFL from Shiraz University. She has taught at many universities and is the faculty member of Amirkabir University of Technology since 2017. Her areas of interest are L2 academic literacy, teacher education, technology-enhanced language learning (TELL), computer-assisted language learning (CALL), discourse and content analysis and historical linguistics.

About the Contributors

Yücel Gelişli holds a Bachelor's degree in Department of Curriculum and Instruction from Gazi Education Faculty of Gazi University, Master's degree in Curriculum Development from the Social Sciences Institute of Balıkesir University, and PhD in Curriculum and Instruction (Social and Historical Foundations of Education) from the Social Sciences Institute of Ankara University. In 2011, he has become a professor in the department of Curriculum and Instruction in Education Sciences of Gazi Faculty of Education in Gazi University. His main research interests are Curriculum Development, Teacher Training System and Turkish History of Education.

Géraldine Heilporn is an Assistant Professor in Educational Technology in the Department of Teaching and Learning Studies at the Faculty of Education at Université Laval. Her research interests focus on technology use in teaching and learning, student engagement, and inclusive pedagogical strategies from secondary school to university, as well as blended and online learning in postsecondary settings. Her research aims to support engagement, learning, and inclusion of all learners with increasingly diverse needs.

Galip Kartal is an accomplished Associate Professor in the Department of English Language Teaching at Necmettin Erbakan University in Konya, Turkey. He holds a BA, MA, and PhD in English Language Teaching, reflecting his extensive expertise in the field. Dr. Kartal's research interests span teaching vocabulary, innovative language learning and teaching techniques, and second language teacher education with a focus on professional development. In recent years, he has also explored the potential of AI-supported language teaching to transform traditional instructional methods and improve student outcomes. As a dedicated educator and researcher, Dr. Kartal continues to make significant contributions to the field of English Language Teaching, shaping the future of language education for teachers and learners alike.

Fatma Kimsesiz has B.E., M.E., and Ph.D degrees from Atatürk University, Erzurum, Turkey in 2007, 2012, and 2017, respectively. She has been teaching English as a foreign language for about 17 years in Türkiye. She has been with the School of Foreign Languages, Kırşehir Ahi Evran University where she has been performing as an Asst. Prof. for 6 years. Her main areas of research include teaching English as a foreign language, teaching English to young learners, comparative studies across Turkish and English, and vocabulary teaching in EFL classes. She published a book, a number of book chapters, and articles that cover her research areas.

About the Contributors

Betul Kinik is an assistant professor doctor at İnönü University, Department of English Language Education. She holds a BA, MA, and PhD in English Language Teaching. In addition to publishing and presenting internationally, she is one of the editors in-chief of the Journal of Language Teaching and Learning. Her research areas are sociocultural theory, academic discourse socialization, and online pedagogies.

Mourad Majdoub is a PhD candidate in Educational Technology in the Department of Teaching and Learning Studies at the Faculty of Education at Université Laval. I am currently working as a research assistant in various projects. I am also an ESL teacher with more than 20 years of working experience.

Şenol Orakcı is an associate professor in the Department of Curriculum and Instruction at Aksaray University in Turkey. His scholarship focuses on teacher education, curriculum studies, and international education. He has published several books, book chapters, articles and conference papers in the field of Curriculum and Instruction.

Gülşah Öz has been working as a Research Assistant at the Department of Foreign Languages Education, Aksaray University, Turkey. Her academic background mainly consists of English Language Teaching. She graduated from Çukurova University and got her MA degree from Çağ University. Then, she started her PhD at Çukurova University in 2020 and she is still a PhD student. She is especially interested in multiculturalism, social justice and equity in education, language teachers' education, foreign language teaching.

Sibel Kahraman-Özkurt holding a PhD works as a research assistant at the Foreign Languages Education Department of Pamukkale University. Her research interests include second language acquisition, teacher autonomy, use of technology in language education, and continuing professional development. She is currently giving lectures on language acquisition, computer-assisted language learning (CALL) and language skills.

Tugba Elif Toprak-Yildiz is an associate professor at the Faculty of Science and Letters, Department of English and Literature, Izmir Democracy University, Turkiye. Dr. Toprak-Yildiz is interested in using multidimensional psychometric models to examine language comprehension and processing in individuals. Her work particularly focuses on diagnostic language assessment and combines methods and techniques from several areas, such as the learning sciences, cognitive science, and natural language processing.

About the Contributors

Ümran Üstünbaş is an assistant professor at Zonguldak Bülent Ecevit University, Ereğli Faculty of Education, English Language Teaching Department, Türkiye. Before being appointed as an assistant professor, she worked as an English instructor at School of Foreign Languages of the same university. She earned her BA in English Language Teaching (ELT) from Anadolu University, Türkiye, MA in TEFL from Bilkent University, Türkiye and PhD in ELT from Hacettepe University, Türkiye. Her research interests are teacher education and training, L2 writing and pragmatics on which she has publications. Her recent research has centered around AI use in language learning and teaching.

Mohamad Zreik, a Postdoctoral Fellow at Sun Yat-sen University, is a recognized scholar in International Relations, specializing in China's Arab-region foreign policy. His recent work in soft power diplomacy compares China's methods in the Middle East and East Asia. His extensive knowledge spans Middle Eastern Studies, China-Arab relations, East Asian and Asian Affairs, Eurasian geopolitics, and Political Economy, providing him a unique viewpoint in his field. Dr. Zreik is a proud recipient of a PhD from Central China Normal University (Wuhan). He's written numerous acclaimed papers, many focusing on China's Belt and Road Initiative and its Arab-region impact. His groundbreaking research has established him as a leading expert in his field. Presently, he furthers his research on China's soft power diplomacy tactics at Sun Yat-sen University. His significant contributions make him a crucial figure in understanding contemporary international relations.

Index

A

Achievement Tests 91-93, 95-97, 114
Adaptive Learning Systems 11, 20
Artificial Intelligence (AI) 1-4, 7, 9-14, 20, 49, 61, 70, 90, 93, 115-119, 129, 133, 195, 216-217, 221, 225, 227-228, 234
Asynchronous Online Learning 258
Augmented Reality (AR) 1-2, 5-8, 10-14, 20, 146, 154, 158
automated scoring 205, 217, 219-222, 224-227
automated speech 216-229, 234
Automated Speech Recognition 216-217, 220-222, 224, 228
Automated Speech Scoring 216-220, 222-229, 234
autonomous learners 21-22, 25-26, 28, 30, 116, 123, 262
Autonomous Learning 21-22, 24-31, 33, 36, 39-40, 47, 76, 82, 158, 226, 263, 265, 267, 276

B

Blended Learning 116, 236-237, 240, 258

C

Chatbots 3-4, 50, 53, 71-78, 115, 196-197
ChatGPT 1, 7-10, 13-15, 20, 48-50, 55-64, 68, 70-83, 90, 115-122, 124-129, 133, 194-207, 209
Corrective Feedback 95, 115-119, 121-122, 129, 133, 137, 153

critical thinking 9, 25, 56, 71, 78, 81, 118, 155, 186, 188

D

Digital Equity 12, 20
Digital Literacy 12-13, 15, 20, 117, 125, 128-129, 133, 245
Digital pedagogy 235
digital picture 174-183, 187-188, 193
digital picture books 174-183, 187-188
Digital practices 263, 268, 276
digital tools 12, 20, 37, 68, 91, 93, 98-101, 108, 116-117, 122, 124-128, 138, 178, 240, 250, 252, 261, 269, 271, 275-276
digital world 117, 119, 129
Distance Education 21, 29, 31-34, 36, 39, 47, 264
Distance Learning 21, 33, 47, 258

E

Educational Policy 1, 3, 12, 14
Educational Technology 8, 31, 68, 144
English Teachers 48-50, 56-58, 63-64, 69, 183

F

Foreign Language Education 23, 30-31, 47, 49, 235, 246, 262
Foreign Language Teaching 21, 23, 28, 177, 187, 236, 240-241, 244, 246
Formal Assessment 94, 114
Formative Assessment 93-95, 98, 101, 104,

Index

107, 114, 218

G

Gamification 101, 134-136, 138-144, 146-147, 151-159, 161, 264, 274

H

human rater 194, 198-205, 208-209
HyFlex Teaching 235-237, 239-252, 259

I

Informal Assessment 94, 114
In-Service English Teachers 48-50, 56-58, 63, 69
Interactional Competence 225, 228, 234

L

L2 Learning 129, 134-143, 151-152, 154-155, 157, 159-161
L2 Writing 77, 82, 137, 140
Language Assessment 93-95, 98-99, 101, 107-108, 114, 216, 218-219, 221, 226-228
language education 2-3, 7-8, 11, 14-15, 23-24, 30-31, 47, 49-50, 53-57, 129, 196, 219-220, 235, 246, 262
Language Learning 2, 5-6, 8-9, 13, 15, 21-22, 24-27, 32, 39-40, 49, 53-54, 69-70, 73-75, 77, 83, 116-122, 127, 129, 135, 137-139, 141, 143-144, 146-147, 151-152, 157-158, 174, 179, 218, 235, 237, 239-241, 244, 248-250, 252, 260-263, 266-269, 273, 276
Language Learning Autonomy 21, 32
Language Pedagogy 1, 13, 36, 57, 69
language teaching 2, 15, 21, 23-24, 26, 28, 49-50, 53, 56-57, 60, 62, 71, 73, 80-81, 83, 92, 98-99, 101-102, 104, 106-108, 115, 154, 177, 187, 194, 199-200, 226, 236, 240-241, 244, 246
Large Language Models 72, 90
Learner Autonomy 10, 12-14, 20-21, 33-34, 47, 117, 122, 128, 133, 151, 178, 236,

249, 262, 276
Literature Review 51, 63, 134, 136, 141, 156, 262, 269

M

Metaverse 1-2, 7-10, 12-15, 20
mobile-assisted language learning 268, 273

N

Natural Language Processing 53, 71, 73, 90, 195, 216-220, 227-228, 234
N-Gram 234

P

Pedagogical Strategy 14, 20
Personalized Learning 3, 5, 48, 51, 53, 55-56, 69, 74, 76, 141
Personalized Learning Experiences 51, 56, 69
picture books 174-183, 186-188
Professional Development 12, 26, 39, 48-50, 54-58, 60-64, 69, 82

S

Second Language Acquisition 136, 141, 144
self-directed language learning 262-263, 267-269, 273, 275
Self-Efficacy 76, 82, 117, 122, 128, 133, 137-138, 197, 246, 252, 267
Self-Regulated Learning 117, 122, 128, 133, 141, 262-263
Speech Processing 217, 222, 226, 228, 234
Speech Recognition 216-217, 219-224, 227-228, 234
Students' Creativity 70, 81, 83
Summative Assessment 95, 98, 114, 225
Synchronous Online Learning 259

T

Teacher Training 12, 14-15, 28, 55
Teachers' Creativity 81
Technological Assessment Tools 11

Index

technology-based learning 135, 250
Theories of Distance Learning 47

V

Virtual Reality (VR) 20, 141
vocabulary acquisition 76, 179-180, 182, 266

W

writing assessment 194, 196, 207, 209

Written Corrective Feedback 116, 118-119, 121, 129, 133

Y

young learners 174-175, 178, 182-183, 187-188

Recommended Reference Books

IGI Global's reference books are available in three unique pricing formats:
Print Only, E-Book Only, or Print + E-Book.
Order direct through IGI Global's Online Bookstore at **www.igi-global.com** or through your preferred provider.

Online Distance Learning Course Design and Multimedia in E-Learning
ISBN: 9781799897064
EISBN: 9781799897088
© 2022; 302 pp.
List Price: US$ 215

Global and Transformative Approaches Toward Linguistic Diversity
ISBN: 9781799889854
EISBN: 9781799889878
© 2022; 383 pp.
List Price: US$ 215

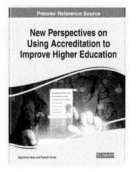

New Perspectives on Using Accreditation to Improve Higher Education
ISBN: 9781668451953
EISBN: 9781668451960
© 2022; 300 pp.
List Price: US$ 215

Impact of School Shootings on Classroom Culture, Curriculum, and Learning
ISBN: 9781799852001
EISBN: 9781799852018
© 2022; 355 pp.
List Price: US$ 215

Modern Reading Practices and Collaboration Between Schools, Family, and Community
ISBN: 9781799897507
EISBN: 9781799897521
© 2022; 304 pp.
List Price: US$ 215

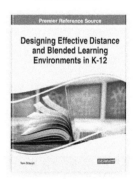

Designing Effective Distance and Blended Learning Environments in K-12
ISBN: 9781799868293
EISBN: 9781799868316
© 2022; 389 pp.
List Price: US$ 215

Do you want to stay current on the latest research trends, product announcements, news, and special offers?
Join IGI Global's mailing list to receive customized recommendations, exclusive discounts, and more.
Sign up at: **www.igi-global.com/newsletters**

Publisher of Timely, Peer-Reviewed Inclusive Research Since 1988

IGI Global
PUBLISHER of TIMELY KNOWLEDGE

www.igi-global.com   Sign up at www.igi-global.com/newsletters   facebook.com/igiglobal   twitter.com/igiglobal

Ensure Quality Research is Introduced to the Academic Community

Become an Evaluator for IGI Global Authored Book Projects

   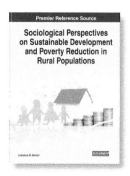

The overall success of an authored book project is dependent on quality and timely manuscript evaluations.

Applications and Inquiries may be sent to:
development@igi-global.com

Applicants must have a doctorate (or equivalent degree) as well as publishing, research, and reviewing experience. Authored Book Evaluators are appointed for one-year terms and are expected to complete at least three evaluations per term. Upon successful completion of this term, evaluators can be considered for an additional term.

If you have a colleague that may be interested in this opportunity, we encourage you to share this information with them.

Easily Identify, Acquire, and Utilize Published
Peer-Reviewed Findings in Support of Your Current Research

IGI Global OnDemand

Purchase Individual IGI Global OnDemand Book Chapters and Journal Articles

For More Information:
www.igi-global.com/e-resources/ondemand/

Browse through 150,000+ Articles and Chapters!

Find specific research related to your current studies and projects that have been contributed by international researchers from prestigious institutions, including:

- Accurate and Advanced Search
- Affordably Acquire Research
- Instantly Access Your Content
- Benefit from the InfoSci Platform Features

It really provides an excellent entry into the research literature of the field. It presents a manageable number of highly relevant sources on topics of interest to a wide range of researchers. The sources are scholarly, but also accessible to 'practitioners'.

- Ms. Lisa Stimatz, MLS, University of North Carolina at Chapel Hill, USA

Interested in Additional Savings?

Subscribe to
IGI Global OnDemand

Learn More

Acquire content from over 128,000+ research-focused book chapters and 33,000+ scholarly journal articles for as low as US$ 5 per article/chapter (original retail price for an article/chapter: US$ 37.50).

7,300+ E-BOOKS.
ADVANCED RESEARCH.
INCLUSIVE & AFFORDABLE.

IGI Global e-Book Collection

- **Flexible Purchasing Options** (Perpetual, Subscription, EBA, etc.)
- Multi-Year Agreements with **No Price Increases** Guaranteed
- **No Additional Charge** for Multi-User Licensing
- No Maintenance, Hosting, or Archiving Fees
- Continually Enhanced & Innovated **Accessibility Compliance Features** (WCAG)

Handbook of Research on Digital Transformation, Industry Use Cases, and the Impact of Disruptive Technologies
ISBN: 9781799877127
EISBN: 9781799877141

Handbook of Research on New Investigations in Artificial Life, AI, and Machine Learning
ISBN: 9781799886860
EISBN: 9781799886877

Handbook of Research on Future of Work and Education
ISBN: 9781799882756
EISBN: 9781799882770

Research Anthology on Physical and Intellectual Disabilities in an Inclusive Society (4 Vols.)
ISBN: 9781668435427
EISBN: 9781668435434

Innovative Economic, Social, and Environmental Practices for Progressing Future Sustainability
ISBN: 9781799895909
EISBN: 9781799895923

Applied Guide for Event Study Research in Supply Chain Management
ISBN: 9781799889694
EISBN: 9781799889717

Mental Health and Wellness in Healthcare Workers
ISBN: 9781799888130
EISBN: 9781799888147

Clean Technologies and Sustainable Development in Civil Engineering
ISBN: 9781799898108
EISBN: 9781799898122

Request More Information, or Recommend the IGI Global e-Book Collection to Your Institution's Librarian

---

For More Information or to Request a Free Trial, Contact IGI Global's e-Collections Team: eresources@igi-global.com | 1-866-342-6657 ext. 100 | 717-533-8845 ext. 100

Are You Ready to Publish Your Research?

IGI Global — PUBLISHER of TIMELY KNOWLEDGE

IGI Global offers book authorship and editorship opportunities across 11 subject areas, including business, computer science, education, science and engineering, social sciences, and more!

Benefits of Publishing with IGI Global:

- Free one-on-one editorial and promotional support.
- Expedited publishing timelines that can take your book from start to finish in less than one (1) year.
- Choose from a variety of formats, including Edited and Authored References, Handbooks of Research, Encyclopedias, and Research Insights.
- Utilize IGI Global's eEditorial Discovery® submission system in support of conducting the submission and double-blind peer review process.
- IGI Global maintains a strict adherence to ethical practices due in part to our full membership with the Committee on Publication Ethics (COPE).
- Indexing potential in prestigious indices such as Scopus®, Web of Science™, PsycINFO®, and ERIC – Education Resources Information Center.
- Ability to connect your ORCID iD to your IGI Global publications.
- Earn honorariums and royalties on your full book publications as well as complimentary content and exclusive discounts.

Join Your Colleagues from Prestigious Institutions, Including:

Australian National University
Massachusetts Institute of Technology
Johns Hopkins University
Tsinghua University
Harvard University
Columbia University in the City of New York

Learn More at: www.igi-global.com/publish
or by Contacting the Acquisitions Department at: acquisition@igi-global.com

Individual Article & Chapter Downloads
US$ 29.50/each

Easily Identify, Acquire, and Utilize Published Peer-Reviewed Findings in Support of Your Current Research

- Browse Over **170,000+ Articles & Chapters**
- **Accurate & Advanced** Search
- Affordably Acquire **International Research**
- **Instantly Access** Your Content
- Benefit from the **InfoSci® Platform Features**

THE UNIVERSITY *of* NORTH CAROLINA *at* CHAPEL HILL

" It really provides an excellent entry into the research literature of the field. It presents a manageable number of highly relevant sources on topics of interest to a wide range of researchers. The sources are scholarly, but also accessible to 'practitioners'. "

- Ms. Lisa Stimatz, MLS, University of North Carolina at Chapel Hill, USA

Interested in Additional Savings?

Subscribe to
IGI Global OnDemand *Plus*

Learn More

Acquire content from over 128,000+ research-focused book chapters and 33,000+ scholarly journal articles for as low as US$ 5 per article/chapter (original retail price for an article/chapter: US$ 37.50).

IGI Global Proudly Partners with

Editorial Services

Providing you with High-Quality, Affordable, and Expeditious Editorial Support from Manuscript Development to Publication

Copy Editing & Proofreading

Perfect your research paper before publication. Our expert editors will correct faulty spelling, grammar, punctuation, and word usage.

Scientific & Scholarly Editing

Increase your chances of being published. Our expert editors will aid in strengthening the quality of your research before submission.

Figure, Table, Chart & Equation Conversions

Enhance the visual elements of your research. Let our professional designers produce or correct your figures before final submission.

Journal Recommendation

Save time and money when you rely on our expert journal selectors to provide you with a comprehensive journal recommendation report.

Order now to receive an automatic **10% Academic Discount** on all your editorial needs.

Scan the QR Code to Learn More

Upload Your Manuscript, Select Your Desired Editorial Service, and Receive a Free Instant Quote

Email: customerservice@econtentpro.com

econtentpro.com

Milton Keynes UK
Ingram Content Group UK Ltd.
UKHW051559021224
3319UKWH00046B/1424